LOEB CLASSICAL LIBRARY

FOUNDED BY JAMES LOEB 1911

EDITED BY

JEFFREY HENDERSON

PLAUTUS

V

LCL 328

PLAUTUS

STICHUS · THREE-DOLLAR
DAY · TRUCULENTUS ·
THE TALE OF A
TRAVELING-BAG ·
FRAGMENTS

EDITED AND TRANSLATED BY

WOLFGANG DE MELO

HARVARD UNIVERSITY PRESS
CAMBRIDGE, MASSACHUSETTS
LONDON, ENGLAND
2013

YBP 5/2013 24.00

First published 2013

LOEB CLASSICAL LIBRARY® is a registered trademark
of the President and Fellows of Harvard College

Library of Congress Control Number 2010924480
CIP data available from the Library of Congress

ISBN 978-0-674-99681-6

Composed in ZephGreek and ZephText by
Technologies 'N Typography, Merrimac, Massachusetts.
Printed on acid-free paper and bound by
The Maple-Vail Book Manufacturing Group

CONTENTS

To my wife and daughter

PREFACE

This final volume of the Loeb Plautus contains three complete comedies, the *Stichus*, *Trinummus*, and *Truculentus*, as well as the remains of the *Vidularia*, only transmitted in the Ambrosian palimpsest, and the fragments of the plays outside the Varronian canon. Added together, the *Vidularia* and the fragments contain far fewer lines than the shortest complete Plautine comedy; yet it took me as long to finish the *Vidularia* and the fragments as it did to finish the rest of the volume. The reason is that because we often lack context, fragments are usually open to more than one interpretation. Meter, grammar, and literary aspects can all be uncertain at the same time. For the *Vidularia*, plot reconstruction is a difficult undertaking, but not an entirely doomed one, which is why I present a rough outline of its structure. For the plays outside the Varronian canon, plot reconstruction is impossible, so that I have restricted myself to presenting fragments together with the source texts in which they are embedded. Most of the fragments are citations by ancient grammarians and lexicographers, who were typically more interested in peculiarities than in regularities of usage. Thus it comes as no surprise that the linguistic features of the fragments are interesting but do not represent typical Plautine diction.

Among the three complete comedies in this volume,

the *Trinummus* is undoubtedly the most beautiful. Its main theme of sincere and reliable friendship makes it resemble the *Captivi*, which Lindsay called the "king of comedies." The *Stichus*, one of only two Plautine plays that can be dated with certainty, has relatively little plot, but is rather a concatenation of entertaining scenes. And in the *Truculentus*, a play often criticized for its moral depravity in the past, Plautus foreshadows Roman satire.

Just as in the *Trinummus* Callicles remains unwaveringly loyal to Charmides during his three years abroad, my colleagues and friends in England have supported me during the almost three years I have by now spent in Belgium. I am deeply grateful to John Trappes-Lomax for all his help. Yet again he has patiently and diligently read all my Latin and English texts and improved them in many places—*tu ex amicis certis mi es certissumus*. The advice given by Jim Adams has been, as always, invaluable; I owe him far more than can be said here. Peter Brown has answered many questions I had with regard to meter and staging, and I have learned a great deal from him. As before, Panagiotis Filos has had to put up with queries concerning unusual Greek names sent to him in Cyprus at late hours. The editors and staff at Harvard University Press have been outstanding throughout and have helped me promptly and efficiently with all five volumes; in particular, I would like to thank Richard Thomas, Jeffrey Henderson, Ian Stevenson, Liz Duvall, and Cheryl Lincoln. But the greatest support has come from my wife and daughter, who have made my work on Plautus joyful; this book is dedicated to both of them.

STICHUS

INTRODUCTORY NOTE

Like the *Pseudolus*, the *Stichus* has been transmitted with a stage record; but the record for the *Stichus* is much more informative than that for the *Pseudolus*. It tells us that our play was first staged during the Plebeian Games when Gaius Sulpicius and Gaius Aurelius were consuls, which means that this performance took place in November 200 BC. The stage record also states that the Greek original of the *Stichus* was Menander's *Adelphoe*, "The Brothers." As Menander wrote two plays called *Adelphoe*, they received additional names to distinguish between them. The first *Adelphoe* was also called *Philadelphoi*, "Brothers Devoted to Each Other," while the second *Adelphoe* had the alternative title *Homopatrioi*, "Sons of the Same Father." It is highly likely that the *Stichus* goes back to the first *Adelphoe*. The reason is that Terence also wrote a play called *Adelphoe*, an adaptation of a Menandrean original; and the original of Terence's play seems to have been the second *Adelphoe*, as the correspondence between a Greek fragment (transmitted in the scholia to Plato's *Phaedrus* 279c) and Ter. *Ad*. 804 shows. Now there was a convention in Terence's day that a Greek play adapted by one Roman playwright could not be used by another; when Terence did so on one occasion, he had to apologize and state that this was an oversight on his part (*Eun*. 25–28). Consequently it seems improbable that the model for the *Stichus* could have been the second *Adelphoe*.

Livy supplements the information from the stage record in an interesting way; he notes that the Plebeian Games, and thus also the *Stichus*, were repeated three times (31.50.3). Such repetitions were made for religious reasons; theater performances formed part of the ceremonies, and if a mistake had been made in one ritual, everything had to be repeated. But there can be little doubt that in general more repetitions were made than strictly necessary and that the true reason behind many of them was the desire of the officials who had commissioned the comedies to ingratiate themselves with the people. The three repetitions of the *Stichus* thus may indicate the popularity of this play.

This popularity has baffled many modern scholars, because the *Stichus* contains very little action; neither is there an intrigue against a rich old man, nor is a slave girl discovered to be a freeborn virgin. The plot, if it can be so called, consists of loosely connected scenes.

The play begins with the dialogue between two sisters (ll. 1–47; ll. 48–57 are to be excluded). The elder one, Panegyris, is married to a man called Epignomus. The younger one is married to his brother Pamphilippus. This younger sister remains unnamed in the Palatine manuscripts, which may reflect the original situation. Perhaps simply in order to avoid confusion with her sister, she is called Pamphila in the Ambrosian palimpsest, a name that could have been chosen because of its similarity to her husband's name. For the sake of clarity I follow the palimpsest.

The two sisters are deeply worried. Their husbands

had lost their wealth through their luxurious lifestyle, including frequent dinners with their hanger-on Gelasimus. Three years ago they left Athens in order to earn money as mercenaries and to start trading with what they earned. But there has been no news from them. So Antipho, the women's father, from whom the two men did not part on good terms, has hinted that he wants to take his daughters home and marry them to husbands who can provide for them. But the women do not want to remarry. Pamphila strongly emphasizes her duty toward her husband, while Panegyris also takes her duty toward her father into consideration. Finally, they decide not to fight their father openly but to convince him through clever reasoning.

At the beginning of the dialogue Panegyris compares herself and her sister to Penelope, the wife of Ulysses, who had remained faithful to her husband despite his very long absence; at the end of the conversation it becomes apparent that the comparison is apt on another level as well: Penelope had kept her suitors at arm's length by promising to remarry after finishing her father-in-law's funerary shroud, but she had undone her weaving every night. Similarly, the two women in our play want to give the impression of obeying their father, but they are actually plotting to frustrate his plans.

The next scene (ll. 58–154) shows that the women's worries were justified: Antipho comes over to persuade his daughters to remarry. It is subtly ironic that he complains about his slaves not minding their duties but then goes on to tell his daughters to leave their husbands and thereby to abandon a far more important duty. Calculating as he is, Antipho does not give orders to his daughters; instead, he tells them that he wants to remarry now that he is a

widower and that he needs their advice. His plan is to use
their advice on remarriage against them, but the women
do not fall into this trap and Antipho has to leave without
accomplishing what he wanted. The scene ends with Pan-
egyris sending her slave girl Crocotium to Gelasimus, who
is to come to Panegyris at once. Panegyris plans to send
him to the harbor to see if any ship has arrived. Even
though she already has the slave boy Pinacium at the har-
bor, who sits there every day to keep watch, her action is
not as strange as a number of commentators have asserted;
now that Antipho has made his wishes clear, an emergency
situation has arisen, and Panegyris is not content with only
Pinacium's services.

Immediately after Crocotium is sent out, Gelasimus
appears and provides some comic relief, first in a mono-
logue occasionally punctured by asides from an eaves-
dropping Crocotium (ll. 155–236) and then in a light-
hearted dialogue between the two (ll. 237–73). Just when
Gelasimus wants to go to see Panegyris, he spots Pina-
cium, who is running home.

What is the second act in modern editions (ll. 274–401)
begins with a typically pompous "running-slave mono-
logue" by Pinacium, who talks about the importance of his
message and his resultant hurry. He does indeed have im-
portant news: the husband of Panegyris has just arrived in
the harbor, and he has acquired enormous wealth. Pina-
cium loudly knocks at his mistress's door and rudely re-
fuses to tell Gelasimus the meaning of his behavior. When
Panegyris appears, he does not inform her immediately
but instigates a major housecleaning operation, in which
Gelasimus hesitantly participates. Finally, Pinacium says
that Epignomus has arrived with his newly found riches

5

and that Pamphilippus, equally successful, will arrive soon. Both Panegyris and Gelasimus are overjoyed, but Gelasimus' happiness turns to worry and despair when Pinacium claims that Epignomus has brought new hangers-on with him and Panegyris curtly sends him away.

It is not before the third act (ll. 402–504) that we meet Stichus, the slave after whom the play is named. He comes on stage together with his master, Epignomus, who thanks the gods for his safe arrival and states that he has made peace with Antipho, which was unproblematic because Antipho saw the profits he had made. Epignomus then wants to give Stichus another job. But Stichus asks if he may take this one day off after such long hardships, and Epignomus not only agrees but also presents him with a jar of wine. Stichus has already planned how to spend his holiday. He and Sangarinus,[1] a slave of Pamphilippus who was also abroad with his master, have the same girlfriend, Stephanium, Pamphila's slave girl who stayed behind with her mistress. Now Stichus and Sangarinus want to have a homecoming banquet with her and enjoy wine, food, and love. Stichus goes in to make the necessary preparations, and Gelasimus returns to meet Epignomus. Gelasimus tries his best to get a dinner invitation, but Epignomus, who does not want to return to his previous lifestyle, makes it very clear that he does not want him.

In the fourth act (ll. 505–640), we encounter Pamphilippus, the milder of the two brothers. He returns from

[1] In l. 433 he is referred to as "the Syrian Sangarinus," but the name comes from Asia Minor. The name is consistently written Sangarinus in the manuscripts, but sometimes the form Sagarinus, which occurs in inscriptions, is required by the meter.

the harbor with Antipho, with whom he, too, has made peace.[2] They meet Epignomus, whom Antipho tries to persuade in a not very convincing attempt at subtlety to part with at least one of his new slave girls; Antipho wants to have a concubine, and what is more, he hopes that Epignomus will also provide her cost of living. Epignomus first mocks him, but after Antipho has left, he tells his brother that he will comply. Gelasimus, however, who now attempts to get a dinner invitation from Pamphilippus, gets the cold shoulder again.

The rest of the play (ll. 641–775) consists of the slaves' banquet. Epignomus and his brother dine in the former's house with their wives and father-in-law, while the slaves enjoy their banquet in front of the house of Pamphilippus. They drink and perform erotic dances, first on their own, then with Stephanium.

Given that the production notice states explicitly that the model for the *Stichus* was a play by Menander, it comes as a surprise that it deviates so much in its structure from what we know of Menandrean comedy. Thus many scholars have tried to find out which structural elements are Menandrean and which are Plautine. There is broad consensus that the fifth act, the slaves' banquet, is Plautine, although it is generally assumed that the idea behind

---

[2] In l. 143 Antipho announced that he will go to see his friends, presumably in the forum (exit on the right). The fact that he is now coming from the harbor (exit on the left) constitutes a violation of ancient stage conventions because characters normally re-enter on the side on which they left before; but it is only a minor violation: presumably he could have reached the harbor on a different route.

this banquet was taken from Menander, who probably had a celebration of the masters with their wives instead; but the sight of the ruling classes getting drunk and behaving bawdily may have been too much for Roman sensitivities.

The arguments in favor of this view are convincing. It is rather odd that Sangarinus does not arrive before ll. 649–50, much later than his master; had this happened in Menander, an explanation would almost certainly have been given. As Plautus does not normally remove such explanations, and as Sangarinus has no function other than participating in the slaves' banquet, it seems that this character is a purely Plautine invention. Another oddity should be noted as well. After Epignomus has said his prayer of thanksgiving for his safe arrival, there is a passage apparently inserted by Plautus (ll. 419–53): a dialogue between Epignomus and Stichus (419–35) and then a monologue by Stichus (436–53), during which Epignomus remains on stage.[3] That Epignomus stays idle during the entire monologue is rather awkward, and it is a reasonable assumption that Menander would have handled the situation better. Plautus seems to have inserted this passage merely to prepare the audience for the slaves' banquet.

It is much more difficult to determine what else is Plautine addition. Vogt-Spira believes that in Menander the two brothers became poor through no fault of their

[3] Epignomus cannot have gone inside during the monologue; ll. 523–6 must be spoken when he leaves his house for the first time after his arrival, which means that when he is going inside after l. 496, he is doing so for the first time.

own, otherwise the happy ending would not be deserved. On that view the entertaining but detrimental Gelasimus has no place in the original. According to Vogt-Spira, the Menandrean Antipho is acting out of worry and love for his daughters, not because he is greedy; his libidinous and other negative characteristics are Plautine ornamentation. Although this theory is not without appeal, Vogt-Spira's ideas cannot be upheld. If in addition to the slaves' banquet not even the passages with Gelasimus or Antipho's attempt to get a concubine can be maintained for the original, not much remains beyond the first act. But then it would be strange that the stage record states that the original of our play is Menander's *Adelphoe*.

The question remains why the *Stichus* was popular. It is likely that in Menander the conflict between Antipho and his sons-in-law was far more central and made for more interesting dialogue. Why would Plautus relegate the reconciliation scenes to such a marginal place? Wagenvoort has argued convincingly that in 200 BC, the year of the first performance of our comedy, an atmosphere of general joy prevailed: the Romans had won a difficult victory over Hannibal, and an audience with many returning soldiers would not have had the patience to sit through a play with a complicated plot. But the happy reunion of husbands and wives must have been a common occurrence and its portrayal would have been welcome. Of course the political situation of Rome was never straightforward, and Owens is right to point out that in the same year the senate was already preparing for war against Philip V of Macedon. But it would probably go too far to assert, with Owens, that the common people identified with Gelasimus, who is said to be neglected unfairly by the brothers, who would represent the politicians in favor of the war. Plautus was not a political writer, and the average Roman must have felt that Gelasimus got his just deserts, having wrecked the brothers' fortunes and then having the cheek to ask Epignomus for a meal even before he can see his wife.

Finally, it should be mentioned that the *Adelphoe* by Menander may have contained a parody of Plato's *Symposium*, which would not have been understood by the average theatergoer in Plautus' day: Gelasimus jokes in ll. 155–70 that Hunger was his mother and that he is now carrying his mother in his belly without being able to give birth to her. Fraenkel had assumed that this joke had to be Plautine, as the Greek word for hunger, *limos*, is masculine, at least in the Attic dialect. But, as Leitão points out, Menander could have made the same joke with a different word for hunger, *peina* or *peine*, a word which is close enough to *penia*, "need." In the famous speech of Diotima in the *Symposium*, *Penia* is the mother of *Eros*, "Love" (203b–c), and it is also said that philosophers are pregnant in their soul, giving birth to thought, poetry, and so on (209a). Ultimately, it cannot be proved that Gelasimus' joke was already in Menander and, if so, that it was essentially a parody of Plato; but it is an intriguing thought.

SELECT BIBLIOGRAPHY

Editions and Commentaries

Fennell, C. A. M. (1893), *T. Macci Plauti Stichus: Edited with Introduction and Notes* (Cambridge).

Petersmann, H. (1973), *T. Maccius Plautus: Stichus; Einleitung, Text, Kommentar* (Heidelberg).

Tardin Cardoso, I. (2006), *Estico de Plauto* (Campinas).

Criticism

Arnott, W. G. (1972), "Targets, Techniques, and Tradition in Plautus' *Stichus*," in *Bulletin of the Institute for Classical Studies* 19: 54–79.

Enk, P. J. (1916), "De Stichi Plautinae compositione," in *Mnemosyne* NS 44: 18–44.

Gilleland, M. E. (1977), "Plautus, *Stichus* 617," in *American Journal of Philology* 98: 355.

Hiltbrunner, O. (1945), "Ein plautinisches Wortspiel (Stich. 173)," in *Museum Helveticum* 2: 28–32.

Krauss, A. N. (2008), "Panegyris Channels Penelope: *Mêtis* and *Pietas* in Plautus's *Stichus*," in *Helios* 35: 28–47.

Leitão, D. D. (1997), "Plautus, *Stichus* 155 ff.: A Greek Parody of Plato's *Symposium*?," in *Mnemosyne* NS 50: 271–80.

Owens, W. M. (2000), "Plautus' *Stichus* and the Political Crisis of 200 B.C.," in *American Journal of Philology* 121: 385–407.

Petrone, G. (1977), *Morale e antimorale nelle commedie di Plauto: ricerche sullo Stichus* (Palermo).

Vogt-Spira, G. (1991), "Stichus oder Ein Parasit wird Hauptperson," in E. Lefèvre, E. Stärk, G. Vogt-Spira (eds.), *Plautus barbarus: Sechs Kapitel zur Originalität des Plautus* (Tübingen), 163–74.

Wagenvoort, H. (1932), "De Sticho Plautina," in *Mnemosyne* NS 59: 309–12.

STICHVS

DIDASCALIA

⟨T. MACCI PLAVTI STICHVS.⟩
GRAECA ADELPHOE MENANDRV.
ACTA LVDIS PLEBEIS
CN. BAEBIO C. TERENTIO AED. PL.
5 ⟨EGIT⟩
T. PVBLILIVS PELLIO.
⟨MODVLATVS EST⟩
MARCIPOR OPPII
TIBIIS SARRANIS TOTAM.
10 ***
C. SVLPICIO C. AVRELIO COS.

did. 1, 5, 7 *suppl. Ritschl*

STICHUS

STAGE RECORD

The *Stichus* by Titus Maccius Plautus.
Greek play: Menander's *Adelphoe.*
Staged at the Plebeian Games
when Gnaeus Baebius and Gaius Terentius were plebeian ae-
diles.[1]
Put on stage by   5
Titus Publilius Pellio.
Set to music by
Marcipor, slave of Oppius,
in its entirety for the Sarranian flute.[2]
***   10

when Gaius Sulpicius and Gaius Aurelius were consuls.

[1] Aediles were Roman officials in charge of public games and mar-
kets; the plebeian aediles, as opposed to the curule aediles, were the
ones chosen by the common people.
[2] The Sarranian flute, named after the Phoenician city Sarra (Sor),
better known as Tyre, has two pipes of equal length.

ARGVMENTVM I

duas soror es ***
duo f‹ratres› ***
rem quaer‹unt› ***
***
5   soror‹es› ***
pa‹ter› ***
r***
fac***
***

ARGVMENTVM II

Senex castigat filias quod eae uiros
Tam perseuerent peregrinantis pauperes
Ita sustinere fratres nec relinquere;
Contraque uerbis delenitur commodis
5   Habere ut sineret quos semel nactae forent.
Viri reueniunt opibus aucti trans mare;
Suam quisque retinet ac Sticho ludus datur.

arg. 1 *solum fertur in A*   *suppl. Studemund*
arg. 2 *solum fertur in P*

14

PLOT SUMMARY 1

Two sisters *** two brothers *** they seek to make money ***
the sisters *** the father ***.   5

PLOT SUMMARY 2

An old man reproaches his daughters because they persist so
firmly in supporting and not leaving their husbands, impover-
ished brothers traveling abroad; and yet he is softened up by
agreeable words so that he lets them keep the husbands that   5
they have once acquired. The husbands return, enriched with
wealth on the other side of the sea. Each retains his wife and
Stichus is given the opportunity to have fun.

PERSONAE

PANEGYRIS uxor Epignomi
PAMPHILA uxor Pamphilippi
ANTIPHO senex
GELASIMVS parasitus
CROCOTIVM ancilla
PINACIVM puer
EPIGNOMVS frater
PAMPHILIPPVS frater
STICHVS seruos
SA(N)GARINVS seruos
STEPHANIVM ancilla

SCAENA

Athenis

CHARACTERS

PANEGYRIS wife of Epignomus; elder daughter of Antipho

PAMPHILA wife of Pamphilippus; younger daughter of Antipho

ANTIPHO an old man; of good reputation, but dubious character

GELASIMUS a hanger-on; used to entertain Epignomus and Pamphilippus

CROCOTIUM a slave girl; works for Panegyris

PINACIUM a slave boy; belongs to Epignomus and Panegyris

EPIGNOMUS brother of Pamphilippus

PAMPHILIPPUS brother of Epignomus

STICHUS a slave; belongs to Epignomus

SA(N)GARINUS a slave; belongs to Pamphilippus

STEPHANIUM a slave girl; girlfriend of both Stichus and Sangarinus

STAGING

The stage represents a street in Athens. On it are the houses of Epignomus, to the left, of Pamphilippus, in the middle, and of Antipho, to the right. The street leads to the harbor on the left and to the city center on the right.

ACTVS I

I. i: PANEGYRIS. PAMPHILA

1	PAN	credo ego miseram
1ᵃ		fuisse Penelopam,
2		soror, suo ex animo,
2ᵃ		quae tam diu uidua
3		uiro suo caruit;
3ᵃ		nam nos eius animum
		de nostris factis noscimus, quarum uiri hinc ap- sunt,
5		quorumque nos negotiis apsentum, ita ut aequom est,
		sollicitae noctes et dies, soror, sumus semper.
7	PAMPHILA	nostrum officium
7ᵃ		nos facere aequom est
8		neque id magis facimus
8ᵃ		quam nos monet pietas.
		sed hic, soror, assidedum: multa uolo tecum
10		loqui de re uiri.
10ᵃ	PAN	saluene, amabo?
	PAMPHILA	spero quidem et uolo; sed hoc, soror, crucior
		patrem tuom meumque adeo, unice qui unus
		ciuibus ex omnibus probus perhibetur,
		eum nunc improbi uiri officio uti,
15		uiris qui tantas apsentibus nostris
		facit iniurias immerito

18

STICHUS

ACT ONE

*Enter PANEGYRIS and PAMPHILA from the former's house;
they stand in front of a comfortable couch and a wooden
bench.*

PAN   I believe that Penelope[3] was wretched in her heart,
my sister, as she was desolate through her husband's
absence for so long; we can understand her state of
mind from our experience, since our husbands are
away from here and we are always, day and night,   5
worried about their business in their absence, as it
is right, my sister.

PAMPHILA It's right for us to do our duty, and we aren't
doing it more than loyalty admonishes us to. But do
sit down here, my sister; I want to discuss many
things with you about our husband situation. (*they*   10
take a seat on the couch)

PAN   Is all well, please?

PAMPHILA (*begins to cry*) I hope so and wish for it; but,
my sister, it pains me that your father, and mine, the
man who is considered by far the most righteous
among all the citizens, is now acting the part of an
unrighteous man: he does such great injustices to   15
our absent husbands, and undeservedly so, and he

---

[3] The faithful wife of Ulysses, who waited for him while he
was fighting against Troy and then trying to get home.

nosque ab eis abducere uolt.
haec res uitae me, soror, saturant,
haec mi diuidiae et senio sunt.

20 PAN ne lacruma, soror, neu tuo id animo
fac quod tibi [tuos] pater facere minatur:
spes est eum melius facturum.
noui ego illum: ioculo istaec dicit,
neque ille sibi mereat Persarum

25 montis, qui esse aurei perhibentur,
ut istuc faciat quod tu metuis.
tamen si faciat, minime irasci
decet neque id immerito eueniet.
nam uiri nostri domo ut abierunt

30 hic tertius annus—
PAMPHILA   ita ut memoras.
PAN —quom ipsi interea uiuant, ualeant,
ubi sint, quid agant, ecquid agant
nec participant nos nec redeunt.

34–35 PAMPHILA an id doles, soror, quia illi suom officium
non colunt, quom tu tuom facis?
PAN   ita pol.
PAMPHILA tace sis, caue sis audiam ego istuc
posthac ex te.
PAN   nam quid iam?
PAMPHILA quia pol meo animo omnis sapientis

40 suom officium aequom est colere et facere.
quam ob rem ego te hoc, soror, tam etsi es maior,
moneo ut tuom memineris officium:
etsi illi improbi sint atque aliter

21 tuos *del. Bothe*

wants to take us away from them. This situation makes
me weary of life, my sister, and causes me agony and
distress.

PAN Stop crying, my sister, and don't inflict on your heart that 20
distress which our father is threatening to cause you.
There's hope that he'll act better. I know him: he said it
in jest and wouldn't gain the fabled Persian mountains 25
made of gold[4] on condition of doing what you're afraid
of. Still, should he do it, we ought not to be angry with
him, and it won't happen without good reason: this is the
third year since our husbands left home— 30

PAMPHILA (*interrupting*) Precisely as you say.

PAN —that they aren't returning and don't let us know
whether in the meantime they themselves are alive and
in good health, where they are, what they're doing, if
they're doing anything.

PAMPHILA Are you upset, my sister, because they aren't honor- 35
ing their duty, while you are doing yours?

PAN Yes, indeed.

PAMPHILA Please be quiet and please make sure that I won't
hear that from you hereafter.

PAN Why is that?

PAMPHILA Because in my opinion all the wise ought to honor 40
and do their duty. For this reason, my sister, I remind
you, even though you are the older one, to remember
your duty. Even if they should be disloyal and fail to treat

---

[4] The mountains of gold were proverbial (cf. e.g., Aristophanes,
Ach. 82). The Persians were associated with wealth, but not necessarily
with those mountains.

nos faciant quam aequom est, tam pol,
45   ne quid magis sit ***
45^a *** omnibus obnixe opibus
nostrum officium meminisse decet.

PAN   placet: taceo.

PAMPHILA   at memineris facito.

[PAN nolo ego, soror, me credi esse immemorem uiri,
neque ille eos honores mihi quos habuit perdidit;
50   nam pol mihi grata acceptaque huiust benignitas.
et me quidem haec condicio nunc non paenitet
neque est quor [non] studeam has nuptias mutarier;
uerum postremo in patris potestate est situm:
faciendum id nobis quod parentes imperant.
55 PAMPHILA scio atque in cogitando maerore augeor,
nam propemodum iam ostendit suam sententiam.

PAN   igitur quaeramus nobis quid facto usus sit.]

I. ii: ANTIPHO. PANEGYRIS. PAMPHILA

ANT qui manet ut moneatur semper seruos homo officium
suom
nec uoluntate id facere meminit, seruos is habitu hau
probust.
60   uos meministis quotcalendis petere demensum cibum:
qui minus meministis quod opus sit facto facere in ae-
dibus?
iam quidem in suo quicque loco nisi erit mihi situm
supellectilis,
quom ego reuortar, uos monumentis commonefaciam
bubulis.
non homines habitare mecum mi hic uidentur, sed
sues.

44 nos Ω, nobis *Guyet*, in nos *Pius*

us as they should, still, so that nothing worse will hap-
pen *** we ought to remember our duty with determi- 45
nation and all our strength.

PAN   Agreed; I'm silent.

PAMPHILA   But do remember it.

[PAN   My sister, I don't want you to believe that I'm forgetful
of my husband, and he hasn't wasted the marks of es-
teem he bestowed upon me; his kindness is welcome and 50
loved by me. I don't regret this match now and I have no
reason why I should be keen to have this marriage re-
placed by another one. But in the end it lies in our fa-
ther's power. We have to do what our parents tell us to.

PAMPHILA   I know, and I'm filled with sadness when I think 55
about it: he's practically shown us his decision already.

PAN   Then let's consider what we need to do.]

Enter ANTIPHO *from his house.*

ANT   (*into the house*) A slave who always waits to be reminded
of his duty and doesn't remember to do it voluntarily is
a slave who isn't worth keeping. You fellows remem- 60
ber to demand your rations of food on the first of every
month; why don't you remember to do in the house what
needs to be done? Now unless every piece of household
equipment is put in its proper place when I return, I'll
remind you with reminders of cowhide.[5] Not humans,
but pigs seem to live here with me. Do make sure that 65

---

[5] I.e., whips.

45–45[a] sit *A*, simus *P*   *post hoc lacunam statuit Leo*
48–57 *uersus non feruntur in A*   52 non *del. Guyet*

65   facite sultis nitidae ut aedes meae sint, quom redeam
        domum.
    iam ego domi adero: ad meam maiorem filiam inuiso
        modo;
    siquis me quaeret, ind' uocatote aliqui; aut iam egomet
        hic ero.

PAMPHILA quid agimus, soror, si offirmabit pater aduorsum
        nos?

PAN   pati
    nos oportet quod ille faciat, quoius potestas plus po-
       test.

70   exorando, haud aduorsando sumendam operam censeo:
    gratiam per si petimus, spero ab eo impetrassere;
    aduorsari sine dedecore et scelere summo hau possu-
       mus,
    neque equidem id factura nec tu ut facias consilium
       dabo,
    uerum ut exoremus. noui ego nostros: exorabilest.

75 ANT principium ego quo pacto cum illis occipiam, id ratioci-
       nor:
    utrum ego perplexim lacessam oratione ad hunc mo-
       dum,
    quasi numquam quicquam in eas simulem, an quasi
       quid indaudiuerim
    eas in se meruisse culpam; an potius temptem leniter
    an minaciter? scio litis fore—ego meas noui optume—

80   si manere hic sese malint potius quam alio nubere.
    non faciam. quid mi opust decurso aetatis spatio cum
       ⟨m⟩eis
    gerere bellum, quom nil quam ob rem id faciam
       meruisse arbitror?

24

my house is spick and span when I return home. I'll be home soon; I'm just going round to see my elder daughter. If anyone is looking for me, some of you must call me from there; at any rate I'll be back soon. (*begins to walk over*)

PAMPHILA What are we to do, my sister, if our father decides not to give in to us?

PAN We ought to accept what is done by the man who has more authority. I think we should make an effort to en- 70 treat and not to oppose him. If we seek it in a friendly manner, I hope that we shall achieve it from him. We cannot oppose him without very great disgrace and wickedness; I for one am not going to do it and I won't advise you to do it, but rather, we should entreat him. I know our men: he's capable of being won over by entreaty. (*they walk away a little*)

ANT (*to himself*) I'm considering the beginning, how I should 75 start with them: should I vex them with my speech obscurely like this, as if I were never accusing them at all, or as if I'd heard something, that they'd become guilty; in other words, had I better handle them gently or threateningly? I know there will be arguments—I know my girls perfectly—if they prefer staying here to getting 80 married to different men. I won't do it. What's the use of waging war with my girls now that I've reached the end of the course of my life, when I don't think they've done anything for which they deserve my doing this? No,

---

71 gratiam per *A*, gratiam a patre *P*

77 in eas simulem *P*, adeo adsimulem *A*   an quasi quid *A*, quasi nihil *P*

81 eis *Ω*, meis *Loman*

25

83	minime, nolo turbas, sed hoc mihi optumum factu arbitror:
85	perplexabiliter earum hodie perpauefaciam pectora.
84	sic faciam: assimulabo quasi quam culpam in sese ammiserint.
86	postid [agam] igitur deinde, ut animus meus erit, faciam palam.
	multa scio faciunda uerba. ibo intro. sed aperta est foris.

PAMPHILA certo enim mi paternae uocis sonitus auris accidit.

PAN is est ecastor. ferre aduorsum homini occupemus osculum.

90 PAMPHILA salue, mi pater.

ANT   et uos ambae. ilico agite assidite.

PAMPHILA osculum—

ANT   sat est osculi mi uostri.

PAN   qui, amabo, pater?

ANT quia ita meae animae salsura euenit.

PAMPHILA   asside hic, pater.

ANT non sedeo istic, uos sedete; ego sedero in subsellio.

PAN mane, puluinum—

ANT   bene procuras. mi satis sic fultum est. sede.

95 PAMPHILA sine, pater.

ANT   quid opust?

PAN   opust.

ANT   morem tibi geram. atque hoc est satis.

PAMPHILA numquam enim nimis curare possunt suom parentem filiae.

85 *ante 84 pos. Petersmann*
86 agam *del. Ritschl*

I don't want commotions; rather, I think this is the best
thing for me to do: I'll frighten their hearts in a confusing   85
manner today. I'll act like this: I'll pretend that they've
committed some offense. Then, after that, I'll reveal
what my feelings are. I know that I'll have to use a lot
of words. (*walks to the door of Pamphila's house with-
out seeing his daughters*) I'll go inside. But the door is
open.

PAMPHILA (*to Panegyris*) Certainly the sound of our father's
voice has reached my ears.

PAN It's him indeed. Let's be quick to go and give him a kiss.
(*they approach*)

PAMPHILA Greetings, my dear father.   90

ANT And mine to you both. Go on, sit down where you are.

PAMPHILA A kiss—(*they embrace him and kiss his cheeks*)

ANT (*interrupting*) I've had enough of your kissing.

PAN How so, please, father?

ANT Because that's how my breath has been salted.[6]

PAMPHILA Do sit down here, father. (*points to the couch*)

ANT I won't sit there; you two should sit there. I'll sit on the
bench. (*does so*)

PAN Wait, a cushion—(*brings one*)

ANT (*interrupting*) You're taking good care of me, but I'm
propped up enough. Sit.

PAMPHILA (*with another cushion*) Allow me, father.   95

ANT What's it necessary for?

PAN It is necessary.

ANT I'll humor you. And this is enough. (*they sit down*)

PAMPHILA Well, daughters can never look after their father

---

[6] The girls' cheeks are still wet with tears, hence the reference to
salting.

quem aequiust nos potiorem habere quam te?
postidea, pater,
uiros nostros, quibus tu uoluisti ess' nos matres fami-
lias.

ANT   bonas ut aequom est facere facitis, quom tamen apsen-
tis uiros

100   perinde habetis quasi praesentes sint.

PAMPHILA   pudicitia est, pater,
eos nos magnuficare qui nos socias sumpserunt sibi.

ANT   num quis hic est alienus nostris dictis auceps auribus?

PAN   nullus praeter nosque teque.

ANT   uostrum animum adhiberi uolo;
nam ego ad uos nunc imperitus rerum et morum mu-
lierum

105   discipulus uenio ad magistras: quibus matronas mori-
bus

quae optumae sunt esse oportet? sed utraque ut dicat
mihi.

PAMPHILA   quid istuc est quod huc exquisitum mulierum
mores uenis?

ANT   pol ego uxorem quaero, postquam uostra mater mortua
est.

PAMPHILA   facile inuenies et peiorem et peius moratam,
pater,

110   quam illa fuit: meliorem nec tu reperies nec Sol uidet.

ANT   at ego ex te exquiro atque ex istac tua sorore.

PAMPHILA   edepol, pater,
scio ut oportet esse; si sint ita ut ego aequom censeo.

ANT   uolo scire ergo ut aequom censes.

100 perinde *P*, proinde *A*   sint *P*, sient *A*

too much. Who would it be right for us to treat better
than you? And next to you, father, our husbands, whose
wives you wanted us to be.

ANT   You're acting the way good women ought to act, since
you treat your husbands as if they were present, absent   100
though they are.

PAMPHILA   It's only right, father, to honor the men who have
taken us as their partners.

ANT   Is there any stranger here bird-catching our words with
his ears?

PAN   There's no one besides us and you.

ANT   I want you two to pay attention; I'm coming to you now
as someone inexperienced in the ways and characters of   105
women, as a male pupil to his female teachers: what
character should those married women have who are
best? But each of you must tell me separately.

PAMPHILA   What do you mean by saying that you're coming
here to ask us about the characters of women?

ANT   I'm looking for a wife, now that your mother has died.

PAMPHILA   Father, you'll easily find one who is worse and has
a worse character than she had; you won't find a better   110
one, nor can Sol[7] see one.

ANT   Still, I'm asking you and your sister there.

PAMPHILA   Goodness, father, I know what they should be like,
if they're the way I believe they ought to be.

ANT   I want to know then how you believe they ought to be.

_____
[7] The sun god, who sees everything.

PAMPHILA   ut, per urbem quom ambulent,
         omnibus os opturent, ne quis merito male dicat sibi.

115   ANT   dic uicissim nunciam tu.

        PAN   quid uis tibi dicam, pater?

        ANT   ubi facillime spectatur mulier quae ingenio est bono?

        PAN   quoi male faciundi est potestas, quae ne id faciat tem-
              perat.

        ANT   hau male istuc! age tu altera, utra siet condicio pensior,
              uirginemne an uiduam habere?

PAMPHILA   quanta mea sapientia est,

120   ex malis multis malum quod minimum est, id minime
              est malum.

        ANT   qui potis est mulier uitare uitiis?

PAMPHILA   ut cottidie
         pridie caueat ne faciat quod pigeat postridie.

        ANT   quae tibi mulier uidetur multo sapientissuma?

        PAN   quae tamen, quom res secundae sunt, se poterit
              noscere,

125   et illa quae aequo animo patietur sibi esse peius quam
              fuit.

        ANT   edepol uos lepide temptaui uostrumque ingenium in-
              geni.
              sed hoc est quod ad uos uenio quodque esse ambas
              conuentas uolo:
              mi auctores ita sunt amici, ut uos hinc abducam do-
              mum.

PAMPHILA   at enim nos quarum res agitur aliter auctores su-
         mus.

130   nam aut olim, nisi tibi placebant, non datas oportuit
         aut nunc non aequom est abduci, pater, illisce apsenti-
         bus.

118–20 *uersus del.* Leo   118 sit Ω, siet *Lindsay*

PAMPHILA When they're walking through town, they should close everybody's mouth, so that no one may slander them deservedly.

ANT *(to Panegyris)* Now you must tell me in turn.   115

PAN What do you want me to tell you, father?

ANT How can one most easily spot a woman who is good-natured?

PAN If a woman has the opportunity to act badly and refrains from acting so.

ANT Not bad, that! Come on, you other one, which match is preferable, having a virgin or a widow?

PAMPHILA In my experience, the evil that's the least among   120
the many is evil to the smallest degree.

ANT How can a woman steer clear of faults?

PAMPHILA Every day she should be on her guard not to do anything the day before that she would regret the next day.

ANT *(to Panegyris)* What woman seems by far the wisest to you?

PAN The one who'll still be able to know herself during prosperity, and the one who bears it calmly when she's in a   125
worse situation than she was.

ANT I've tested you two and the nature of your nature delightfully. But this is the reason why I'm coming to you and why I want to meet you both: my friends advise me to take you home, away from here.

PAMPHILA But we, whose situation is at stake, advise you differently: either we ought not to have been given in mar-   130
riage to the men back then, if you didn't like them, or else it isn't right for us to be taken away now in their absence, father.

ANT   uosne ego patiar cum mendicis nuptas me uiuo uiris?

PAMPHILA   placet ille meus mi mendicus: suos rex reginae
      placet.

    idem animust in paupertate qui olim in diuitiis fuit.

135   ANT   uos' latrones et mendicos homines magni penditis?

PAMPHILA   non tu me argento dedisti, opinor, nuptum, sed
      uiro.

ANT   quid illos exspectatis qui abhinc iam abierunt trien-
      nium?

    quin uos capitis condicionem ex pessuma primariam?

PAN   stultitia est, pater, uenatum ducere inuitas canes.

140   hostis est uxor inuita quae ad uirum nuptum datur.

ANT   certumne est neutram uostrarum persequi imperium
      patris?

PAN   persequimur, nam quo dedisti nuptum abire nolumus.

ANT   bene ualete. ibo atque amicis uostra consilia eloquar.

PAN   probiores credo arbitrabunt, si probis narraueris.

145   ANT   curate igitur familiarem rem ut potestis optume.

PAN   nunc places, quom recte monstras; nunc tibi ausculta-
      bimus.

    nunc, soror, abeamus intro.

PAMPHILA   immo interuisam domum.

    si a uiro tibi forte ueniet nuntius, facito ut sciam.

133 *uel* illic

ANT   Am I to bear it that you two are married to beggars while I'm alive?

PAMPHILA   I like that beggar of mine: a queen likes her king. I have the same attitude in poverty as I once had in wealth.

ANT   Do you two have a high opinion of mercenaries and beggars?   135

PAMPHILA   You didn't give me in marriage to money, I think, but to a man.

ANT   Why are you still waiting for them when they've already been away for three years? Why won't you accept a first-rate match instead of an utterly wretched one?

PAN   Father, it's stupidity to take dogs hunting against their will. A wife who is given in marriage to a man against her   140 will is his enemy.

ANT   Is it your decision that neither of you will follow her father's command?

PAN   We are following it, because we don't want to leave the men you gave us in marriage to.

ANT   Goodbye. I'll go and tell my friends your plans.

PAN   I believe they'll consider us more honorable, if they are honorable themselves.

ANT   Then look after the household affairs as best you can.   145

PAN   Now that you're making rightful suggestions, we approve; now we'll obey you.

Exit ANTIPHO *to the right.*

PAN   Now let's go inside, my sister.

PAMPHILA   No, I'll go and check on my home. If by chance a message comes to you from your husband, let me know.

PAN neque ego te celabo, nec tu me celassis quod scias.
150 eho, Crocotium! i, parasitum Gelasimum huc arcessito,
tecum adduce; nam illum ecastor mittere ad portum
    uolo,
si quae forte ex Asia nauis heri aut hodie uenerit.
nam dies totos apud portum seruos unus assidet;
sed tamen uolo interuisi. propera atque actutum redi.

I. iii: GELASIMVS. CROCOTIVM

155 GEL Famem ego fuisse suspicor matrem mihi,
nam postquam natus sum satur numquam fui.
157 nec quisquam melius referet matri gratiam
[157ᵃ quam ego meae matri refero . . . inuitissumus]
nec rettulit quam ego refero meae matri Fami.
nam illaec me in aluo menses gestauit decem,
160 at ego illam in aluo gesto plus annos decem.
atque illa puerum me gestauit paruolum,
quo minus laboris cepisse illam existumo:
ego non pauxillulam in utero gesto Famem,
uerum hercle multo maxumam et grauissumam;
165 uteri dolores mi [ob]oriuntur cottidie,
sed matrem parere nequeo nec quid agam scio.
⟨atque⟩ auditaui saepe hoc uolgo dicier
solere elephantum grauidam perpetuos decem
esse annos; eius ex semine haec certo est Fames,

157ᵃ *del. Seyffert*
158 *non fertur in A (sed in P et Charisio), del. Lindsay*
159 illa me Ω, illaec me *Lindsay in apparatu*, me illa *Pylades*
165 oboriuntur Ω, oriuntur *Bentley* dolores mi uteri oboriuntur
Pariente 167 atque *add. Leo*

---

8 Asia Minor, i.e., today's Turkey.

PAN   I won't conceal it from you, and you mustn't conceal from me what you learn.

Exit PAMPHILA into her house.

PAN   Hey, Crocotium!   150

Enter CROCOTIUM from the house of Panegyris.

PAN   Go, fetch the hanger-on Gelasimus, and bring him along with you; I want to send him to the harbor, if by chance any ship has come here from Asia[8] yesterday or today; one slave is sitting at the harbor every day, but still I want someone to go and check. Hurry and return at once.

Exit PANEGYRIS into her house.
Enter GELASIMUS from the right, without noticing Crocotium.

GEL   I suspect that Hunger was my mother: from the time that   155
I was born I've never been full. And no one will repay his mother better [than I am repaying my mother . . . completely against my will] or has repaid her better than I repay my mother, Hunger: she carried me in her belly for ten months,[9] whereas I have been carrying her in my   160
belly for over ten years. And she carried me as a tiny baby, which is why I think she had less trouble; I am not carrying a tiny Hunger in my belly, but the greatest and heaviest by far. Every day I get pangs in my stomach, but   165
I can't give birth to my mother and I don't know what to do. And I've often heard the common saying that an el-

---

[9] Lunar months rather than calendar months.

170	nam iam compluris annos utero haeret meo.
	nunc si ridiculum hominem quaerat quispiam,
	uenalis ego sum cum ornamentis omnibus;
	inanimentis explementum quaerito.
174	Gelasimo nomen mi indidit paruo pater,
176	quia ind' iam a pusillo puero ridiculus fui.
175	propter pauperiem hoc adeo nomen repperi,
177	eo quia paupertas fecit ridiculus forem;
	nam illa artis omnis perdocet, ubi quem attigit.
	per annonam caram dixit me natum pater:
180	propterea, credo, nunc esurio acrius.
	sed generi nostro haec reddita est benignitas:
	nulli negare soleo, siquis me esum uocat.
	oratio una interiit hominum pessume,
	atque optuma hercle meo animo et scitissuma,
185	qua ante utebantur: "ueni illo ad cenam, sic face,
	promitte uero, ne grauare. est commodum?
	uolo inquam fieri, non amittam quin eas."
	nunc reppererunt iam ei uerbo uicarium—
	nihili quidem hercle uerbum est ac uilissumum:
190	"uocem te ad cenam nisi egomet cenem foris."
	ei hercle ego uerbo lumbos diffractos uelim,
	ni uere perierit, si cenassit domi.
	haec uerba subigunt me uti mores barbaros

176 *ante 175 posuit Acidalius*
193 me ut Ω, me uti *Bothe*, med ut *Lindsay*

---

10 A common, but mistaken belief in antiquity (cf. e.g., Plin. *nat.* 8.28), yet not without basis in reality: elephant pregnancies last remarkably long, on average just under two years.

11 A wordplay. Suffixes in *-mentum* denote types of speech or edible things. The *inanimenta* or "emptiments" mentioned by Gelasimus re-

ephant is normally pregnant for an entire ten years;[10] that's the breed this Hunger is certainly from: it's been attached to my belly for several years already.   170

Now if anyone should be looking for a jester, I'm for sale with all my equipment. I'm looking for fulfillment for my emptiments.[11] My father gave me the name Gelasimus when I was small, because I was funny right from the time I was a tiny tot.[12] In addition I found this name   175 because of my poverty, because poverty caused my being funny; it teaches all skills whenever it gets hold of someone. My father said I was born when the price of grain was high. That's the reason I think I'm suffering from   180 sharper pangs of hunger now. But our family has been given this kindness as compensation: I'm not in the habit of saying no to anyone if he invites me to eat. Now one type of speech of the people has perished most wretchedly, and in my opinion it was the best and smartest one, which they used before: "come over to dinner, do, prom-   185 ise it in truth, stop objecting. Is it convenient? I tell you, I want it done, I won't let you avoid coming." Now they've found a substitute for this phrase—a worthless and most despicable phrase at that: "I'd invite you to   190 dinner if I weren't eating out myself." I'd really like this word's loins broken, unless it's truly dead, if he eats at home.[13] These phrases are forcing me to learn barbarian

fer to his jokes, which have no substance to them, but he also jocularly transfers the word to a new sphere, his hunger. The *explementum* refers to food.   [12] *Gelasimus* means "funny."

[13] Somewhat obscure. The meaning seems to be that eating out is just an excuse for not inviting the hanger-on, but that the man who makes this excuse will actually still eat at home; so the excuse should be punished severely or even die.

		discam atque ut faciam praeconis compendium
195		itaque auctionem praedicem ipse ut uenditem.
	CRO	hic ille est parasitus quem arcessitum missa sum.
		quae loquitur auscultabo prius quam colloquar.
	GEL	sed curiosi sunt hic complures mali,
		alienas res qui curant studio maxumo,
200		quibus ipsis nulla est res quam procurent sua:
		i quando quem auctionem facturum sciunt,
		adeunt, perquirunt quid siet causae ilico:
		alienum aes cogat an pararit praedium,
		uxorin sit reddenda dos diuortio.
205		eos omnis tam etsi hercle haud indignos iudico
		qui multum miseri sint, laborent, nil moror:
		dicam auctionis causam, ut damno gaudeant;
208		nam curiosus nemo est quin sit maleuolus.
[208ᵃ		ipse egomet quam ob rem auctionem praedicem.]
		damna euenerunt maxuma misero mihi,
210		ita me mancupia miserum affecerunt male,
		potationes plurumae demortuae;
		quot adeo cenae quas defleui mortuae,
		quot potiones mulsi, quae autem prandia,
		quae inter continuom perdidi triennium!
215		prae maerore adeo miser atque aegritudine
		consenui; paene sum fame emortuos.
	CRO	ridiculus aeque nullus est, quando esurit.
	GEL	nunc auctionem facere decretum est mihi:
		foras necessum est quicquid habeo uendere.

195 uenditem *A*, me ueni item *P*, ueneam *Gronovius*
202 siet causae Ω, sit causai *Leo*
208ᵃ *uersum om. A*

customs, to save the cost of an auctioneer, and thus to announce an auction myself in order to sell myself. 195

CRO (*aside*) This is that hanger-on who I was sent to fetch. I'll listen to what he says before I address him.

GEL But here there are many crooked meddlers, who meddle in other people's business with greatest enthusiasm, and who don't have anything of their own to meddle with. When they know that someone's going to hold an auction, they instantly approach him and ask what the reason is: whether debt is forcing him to or whether he has bought land, or whether he has to return his wife's dowry to her because of a divorce. Even if I judge that they all deserve to be very wretched and to suffer, I don't care: I'll state the reason for the auction so that they may be happy about my loss; there's no meddler who isn't malevolent. [The reason why I myself am announcing an auction.] 200 205

Poor me, I've made very great losses, that's how wretchedly my slaves[14] have behaved toward me and very many drinking sessions have died. What's more, how many dinners are there whose death I've grieved over, how many drinks of honey wine, and how many lunches which I've lost during the last three years! Poor me, out of sadness and grief I've grown old; I'm almost dead from hunger. 210 215

CRO (*aside*) Nobody is as funny as him when he's hungry.

GEL Now I'm resolved to hold an auction; I have to sell away to strangers whatever I have.

[14] The slaves are his meals.

220		adeste sultis, praeda erit praesentium.
		logos ridiculos uendo. age licemini.
		qui cena poscit? ecqui poscit prandio?
		Hercules te amabit—prandio, cena tibi.
		ehem, annuistin? nemo meliores dabit,
225		nulli meliores esse parasito sinam.
		uel unctiones Graecas sudatorias
		uendo uel alias malacas, crapularias;
		cauillationes, assentatiunculas,
		ac periuratiunculas parasiticas;
230		robiginosam strigilim, ampullam rubidam,
		parasitum inanem quo recondas reliquias.
		haec ueniisse iam opus est quantum potest,
		ut decumam partem Herculi polluceam.
234– 35	CRO	ecastor auctionem hau magni preti!
		adhaesit homini ad infumum uentrem fames.
		adibo ad hominem.
	GEL	quis haec est quae aduorsum it mihi?
		Epignomi ancilla haec quidem est Crocotium.
	CRO	Gelasime, salue.
	GEL	non id est nomen mihi.
240	CRO	certo mecastor id fuit nomen tibi.
	GEL	fuit disertim, uerum id usu perdidi:
		nunc Miccotrogus nomine e uero uocor.
	CRO	eu ecastor!
		risi ted hodie multum.
	GEL	quando aut quo in loco?

225 *uersum secl. Guyet*

---

[15] Fest. 318 L. states that flasks which are *rubidae* are made of
leather and are full of creases (and thus presumably worn out).

(*to the audience*) Do attend, the booty will belong to 220
those present! I'm selling jokes. Come on, make a bid.
Who wants to buy them for the price of a dinner? Does
anyone want to buy them for the price of a lunch? (*to
someone in the audience*) Hercules will love you—for a
lunch and a dinner for you. (*to someone else*) Oh, have
you nodded a yes? No one will give you better ones, I 225
won't let any hanger-on have better ones. (*to the whole
audience again*) I'm selling Greek sudorific ointments,
or other, emollient ones against hangover; little pieces of
jest, flatteries, and a hanger-on's perjuries; a rusty oil 230
scraper, a red-brown[15] flask, and an empty hanger-on to
bury your leftovers in. These need to be sold now as
quickly as possible so that I may offer up a tithe to Her-
cules.[16]

CRO   (*aside*) Goodness, an auction of little worth! Hunger has 235
got itself attached to the pit of his stomach. I'll approach
him.

GEL   (*spotting her*) Who is this woman who is coming toward
me? It's the slave girl of Epignomus, Crocotium.

CRO   My greetings, Gelasimus.

GEL   That's not my name.

CRO   It certainly was your name. 240

GEL   It surely was, but I wore it out; now I'm truthfully called
Miccotrogus by name.[17]

CRO   Goodness! I've laughed at you a lot today.

GEL   When or in what place?

---

[16] Tithes were regularly given to Hercules to thank him for business
success.

[17] The name means "small biter."

245	CRO	hic quom auctionem praedicabas—
	GEL	pessuma,
		eho an audiuisti?
	CRO	—te quidem dignissumam.
	GEL	quo nunc is?
	CRO	ad te.
	GEL	quid uenis?
	CRO	Panegyris
		rogare iussit te nunc opere maxumo
		mecum simitu ut ires ad sese domum.
250	GEL	ego illo mehercle uero eo quantum potest.
		iamne exta cocta sunt? quot agnis fecerat?
	CRO	illaquidem nullum sacruficauit.
	GEL	quo modo?
		quid igitur me uolt?
	CRO	tritici modios decem
		rogare, opinor[, te uolt].
	GEL	mene, ut ab sese petam?
255	CRO	immo ut ⟨tu⟩ a uobis mutuom nobis dares.
	GEL	nega esse quod dem nec mihi nec mutuom
		neque aliud quicquam nisi hoc quod habeo pallium;
		linguam quoque etiam uendidi datariam.
	CRO	au!
260		nullan tibi lingua est?
	GEL	quae quidem dicat "dabo";
		uentri reliqui eccam quae dicat "cedo."
	CRO	malum quidem si uis—
	GEL	haec eadem dicit tibi.
	CRO	quid nunc? ituru's an non?

248 te ut Ω, te nunc *Guyet*, ted hoc *Bugge*
254 te uolt *del. Gruterus*

| CRO | Here, when you were announcing your auction— | 245 |

CRO   Here, when you were announcing your auction—   245

GEL   (*interrupting*) You crook, hey, did you listen to it?

CRO   —which was worthy of yourself.

GEL   Where are you going now?

CRO   To you.

GEL   Why are you coming to me?

CRO   Panegyris told me to ask you earnestly now to come along with me home to her.

GEL   I'm indeed going there as quickly as possible. Are the innards cooked already?[18] How many lambs did she sacrifice?   250

CRO   She didn't sacrifice at all.

GEL   How do you mean? Why does she want me then?

CRO   To ask you for ten pecks[19] of wheat, I think.

GEL   Me, so that I demand them from her?

CRO   No, so that you would lend them to us from yourself.   255

GEL   Say to her that I don't have anything to give on loan or anything else except for this cloak that I have. I've even sold my tongue that had to do with giving.

CRO   Oh! Don't you have any tongue?   260

GEL   At least none to say "I'll give"; but look, I left my belly one to say "give." (*sticks out his tongue*)

CRO   If you want a thrashing—

GEL   (*interrupting*) My tongue says the same to you.

CRO   Well then? Are you going to come or not?

---

[18] After the sacrifice most meat was consumed by the participants.   [19] A dry measure roughly equivalent to nine liters.

---

255 tu *add. Goetz*   a uobis *A*, abs te *P*
256 nega *A*, negato *P*

GEL   abi sane domum,

264–65   iam illo uenturum dicito. propera atque abi.

demiror quid illaec me ad se arcessi iusserit,
quae numquam iussit me ad se arcessi ante hunc diem
postquam uir abiit eius. miror quid siet,
nisi ut periclum fiat: uisam quid uelit.

270   sed eccum Pinacium eius puerum. hoc uide,
satin ut facete, atque ex pictura astitit?
ne iste edepol uinum poculo pauxillulo
saepe exanclauit submerum scitissume.

ACTVS II

II. i: PINACIVM. GELASIMVS

PIN   Mercurius, Iouis qui nuntius perhibetur, numquam ae-
       que patri

275   suo nuntium lepidum attulit quam ego nunc meae erae
       nuntiabo:

itaque onustum pectus porto laetitia lubentiaque
nec lubet nisi gloriose quicquam proloqui profecto.
amoenitates omnium uenerum et uenustatum affero
ripisque superat mi atque abundat pectus laetitia
       meum.

280   propera, Pinacium, pedes hortare, honesta dicta fac-
       tis—

nunc tibi potestas adipiscendi est gloriam, laudem, de-
       cus—

eraeque egenti subueni [—benefacta maiorum
       tuom—]

282 genti Ω, egenti Z   benefacta maiorum (malorum *AB*) tuum (tuorum *CD*) Ω, *del. Ritschl*

GEL Do go home and tell her that I'm going there now. Hurry   265
     and leave.

Exit CROCOTIUM *into the house of Panegyris.*

GEL I wonder why she had me summoned to her; before this
     day she never had me summoned to her, after her hus-
     band left. I wonder what's the matter, except that she
     wants to test me. I'll go and see what she wants. (*looks*   270
     around) But look, Pinacium, her slave boy. Look at this:
     hasn't he taken a charming stance, like in a painting?[20]
     Really, he's often ladled out nearly undiluted wine with
     his tiny cup in a very delightful way.

ACT TWO

Enter PINACIUM *from the left, in such a hurry that he does not
notice anyone; he is carrying his fishing gear.*

PIN Mercury, who is said to be Jupiter's messenger, never
     brought his father a message as delightful as the one I'll   275
     now announce to my mistress: so laden with happiness
     and pleasure is the breast I'm carrying; indeed I don't
     want to say anything except in a boastful manner. I'm
     bringing the delights of all charms and graces, and my
     breast overflows its banks with joy. Hurry, Pinacium,   280
     urge on your feet, do credit to your words by your ac-
     tions—now you have the chance to gain glory, laud, and
     honor—and bring help to your poor mistress in need,
     [—the good deeds of your ancestors—] who is waiting

[20] Greek *pinakion* can mean "picture."

quae misera in exspectatione est Epignomi aduentum
uiri.

proinde ut decet amat uirum suom, cupide expetit.

nunc, Pinacium,

285   age ut placet, curre ut lubet, caue quemquam flocci fe-
ceris,

cubitis depulsa de uia, tranquillam concinna uiam;

si rex opstabit obuiam, regem ipsum prius peruortito.

288   GEL   quidnam dicam Pinacium

288ᵃ   lasciuibundum tam lubentem currere?

harundinem fert sportulamque et hamulum piscarium.

290   PIN   sed tandem, opinor, aequiust eram mihi esse supplicem

atque oratores mittere ad me donaque ex auro et qua-
drigas

qui uehar, nam pedibus ire non queo. ergo iam reuor-
tar.

ad me adiri et supplicari egomet mihi aequom censeo.

an uero nugas censeas, nihil esse quod ego nunc scio?

295   tantum a portu apporto bonum, tam gaudium grande
affero,

uix ipsa domina hoc, ut scias, exoptare ab dis audeat.

nunc ultro id deportem? hau placet neque id uiri offi-
cium arbitror.

sic hoc uidetur mihi magis meo conuenire huic nuntio:

aduorsum ueniat, opsecret se ut nuntio hoc impertiam;

300   secundas fortunas decent superbiae.

sed tandem quom recogito, qui potuit scire haec scire
me?

non enim possum quin reuortar, quin loquar, quin edis-
sertem

288ᵃ lubentem *A*, lubenter *P*

46

for the arrival of her husband Epignomus. Just as she ought to, she loves her husband and eagerly longs for him. Now, Pinacium, go on as you like, run as you like, and make sure you don't care a straw about anyone. Push them off the street with your elbows, render the street calm. If a king stands in your way, knock down the king himself first. 285

GEL *(aside)* Why on earth should I say Pinacium is running so friskily and so eagerly? He's carrying his fishing rod, a basket, and a fishhook.

PIN But in the end I think it's more appropriate for my mis- 290 tress to entreat me and to send envoys to me, gifts of gold, and a chariot for me to drive in: I can't walk on foot. So now I'll go back. I think it's fair that I should be approached and entreated. Or would you really consider it nonsense and believe that what I know now amounts to nothing? I'm bringing such a great good from the harbor 295 and such great joy, my mistress herself, just so that you know, would hardly dare to wish for it from the gods. Should I now bring it to her of my own accord? I don't like it and I don't consider it the way to behave for a man. This seems to me to be more appropriate for this message of mine: let her come toward me and beg me to share this news with her. Displays of pride suit good 300 fortunes. *(turns toward the harbor again)*

But in the end, when I think about it, how could she have known that I know this? I really can't help returning, speaking, explaining, freeing my mistress from

---

292 nam Ω, iam *FZ*
296 ni scias *A*, ne si sciat *B*, nisi sciat *CD*, ut scias *Leo*

eramque ex maerore eximam, bene facta maiorum
meum

exaugeam atque illam augeam insperato, opportuno
bono:

305   contundam facta Talthybi contemnamque omnis nun-
tios;

simulque [ad] cursuram meditabor [me] ad ludos
Olympios.

sed spatium hoc occidit: breue est curriculo; quam me
paenitet!

quid hoc? occlusam ianuam uideo. ibo et pultabo fores.

309   aperite atque approperate, fores

309ᵃ   facite ut pateant, remouete moram;

310   nimis haec res sine cura geritur.

310ᵃ   uide quam dudum hic asto et pulto.

311   somnone operam datis? experiar

311ᵃ   fores an cubiti ac pedes plus ualeant.

312   nimis uellem hae fores erum fugissent,

312ᵃ   ea causa ut haberent malum magnum;

defessus sum pultando.

hoc postremum est. uae uobis!

315   GEL   ibo atque hunc compellabo.

saluos sis.

     PIN   et tu salue.

     GEL   iam tu piscator factu's?

     PIN   quam pridem non edisti?

     GEL   unde is? quid fers? quid festinas?

320   PIN   tua quod nil refert, ne cures.

304 domo *A*, modo *P*, bono *Gulielmus*
306 ad *et* me *del. Ritschl*
311ᵃ an pedes Ω, ac pedes *Loman*

her misery, increasing the good deeds of my ancestors,
and providing her with unhoped-for, timely good news.
(*turns again and runs*) I'll outdo the deeds of Talthy-   305
bius[21] and despise all messengers; and at the same time
I'll practice running for the Olympic games. (*reaches the
house of Panegyris*) But this distance has come to an end.
It's too short for a run; how sad! What's this? I can see
that the door is locked. I'll go and knock at it. (*does so
very loudly*) Open up and hurry up, make sure that the
door is wide open, get rid of delay! (*to the audience*) This   310
business is being done far too carelessly. Look how long
I've been standing here and knocking. (*into the house
again*) Are you diligently occupied in sleep? I'll try
whether the door or my elbows and feet are stronger.
(*hits very hard*) I very much wish that this door had fled
from its master, so that it would get a great thrashing for
it; I'm tired from knocking. This is the last time. (*hits the
door*) Curse you!

GEL   (*aside*) I'll go and address him. (*loudly*) My greetings to   315
you.

PIN   And mine to you.

GEL   Have you become a fisherman now?

PIN   For how long haven't you eaten?

GEL   Where are you coming from? What are you bringing?
Why are you in a rush?

PIN   You shouldn't busy yourself with what's none of your   320
business.

---

[21] In Homer, he was the messenger of King Agamemnon.

312ᵃ manum Ω, malum magnum *Hermann*

	GEL	quid istic inest?
	PIN	quas tu edes colubras.
	GEL	quid tam iracundu's?
	PIN	si in te
		pudor assit, non me appelles.
	GEL	possum scire ex te uerum?
325	PIN	potes: hodie non cenabis.

II. ii: PANEGYRIS. GELASIMVS. PINACIVM

326	PAN	quisnam, opsecro, has frangit fores? ubi ⟨is⟩ est?
326ᵃ		tune haec facis? tun mi huc hostis uenis?
327	GEL	salue, tuo arcessitu uenio huc.
327ᵃ	PAN	ean gratia fores effringis?
328	GEL	tuos inclama, tui delinquont:
328ᵃ		ego quid me uelles uisebam;
329		nam mequidem harum miserebat.
	PIN	er-
329ᵃ		go auxilium propere latum est.
330	PAN	quisnam hic loquitur tam prope nos?
	PIN	Pinacium.
	PAN	ubi is est?
	PIN	respice ad me et relinque egentem parasitum, Panegy-ris.
	PAN	Pinacium.
	PIN	istuc indiderunt nomen maiores mihi.
	PAN	quid agis?
	PIN	quid agam rogitas?
	PAN	quidni rogitem?
	PIN	quid mecum est tibi?
	PAN	min fastidis, propudiose? eloquere propere, Pinacium.

326 ubist *A*, ubi est *P*, ubi is est *Spengel*

50

GEL What's in there? (*points at the basket*)

PIN Snakes that you'll eat.

GEL Why are you so angry?

PIN If you had any shame, you wouldn't address me.

GEL Can I learn the truth from you?

PIN Yes, you can: you won't have dinner today.   325

Enter PANEGYRIS *from her house, without noticing her slave.*

PAN Who on earth is breaking this door, please? Where is he?
     (*to Gelasimus*) Are you doing this? Have you come here
     as my enemy?

GEL My greetings, I've come here on your summons.

PAN Is that why you're breaking down the door?

GEL Scold your own people, it's your own people who are at
     fault; I was coming to see what you wanted me for: *I* had
     pity on the door.

PIN That's why help was brought quickly.

PAN Who is speaking here so close to us?   330

PIN Pinacium.

PAN Where is he?

PIN (*stepping forward*) Look at me and leave the impover-
     ished hanger-on alone, Panegyris.

PAN Pinacium!

PIN That's the name my ancestors have given me.

PAN What are you up to?

PIN You ask what I'm up to?

PAN Why shouldn't I ask?

PIN What business have you with me?

PAN Are you putting on airs with me, you shameless creature?
     Tell me quickly, Pinacium.

335	PIN	iube me omittere igitur hos qui retinent.
	PAN	qui retinent?
	PIN	rogas?
		omnia membra lassitudo mihi tenet—
	PAN	linguam quidem
		sat scio tibi non tenere.
	PIN	—ita celeri curriculo fui
		propere a portu tui honoris causa.
	PAN	ecquid apportas boni?
	PIN	nimio apporto multo tanta plus quam speras.
	PAN	salua sum.
340	PIN	at ego perii, quoi medullas lassitudo perbibit.
	GEL	quid ego, quoi misero medullas uentris percepit fames?
	PAN	ecquem conuenisti?
	PIN	multos.
	PAN	at uirum?
	PIN	equidem plurumos:
		uerum ex multis nequiorem nullum quam hic est.
	GEL	quo modo?
		iam dudum ego istum patior dicere iniuste mihi.
345		praeterhac si me irritassis—
	PIN	edepol esuries male.
	GEL	animum inducam ut istuc uerum te elocutum esse arbitrer.
	PIN	munditias uolo fieri. efferte huc scopas simulque harundinem,
		ut operam omnem araneorum perdam et texturam improbem
		deiciamque eorum omnis telas.

339 nimio inparti *P*, nimiamres *A*, nimio adporto *Ritschl*

PIN	Then have those who are holding me back let go of me.	335
PAN	Who are the ones holding you back?	
PIN	You ask? Exhaustion has all my limbs in its grip—	
PAN	(*interrupting*) I know well enough that it doesn't have your tongue in its grip.	
PIN	—that's how quickly I've been hurrying from the harbor out of respect for you.	
PAN	Are you bringing me anything good?	
PIN	I'm bringing many times more good than you hope for.	
PAN	I'm saved!	
PIN	But I am dead: exhaustion has drunk up my vitals.	340
GEL	What about me, the vitals of whose stomach hunger has gripped, poor me?	
PAN	(*ignoring Gelasimus*) Have you met anyone?	
PIN	A lot of people.	
PAN	But a man?[22]	
PIN	Very many; yet among the many none more worthless than this man here is. (*points at Gelasimus*)	
GEL	How do you mean? (*to Panegyris*) For a long time now I've tolerated him insulting me. (*to Gelasimus*) If you provoke me further—	345
PIN	(*interrupting*) You'll starve terribly.	
GEL	I'll persuade myself to think that you've spoken the truth.	
PIN	(*into the house*) I want tidiness to be created. Bring out brooms and with them a pole so that I may destroy every work of the spiders, remove their weaving, and throw down all their webs. (*slaves bring out cleaning equipment and wait for further orders*)	

[22] Latin *uir* is ambiguous between "man" and "husband." As no possessive pronoun is used here, the ambiguity is all the more striking.

	GEL	miseri algebunt postea.
350	PIN	quid? illos itidemne esse censes quasi te cum ueste unica?

cape illas scopas.

	GEL	capiam.
	PIN	hoc egomet, tu hoc conuorre.
	GEL	ego fecero.
	PIN	ecquis huc effert nassiternam cum aqua?
	GEL	sine suffragio

populi tamen aedilitatem hic quidem gerit.

	PIN	age tu ocius

finge humum, consperge ante aedis.

	GEL	faciam.
	PIN	factum oportuit.
355	PIN	ego hinc araneas de foribus deiciam et de pariete.
	GEL	edepol rem negotiosam!
	PAN	quid sit nil etiam scio,

nisi forte hospites uenturi sunt.

	PIN	⟨uos⟩ lectos sternite.
	GEL	principium placet de lectis.
	PIN	alii ligna caedite,

alii piscis depurgate quos piscatu rettuli,

360		pernam et glandium deicite.
	GEL	hic hercle homo nimium sapit.
	PAN	non ecastor, ut ego opinor, satis erae morem geris.
	PIN	immo res omnis relictas habeo prae quod tu uelis.
	PAN	tum tu igitur, qua causa missus es ad portum, id expedi.

354 pinge Ω, finge *Bugge*
357 uos *add. Weise*
359 piscator attulit Ω, piscatu rettuli *Lipsius*

GEL The poor creatures will feel cold afterward.

PIN What? Do you think they're like you with one single 350
     outfit? Take that broom.

GEL Yes. (*does so*)

PIN I'll sweep this, you sweep that.

GEL I'll do so. (*both start cleaning*)

PIN (*into the house*) Is anyone bringing out a can with water?
     (*someone does so*)

GEL This chap has the aedileship, even without the people's
     vote.

PIN Go on, you tidy the floor quickly, sprinkle water in front
     of the house.

GEL I'll do so.

PIN It ought to have been done already. I'll remove the cob- 355
     webs from the door and the wall.

GEL Goodness, what a laborious business!

PAN (*to herself*) Even now I don't know what's going on, un-
     less by chance some guests are going to arrive.

PIN (*to servants*) You, put coverings on the couches. (*they
     obey and go back in*)

GEL I like the beginning about the couches.

PIN Some must cut wood, others must clean the fish I brought
     back from fishing and must take down the ham and 360
     sweetbread.

GEL This chap is terribly sensible.

PAN (*to Pinacium*) You really aren't obeying your mistress
     well enough, I think.

PIN On the contrary, I regard everything as of no account by
     comparison with what you want.

PAN Then tell me about the job you were sent to the harbor
     for.

PIN   dicam. postquam me misisti ad portum cum luci simul,
365   commodum radiosus sese sol superabat ex mari.
      dum percontor portitores, ecquae nauis uenerit
      ex Asia, negant uenisse, conspicatus sum interim
      cercurum, quo ego me maiorem non uidisse censeo.
      in portum uento secundo, uelo passo peruenit.
370   alius alium percontamur: "quoia est nauis? quid uehit?"
      interibi Epignomum conspicio tuom uirum et seruom
        Stichum.

PAN   hem quid? Epignomum elocutu's?
PIN   tuom uirum.
GEL   et uitam meam.
PIN   uenit, inquam.
PAN   tutin ipsus ipsum uidisti?
PIN   lubens.
      argenti aurique aduexit nimium.
GEL   nimis factum bene!
375   hercle uero capiam scopas atque hoc conuorram lu-
        bens.
PIN   lanam purpuramque multam.
GEL   est qui uentrem uestiam.
PIN   lectos eburatos, auratos.
GEL   accubabo regie.
PIN   tum Babylonica et peristroma, tonsilia et tappetia
      aduexit, nimium bonae rei.
GEL   hercle rem gestam bene!
380 PIN   poste, ut occepi narrare, fidicinas, tibicinas,
      sambucas aduexit secum forma eximia.
GEL   eugepae!
      quando adbibero, alludiabo: tum sum ridiculissumus.

PIN   I will. After you sent me to the harbor at first light, the   365
sun, all resplendent, was just then rising from the sea.
While I was asking the customs officers if any ship had
come from Asia and they were saying that none had
come, I spotted the biggest chipper that I think I've ever
seen. It enters the harbor with a favorable wind, full sail.
We ask one another: "Whose ship is it? What is it carry-   370
ing?" Meanwhile I spot Epignomus, your husband, and
his slave Stichus.

PAN   Oh! What? Did you say Epignomus?

PIN   Yes, your husband.

GEL   And my livelihood.

PIN   (*ignoring Gelasimus*) He's come, I'm telling you.

PAN   Did you see him face to face?

PIN   Yes, with pleasure. He's brought a great deal of silver and
gold.

GEL   Excellent! Really, I'll take the broom and sweep this up   375
with pleasure. (*starts cleaning again*)

PIN   A lot of wool and purple cloth.

GEL   I have something to clothe my belly with.

PIN   Couches adorned with ivory and gold.

GEL   I'll recline at table like a king.

PIN   Next, he's brought Babylonian tapestries and draperies,
smooth fabrics and rugs, terribly good.

GEL   How successful he's been!

PIN   Then, as I began to say, he's brought along lyre girls, flute   380
girls, and harp girls of outstanding beauty.

GEL   Hurray! When I've drunk freely, I'll frolic; then I'm fun-
niest.

PIN	poste unguenta multigenerum multa.
GEL	non uendo logos.

iam ‹iam› non facio auctionem, mi optigit hereditas:
385 maleuoli perquisitores auctionum perierint.
Hercules, decumam esse adauctam tibi quam uoui gra-
tulor.
spes est tandem aliquando importunam exigere ex
utero Famem.

PIN	poste autem aduexit parasitos secum—
GEL	ei, perii miser!
PIN	—ridiculissumos.
GEL	reuorram hercle hoc quod conuorri modo.
390 PAN	uidistin uirum sororis Pamphilum?
PIN	non.
PAN	non adest?
PIN	immo uenisse eum simitu aiebat ille; ego huc citus

praecucurri, ut nuntiarem nuntium exoptabilem.

GEL	uenales logi sunt illi quos negabam uendere.

ilicet, iam meo malo est quod maleuolentes gaudeant.
395 Hercules, qui deus sis, sane discessisti non bene.

PAN	i intro, Pinacium, iube famulos rem diuinam mi appa-

rent.
bene uale.

GEL	uin amministrem?
PAN	sat seruorum habeo domi.

384 iam *add. Bothe*
396 famulos *P*, famulis *A*

---

[23] A hypocoristic form of *Pamphilippus*.

PIN Then, many ointments of many types.

GEL I'm not selling my witticisms now. I'm not holding an
     auction any more, I've got hold of an inheritance. May   385
     the malevolent auction hunters be ruined! Hercules, I
     congratulate you on having the tithe increased which I
     vowed to you. There's hope at last that at some point I'll
     drive relentless Hunger out of my belly.

PIN But then he's brought hangers-on with him—

GEL (interrupting) Dear me, I'm dead, wretch that I am!

PIN —and very funny ones at that.

GEL I'll unsweep what I've just swept up.

PAN (still ignoring Gelasimus) Did you see my sister's hus-   390
     band, Pamphilus?[23]

PIN No.

PAN He isn't here?

PIN No, my master said he'd come at the same time. I ran
     ahead here quickly to announce the welcome news.

GEL Those witticisms that I said I wouldn't sell are on sale
     again. It's all up; now because of my misfortune there's
     something malevolent people can rejoice over. Hercules,   395
     considering that you're a god, you really haven't come
     off well.

PAN Go in, Pinacium, have the servants prepare a sacrifice for
     me.

Exit PINACIUM *into the house.*

PAN (to Gelasimus) Goodbye.

GEL Don't you want me to assist?

PAN I have enough slaves at home.

Exit PANEGYRIS *into her house.*

GEL   enim uero, Gelasime, opinor prouenisti futtile,
         si neque ille adest neque hic qui uenit quicquam
            subuenit.
400   ibo intro ad libros et discam de dictis melioribus;
         nam ni illos homines expello, ego occidi planissume.

ACTVS III

III. i: EPIGNOMVS. STICHVS

EPI   quom bene re gesta saluos conuortor domum,
         Neptuno gratis habeo et Tempestatibus;
         simul Mercurio, qui me in mercimoniis
405   iuuit lucrisque quadruplicauit rem meam.
         olim quos abiens affeci aegrimonia,
         eos nunc laetantis faciam aduentu meo.
         nam iam Antiphonem conueni affinem meum
         cumque eo reueni ex inimicitia in gratiam.
410   uidete, quaeso, quid potest pecunia:
         quoniam bene gesta re rediisse me uidet
         magnasque apportauisse diuitias domum,
         sine aduocatis ibidem in cercuro in stega
         in amicitiam atque in gratiam conuortimus.
415   et is hodie apud me cenat et frater meus;
         nam heri ambo in uno portu fuimus, sed mea
         hodie soluta est nauis aliquanto prius.
         age abduce hasce intro quas mecum adduxi, Stiche.
STI   ere, si ego taceam seu loquar, scio scire te
420   quam multas tecum miserias mulcauerim.
         nunc hunc diem unum ex illis multis miseriis

GEL   Really, Gelasimus, I think you've wasted your pains, inasmuch as that other one isn't here and the one who has come isn't coming to your help. I'll go in to my books and   400 learn from among the better jests; unless I drive those people away, I'm most obviously dead.

Exit GELASIMUS *to the right.*

ACT THREE

Enter EPIGNOMUS *and* STICHUS *from the left, followed by slave girls in exotic dress.*

EPI   I give thanks to Neptune and the Weather goddesses for letting me return home successful and safe; and also to Mercury, who helped me in my business affairs and in-   405 creased my possessions fourfold with profit. The people I once made sad by my leaving I shall now make happy by returning: I've already met my relation Antipho and have returned from enmity to favor in his eyes. Please   410 see what money can do: now that he sees that I've come back successful and that I've brought home great riches, we returned to friendship and goodwill without any mediating parties on the ship's deck straightaway. And he   415 dines with me today, and also my brother; yesterday we were both in one and the same harbor, but my ship set sail a bit earlier today. (*to Stichus*) Go on, take these girls inside whom I brought along with me, Stichus.

STI   Master, whether I'm silent or whether I speak, I know that you know how many hardships I've given a hard   420 time to with you. Now for this one day in recompense

61

		uolo me eleutheria capere aduenientem domum.
	EPI	et ius et aequom postulas: sumas, Stiche.
		in hunc diem te nil moror; abi quo lubet.
425		cadum tibi ueteris uini propino.
	STI	papae!
		ducam hodie amicam.
	EPI	uel decem, dum de tuo.
	STI	quid? hoc etiam unum?
	EPI	quid id autem unum est? expedi.
	STI	ad cenam ibone?
	‹EPI	‹si uoca›tu's, censeo.
	STI	sic hoc placet; uoca‹tus necn›e nil moror.
430	EPI	ubi cenas hodie?
	STI	sic hanc rationem institi:
		amicam ego habeo Stephanium hinc ex proxumo,
		tui fratris ancillam: eo condicam symbolam
		ad cenam ad eius conseruom Sangarinum Syrum.
		eadem est amica ambobus, riuales sumus.
435	EPI	age abduce hasce intro. hunc tibi dedo diem.
	STI	meam culpam habeto, nisi probe excruciauero.
		iam hercle ego per hortum ad amicam transibo meam
		mi hanc occupatum noctem; eadem symbolam
		dabo et iubebo ad Sangarinum cenam coqui.
440		aut egomet ibo atque opsonabo opsonium.
		[Sangarinus scio iam hic aderit cum domino suo.

428 ‹EPI ‹si uoca›tu's *Loewe*

429 roga‹tu necn›e *Studemund*, uoca‹tus necn›e *Petersmann*

432 ancillam *P*, ancillulam *A*   ei condicam ad symbolam *T*, eo condici in symbolam *ceteri Palatini*, eo conduxi in symbolam *A*, eo condicam symbolam *Petersmann*

441–45 *uersus non feruntur in P*

for those many afflictions I want to celebrate the Festival of Liberty[24] on my arrival home.

EPI What you say is just and fair; have it, Stichus. For this day I dismiss you: go where you like. I contribute a jar 425 of old wine as a toast to you.

STI Wow! I'll hire a girlfriend today.

EPI Ten, if you like, so long as it's from your own money.

STI Well? Can I ask you one more thing?

EPI Well, what is this one more thing? Tell me.

STI Shall I dine out?

EPI If you're invited, I think yes.

STI That's how I like it. I don't care whether I'm invited or not.

EPI Where are you dining today? 430

STI I've come up with this plan like this: I have Stephanium as my girlfriend, from here next door, your brother's slave girl; to her I'll fix a contribution for a dinner at her fellow-slave's place, the Syrian Sangarinus. Both of us have the same girlfriend, we're rivals.

EPI Go on, take these girls inside. I'm handing this day over 435 to you.

STI Lay the blame on me if I don't torture it properly. (*to the audience*) Now I'll go over to my girlfriend through the garden in order to secure this night for myself; at the same time I'll give her my share of the money and have a dinner cooked at Sangarinus' place. Alternatively, I'll 440 go myself and buy provisions. [I know Sangarinus will be here with his master shortly. If a slave doesn't go to din-

---

[24] Originally a festival celebrating the victory over the Persians at Plataeae, here used comically for a private celebration during which the slaves are free to act as they please.

seruos homo qui ‹ni›s‹i te›m‹p›er‹i a›d cenam meat,
aduorsitores pol cum uerberibus decet
dari, uti eum uerberabundi adducant domum.
445   parata res faciam ut sit. egomet me moror.]
atque id ne uos miremini, homines seruolos
potare, amare, atque ad cenam condicere:
licet haec Athenis nobis. sed quom cogito,
potius quam inuidiam inueniam, est etiam hic ostium
450   aliud, posticum nostrarum harunc aedium:
[450ᵃ   posticam partem magis utuntur aedium:]
ea ibo opsonatum, eadem referam opsonium:
per hortum utroque commeatus continet.
ite hac secundum uos me. ego hunc lacero diem.

III. ii: GELASIMVS. EPIGNOMVS

GEL   libros inspexi; tam confido quam potis
455   me meum optenturum regem ridiculis meis.
nunc interuiso iamne a portu aduenerit,
ut eum aduenientem meis dictis deleniam.
EPI   hicquidem Gelasimus est parasitus qui uenit.
GEL   auspicio ‹hercle› hodie optumo exiui foras:
460   mustela murem apstulit praeter pedes;
quom strena ‹mi› opscaeuauit, spectatum hoc mihi est.
nam ut illa uitam repperit hodie sibi,
item me spero facturum: augurium hac facit.

442 qui ‹ni›s‹i te›m‹p›er‹i a›d *Studemund*
444 uerberabundum abducant *A*, uerberabundi adducant *Bugge*
450ᵃ *non fertur in A*
455 meis *P*, logis *A*
459 hercle *add. Ritschl*
461 mi *add. Ritschl*

ner in good time, he ought to be given attendants with
rods so that they may take him home, flogging him as
they go. I'll make sure that it's prepared. I'm wasting my   445
time.] And so that you won't be surprised that slaves
drink, make love, and make dinner arrangements, we're
allowed to do this in Athens. But when I think about it,
rather than that I should meet with envy, there's also
another door here, a backdoor of our house here: [they   450
use the back part of the house more:] that's where I'll go
to buy provisions, and I'll bring back the provisions the
same way; there's a continuous path through the garden
in both directions. (*to the girls*) Go this way behind me.
I'm frittering this day away.

Exit STICHUS *into the house of Epignomus, followed by the
slave girls.*
Enter GELASIMUS *from the right.*

GEL   (*to the audience*) I've consulted my books; I'm as confi-
      dent as is possible that I'll hold on to my patron through   455
      my jokes. Now I'm having a look to see if he's already
      returned from the harbor, so that I may soften him up
      on his arrival with my jests.
EPI   This is the hanger-on Gelasimus who is coming.
GEL   (*still to the audience*) I've come outside with a very good
      augury today: a weasel carried a mouse past my feet;   460
      when this good omen appeared for me, this is what I
      decided.[25] Yes, just as the weasel found a livelihood for
      itself today, so do I hope to act in the same way. My

[25] A weasel was normally considered a bad sign (cf. Arist. *Eccl.*
792).

        Epignomus hicquidem est qui astat. ibo atque alloquar.

465   Epignome, ut ego nunc te conspicio lubens!

        ut prae laetitia lacrumae prosiliunt mihi!

        ualuistin usque?

EPI   sustentatum est sedulo.

GEL   propino tibi salutem plenis . . . faucibus.

EPI   bene atque amice dicis. di dent quae uelis.

470   GEL   ***

EPI   cenem illi apud te?

GEL   quoniam saluos aduenis.

EPI   locata est opera nunc quidem; tam gratia est.

GEL   promitte.

EPI   certum est.

GEL   sic face inquam.

EPI   certa rest.

GEL   lubente me hercle facies.

EPI   idem ego istuc scio.

475   quando usus ueniet, fiet.

GEL   nunc ergo usus est.

EPI   non edepol possum.

GEL   quid grauare? censeas.

        nescioquid uero habeo in mundo.

EPI   i modo,

        alium conuiuam quaerito tibi in hunc diem.

GEL   quin tu promittis?

EPI   non grauer si possiem.

480   GEL   unum quidem hercle certo promitto tibi:

        lubens accipiam certo, si promiseris.

---

    470 propter 483 suspicatus est Ritschl uersum excidisse quo Gelasi-mus Epignomum ad cenam uocaret

	portent supports this. This is Epignomus who is standing here. I'll go and address him. (*loudly*) Epignomus, how happy I am to see you now! How my tears are gushing forth out of joy! Have you been well throughout?	465
EPI	I've taken good care of myself.	
GEL	I'm drinking to your health with a full . . . gullet.	
EPI	It's kind and friendly of you to say so. May the gods grant what you wish.	
GEL	***	470
EPI	I should dine there at your place?	
GEL	Since you've arrived safely.	
EPI	My services are engaged at present; much obliged to you all the same.	
GEL	Promise.	
EPI	I'm resolved.	
GEL	Do, I insist.	
EPI	It's settled.	
GEL	You'll really do me a pleasure.	
EPI	That I know too. When the need arises, it'll be done.	475
GEL	Then there's need now.	
EPI	I really can't.	
GEL	Why are you objecting? Reconsider it. Seriously, I have something in store for you.	
EPI	Just go, find yourself another table companion for to-day.	
GEL	Why won't you promise?	
EPI	I wouldn't object if I could.	
GEL	One thing I promise you for certain: I'll accept with pleasure for certain, if you promise.	480

---

471 *personas sic distribuit Ritschl*   473 res *A*, res est *P*, rest
Lindsay   474 hercle me Ω, *transp. Camerarius*

482	EPI	ualeas.
	GEL	certumne est?
	EPI	certum. cenabo domi.
484	GEL	sed quoniam nil processit hac, ego iuero
485		apertiore magis uia; ita plane loquar:
483		quando quidem tu ad me non uis promittere,
486		uin ad te ad cenam ueniam?
	EPI	si possim uelim;
		uerum hic apud me cenant alieni nouem.
	GEL	hau postulo equidem med in lecto accumbere:
		scis tu med esse unisubselli uirum.
490	EPI	at ei oratores sunt populi, summi uiri;
		Ambracia ueniunt huc legati publice.
	GEL	ergo oratores populi, summates uiri,
		summi accubent, ego infumatis infumus.
	EPI	haud aequom est te inter oratores accipi.
495	GEL	equidem hercle orator sum, sed procedit parum.
		cras de reliquiis nos uolo—
	EPI	multum uale.
	GEL	perii hercle uero plane, nihil obnoxie.
		uno Gelasimo minus est quam dudum fuit.
		certum est mustelae posthac numquam credere,

484–85 *solum feruntur in A; ante 483 pos. Bothe*

484 processitat ego hac *A*, processit hac ego *Goetz*, processi sat ego hac *Seyffert*

496 *totum uersum Epignomo dat P, sed spatium ante* multum *exstat in A*

---

[26] This is the number required to fill all the couches.

[27] A bench for sitting, thus much less comfortable than the couches on which the other guests lie.

EPI   Goodbye.

GEL   Are you resolved?

EPI   Yes, I am resolved. I'll dine at home.

GEL   But as there was no success this way, I'll go on a more   485
open road instead; I'll speak plainly like this: since you
don't want to promise to come to me, do you want me to
come to dinner to you?

EPI   If I could, I would; but here at my place nine[26] foreigners
are dining.

GEL   I don't expect to lie down on a couch; you know that I'm
a man of the single bench.[27]

EPI   But they're public ambassadors, men of the highest rank;   490
they're coming here from Ambracia[28] as envoys of the
state.

GEL   Then the public ambassadors, the men of the highest
rank, will lie at the high end, and I, a man of the lowest
rank, will lie at the lowest end.

EPI   It isn't right that you should be entertained among am-
bassadors.

GEL   I for one am an ambassador, but I'm getting on badly.   495
From the leftovers I'd like us tomorrow—

EPI   (*interrupting*) I wish you a very good day.

Exit EPIGNOMUS into his house.

GEL   I've perished truly and plainly, with nothing preventing
it. There's one Gelasimus less than there was a while ago.
I'm resolved never to trust a weasel again from now on:

[28] A Greek city, later (in 189 BC) captured by M. Fulvius No-
bilior.

500 nam incertiorem nullam noui bestiam;
    quaen eapse deciens in die mutat locum,
    ea ego auspicaui in re capitali mea?
    certum est amicos conuocare, ut consulam
    qua lege nunc me . . . esurire oporteat.

ACTVS IV

IV. i: ANTIPHO. PAMPHILIPPVS. EPIGNOMVS

505 ANT ita me di bene ament measque mihi bene seruassint fi-
     lias,
    ut mi uolup est, Pamphilippe, quia uos in patriam do-
     mum
    rediisse uideo bene gesta re ambos, te et fratrem tuom.
  PAMPHILI satis aps te accipiam, nisi uideam mihi te amicum
     esse, Antipho;
    nunc quia te amicum mi experior esse, credetur tibi.
510 ANT uocem ego te ad me ad cenam, frater tuos ni dixisset
     mihi
    te apud se cenaturum esse hodie, quom me ad se ad
     cenam uocat.
    et magis par fuerat me uobis dare cenam aduenienti-
     bus
    quam me ad illum promittere, nisi nollem ei aduorsa-
     rier.
    nunc me gratiam aps te inire uerbis nil desidero:
515 cras apud me eritis et tu et ille cum uostris uxoribus.

---

502 auspicaui in *CD et Nonius*, auspicauin *B*, auspicabi in *A*
 509 quia *P*, quoniam *A* te amicum mihi *P*, ex te mihi cum *A* cred-
itur Ω, credetur *Bothe*

I don't know any less reliable animal. Did I seek omens 500
in a matter of life and death for me through an animal
that changes its place ten times a day? I'm resolved to
assemble my friends in order to consult them on which
terms now I . . . ought to starve.

Exit GELASIMUS to the right.

ACT FOUR

Enter ANTIPHO and PAMPHILIPPUS from the left.

ANT   As truly as the gods may love me well and keep my 505
       daughters well for me, Pamphilippus, it is a pleasure for
       me to see that you've both, you and your brother, re-
       turned home to our country conducting your business so
       successfully.

PAMPHILI I'd take security from you, if I didn't see that you're
       friendly toward me, Antipho; now that I realize that
       you're friendly toward me, I'll take your word for it.

ANT   I'd invite you to my place for dinner, if your brother 510
       hadn't told me that you're going to dine at his place to-
       day, when he was inviting me to his place to dinner. And
       it would have been more appropriate for me to give you
       two dinner on your arrival than to accept his invitation,
       but I wouldn't have wished to oppose him. Now I have
       no desire to get your goodwill through mere words: to- 515
       morrow both you and he will be at my place together
       with your wives.

PAMPHILI at apud me perendie. nam ille heri me iam uo-
cauerat
in hunc diem. sed satin ego tecum pacificatus sum, An-
tipho?

ANT quando ita rem gessistis ut uos uelle amicosque adde-
cet,
pax commerxque est uobis mecum. nam hoc tu facito
ut cogites:

520 ut quoique homini res parata est, perinde amicis utitur:
si res firma, ‹item› firmi amici sunt; sin res laxe labat,
itidem amici collabascunt: res amicos inuenit.

EPI iam redeo. nimia est uoluptas, ubi diu afueris domo,
domum ubi redieris, si [t]ibi nulla est aegritudo animo
obuiam.

525 nam ita me apsente familiarem rem uxor curauit
meam,
omnium me exilem atque inanem fecit aegritudinum.
sed eccum fratrem Pamphilippum, incedit cum socero
suo.

PAMPHILI quid agitur, Epignome?

EPI quid tu? quam dudum in portum uenis?

PAMPHILI hau longissume postilla.

EPI iam iste est tranquillus tibi?

530 ANT magis quam mare quo ambo estis uecti.

EPI facis ut alias res soles.
hodien exoneramus nauem, frater?

PAMPHILI clementer uolo.
nos potius oneremus nosmet uicissatim uoluptatibus.
quam mox cocta est cena? impransus ego sum.

EPI abi intro ad me et laua.

521 item *propter spatium in A inuentum add. Studemund*
524 tibi Ω, ibi *Acidalius*   529 huc Ω, hau *Guyet*

PAMPHILI But at my place the day after tomorrow; he'd al-
ready invited me yesterday for today. But have I made
peace with you sufficiently, Antipho?

ANT Since you two conducted your business the way you and
your friends ought to wish, I have peace and friendly
relations with you; do think about this: each man has   520
friends just as he has possessions at hand. If his posses-
sions are stable, his friends are stable, too; if his posses-
sions waver wildly, his friends begin to waver, too. Pos-
sessions find friends.

Enter EPIGNOMUS *from his house.*

EPI (*into the house*) I'll be back directly. (*to the audience*) It's
an enormous joy if after your long absence from home
and after your return home no sorrow reaches your
heart: my wife looked after my affairs in such a way in   525
my absence that she made me free and empty of all
sorrows. But look, my brother Pamphilippus is walking
along with his father-in-law.

PAMPHILI How are you, Epignomus?

EPI And how are you? How long ago did you come into har-
bor?

PAMPHILI Not long at all after you.

EPI Is that chap calm toward you now? (*points to Antipho*)

ANT More so than the sea you both traveled on.   530

EPI (*to Antipho*) You're always the same. (*to Pamphilippus*)
Should we unload the ship today, my brother?

PAMPHILI Gently, please. Rather, let's load ourselves up with
pleasures for a change. How soon is dinner cooked? I
haven't had lunch.

EPI Go in to my place and have a bath.

PAMPHILI deos salutatum atque uxorem modo intro deuortor
domum;

535 haec si ita ut uolo conficio, continuo ad te transeo.

EPI apud nos eccillam festinat cum sorore uxor tua.

PAMPHILI optume est, iam istoc morai minus erit. iam ego
apud te ero.

ANT prius quam abis, praesente ted huic apologum agere
unum uolo.

PAMPHILI maxume.

ANT   fuit olim, quasi ego sum, senex; ei filiae

540 duae erant, quasi nunc meae sunt; eae erant duobus
nuptae fratribus,

quasi nunc meae sunt uobis.

EPI   miror quo euasurust apologus.

ANT erant minori illi adulescenti fidicina et tibicina,

peregre aduexerat, quasi nunc tu; sed ille erat caeleps
senex,

quasi ego nunc sum.

EPI   perge porro. praesens hicquidem est apologus.

545 ANT deind' senex ille illi dixit, quoius erat tibicina,

quasi ego nunc tibi dico—

EPI   ausculto atque animum aduorto sedulo.

ANT "ego tibi meam filiam bene quicum cubitares dedi:

nunc mihi reddi ego aequom esse aps te quicum cubi-
tem censeo."

EPI quis istuc dicit? an ille quasi tu?

ANT   quasi ego nunc dico tibi.

550 "immo duas dabo," inquit ille adulescens, "una si pa-
rum est;

et si duarum paenitebit," inquit, "addentur duae."

537 morae Ω, morai *Lachmann*

PAMPHILI I'll just pop in at home to greet the gods and my
       wife; if I finish this the way I want to, I'll come over to   535
       you at once.

EPI Look, your wife is bustling around at our place with her
       sister.

PAMPHILI That's excellent; because of that there will be less
       delay now. I'll be with you in a moment.

ANT Before you leave, I want to tell this chap (*points to Epi-
       gnomus*) one story in your presence.

PAMPHILI Absolutely.

ANT Once upon a time there was an old man, the same as I
       am; he had two daughters, the same as I do now; they   540
       were married to two brothers, the same as mine are now
       married to you.

EPI I wonder what this story is going to get at.

ANT That younger man had a lyre girl and a flute girl; he'd
       brought them from abroad, the same as you now. But
       that old man was widowed, the same as I am now.

EPI Continue further. This story is very much to the point.

ANT Then that old man said to the one the flute girl belonged   545
       to, the same as I'm now saying to you—

EPI (*interrupting*) I'm listening and paying attention care-
       fully.

ANT "I've given you my daughter so that you could sleep
       pleasantly with her; now I think it's fair that I should be
       given someone by you in return so that I can sleep with
       her."

EPI Who says that? That one the same as you?

ANT Now I'm speaking to you as the one the same as me. "No,   550
       I'll give you two," says that young man, "if one is too
       little; and if you're not content with two," he says, "two
       more will be added."

EPI quis istuc quaeso? an ille quasi ego?

ANT   is ipse quasi tu. ⟨tum⟩ senex
 ille quasi ego "si uis," inquit "quattuor sane dato,
 dum equidem hercle quod edint addas, meum ne
   contruncent cibum."

555 EPI uidelicet parcum fuisse illum senem, qui ⟨id⟩ dixerit,
 quom ille illum, qui pollicetur, etiam cibum poposcerit.

ANT uidelicet [non] nequam fuisse illum adulescentem, qui
   ilico
 ubi ille poscit denegarit dare se granum tritici.
 hercle qui aequom postulabat ill' senex, quando qui-
   dem

560 filiae illae dederat dotem, accipere pro tibicina.

EPI hercle illequidem certo adulescens docte uorsutus fuit,
 qui seni illi concubinam dare dotatam noluit.

ANT senex quidem uoluit, si posset, indipisci de cibo;
 quia nequit, qua lege licuit uelle dixit fieri.

565 "fiat," ille inquit adulescens. "facis benigne," inquit se-
   nex.
 "habeon rem pactam?" inquit. "faciam ita," inquit, "ut
   fieri uoles."
 sed ego ibo intro et gratulabor uostrum aduentum filiis.
 post lauatum in pyelum ibo, ibi fouebo senectutem
   meam.
 post ubi lauero, otiosus uos opperiar accubans.

---

552 tum *add. Acidalius*   554 edant *P*, edint *Acidalius*
555 id *add. Loman*   556 quom/quoniam (qm *CD*, q̃o *B*) ille
illi pollicetur qui eum *P, corr. Petersmann*
 557 non fuisse illum nequam *P*, [non] nequam fuisse illum *Loman*
558 denegauit *P*, denegarit *Acidalius*

EPI   Who says that, please? That one the same as me?

ANT   The very man, the one the same as you. Then that old man the same as me says, "if you wish, do give me four, so long as you provide them with enough to eat, so that they won't gobble up my food."

EPI   Since he said this, it's obvious that that old man was a   555 miser, as he even asked for food from the man who made him the promise.

ANT   No, it's obvious that that young man was a good-for-nothing, since he immediately said he wouldn't give a grain of wheat when that man made the request. Seriously, since that old man had given a dowry to his daughter, he demanded only what's fair, to receive one for the   560 flute girl.

EPI   Really, that young man was certainly cunningly clever, since he didn't want to give that old man a concubine with a dowry.

ANT   Well, the old man wanted to gain his point about the food, if he could; as he couldn't, he said he wanted it to be done on any terms allowed. "Yes," said that young   565 man. "That's kind of you," said the old one. "Have I got it settled?" he said. "I'll act the way you want it done," said the other. (*after a pause*) But I'll go in and congratulate my daughters on your arrival. Then I'll go to the bathtub to wash; there I'll soothe my old age. Then, when I've washed, I'll wait for you at my leisure and reclining at table.

Exit ANTIPHO *into the house of Epignomus.*

---

568 postea ibo lauatum in pyelum *P*, poste ibo lautum in pyelum *Fleckeisen*, post lauatum in pyelum ibo *Havet*

570 PAMPHILI graphicum mortalem Antiphonem! ut apologum
　　　　　 fecit quam fabre!

EPI　　 etiam nunc scelestus sese ducit pro adulescentulo.
　　　　 dabitur homini amica, noctu quae in lecto occentet se-
　　　　 nem.

PAMPHILI namque edepol aliud quidem illi quid amica opus
　　　　　 sit nescio.

　　　　 sed quid agit parasitus noster Gelasimus? etiam ualet?

575 EPI　 uidi edepol hominem hau perdudum.

PAMPHILI　　　　　　　　　　　　　　　　 quid agit?

EPI　　　　　　　　　　　　　　　　　　 quod famelicus.

PAMPHILI quin uocasti hominem ad ⟨te ad⟩ cenam?

EPI　　　　　　　　　　　 nequid adueniens perderem.

　　　　 atque eccum tibi lupum in sermone: praesens esuriens
　　　　 adest.

PAMPHILI ludificemur hominem.

EPI　　　　　　　　　　　 capti consili memorem mones.

　　　 IV. ii: GELASIMVS. PAMPHILIPPVS. EPIGNOMVS

GEL　 sed ita ut occepi narrare uobis: quom hic non affui,

580　　 cum amicis deliberaui iam et cum cognatis meis.
　　　　 ita mi auctores fuere, ut egomet me hodie iugula-
　　　　 rem . . . fame.
　　　　 sed uideone ego Pamphilippum cum fratre Epignomo?
　　　　 atque is est.
　　　　 aggrediar hominem. ⟨o⟩ sperate Pamphilippe, o spes
　　　　 mea,

571 esse *P*, sese *Dousa*, se esse *Acidalius*
572 acentet *B*, accendet *CD*, occentet *Pistoris*
576 te ad *add. Ritschl*
583 o *add. Loman*

78

PAMPHILI What a remarkable fellow Antipho is! How skillfully 570
    he made up his story!

EPI The rascal still takes himself for a youth. The old chap
    will get a girlfriend to sing for him in bed at night.

PAMPHILI Yes, I really don't know any other reason why he'd
    need a girlfriend. But how is our hanger-on Gelasimus?
    Is he still well?

EPI I saw him not long ago. 575

PAMPHILI How does he fare?

EPI Like a starveling.

PAMPHILI Why didn't you invite him to your place for din-
    ner?

EPI In order not to lose anything on my arrival. And look,
    here you have the wolf in the fable:[29] he's present, hun-
    gry.

PAMPHILI Let's make fun of him.

EPI You're reminding someone who remembers the plan
    that has been made.

Enter GELASIMUS from the right.

GEL *(to the audience)* But as I began to tell you: when I wasn't
    here, I had a discussion with my friends now and with 580
    my relatives. They advised me to cut my throat today . . .
    through hunger. But am I seeing Pamphilippus with his
    brother Epignomus? Yes, it's him. I'll approach him.
    (does so) O hoped-for Pamphilippus, O my hope, O my

---

[29] A proverbial expression, much like our "speak of the devil (and
the devil shall come)."

o mea uita, o mea uoluptas, salue! saluom gaudeo
585   peregre te in patriam rediisse.

PAMPHILI   credo; salue, Gelasime.

GEL   ualuistin bene?

PAMPHILI   sustentatum est sedulo.

GEL   edepol gaudeo.

edepol ne ego nunc mihi medimnum mille esse argenti
uelim.

EPI   quid eo tibi opust?

GEL   hunc hercle ad cenam ut uocem, te non uocem.

EPI   aduorsum te fabulare.

GEL   illud quidem, ambos ut uocem;
590   et simi⟨tu⟩ equidem hau maligne uos inuitassem do-
mum

ad me, sed ⟨mi⟩ ipsi do⟨mi me⟩ae nihil est. atque hoc
scitis uos.

EPI   edepol te uocem lubenter, si superfiat locus.

GEL   quin tum stans opstrusero aliquid strenue.

EPI   immo unum hoc potest—

GEL   quid?

EPI   ubi conuiuae abierint, tum uenias.

GEL   uae aetati tuae!
595 EPI   uasa lautum, non ad cenam dico.

GEL   di te perduint!

quid ais, Pamphilippe?

PAMPHILI   ad cenam hercle alio promisi foras.

GEL   quid, "foras"?

585 credo (*uel* saluo?) *A* (*nota personae praecedit*), saluum *P* (*nota personae sequitur*)   590–91 *solum feruntur in A*

590 equidem simi* *A*, equidem simitu *Studemund, transp. Lindsay*   591 *hi ipsi do***ae *A*, mihi ipsi domi meae *Studemund*

life, O my pleasure, my greetings! I'm glad you've re-
turned safely to our country from abroad.   585

PAMPHILI   I believe you. My greetings, Gelasimus.

GEL   Have you been well?

PAMPHILI   I've taken good care of myself.

GEL   I'm really glad. Honestly, now I'd like to have a thousand
bushels[30] of silver.

EPI   What do you need that for?

GEL   In order to invite him for dinner (*points to Pamphilip-
pus*), and not to invite you.

EPI   You're talking to your own disadvantage.

GEL   I mean, in order to invite you both; and I wouldn't have   590
grudged inviting you together to my home, but I myself
have nothing at home. And you two know this.

EPI   I'd invite you with pleasure, if there were any room
left.

GEL   Then I'll thrust something down energetically while
standing up.

EPI   No, but this one thing is possible—

GEL   (*interrupting*) What?

EPI   Come when the guests have left.

GEL   Curse you!

EPI   To wash dishes, I mean, not for dinner.   595

GEL   (*to Epignomus*) May the gods ruin you! (*to Pamphilip-
pus*) What do you say, Pamphilippus?

PAMPHILI   I've promised to go out somewhere for dinner.

GEL   What, "out"?

---

[30] A dry measure roughly equivalent to 54 liters.

PAMPHILI	foras hercle uero.
GEL	qui malum tibi lasso lubet

foris cenare?

PAMPHILI utrum tu censes?

GEL iuben domi cenam coqui

atque ad illum renuntiari?

PAMPHILI solus cenabo domi?

600 GEL non enim solus: me uocato.

PAMPHILI at ille ne suscenseat,

mea qui causa sumptum fecit.

GEL facile excusari potest.

mihi modo ausculta, iube cenam domi coqui.

EPI non me quidem

faciet auctore hodie ut illum decipiat.

GEL non tu hinc abis?

nisi me non perspicere censes quid agas. caue sis tu

tibi,

605 nam illic homo tuam hereditatem inhiat quasi esuriens

lupus.

non tu scis quam . . . efflictentur homines noctu hic in

uia?

PAMPHILI tanto pluris qui defendant ire aduorsum iussero.

EPI non it, non it, quia tanto opere suades ne ebitat.

⟨GEL⟩ iube

domi mi tibique tuaeque uxori celeriter cenam coqui.

610 si hercle faxis, non opinor dices deceptum fore.

PAMPHILI per hanc tibi cenam incenato, Gelasime, esse ho-

die licet.

82

PAMPHILI Yes, out.

GEL Why the deuce do you wish to dine out when you're tired?

PAMPHILI What do you think I should do?

GEL Won't you have a dinner cooked at home and your regrets sent to your host's house?

PAMPHILI Will I dine at home alone?

GEL No, not alone: invite me.   600

PAMPHILI But I'm afraid that the man who has spent money for my sake might be upset.

GEL An excuse can be made easily. Just listen to me, have dinner cooked at home.

EPI He won't be acting on my advice today in deceiving him.

GEL (*to Epignomus*) Won't you go away from here? Unless you think I don't see through what you're up to. (*to Pamphilippus*) Do watch out for yourself: that fellow is gaping at your inheritance like a hungry wolf. Don't you know how . . . people are murdered here in the street at night?   605

PAMPHILI All the more servants I shall tell to come toward me[31] to defend me.

EPI (*teasing*) He isn't going, he isn't going, because you advise him so strongly not to go out.

GEL (*to Pamphilippus*) Have a dinner cooked at home quickly, for myself and you and your wife. If you do so, I don't think you'll say you've been deceived.   610

PAMPHILI As far as this dinner is concerned, Gelasimus, you can remain without dinner today.

31 It was customary that masters would not go home alone after drinking; slaves had to come and pick them up.

GEL	ibisne ad cenam foras?
PAMPHILI	apud fratrem ceno in proxumo.
GEL	certumne est?
PAMPHILI	certum.
GEL	edepol te hodie lapide percussum uelim.
PAMPHILI	non metuo: per hortum transibo, hau prodibo in

    publicum.

615 EPI	quid ais, Gelasime?
GEL	oratores tu accipis, habeas tibi.
EPI	tua pol refert.
GEL	enim, si quidem mea refert, opera utere.
EPI	posse edepol tibi opinor etiam uni locum condi

    p⟨erbon⟩um
    ubi accubes.

PAMPHILI	sane faciundum censeo.
GEL	o lux oppidi!
EPI	si arte poteris accubare.
GEL	uel inter cuneos ferreos

620   tantillum loculi ubi catellus cubet, id mi sat erit loci.

EPI	exorabo aliquo modo. ueni.
GEL	hucine?
EPI	immo in carcerem;

    nam hic quidem genium meliorem tuom non facies.
    eamus, tu.

PAMPHILI	deos salutabo modo, poste ad te continuo transeo.
GEL	quid igitur?
EPI	dixi equidem in carcerem ires.

   614 non prodibo Ω, haud prodibo *Müller*
   617 condi p -um *A*, conspicor *P*, condi p⟨erbon⟩um *Gilleland*,
condi p⟨aruol⟩um *Petersmann*
   620 saeeris est *A*, saterest *P*, sat erit *Bothe*

84

GEL   Will you go out for dinner?

PAMPHILI   I'm dining at my brother's next door.

GEL   Is that your decision?

PAMPHILI   Yes.

GEL   I really hope you'll be murdered with a rock today.

PAMPHILI   I'm not afraid; I'll go over through the garden, I won't go out in the open.

EPI   What do you say, Gelasimus?   615

GEL   You're entertaining ambassadors, have them for yourself.

EPI   It's in your interest.

GEL   Well, if it is indeed in my interest, accept my services.

EPI   I think an excellent space can be made for one man like yourself to recline in.

PAMPHILI   I do think this ought to be done.

GEL   O light of the town!

EPI   If you can recline in a small space.

GEL   Even the tiny space between iron bars where a puppy   620
lies will be enough space for me.

EPI   I'll persuade them somehow. Come.

GEL   Here? (*points to the house of Epignomus*)

EPI   No, into prison; here you won't improve your lot. (*to Pamphilippus*) Let's go.

PAMPHILI   I'll just greet the gods, then I'll come over to you at once.

Exit PAMPHILIPPUS *into his house.*

GEL   Well then?

EPI   I've told you to go to prison.

	GEL	quin si iusseris,
625		eo quoque ibo.
	EPI	di immortales! hicquidem pol summam in crucem
		cena aut prandio perduci potest.
	GEL	ita ingenium meum est:
		quicumuis depugno multo facilius quam cum fame.
	EPI	dum parasitus mi atque fratri fuisti, rem confregimus.
	GEL	non ego isti apud te—?
	EPI	satis spectata est mihi iam tua felicitas;
630–		nunc ego nolo ex Gelasimo mi fieri te Catagelasimum.
31	GEL	iamne abierunt? Gelasime, uide, nunc consilio capto
		opust.
633–		egone? tune. mihine? tibine. uiden ut annona est
35		grauis?
		uiden benignitates hominum ut periere et prothymiae?
		uiden ridiculos nihili fieri atque ipsos parasitarier?
		numquam edepol me uiuom quisquam in crastinum
		inspiciet diem;
		nam mihi iam intus potione iuncea onerabo gulam
640		neque ego hoc committam ut me esse homines mor-
		tuom dicant fame.

632 nunc consilio capto opust *A*, quid es capturus consili *P*
633–35 uides Ω, uiden *Fleckeisen*   636 ut *A*, *om. P*

GEL If you tell me to, I'll go there as well.   625

EPI Immortal gods! This chap could be led to the top of a cross for a dinner or a lunch.

GEL That's what my character is like: I fight much more easily with anything else than with hunger.

EPI As long as you were my and my brother's hanger-on, we wrecked our wealth.

GEL There at your place, wasn't I—

EPI (*interrupting*) The good luck you bring is sufficiently known to me. Now I don't want you to turn from Gelasi- 630 mus to Catagelasimus[32] toward me.

Exit EPIGNOMUS into his house.

GEL Have they left already? Gelasimus, watch out, now you need to hatch a plan. I? You. For myself? For yourself. 635 Can't you see how oppressive the cost of bread is? Can't you see how people's acts of kindness and friendliness have disappeared? Can't you see how jesters are considered worthless and their patrons act as hangers-on themselves? Never will anyone see me alive come tomorrow: I'll go inside, burden my gullet with a drink of rushes,[33] and won't let it come to this that people say I've died 640 from hunger.

Exit GELASIMUS to the right.

[32] The name *Gelasimus*, "funny, laughable," is based on the Greek verb *gelan*, "laugh." Catagelasimus is based on *katagelan*, "laugh at somebody."

[33] Rushes were used for making ropes; Gelasimus says that he wants to hang himself.

ACTVS V

V. i: STICHVS

STI   more hoc fit atque stulte mea sententia:
si quem hominem exspectant, eum solent prouisere;
qui hercle illa causa ocius nihilo uenit.
idem ego nunc facio, qui prouiso Sagarinum,
645   qui nihilo citius ueniet tamen hac gratia.
iam hercle ego decumbam solus, si ille huc non uenit.
cadum modo hinc a me huc cum uino transferam,
postidea accumbam. quasi nix tabescit dies.

V. ii: SANGARINVS. STICHVS

SANG saluete, Athenae, quae nutrices Graeciae,
650   ⟨o⟩ terra erilis patria, te uideo lubens.
sed amica mea et conserua quid agat Stephanium
curae est, ut ualeat. nam Sticho mandaueram
salutem ut nuntiaret atque ei ut diceret
me hodie uenturum, ut cenam coqueret temperi.
655   sed Stichus est hicquidem.
STI   fecisti, ere, facetias,
quom hoc donauisti dono tuom seruom Stichum.
pro di immortales! quot ego uoluptates fero,
quot risiones, quot iocos, quot sauia,
saltationes, blanditias, prothymias!

648 post⟨id⟩ea *Ritschl*
650 o *add. Loman*

ACT FIVE

Enter STICHUS *from the house of Pamphilippus, setting up a bench.*

STI   This is done stupidly and idiotically in my opinion: when people expect someone, they tend to keep watch for him; yet he doesn't come any faster on that account. I'm now doing the same; I'm keeping watch for Sangarinus, who   645 still won't come any faster for this reason. Soon I'll recline at table alone, if he doesn't come here. I'll just bring the jar with wine over from my place, then I'll recline. The day is melting away like snow.

Exit STICHUS *into the house of Epignomus.*
Enter SANGARINUS *from the left.*

SANG Greetings, Athens, you who are the nurse of Greece; o   650 land of my master, I see you with pleasure. But I'm worried how my girlfriend and fellow-slave Stephanium is doing and how she's faring; I'd charged Stichus to give her my greetings and to tell her that I was going to come today, so that she might cook dinner in good time.   655

Enter STICHUS *from the house of Epignomus with a big jar of wine.*

SANG But this is Stichus.

STI   Master, you did a delightful deed when you presented your slave Stichus with this gift. Immortal gods! How many joys I'm carrying, how much laughter, how many jokes, how many kisses, dances, allurements, and acts of kindness!

660 SANG Stiche.

STI   hem!

SANG   quid fit?

STI   eugae! Sangarine lepidissume,

     fero conuiuam Dionysum mihique et tibi.

     namque edepol cena cocta est, locus liber datust

     mihi et tibi apud uos—nam apud nos est conuiuium,

     ibi uoster cenat cum uxore adeo et Antipho,

665   ibidem erus est noster—, hoc mihi dono datum est.

SANG quis somniauit aurum?

STI   quid id ad te attinet?

     proin tu lauare propera.

SANG   lautus sum.

STI   optume.

     [sequere ergo hac me intro, ⟨Sangarine⟩.

SANG   ego uero sequor.]

STI   uolo eluamus hodie, peregrina omnia

670   relinque, Athenas nunc colamus. sequere me.

SANG sequor et domum redeundi principium placet.

     bona scaeua strenaque obuiam occessit mihi.

V. iii: STEPHANIVM

STE   mirum uideri nemini uostrum uolo, spectatores,

674–   quid ego hinc quae illic habito exeam: faciam uos cer-
75   tiores.

     domo dudum huc arcessita sum, ⟨nam⟩ quoniam nun-
       tiatum est

     istarum uenturos uiros, ibi festinamus omnes;

668 Sangarine *add. Ritschl*   *uersum secl. Leo*
676 nam *add. Ritschl*

SANG Stichus! 660

STI Oh!

SANG How are things?

STI Hurray! Most delightful Sangarinus, I'm bringing Dio-
nysus[34] as guest for me and you. Yes, dinner is cooked
and you and I have been given a free space at your place
—well, at our place there is a banquet, there your master
is dining with his wife besides and Antipho, and our 665
master is in the same place—and this has been given as
a gift to me. (*points to the wine*)

SANG Who has dreamed up the gold?

STI What does it matter to you? So be quick to wash.

SANG I am washed.

STI Perfect. [Then follow me inside this way, Sangarinus.

SANG Yes indeed.]

STI I want us to be purified today; leave everything foreign 670
behind; let's live in Athens now. Follow me.

SANG Yes, I'm following you, and I like the start of our return
home. A good omen and favorable sign have come my
way.

*Exeunt STICHUS and SANGARINUS into the house of Pamphilip-
pus.*
Enter STEPHANIUM from the house of Epignomus.

STE I don't want it to seem strange to any of you, spectators,
why I, who live over there, am coming out from here; I'll 675
let you know. A while ago I was summoned from home
to this place: when it was announced that these women's
husbands were going to come, we all bustled about;

---

[34] The god of wine, here used metonymically for the wine itself.

lectis sternendis studuimus munditiisque apparandis.
inter illud tamen negotium meis curaui amicis
680 Sticho et conseruo Sagarino meo cena cocta ut esset.
Stichus opsonatust, ceterum ego curam do: id
allegaui‹t›.
nunc ibo hinc et amicos meos curabo hic aduenientis.

V. iv: SANGARINVS. STICHVS

SANG agite ite foras: ferte pompam. cado te praeficio, Stiche.
omnibus modis temptare certum est nostrum hodie
conuiuium.
685 ita me di ament, lepide accipimur quom hoc recipimur
in loco.
quisquis praetereat, comissatum uolo uocari.
STI   conuenit,
dum quidem hercle quisque ‹ueniet› ueniat cum uino
suo.
nam hinc quidem hodie polluctura praeter nos [iac-
tura] da[bi]tur nemini.
nosmet inter nos ministremus monotropi.
SANG   hoc conuiuium est
690 pro opibus nostris satis commodule nucibus, fabulis, fi-
culis,
olea, enthryptillo, lupillo comminuto, crustulo.
STI satiust seruo homini modeste [melius] facere sumptum
quam ampliter.
suom quemque decet: quibus diuitiae domi sunt, sca-
phiis, cantharis,

680 *uel* Sangarino *si* meo *cum synizesi legas*
681 allegaui‹t› *Goetz*   687 ueniet *add. Goetz*
688 iactura *del. Ritschl*   da[bi]tur *Lindsay*

we were busy spreading the couches and cleaning up.
Still, during that business I took care that dinner would
be cooked for my boyfriends, Stichus and my fellow-   680
slave Sangarinus. Stichus has bought the food, I'm taking
care of the rest; that's what he commissioned. Now I'll
go away and look after my boyfriends here on their ar-
rival.

Exit STEPHANIUM *into the house of Pamphilippus.*
Enter SANGARINUS *and* STICHUS *from the house of Pamphilip-*
pus with the wine, water, some cups, and a few nibbles.

SANG Go on, come out; bring the supply train. I put you in
      charge of the jug, Stichus. I'm resolved to put our ban-
      quet through all sorts of paces today. As truly as the gods   685
      may love me, we're being entertained delightfully while
      we're being entertained in this place. I want everybody
      who walks past to be invited to join the revelry.
STI   Agreed, so long as everybody who comes, comes with his
      own wine: nobody besides us is given a serving from this
      today. We'll wait on each other exclusively.
SANG This banquet is good enough for our means, with nuts,   690
      little beans, little figs, olives, little cakes, tiny lupine
      seeds, and pastries.
STI   For a slave it's better to spend money in moderation
      rather than in excess. What each man's station allows him
      suits him best. Those who have wealth at home, drink

---

691 oleae in tripillo *A*, oleae interiplio *P*, olea entriptillo *Hiltbrun-*
ner   692 sat est Ω *et Nonius*, satiust *Guyet*   melius *P, A non*
legitur (sed habet spatium), om. Nonius

693 quemque *P*, quique *A*   scaphio et Ω, scaphiis *Bothe*

batiocis bibunt, at nos nostro Samiolo poterio:

695 tamen bibimus nos, tamen efficimus pro opibus nostra
moenia.

SANG   mica uter utrubi accumbamus.

STI   abi tu sane superior.

atque adeo ut tu scire possis, pacto ego hoc tecum
diuido:

uide, utram tibi lubet etiam nunc capere, cape prouin-
ciam.

SANG   quid istuc est prouinciae?

STI   utrum Fontine an Libero

700 imperium te inhibere mauis?

SANG   nimio liquido Libero.

sed amica mea et tua dum cenat dumqu' se exornat,
nos uolo

[tamen] ludere inter nos. strategum te facio huic
conuiuio.

STI   nimium lepide in mentem uenit: potius quam in sub-
sellio

cynice hic accipimur quam in lectis.

SANG   immo enim nimio hic dulcius.

705 sed interim, stratege noster, quor hic cessat cantharus?

uide quot cyathos bibimus.

STI   tot quot digiti tibi sunt in manu.

cantio Graeca est: ἢ πέντ' ἢ τρία πῖν' ἢ μὴ τέτταρα.

696 amica *P*, m*cem *A*, mica *Lindsay*, amicam *Exon*
699 prouinciae *P*, prouinciai *Leo*   701 cenat *P*, cessat *Goetz*
702 tamen *del. Guyet*   703 quam *del. Saracenus*
  704 hic[1] *om. P*   lecticis Ω, lectis *Pius*   hic dulcius *A*, hic magis est
dulcius *P*

from good beakers, tankards, and goblets, but we, from
our little Samian[35] cups; all the same, we do drink, all the   695
same, we do perform our functions as our means allow.

SANG Play the morra game[36] as to which of us should recline
where.

STI You should absolutely go to the top. And just so that you
may know, I'm sharing with you in this way: look and take
whichever province[37] you want to take now.

SANG What province is that?

STI Do you prefer to exert authority over Fons or over   700
Liber?[38]

SANG I much prefer to do so over liquid Liber. But while my
and your girlfriend is eating and while she's dressing up,
I want us to have fun among ourselves. For this banquet
I make you commander.

STI I've had an absolutely delightful idea: like Cynic phi-
losophers[39] we're being entertained on a bench rather
than on couches.

SANG Indeed, it's much more pleasant here. But, our com-   705
mander, why is the bowl resting in the meantime? See
how many cups we're drinking.

STI As many as you have fingers on a hand. There's a Greek
song: drink five or three, but not four.[40]

---

[35] Samian earthenware was proverbially cheap.

[36] An ancient hand game sometimes played to decide issues.

[37] A reference to the distribution of provinces among former mag-
istrates.   [38] The two deities stand for water and wine, respectively;
Romans and Greeks did not normally drink their wine undiluted.

[39] The Cynic school of philosophy goes back to Diogenes of Sinope
(fourth century BC), who rejected the comforts of civilization.

[40] An uneven number was considered to bring good luck.

SANG tibi propino. decumam a fonte tibi tute inde, si sapis.
bene uos, bene nos, bene te, bene me, bene nostram
etiam Stephanium!

[710 STI bibe si bibis.

SANG   non mora erit apud me.

STI   edepol conuiui sat est,
modo nostra huc amica accedat: id abest, aliud nil
abest.]

STI lepide hoc actum est. tibi propino cantharum. uinum
tu habes.

SANG nimis uellem aliquid pulpamenti.

STI   si horum quae assunt paenitet,
nihil est. tene aquam.

SANG   melius dicis; nil moror cuppedia.

715 bibe, tibicen. age siquid agis, bibendum hercle hoc est,
ne nega.
quid hic fastidis quod faciundum uides esse tibi? quin
bibis?
[age si quid agis, accipe inquam. hoc non impendet
publicum?]
haud tuom istuc est te uereri. eripe ex ore tibias.

STI ubi illic biberit, uel seruato meum modum uel tu dato.

708 decumam a *B*, decuma *CD*, decumum a *A*
710–11 *uersus secl. Langen*
717 non hoc *P, transp. Acidalius   uersum del. Petersmann*

---

[41] As there are five cups of wine, this means the addition of half a
cup of water. The slaves are thus barely diluting their wine.

SANG *(pouring wine into a mixing bowl)* I'm drinking a toast to you. You'd better put one-tenth from the water jug in for yourself.[41] *(Stichus does so, and Sangarinus and Stichus take cups)* Good health to you all, good health to us, good health to you, good health to me, good health also to our Stephanium! *(they drink)*

[STI   Drink if you're going to drink.   710

SANG There won't be any delay on my part.

STI   Goodness, I've had enough of the banquet; if only our girlfriend were to come here. That's missing, nothing else is missing.]

STI   This has been done delightfully. I'm toasting a bowl to you. You have the wine.

SANG *(as he is filling the mixing bowl)* I'd really like some hors d'oeuvres.

STI   There aren't any if you aren't satisfied with what's here already. Take some water. *(pours it in)*

SANG You're right; I'm not bothered about delicacies. *(tries to   715 pass the drink to the piper)* Drink, piper. Do it, if you're doing anything, you have to drink this, stop refusing. Why are you scorning what you can see you have to do? Why won't you drink? [Act if you're going to act, take this, I'm telling you. Won't the public pay for this?] That bashfulness of yours is not your true character. Pull the pipes from your mouth.

The piper obeys and begins to drink.[42]

STI   When he's had his drink, either stick to my measure or

---

[42] Despite the absence of musical accompaniment, the recitative continues, as the meter shows.

720   nolo ego nos prorsum ‹hoc› ebibere. nulli rei erimus
             postea;

        namque edepol quam uis desubito uel cadus uorti po-
             test.

SANG   quid igitur? quamquam grauatus fuisti, non nocuit ta-
             men.

723   age,

723ᵃ   tibicen, quando bibisti, refer ad labeas tibias.

        suffla celeriter tibi buccas quasi proserpens bestia.

725   agedum, Stiche, uter demutassit, poculo multabitur.

STI   bonum ius dicis. impetrare oportet qui aequom postu-
             lat.

SANG age ergo opserua. si peccassis, multam hic retinebo
             ilico.

STI   optumum atque aequissumum oras. em tibi hoc pri-
             mum omnium.

        haec facetia est, amare inter se riualis duos,

730   uno cantharo potare, unum scortum ducere.

        hoc memorabile est: ego tu sum, tu es ego, unianimi
             sumus,

        unam amicam amamus ambo, mecum ubi est, tecum
             est tamen;

        tecum ubi autem est, mecum ibi autem est: neuter
             ‹ne›utri inuidet.

SANG ohe, iam satis! nolo optaedescat; alium ludum nunc
             uolo.

720 prosumo (pro summo *CD*) bibere *P*, prosum ‹hoc› ebibere
Müller

733 ‹ne›utri *Kellerhoff*

distribute your own.[43] I don't want us to drink this up   720
altogether. We'll be fit for nothing afterward; even a jar
can be tipped up as quickly as you like.[44]

SANG *(to the piper)* Well then? Even though you objected, it
didn't hurt you. Go on, piper, now that you've had your
drink, return the pipes to your lips. Inflate your cheeks
quickly like a serpent.

The piper begins to play again.

SANG Come on, Stichus, whichever of us makes a slip will for-   725
feit a cup.

STI What you say is perfectly right. Someone who demands
what's fair ought to get it.

SANG Go on then, watch. *(makes a dance move)* If you make a
slip, I'll retain the fine here on the spot.

STI What you ask is absolutely right and fair. Here you are,
this is the first performance of all. *(starts dancing)* This
is an amusing thing, that two rivals love each other, drink   730
from one single cup, and hire one single prostitute. This
is remarkable: I am you, you are me, we're in full accord,
we both love one single prostitute, and when she's with
me, she's with you all the same; but when she's with
you, she's there with me. Neither of us is jealous of the
other.

SANG Hey there, enough now! *(Stichus stops)* I don't want it to
get tedious; now I want another game.

---

[43] Stichus is upset because Sangarinus has assumed the role of head
of the banquet.

[44] The jar is emptied by tipping, not by using a ladle.

735	STI	uin amicam huc euocemus? ea saltabit.
	SANG	censeo.
	STI	mea suauis, amabilis, amoena Stephanium, ad amores tuos
		foras egredere, satis mi pulchra es.
	SANG	at enim ‹mihi› pulcherruma.
		STI fac nos hilaros hilariores opera atque aduentu tuo.
739–40	SANG	peregre aduenientes te expetimus, Stephaniscidium, mel meum,
		si amabilitas tibi nostra placet, si tibi ambo accepti sumus.

V. V: STEPHANIVM. STICHVS. SANGARINVS

	STE	morigerabor, meae deliciae. nam ita me Venus amoena amet,
		ut ego huc iam dudum simitu exissem uobiscum foras,
		nisi me uobis exornarem. nam ita est ingenium muliebre:
745		bene quom lauta [est], terta, ornata, ficta est, infecta est tamen;
		nimioque sibi mulier meretrix repperit odium ocius
		sua immunditia quam in perpetuom ut placeat munditia sua.
	STI	nimium lepide fabulata est.
	SANG	Veneris mera est oratio.
	STI	Sangarine.
	SANG	quid est?
	STI	totus doleo.
	SANG	potus? tanto miserior.

737 mihi *add. Acidalius*
742 morem uobis geram *P*, morigerabor *Ritschl*

100

STI   Do you want us to call our girlfriend out here? She will   735
dance.

SANG Yes, I agree.

STI   *(loudly)* My sweet, lovely, pretty Stephanium, come out
to your sweethearts, you're beautiful enough for me.

SANG *(loudly)* But for me you're the most beautiful.

STI   *(loudly)* Make us joyful ones more joyful still by coming
here and performing.

SANG *(loudly)* On our arrival from abroad we seek you, little   740
Stephanium, my honey, if you like our charm and if we're
both welcome to you.

Enter STEPHANIUM from the house of Pamphilippus.

STE   I'll humor you, my darlings: as truly as lovely Venus may
love me, I'd have come out here together with you long
ago, if I hadn't been making myself pretty for you; yes,
a woman's nature is like this: when she's washed well,   745
made neat, decorated, and made up, she's unready none-
theless; and a prostitute finds reproach much more
quickly through absence of neatness than that she should
be liked for good through presence of neatness.

STI   She's talked absolutely delightfully.

SANG It's a speech straight from Venus.

STI   Sangarinus!

SANG What is it?

STI   I'm all in pain.

SANG From drinking?[45] You're all the more wretched.

---

[45] A pun on *totus*, "all," and *potus*, "drunk."

---

745 *est del.* Scaliger   tersa P, terta *Bücheler*

750 STE utrubi accumbo?
     SANG   utrubi tu uis?
     STE   cum ambobus uolo, nam ambos amo.
     STI uapulat peculium, actum est.
     SANG   fugit hoc libertas caput.
     STE date mi locum ubi accumbam, amabo, siquidem placeo.
     STI   tun mihi?
     STE cupio cum utroque.
     STI   ei mihi! bene dispereo. quid ais?
     SANG   quid est?
     STI ita me di ament, numquam enim fiet hodie haec quin
              saltet tamen.
755   age, mulsa mea suauitudo, salta: saltabo ego simul.
     SANG numquam edepol med istoc uinces quin ego ibidem
              pruriam.
     STE siquidem mihi saltandum est, tum uos date bibat tibi-
              cini.
     STI et quidem nobis.
     SANG   tene, tibicen, primum; postidea loci
          si hoc eduxeris, proinde ut consuetu's antehac, celeriter
760   lepidam et suauem cantionem aliquam occupito cinae-
              dicam,
          ubi perpruriscamus usque ex unguiculis. inde huc
              aquam.

              v. vi: SANGARINVS. STICHVS
     SANG tene tu hoc, educe. dudum ⟨hau⟩ placuit potio:

          762 haud *add. Pistoris*

102

STE   In which place am I to recline?   750

SANG In which do you want to?

STE   I want to be with both, because I love you both.

STI   My savings are getting a thrashing, I'm done for.

SANG Freedom is running away from me.

STE   Please give me a place to recline, you two, if you like me.

STI   *I* like *you?*

STE   I wish to do so with each of you.

STI   Dear me! I'm perishing in a good way. What do you say?

SANG What is it?

STI   As truly as the gods may love me, still, she'll never get away with not dancing today. Come on, my honeyed   755 sweetness, dance: I'll dance at the same time.

SANG You'll never get the better of me in that way without me itching in the same place.

STE   If I have to dance, then you two must give something to drink to the flute player.

STI   And to ourselves.

SANG (*pouring some wine*) Piper, take this first; then, when you've drunk it up, quickly play us some nice and sweet lewd tune, just as you used to before, a tune which makes   760 us itch all over down to our fingertips. (*to Stichus*) Put some water in here. (*Stichus obeys*)

The piper stops playing.[46]

SANG (*to the piper*) You, take this and drink it up. (*to the audi-*

---

[46] This time the recitative ends and spoken senarii begin until the piper resumes playing.

nunc minus grauate iam accipit. tene tu. interim,
meus oculus, da mi sauium, dum illic bibit.

765 STI prostibiles<t> tandem? stantem stanti sauium
dare amicum amicae? eugae eugae, sic furi datur!

SANG age, iam infla buccas, nunciam aliquid suauiter.
redd' cantionem ueteri pro ui<no> nouam.

V. vii: SANGARINVS. STICHVS

SANG qui Ionicus aut cinaedicus<t>, qui hoc tale facere pos-
siet?

770 STI si istoc me uorsu uiceris, alio me prouocato.

SANG fac tu hoc modo.

STI   at tu hoc modo.

SANG   babae!

STI   tatae!

SANG   papae!

STI   pax!

SANG nunc pariter ambo. omnis uoco cinaedos contra.
satis esse nobis non magis potis [est] quam fungo im-
ber.

STI intro hinc abeamus nunciam: saltatum satis pro uino
est.

775 uos, spectatores, plaudite atque ite ad uos comissatum.

765 prostibiles<t> *Leo*
768 proui *P*, pro uino *Saracenus*
769 cenedicus *B*, cenydicus *CD*, cynaedicus<t> *Ritschl*
773 est *del. Leo*
775 nos *P*, uos *Palmer*

---

[47] Ionia, the coastal region of what is now Turkey, was considered the home of lascivious dances.

ence) A while ago he didn't like the drink; now he's taking it with less fuss already. (*to the piper*) You, take it. (*as the piper drinks, to Stephanium*) Meanwhile, apple of my eye, give me a kiss while he's drinking.

STI   Is she a street whore then? Should a standing boyfriend   765
give a kiss to his standing girlfriend? Goodness, goodness, that's how it's given to a thief!

SANG   (*to the piper*) Go on, now puff out your cheeks, play something sweet now. Give us a new tune for the old wine.

The piper starts playing again.

SANG   (*whirling around*) How could someone who is an Ionian[47] or a lewd dancer do something like this?

STI   (*also whirling around*) If you get the better of me with   770
that turn, challenge me with another.

SANG   Do it this way.

STI   But you, this way.

SANG   Wow!

STI   Oh!

SANG   Whoa!

STI   Enough! (*they stop*)

SANG   Now both at the same time. (*they start again, this time together*) I challenge all lewd dancers to compete against us. We can no more get enough of it than a mushroom can get enough of rain.

STI   Let's go in now; there's been enough dancing for the wine. (*they stop*) You, spectators, give us your applause   775
and go to your own places to have fun.

TRINUMMUS

INTRODUCTORY NOTE

The *Trinummus*, "Three-Dollar Day," an adaptation of Philemon's *Thesauros*, "The Treasure," used to be a highly popular play in schools, no doubt at least in part because of its moral tone. The comedy is much less widely read nowadays, but undeservedly so, as it is one of the most beautiful of Plautine comedies.

In keeping with the moral sentiment of the play, the prologue is spoken by two allegorical figures, Luxury and her daughter Want, neither of whom has a concrete role in the play itself. Luxury tells us that Lesbonicus, a young man, has wasted his possessions on her, and now that he has nothing left, he has to live with her daughter Want.

Most of the background information is provided in what is the first act in modern editions (ll. 23–222). Lesbonicus' excesses have forced Charmides, his father, to go abroad to do business. In his absence, Charmides has entrusted his son and his daughter to his close friend Callicles; secretly, he has also entrusted a treasure to him, which is buried in the house. It is this treasure that gave the Greek original its name. As Lesbonicus is uncontrollable, he must not find out about the treasure, which Callicles is to use to provide a dowry for the daughter of Charmides in case he does not return. During a brief absence of Callicles, Lesbonicus, having run out of funds, put his father's house up for sale. On his return, Callicles, afraid to lose his friend's treasure, immediately buys the house for a low price, planning to give it back to Charmides once he returns. Lesbonicus and his slave Stasimus now live in an annex of their former house, while the daughter of Charmides remains in the house, together with the daughter of Callicles. Incidentally, the behavior of Lesbonicus shows that the agreement between Charmides and Callicles has no legal basis, otherwise Callicles could simply have forbidden Lesbonicus to put up the property for sale; Lesbonicus acted as if he had already inherited the house.

Naturally, this state of affairs has led to unpleasant rumors. Callicles has lost his good reputation among the citizens because he is believed to have taken advantage of Charmides in his absence. Megaronides, a friend of both Charmides and Callicles, feels impelled to visit the latter in order to reproach him and to persuade him to mend his ways. When Megaronides does not give up his attempt, Callicles finally tells him the truth about the situation, and Megaronides, embarrassed, offers his support.

The second act (ll. 223–601) begins with a song by Lysiteles, a young man who is a friend of Lesbonicus. Lysiteles, who, unlike his friend, has lived his entire youth as a paragon of virtue, is now considering whether a life spent in love affairs or one dedicated to hard work brings more joy in the long run. Having realized that it is hard work that leads to happiness in the long term, he decides that this is the course of life that he wishes to pursue.

When his father, Philto, appears on stage, the dialogue between the two quickly turns from a discussion of virtue to a request from Lysiteles: he wishes to marry the sister of Lesbonicus, and as his friend is now impoverished, he wishes to do so without a dowry. What must strike the modern reader as odd is that no fondness for the girl at all is mentioned in the dialogue between father and son; Lysiteles presents the marriage as something both parties would profit from, Lesbonicus because he is spared a dowry, and Philto and Lysiteles because they will gain a good reputation. Nevertheless, we should not be quick to assume that feelings do not enter into the equation at all; it is simply not a line of argument that would be effective with this type of father. After some hesitation, Philto agrees to the match and is even persuaded to approach Lesbonicus in order to secure the marriage.

When Philto goes to meet Lesbonicus, he witnesses a conversation between him and Stasimus in which they discuss finances. Philto is shocked by the careless approach Lesbonicus takes to money but does not show it in front of him. As soon as he asks the young man for his sister in marriage for his own son, Lesbonicus is upset because he thinks that he is being mocked. But once having realized that Philto is serious, he feels obliged to turn him down because of their difference in wealth. Philto's offer to forgo the traditional dowry is not met with approval by Lesbonicus, who feels that a marriage without a dowry is a disgrace and wishes to endow the girl with a plot of land, the last piece of property he owns. Worried about his master's welfare, Stasimus takes Philto aside and tries to dissuade him from accepting the land on the grounds that it is cursed. Philto goes away after securing an engagement but says that he will leave the discussions about the dowry to the two young friends.

The third act (ll. 602–819) deals exclusively with the

problem of the dowry. On the orders of Lesbonicus, Sta-
simus tells Callicles about the match, mentioning the ab-
sence of a dowry. Callicles is as shocked about the lack of
a dowry as Philto was and decides to consult Megaronides
about how she can receive the treasure without any resul-
tant suspicions and without giving Lesbonicus the chance
to squander this money as well. It is ironic that he does
not learn from Stasimus how keen Lesbonicus is to pro-
vide a dowry, otherwise he could tell him the truth with-
out too great a risk that Lesbonicus would use up this
money; but it is possible that Lesbonicus would be less
high-minded if he actually heard about the gold.

The discussion between the two young men is unsuc-
cessful. Both try to do what is honorable and in the other's
interests; Lesbonicus is as determined to provide a dowry
as Lysiteles is determined not to accept one. As no agree-
ment is reached, the engagement is under threat.

Callicles and Megaronides consider a number of solu-
tions to the problem. Callicles suggests borrowing money
from a friend and repaying it from the treasure after the
marriage, hinting that Megaronides could perhaps pro-
vide it, but Megaronides is not keen. Megaronides has a
different idea, which Callicles accepts. They decide to hire
a sycophant, an impostor, who should pretend to be a busi-
ness associate of Charmides; he should bring two letters,
one for Lesbonicus and one for Callicles; the letter for
Lesbonicus will say that the letter for Callicles, which will
actually be empty, contains a dowry for the girl. The dowry
can then be provided from the treasure without Lesboni-
cus suspecting the truth.

The impostor is hired for three *nummi*, "coins"; this
inherently vague term, in our translation "dollars," prob-

ably refers to sesterces, as three sesterces, roughly equivalent to one Greek tetrobol, would have been the standard payment for a day's unskilled labor. Plautus, who occasionally named his plays after details of minor importance to their plots, called this comedy *Trinummus*, "Three-Dollar Day," because of this insignificant event, no doubt at least in part in order to achieve a comical contrast with the Greek title *Thesauros*, "The Treasure."

By the standards of Roman comedy, the trick of Megaronides and Callicles is unusual in three respects: it is hatched by two old men, not by a young man or, rather, by his slave; it is intended to give money to the victim, not to rob him; and it is a trick that will fail because in the fourth act (ll. 820–1114) Charmides returns. After a prayer (ll. 820–42[b]), which seems to have been expanded somewhat by Plautus, Charmides encounters the sycophant (ll. 843–1007). In the Greek original, which had problems of friendship as its central theme, the main function of this scene must have been to show how Charmides, who returns from a successful yet exhausting stay abroad, suffers new distress and begins to fear for the well-being of his family. Plautus, however, realized the comic potential of the passage and turned it into the funniest scene in the play. Charmides becomes a trickster himself and questions his supposed business associate cleverly, until the sycophant finally gives up and leaves.

In the Greek original, what is now the third scene of the fourth act (ll. 1008–92) must have had a function similar to that of the preceding scene. Charmides meets Stasimus and hears from him that Callicles has bought his house and thrown out his son, which adds to his agony.

Again we can see Plautine expansion and the introduction of ridiculous elements. Stasimus went to the forum to get back some of his private money, which he had lent to a friend. In the Greek text he may have done so to help Lesbonicus provide a dowry with what little he had, while in Plautus the purpose is to get travel provisions (ll. 727–28), as his bankrupt master is likely to go abroad to earn a living; in the Greek the sum is also likely to have been a small amount, whereas in Plautus it is an Attic talent (ll. 1055–56), a sum of money no ordinary slave could have owned. More important, the scene is a typical running-slave passage, with the whole range of moralizing elements of which Plautus was so fond. But it is strange that there is no intrinsic, structural motivation for Stasimus' haste. Plautus seems to have turned the Greek scene into a running-slave scene merely in order to provide some action and the standard criticism of contemporary society.

In l. 1016, Charmides says that the training master of the running slave is his *gurgulio*, his "gullet." Gratwick suggests emending the transmitted *gurgulio* to *Curculio*. If correct, this would provide an extrinsic, meta-theatrical motivation for Stasimus' hurry: Stasimus has lost his ring, like the soldier in the *Curculio*, and is now rushing onto the stage like the eponymous hero of that play. Gratwick remarks that this "is as if Plautus jocosely wishes to imply that during his absence in the Market Stasimus has wandered off into another play taking place elsewhere in Plautinopolis, the same one as that in which Curculio figures" (1981: 342).

But while Gratwick's emendation makes sense, it is by no means necessary. *Gurgulio*, "gullet," is reasonable in

113

its context; Stasimus, who has been drinking, is perhaps not even able to walk straight, which makes his run more comical, and Charmides' statement that Stasimus' gullet is his trainer is a witty explanation of what he sees.[1]

In striking contrast to the preceding passages, the fourth scene of the fourth act (ll. 1093–114) shows clear signs of compression. It contains the confrontation between Charmides and Callicles and the restoration of their friendship. Plautus has so condensed the argument between the two that Callicles does not even explain on stage why he bought the house, even though this is absolutely crucial information. Thus it is strange how easily contented Charmides is. Plautus was clearly not very interested in this scene of reconciliation.

The last act (ll. 1115–89) ties up the remaining loose ends. Lysiteles meets Charmides, and the engagement is confirmed, this time with an appropriate dowry. Lesbonicus shows contrition for his previous behavior and as a corrective measure has to marry the daughter of Callicles.

Legal historians have often wondered whether the procedures in the two weddings are more Greek or more Roman. It is conceivable that in the Greek original Les-

---

[1] It has been suggested that Stasimus, having spent too much time drinking, is in a rush and running very fast, and that Charmides understands that the reason behind Stasimus' hurry is his previous drinking session and subsequent fear of a beating; but unless there is some outward sign of drunkenness, it seems unlikely that Charmides would be able to guess the cause for the slave's haste.

bonicus was not forced to marry, but while such autocratic behavior is in line with the power of a Roman father, it is not unheard of in Greek comedy either. The marriage arrangements of Lysiteles, being of central importance to the plot, are discussed at much greater length and are consequently more interesting. It is a priori likely that Plautus by and large followed his Greek original here, and this is confirmed on closer inspection of individual scenes. The fact that Lysiteles decides to marry and then approaches his father to ask for permission could fit with either Greek or Roman traditions; but later on Lysiteles negotiates with Lesbonicus himself, and this seems more in line with Greek customs. It is notable that Lesbonicus has the power to engage his sister. In Athenian law, if the father has died or gone missing, a woman's brother could engage her without further ado. In Rome he needed the sister's permission. Thus the *Trinummus* reflects Athenian law here as well, unless the girl's assent is implicitly assumed.

When was the *Trinummus* first staged? In l. 990 the new aediles are mentioned. As aediles were always elected in March, the only festival at which they can still be referred to as new is the *ludi Megalenses* in April. Given that dramatic performances did not form part of this feast before 194 BC (Liv. 34.54.3), this year must be our *terminus post quem*. L. 152, where Philippics are mentioned, is in broad agreement with this date: this currency was not well known in Rome before 195 BC. But we can probably be more precise. In l. 542 we hear of Syrian slaves; these only became common after the beginning of the war against Antiochus III in 191 BC. The *Trinummus* is thus one of Plautus' later plays. If the census in l. 872 refers to the censorship of Marcus Claudius Marcellus and Titus Quinctius Flaminius in 189–188 BC, the *Trinummus* was probably staged for the first time in 188 or 187 BC.

SELECT BIBLIOGRAPHY

Editions and Commentaries

Brix, J., and M. Niemeyer (1925), *Ausgewählte Komödien des T. Maccius Plautus für den Schulgebrauch erklärt*, vol. 1: *Trinummus* (Leipzig and Berlin).

Nutting, H. C. (1908), *The Trinummus of Plautus, Edited with Notes and Stage Directions* (Boston).

Criticism

Bridgham, J. M. (1943), "Plautus, *Trinummus* 845," in *Classical Journal* 38: 226–27.

Cole, C. N. (1907), "Plautus *Trin.* 368," in *Classical Journal* 2: 305–6.

Gratwick, A. S. (1981), "Curculio's Last Bow: Plautus, *Trinummus* IV. 3," in *Mnemosyne* NS 34: 331–50.

Green, W. M. (1929), "Greek and Roman Law in the *Trinummus* of Plautus," in *Classical Philology* 24: 183–92.

Hopkins, A. G. (1895), "On a Misunderstood Passage in the *Trinummus* of Plautus, Vs. 642–4," in *Classical Review* 9: 307–9.

Karakasis, E. (2003), "Legal Language in Plautus with Special Reference to *Trinummus*," in *Mnemosyne* NS 56: 194–209.

Muecke, F. (1985), "Names and Players: The Sycophant Scene of the 'Trinummus' (Trin. 4.2)," in *Transactions of the American Philological Association* 115: 167–86.

Prescott, H. W. (1910), "Plautus' *Trinummus* 675," in *Classical Philology* 5: 103–4.

Renkema, E. H. (1930), "Ad Plauti Trinummum," in *Mnemosyne* NS 58: 114–20.

TRINVMMVS

ARGVMENTVM

Thesaurum apstrusum abiens peregre Charmides
Remque omnem amico Callicli mandat suo.
Istoc apsente male rem perdit filius;
Nam et aedis uendit: has mercatur Callicles.
5 **V**irgo indotata soror istius poscitur.
Minus quo cum inuidia ei det dotem Callicles,
Mandat qui dicat aurum ferre se[se] a patre.
Vt uenit ad aedis, hunc deludit Charmides
Senex, ut rediit; quoius nubunt liberi.

arg. 7 sese *P*, se *Camerarius*

THREE-DOLLAR DAY

PLOT SUMMARY

When going abroad, Charmides entrusts a hidden treasure and
all his belongings to his friend Callicles. In the absence of
Charmides, his son wastes his money badly: he even sells the
house. Callicles buys it. His virgin sister is asked for in marriage   5
without a dowry. In order to give her a dowry without caus-
ing offense, Callicles commissions someone to say that he is
bringing gold from her father. When he comes to the house,
old Charmides makes fun of him on his return; his children
marry.

PERSONAE

LVXVRIA cum INOPIA prologus
MEGARONIDES senex
CALLICLES senex
LYSITELES adulescens
PHILTO senex
LESBONICVS adulescens
STASIMVS seruos
CHARMIDES senex
SYCOPHANTA

SCAENA

Athenis

CHARACTERS

LUXURY with WANT speaker of the prologue and her
    daughter; purely allegorical figures with no concrete role
    later on
MEGARONIDES an old man; friend of Callicles and Char-
    mides
CALLICLES an old man; very reliable friend of Charmides
LYSITELES a young man; morally upright
PHILTO an old man; father of Lysiteles
LESBONICUS a young man; essentially good, but wasting
    money without self-restraint
STASIMUS a slave; works for Charmides and Lesbonicus
CHARMIDES an old man; father of Lesbonicus returning
    from abroad
SYCOPHANT a trickster hired by Megaronides and Callicles

STAGING

The stage represents a street in Athens. On it is the house of
Charmides, with a small annex attached to it; this annex can be
reached through a separate door. The houses of Megaronides
and Philto are offstage, the former to the right and the latter to
the left; at least the house of Philto is close by. To the left the
street leads to the harbor and to the right to the city center.

PROLOGVS

LVXVRIA. INOPIA

LVX sequere hac me, gnata, ut munus fungaris tuom.
INO sequor, sed finem fore quem dicam nescio.
LVX adest. em illae sunt aedes, i intro nunciam.
  nunc, ne quis erret uostrum, paucis in uiam
5 deducam, si quidem operam dare promittitis.
  nunc igitur primum quae ego sim et quae illaec siet
  huc quae abiit intro dicam, si animum aduortitis.
  primum mihi Plautus nomen Luxuriae indidit;
  tunc hanc mihi gnatam esse uoluit, Inopiam.
10 sed ea huc quid intro ierit impulsu meo
  accipite et date uociuas auris dum eloquor.
  adulescens quidam est qui in hisce habitat aedibus;
  is rem paternam me adiutrice perdidit.
  quoniam ei qui me aleret nil uideo esse relicui,
15 dedi ei meam gnatam quicum ⟨una⟩ aetatem exigat.
  sed de argumento ne exspectetis fabulae:
  senes qui huc uenient, i rem uobis aperient.

9 tum *P*, tunc *Trappes-Lomax*
15 una *add. Vollbehr*

PROLOGUE

Enter LUXURY *from the right, followed by* WANT.

LUX Follow me this way, my daughter, so that you may do your duty.

WANT Yes, but I don't know what I should say our destination is.

LUX It's here. There, that's the house, go in at once.

Exit WANT *into the house of Charmides.*

LUX (*to the audience*) Now so that none of you will be mistaken, I'll set you on the right track with a few words, if 5
you promise to give me your attention. Now then, first I'll say who I am and who that woman is who went in here, if you pay attention. First, Plautus gave me the name of Luxury; next, he wanted me to have this woman as my daughter, Want. But take in why she went in here 10
at my prompting and give me empty ears while I'm telling you.

   There's a certain young man who lives in this house; with my assistance, he squandered his father's possessions. When I saw that he had nothing left with which to maintain me, I gave him my daughter to spend his life 15
with.

   But don't wait for me to tell you the plot of the play: the old men who'll come here will disclose the matter

huic Graece nomen est Thesauro fabulae:
Philemo scripsit, Plautus uortit barbare,
20   nomen Trinummo fecit, nunc hoc uos rogat
ut liceat possidere hanc nomen fabulam.
tantum est. ualete, adeste cum silentio.

ACTVS I

I. i: MEGARONIDES

MEG   amicum castigare ob meritam noxiam
immoene est facinus, uerum in aetate utile
25   et conducibile. nam ego amicum hodie meum
concastigabo pro commerita noxia,
inuitus, ni id me inuitet ut faciam fides.
nam hic nimium morbus mores inuasit bonos;
ita plerique omnes iam sunt intermortui.
30   sed dum illi aegrotant, interim mores mali
31   quasi herba irrigua succreuere uberrume;
33   eorum licet iam metere messem maxumam,
32   nec quicquam hic nunc est uile nisi mores mali.
34   nimioque hic pluris pauciorum gratiam
35   faciunt pars hominum quam id quod prosit pluribus.
ita uincunt illud conducibile gratiae,
quae in rebus multis opstant odiosaeque sunt
remoramque faciunt rei priuatae et publicae.

33 *ante* 32 *posuit Bücheler*
35 prosint Ω, prosit *Gronovius*

to you. This play is called *Thesauros*[1] in Greek. Phile-
mon wrote it and Plautus translated it into the barbarian
tongue; he gave it the name *Three-Dollar Day* and now   20
asks you that this play may keep this name. That's all.
Farewell, attend quietly.

Exit LUXURY *to the right.*

ACT ONE

Enter MEGARONIDES *from the right.*

MEG Remonstrating with a friend for a wrong committed is a
thankless task, but at times useful and beneficial; today   25
I shall remonstrate with a friend of mine for a wrong
committed, and I'll do so against my will, but my sense
of loyalty requires me to do so. Well, a plague has made
sad inroads upon moral standards here, so much so that
they're pretty much all dead by now. But in the mean-   30
time, while they were ill, moral laxity has sprung up in
great abundance like well-watered weeds. You can now
harvest an enormous crop of it, and nothing is cheap
here these days apart from moral laxity. A part of the
people hold the favor of a minority in higher esteem here   35
than what benefits the majority. In this way expedience
is sacrificed to the desire for favor, which is obstructive
in many things, is hateful, and hinders personal and pub-
lic welfare.

Enter CALLICLES *from the house of Charmides.*

[1] "The Treasure."

I. ii: CALLICLES. MEGARONIDES

CAL   Larem corona nostrum decorari uolo.

40   uxor, uenerare ut nobis haec habitatio

        bona, fausta, felix, fortunataque euenat . . .

        teque ut quam primum possim uideam emortuam.

MEG hic ille est senecta aetate qui factust puer,

        qui ammisit in se culpam castigabilem.

45   aggrediar hominem.

CAL   quoia hic uox prope me sonat?

MEG tui beneuolentis, si ita es ut ego te uolo,

        sin aliter es, inimici atque irati tibi.

CAL   o amice, salue, atque aequalis. ut uales,

        Megaronides?

MEG   et tu edepol salue, Callicles.

50 CAL ualen? ualuistin?

MEG   ualeo et ualui rectius.

CAL   quid agit tua uxor? ut ualet?

MEG   plus quam ego uolo.

CAL   bene hercle est illam tibi ualere et uiuere.

MEG credo hercle te gaudere si quid mi mali est.

CAL   omnibus amicis quod mihi est cupio esse idem.

55 MEG eho tu, tua uxor quid agit?

CAL   immortalis est,

        uiuit uicturaque est.

MEG   bene hercle nuntias,

        deosque oro ut uitae tuae superstes suppetat.

CAL   dum quidem hercle tecum nupta sit, sane uelim.

MEG uin commutemus, tuam ego ducam et tu meam?

60   faxo hau tantillum dederis uerborum mihi.

---

2 The Lar, a tutelary deity who, together with the Penates, was supposed to protect the household and its members.

CAL (*into the house*) I want our Household God[2] to be
adorned with a garland. My wife, pray that our residence   40
may become good, blessed, happy, and successful . . .
(*aside*) and that I may see you dead as quickly as pos-
sible.

MEG (*aside*) This is the man who has become a boy in his old
age and who has committed a wrong deserving remon-
stration. I'll approach him.   45

CAL (*startled*) Whose voice can be heard here near me?

MEG (*approaching*) That of your well-wisher, if you're the way
I wish you to be; but if you're different, that of an enemy
and someone who is angry with you.

CAL Greetings, my friend and contemporary. How are you,
Megaronides?

MEG Greetings to you, too, Callicles.

CAL Are you well? Have you been well?   50

MEG I'm well, but I've been better.

CAL How is your wife? How is her health?

MEG Better than I wish.

CAL It's good that she's alive and well for you.

MEG I do believe that you're happy if I have some misfor-
tune.

CAL I'm keen that all my friends should have the same as
me.

MEG Hey there, how's your own wife?   55

CAL She's immortal; she's alive and always will be.

MEG I'm glad to hear it and I ask the gods that she may outlive
you.

CAL If only she were married to you, I'd wish for it indeed.

MEG Do you want us to swap, so that I marry yours and you
mine? I'll guarantee that you won't have tricked me at   60
all.

	CAL	namque enim tu, credo, me imprudentem obrepseris.
	MEG	ne tu hercle faxo hau nescias quam rem egeris.
	CAL	habeas ut nanctu's: nota mala res optuma est.
		nam ego nunc si ignotam capiam, quid agam nesciam.
65	MEG	edepol proinde ut diu uiuitur, bene uiuitur.
		sed hoc animum aduorte atque aufer ridicularia;
		nam ego dedita opera huc ad te [ad]uenio.
	CAL	quid uenis?
	MEG	malis te ut uerbis multis multum obiurigem.
	CAL	men?
	MEG	numquis est hic alius praeter me atque te?
70	CAL	nemo est.
	MEG	quid tu igitur rogitas tene obiurigem?
		nisi tu me mihimet censes dicturum male.
72		nam si in te aegrotant artes antiquae tuae,
[72ᵃ		sin immutare uis ingenium moribus,]
		aut si demutant mores ingenium tuom
		neque eos antiquos seruas, ast captas nouos,
75		omnibus amicis morbum tu incuties grauem,
		ut te uidere audireque aegroti sient.
	CAL	qui in mentem uenit tibi istaec dicta dicere?
	MEG	quia omnis bonos bonasque accurare addecet
		suspicionem et culpam ut ab se segregent.
80		CAL non potest utrumque fieri.
	MEG	quapropter?

65 bene uiuitur diu Ω, diu uiuitur bene *Acidalius*
67 uenio A, aduenio P
72ᵃ *uersum om.* A
73–74 *del. Ritschl*

CAL (*with irony*) Yes, for you will have taken me by surprise, I suppose.

MEG Seriously, I'll make sure that you know exactly what you've done.

CAL Keep her as you've got hold of her: the evil that's known is the evil that's best; if I were to take on an unfamiliar one now, I wouldn't know what to do.

MEG Yes, one lives best in the way to which one has grown 65
accustomed. But pay attention and stop your jokes; I've come here to you with a definite errand.

CAL Why have you come?

MEG In order to reproach you a lot with a lot of harsh words.

CAL Me?

MEG There isn't anyone here apart from me and you, is there?

CAL No. 70

MEG Then why do you ask if it's you that I'm reproaching? Unless you think that I'm going to denounce myself. Well, if your old ways are sick within you, [if you wish to change your character because of the habits of this age,] or if the habits of this age are changing your character and you aren't preserving those old ones, but taking on new ones, you'll inspire a grave affliction in all 75
your friends, so that it'll make them sick to see and hear you.

CAL Why did you come up with the idea of saying those words?

MEG Because all good men and women ought to make sure that they keep suspicion and offense away from themselves.

CAL Not both of these things can be done. 80

MEG Why?

CAL   rogas?

ne ammittam culpam, ego meo sum promus pectori:
suspicio est in pectore alieno sita.
nam nunc ego si te surrupuisse suspicer
Ioui coronam de capite ex Capitolio

85   qui in columine astat summo: si id non feceris
atque id tamen mi lubeat suspicarier,
qui tu id prohibere me potes ne suspicer?
sed istuc negoti cupio scire quid siet.

MEG haben tu amicum aut familiarem quempiam

90   quoi pectus sapiat?

CAL   edepol hau dicam dolo:
sunt quos scio esse amicos, sunt quos suspicor,
sunt quorum ingenia atque animos nequeo noscere
ad amici partem an ad inimici peruenant;
sed tu ex amicis certis mi es certissumus.

95   si quid scis me fecisse inscite aut improbe,
si id non me accusas, tute ipse obiurgandus es.

MEG scio et, si alia huc causa ad te adueni, aequom postulas.

CAL exspecto si quid dicas.

MEG   primumdum omnium,
male dictitatur tibi uolgo in sermonibus:

100   turpilucricupidum te uocant ciues tui;
tum autem sunt alii qui te uolturium uocant:
hostisne an ciuis comedis parui pendere.
haec quom audio in te dici, eis excrucior miser.

85 quod Ω, qui *Scaliger*
88 cupio scire *A*, scire cupio *P*
103 dicis *P*, dici is *Vahlen*

CAL You ask? I guard my own breast against committing an offense; but suspicion resides in another's breast. For instance, if I were to suspect now that you've stolen the crown from the Capitoline Temple from the head of Jupiter, who stands on the rooftop:[3] if you hadn't done   85 this and if I still wished to suspect it, how could you prevent me from suspecting it? But I'm keen to know what's troubling you.

MEG Do you have any friend or intimate who possesses sound   90 sense?

CAL I'll tell you frankly: there are people whom I know to be friends, there are people whom I suspect to be friends, and there are people of whom I can't find out whether their minds and hearts belong to the side of friend or foe; but of my certain friends you are the most certain. If you   95 know that I've done something in a foolish or inappropriate way and if you don't reproach me for it, you deserve to be rebuked yourself.

MEG I know, and if I've come here to you for any other reason, you have cause for complaint.

CAL I'm waiting to see if you're going to say anything.

MEG Well, first of all you're commonly defamed in conversations: your fellow citizens call you greedy for dishonest   100 gain; then again there are others who call you a vulture, claiming that you care little whether you eat up foreigners or citizens. When I hear this being said against you, I agonize over it, poor me.

---

[3] The temple of Jupiter on the Capitoline Hill, with its statue of the deity on the temple roof, was the most important temple in Rome.

CAL   est atque non est mi in manu, Megaronides:
105   quin dicant, non est; merito ut ne dicant, id est.
MEG   fuitne hic tibi amicus Charmides?
CAL   est et fuit.
    id ita esse ut credas, rem tibi auctorem dabo.
    nam postquam hic eius rem confregit filius
    uidetque ipse ad paupertatem protractum esse se
110   suamque filiam esse adultam uirginem,
    simul eius matrem suamque uxorem mortuam,
    quoniam hinc iturust ipsus in Seleuciam,
    mihi commendauit uirginem gnatam suam
    et rem suam omnem et illum corruptum filium.
115   haec, si mi inimicus esset, credo hau crederet.
MEG   quid tu? adulescentem, quem esse corruptum uides,
    qui tuae mandatus est fide et fiduciae,
    quin eum restituis, quin ad frugem corrigis?
    ei rei operam dare te fuerat aliquanto aequius,
120   si qui probiorem facere posses, non uti
    in eandem tute accederes infamiam
    malumque ut eius cum tuo misceres malo.
CAL   quid feci?
MEG   quod homo nequam.
CAL   non istuc meum est.
MEG   emistin de adulescente has aedis—quid taces?—
125   ubi nunc tute habitas?
CAL   emi atque argentum dedi,
    minas quadraginta, adulescenti ipsi in manum.
MEG   dedistine argentum?

---

4 Seleucia on the Tigris, in what is now Iraq, was one of the biggest
Hellenistic cities.

CAL It is and it isn't in my power, Megaronides: it isn't in my   105
     power to keep them from saying it; but it is in my power
     to keep them from saying it deservedly.

MEG Didn't you have Charmides as a friend here?

CAL I do and I did. In order that you should believe this to
     be the case, I give you a fact as proof: after his son ruined
     his wealth here and he saw that he himself had been
     dragged down to poverty, that his daughter was a grown-   110
     up young woman, and that her mother and his wife was
     dead, at the time when he was about to go to Seleucia,[4]
     he entrusted me with his virgin daughter, his entire pos-
     sessions, and that decadent son of his. If he were my   115
     enemy, I trust he wouldn't have trusted me with this.

MEG Well then? Why don't you change the young man back
     and bring him back to responsible behavior, when you
     can see that he's decadent and when he was entrusted to
     your faith and reliability? This is what would have been
     far more appropriate for you to take care of, to see if you   120
     could in any way make him more decent, not to succumb
     to the same notoriety yourself and mix his depravity with
     yours.

CAL What have I done?

MEG The doings of a crook.

CAL Your words don't describe me.

MEG Didn't you buy this house from the young man—why are
     you quiet?—where you yourself live now?   125

CAL I did buy it and I paid the young man himself cash down,
     forty minas.[5]

MEG You paid him?

---

[5] A very low sum. In *Most.* 645, forty minas is only enough as a deposit for a house.

CAL	factum nec facti piget.
MEG	edepol fide adulescentem mandatum malae!
	dedistine hoc facto ei gladium qui se occideret?
130		quid secus est aut quid interest dare te in manus
	argentum amanti homini adulescenti, animi impoti,
	qui exaedificaret suam incohatam ignauiam?
CAL	non ego illi argentum redderem?
MEG	non redderes
	nec de illo quicquam neque emeres nec uenderes,
135		nec qui deterior esset faceres copiam.
	inconciliastine eum qui mandatust tibi,
	ill' qui mandauit, eum exturbasti ex aedibus?
	edepol mandatum pulchre et curatum probe!
	crede huic tutelam: suam melius rem gesserit.
140	CAL	subigis maledictis me tuis, Megaronides,
	nouo modo adeo, ut quod meae concreditum est
	taciturnitati clam, fide et fiduciae,
	ne enuntiarem quoiquam neu facerem palam—
	ut mihi necesse sit iam id tibi concredere.
145	MEG	mihi quod credideris sumes ubi posiueris.
CAL	circumspicedum te ne quis assit arbiter
	nobis, et quaeso identidem circumspice.
MEG	ausculto si quid dicas.
CAL	si taceas, loquar.
	quoniam hinc est profecturus peregre Charmides,
150		thesaurum demonstrauit mihi in hisce aedibus,
	hic in conclaui quodam; sed circumspice.
MEG	nemo est.
CAL	nummorum Philippeum ad tria milia.

---

6 Three times as much as Callicles has paid for the house.

CAL   I did and I don't regret the deed.

MEG   To what faithlessness the young fellow was entrusted! Haven't you given him a sword with which to kill himself? What else is it, what difference is there, when you give a lovesick young man without self-restraint money into his hands, with which he can complete building the ruin he has begun?   130

CAL   Shouldn't I have paid him?

MEG   No, you shouldn't have, and you shouldn't have bought or sold anything from him or given him the means to be even more depraved. Haven't you got the man who was entrusted to you into trouble and haven't you thrown the man who entrusted him to you out of his house? Goodness, the job was placed into your care beautifully and carried out properly! Trust this chap with the guardianship: he'll look after his own interests better.   135

CAL   Megaronides, with your harsh words you're forcing me, and forcing me unexpectedly, so that what was secretly entrusted to my silence, my faith and reliability, so that I shouldn't tell anyone or make it known—so that I can't avoid entrusting it to you now.   140

MEG   Whatever you entrust me with you'll be able to recover from where you placed it.   145

CAL   Just look around you to make sure that we don't have any witness present, and please, look around again and again.

MEG   (*doing so*) I'm listening, if you're saying anything.

CAL   If you're quiet, I'll speak. When Charmides was about to go abroad, he showed me a treasure in this house, in a certain room here; but do look around.   150

MEG   (*doing so*) There's no one here.

CAL   Around three thousand Philippics.[6] When we were both

135

		id solus solum per amicitiam et per fidem
		flens me opsecrauit suo ne gnato crederem
155		neu quoiquam unde ad eum id posset permanascere.
		nunc si ille huc saluos reuenit, reddam suom sibi;
		si quid eo fuerit, certe illius filiae,
		quae mihi mandata est, habeo dotem unde dem,
		ut eam in se dignam condicionem collocem.
160	MEG	pro di immortales, uerbis paucis quam cito
		alium fecisti me, alius ad te ueneram!
		sed ut occepisti, perge porro proloqui.
	CAL	quid tibi ego dicam, qui illius sapientiam
		et meam fidelitatem et celata omnia
165		paene ille ignauos funditus pessum dedit?
	MEG	quidum?
	CAL	quia, ruri dum sum ego unos sex dies,
		me apsente atque insciente, inconsultu meo,
168		aedis uenalis hasce inscribit litteris.
170	MEG	lupus opseruauit dum dormitarent canes:
169		adesuriuit magis, [et] inhiauit acrius;
171		gregem uniuorsum uoluit totum auortere.
	CAL	fecisset edepol, ni haec praesensisset canes.
		sed nunc rogare ego uicissim te uolo:
		quid fuit officium meum me facere? fac sciam;
175		utrum indicare me ei thesaurum aequom fuit,
		aduorsum quam eius me opsecrauisset pater,
		an ego alium dominum paterer fieri hisce aedibus?
		qui emisset, eius essetne ea pecunia?
		emi egomet potius aedis, argentum dedi
180		thesauri causa, ut saluom amico traderem.
		neque adeo hasce emi mihi neque usurae meae:

169 et *del. Hermann*   *uersum post 170 posuit Vahlen*

alone, he entreated me in tears by our friendship and by
my good faith that I shouldn't entrust this to his son or   155
to anyone from whom it could leak out to him. Now if he
returns here safely, I'll return his possessions to him; if
anything happens to him, I certainly have the means to
give a dowry to his daughter, who was entrusted to me,
so that I can give her in a marriage worthy of her.

MEG   Immortal gods, how quickly you have, with a few words,   160
turned me into a different man from the one that had
come to you! But as you've begun, go on speaking.

CAL   Why should I tell you how that good-for-nothing almost
ruined completely his father's wisdom, my trustworthi-   165
ness, and all our secrets?

MEG   How so?

CAL   Because while I was in the country for a mere six days,
he advertised this house for sale in my absence, without
my knowledge, and without consulting me.

MEG   The wolf waited until the dogs were drowsy. He got hun-   170
grier and gaped more fiercely; he wanted to steal the
entire flock.

CAL   He would have done so, if this dog hadn't got wind of it.
But now I want to ask you in turn: what was it my duty
to do? Let me know. Would it have been right to reveal   175
the treasure to him, against his father's entreaties, or
should I have allowed another to become master of this
house? Should this money have belonged to the man
who'd bought it? I bought the house myself in prefer-
ence to that and paid money for the sake of the treasure,   180
so that I could return it to my friend safely. And I didn't
buy this house for myself or my use either; I bought it

		illi redemi rursum, a me argentum dedi.
		haec sunt: si recte seu peruorse facta sunt,
		ego me fecisse confiteor, Megaronides.
185		em mea malefacta, em meam auaritiam tibi!
		hasc' mihi propter res maledicas famas ferunt.
	MEG	παῦσαι: uicisti castigatorem tuom:
		occlusti linguam, nihil est qui respondeam.
	CAL	nunc ego te quaeso ut me opera et consilio iuues
190		communicesque hanc mecum meam prouinciam.
	MEG	polliceor operam.
	CAL	ergo ubi eris paulo post?
	MEG	domi.
	CAL	numquid uis?
	MEG	cures tuam fidem.
	CAL	fit sedulo.
	MEG	sed quid ais?
	CAL	quid uis?
	MEG	ubi nunc adulescens habet?
	CAL	posticulum hoc recepit, quom aedis uendidit.
195	MEG	istuc uolebam scire. i sane nunciam.
		sed quid ais? quid nunc uirgo? nempe apud te est?
	CAL	ita est,
		iuxtaque eam curo cum mea.
	MEG	recte facis.
	CAL	numquid prius quam abeo me rogaturu's?

186 hasce mihi *A*, hascine me *P*   malas *A*, maledictas *P*, maledicas
Saumaise
192 fit *P*, fiet *A*

back for him and paid from my own pocket. These are
the facts: whether it was done rightly or wrongly, I admit
that I've done it, Megaronides. Here you have my bad   185
deeds, here you have my greed! It's because of these
things that people spread slanderous gossip about me.

MEG   Enough! You've won the day over the one reproaching
you: you've locked up my tongue, I have nothing to give
you an answer with.

CAL   Now I ask you to support me with help and advice and   190
to share this duty of mine with me.

MEG   I promise you my help.

CAL   Then where will you be a little later?

MEG   At home.

CAL   Is there anything you want?

MEG   Look after your good faith.

CAL   Yes, with all my heart. (*turns to go*)

MEG   (*calling him back*) But what do you say?

CAL   What do you want?

MEG   Where does the young fellow live now?

CAL   He reserved this annex for himself when he sold the
house.

MEG   That's what I wanted to know. Do go now. (*just as Cal-*   195
licles turns to go) But what do you say? What about the
girl now? She's with you, isn't she?

CAL   Yes, I'm looking after her along with my own daughter.

MEG   You're doing what's right.

CAL   Are you going to ask me anything else before I leave?

MEG   Goodbye.

Exit CALLICLES *to the right; he will return on a different route
and go into his house from a back entrance.*

MEG   uale.

nihil est profecto stultius nec stolidius
200   nec mendaciloquius neque [adeo] argutum magis,
nec confidentiloquius nec periurius
quam urbani assidui ciues quos scurras uocant.
atque egomet me adeo cum illis una ibidem traho,
qui illorum uerbis falsis acceptor fui,
205   qui omnia se simulant scire nec quicquam sciunt.
207   sciunt id quod in aurem rex reginae dixerit,
208   sciunt quod Iuno fabulata est cum Ioue;
206   quod quisque in animo habet aut habiturust sciunt,
209   quae nec futura nec sunt, tamen illi sciunt.
210   falsone an uero laudent, culpent quem uelint,
non flocci faciunt, dum illud quod lubeat sciant.
omnes mortales hunc aiebant Calliclem
indignum ciuitate ac sese uiuere,
bonis qui hunc adulescentem euortisset suis.
215   ego de eorum uerbis famigeratorum insciens
prosilui amicum castigatum innoxium.
quod si exquiratur usque ab stirpe auctoritas,
und' quicque auditum dicant, nisi id appareat,
famigeratori res sit cum damno et malo,
220   hoc ita si fiat, publico fiat bono,
pauci sint faxim qui sciant quod nesciunt,
occlusioremque habeant stultiloquentiam.

200 adeo *A, om. P*
206 *post 208 posuit Niemeyer*
211 lubeat *P*, lubeant *A*
213 haecesciet *A*, hac esset *P*, ac sese *Gulielmus*, hac esse et *Taub-
mann*   214 suis *P*, omnibus *A*
218 quidquid *A*, quicquid *P*, quidque *Acidalius*

MEG There really isn't anything more stupid and more idiotic, or more lying and more garrulous, or speaking more   200 boldly and with perjury, than the unremitting city-folks they call the men about town. And I count myself in the same category, since I swallowed the false words of those who pretend to know everything and don't know any-   205 thing. They know what the king said into the queen's ear, they know what Juno[7] talked about with Jupiter; they know what everyone has or will have in mind; and what won't be and isn't the case, they know it all the same. They don't care a straw whether it is rightly or wrongly   210 that they praise and find fault with anyone they wish, so long as they may know whatever they like. All mortals said that Callicles here was unworthy of the community and of himself, since he'd cheated this young man out of his possessions. Moved by the words of these gossips I   215 rushed forth without investigation in order to reproach an innocent friend. But if the authority for the claim were examined down to its very roots, from where they say they've heard everything, and if it were a matter of fine and punishment for the gossip if he couldn't pro- duce his source, well, if it were like that, it would be for   220 the public benefit, I'd bet there would be few people who know what they don't know, and that they'd keep their foolish talk more to themselves.

Exit MEGARONIDES *to the right.*

[7] Jupiter's wife.

ACTVS II

II. i: LYSITELES

	LYS	multas res simitu in meo corde uorso,
		multum in cogitando dolorem indipiscor:
225		egomet me coquo et macero et defetigo,
		magister mihi exercitor animus nunc est.
		sed hoc non liquet nec satis cogitatum est
		utram potius harum mihi artem expetessam,
		utram aetati agundae arbitrer firmiorem,
230		amorine me an rei opsequi potius par sit,
		utra in parte plus sit uoluptatis uitae
		ad aetatem agundam.
		de hac re mihi satis hau liquet; nisi hoc sic faciam, opi-
		nor,
		ut utramque rem simul exputem, iudex sim reusque ad
		eam rem.
235		ita faciam, ita placet; omnium primum
		Amoris artis eloquar quem ad modum [se] expediant.
237		numquam Amor quemquam
237ᵃ		nisi cupidum hominem
237ᵇ		postulat se in plagas conicere:
238		eos cupit, eos consectatur;
238ᵃ		subdole [blanditur] ab re consulit,
239		blandiloquentulus, harpago, mendax,
239ᵃ		cuppes, auarus, elegans, despoliator,
240		latebricolarum hominum corruptor,
		[blandus] inops, celatum indagator.
		nam qui amat quod amat quom extemplo
		sauiis sagittatis perculsust,
		ilico res foras labitur, liquitur.
245		"da mihi hoc, mel meum, si me amas, si audes."

ACT TWO

Enter LYSITELES *from the left.*

LYS   I'm turning many things over in my heart at the same time and I'm acquiring much pain while thinking. I'm 225 stirring up, wearing down, and tiring out my own self; my mind is a strict training master for me now. But it isn't clear and hasn't been thought through enough which of the two occupations I should seek and which I should consider more solid for leading my life: should 230 I rather devote myself to love or to industry, and on which side is there more pleasure in life throughout one's years?

    About this matter I'm not clear; but I'll act like this, I think: I'll examine both things at the same time, I'll be judge and defendant for this matter. That's what I'll do, 235 that's how I like it. First of all I'll say how Love's principles turn out.

    Love never demands to ensnare anyone, except a passionate man; those people he desires, those people he follows. He cleverly advises them to their disadvantage, a flattering, rapacious, lying, gluttonous, greedy, luxury-loving thief, ruin of men living in the shadow, destitute, 240 and prying into secrets. Yes, as soon as a man who is in love with the object of his love is pierced by arrowlike kisses, his wealth slips away and melts away. "Give me 245 this, my honey, if you love me and if you want to." Then

---

236 se *A, om.* P
238 eos cupit eos consectatur *P,* eos petit eos sectatur *A*
238ᵃ blanditur *del. Ritschl*   241 blandus *del. Hermann*

ibi ille cuculus: "ocelle mi, fiat:
et istuc et si amplius uis dari, dabitur."
ibi illa pendentem ferit: iam amplius orat;
non satis id est mali, ni amplius ⟨sit⟩ etiam,
250 quod ebibit, quod comest, quod facit sumpti.
nox datur: ducitur familia tota,
252 uestiplica, unctor, auri custos,
252ᵃ flabelliferae, sandaligerulae,
cantrices, cistellatrices,
254 nuntii, renuntii, rap-
254ᵃ tores panis et peni;
255 fit ipse, dum illis comis est, inops amator.
haec ego quom ago cum animo meo et recolo,
ubi qui eget, quam preti sit parui:
apage te, Amor, non places, nil te utor;
quamquam illud est dulce, esse et bibere,
260 Amor amara dat tamen, satis quod sit aegre:
fugit forum, fugitat suos cognatos,
fugat ipsus se ab suo contutu
neque eum sibi amicum uolunt dici.
mille modis, Amor, ignorandu's,
265 procul abhibendu's atque apstandu's;
265ᵃ nam qui in amorem praecipitauit
266 peius perit quasi saxo saliat:
266ᵃ apage te, Amor, tuas res tibi habeto,

249 amplius etiam *P*, etiam amplius *A*, amplius sit etiam *Leo*
252 uestiplice *P*, uestispica *A*, uestispici *Nonius*, uestiplica *Ritschl*
256 cum ago cum meo animo et recolo (rectilo *B*) *P*, quum cum
animo meo reputo *A*
260 aegre sit Ω, *transp. Seyffert*
261 fugit suos *A*, fugat uos *P*, fugitat suos *Spengel*
264 ignorandust *ACD*, ignorandum est *B*, ignorandu's *Leo*

144

that cuckoo says: "Yes, apple of my eye; you'll get that
and anything else if you want to get it." In that situation
she flogs him while he hangs there: immediately she asks
for more. This is not enough trouble, unless there's even
more that she drinks up, eats up, and spends money on.   250
He's granted a night: the whole establishment is hired,
the dress-folder, the masseur, the guardian of jewelry,
the fan-bearers, the sandal-carriers, the female singers,
the maids with treasure boxes, the ones who bring mes-
sages and the ones who bring messages back, the thieves
of bread and sustenance; while the lover is being gener-   255
ous to them, he himself becomes destitute.

When I think it through and go over it in my mind
how little anyone is worth when he's poor, away with you,
Love, I don't like you, I'm not having any dealings with
you. Even though it's nice to eat and drink, Love still   260
gives you bitterness, enough to distress you. The lover
flees from the forum, he flees from his relatives, he puts
himself to flight from his own gaze, and people don't
want him to be called their friend. You should be disre-
garded in a thousand ways, Love, you should be kept far   265
off and held at a distance: the man who falls head over
heels in love perishes in a worse way than if he were to
jump from the Rock.[8] Away with you, Love, have your
own property for yourself,[9] Love, and never be my

[8] The Tarpeian Rock in Rome, from which murderers and other
major criminals were thrown to their death.

[9] A standard divorce formula.

265 adhibendus *A*, adhibendus est (adhibendum est *C¹*) *P*, abhiben-
dus *Acidalius* (*unde* -u's *Leo*) abstandust *A*, aptinendus *B*, abtinendus
CD, abstandu's *Leo*

Amor, mihi amicus ne fuas umquam;
sunt tamen quos miseros maleque habeas,
quos tibi obnoxios fecisti.
270   certum est ad frugem adicere animum,
quamquam ibi [animo] labos grandis capitur.
boni sibi haec expetunt, rem, fidem, honorem,
gloriam, et gratiam: hoc probis pretium est.
eo mi magis lubet cum probis potius
275   quam cum improbis uiuere uanidicis.

II. ii: PHILTO. LYSITELES

PHIL   quo illic homo foras se penetrauit ex
      aedibus?
LYS   pater, assum, impera quiduis,
278   nec tibi ero in mora nec latebrose
278[a]   me aps tuo conspectu occultabo.
PHIL   feceris par tuis ceteris factis,
280   patrem tuom si percoles per pietatem.
nolo ego cum improbis te uiris, gnate mi,
282   neque in uia neque in foro
282[a]   necullum sermonem exsequi.
noui ego hoc saeculum moribus quibus siet:
malus bonum malum esse uolt, ut sit sui similis;
285   turbant, miscent mores mali:
285[a]   rapax, auarus, inuidus;
286   sacrum profanum, publicum
286[a]   priuatum habent, hiulca gens.
287   haec ego doleo, haec
287[a]   sunt quae med excruciant, haec dies
287[b]   noctesque tibi canto ut caueas.
288   quod manu non queunt tangere tantum

friend; still, there are others you can torture and tor-
ment, men you have enslaved.

I'm resolved to turn my mind to industry, however   270
great a toil one takes upon oneself there.

The good strive after these things: wealth, a good
name, a good reputation, fame, and friendly relations;
this is the reward for the decent. I'm all the keener
to live with the decent rather than with indecent chat-   275
terers.

Enter PHILTO *from the left, looking around.*

PHIL   Where out of the house has he made his way to?
LYS   (*approaching*) Father, I'm here, command me anything
      you like, I won't delay you or secretly hide from your
      sight.
PHIL   You'll act in accordance with your other deeds, if you   280
      honor your father with respect. My dear son, I don't want
      you to pursue any conversation with immoral men, ei-
      ther in the street or in the forum. I know what moral
      standards this generation has: the bad man wants the
      good one to be bad, so that he should resemble him; the   285
      bad confuse and mix up our standards: the rapacious, the
      greedy, and the envious man; they consider the sacred as
      profane and the public as private, an insatiable people.
      That's what I feel pain about, that's what torments me,
      that's what I harp on about day and night for you to be
      on your guard against. Only what they can't touch with

---

270 certunst *BCD*, certumst *G*, certa est res *A*   adplicare Ω, adi-
cere *Questa in apparatu*   271 animo *P, om. A*
287ᵇ noctesque *P*, noctes *A*   tibi canto *CD*, canto tibi *AB*

147

288ª fas habent quo manus apstineant,
      cetera: rape, trahe, fuge, late—lacrumas
290   haec mi quom uideo eliciunt,
      quia ego ad hoc genus hominum duraui.
      quin prius me ad pluris penetraui?
      nam hi mores maiorum laudant,
      eosdem lutitant quos collaudant.
295   hisce ego de artibus gratiam facio,
      ne colas neue imbuas ingenium.
      meo modo et moribus uiuito antiquis,
      quae ego tibi praecipio, ea facito.
      nil ego istos moror faeceos mores, turbidos, quibus
          boni dedecorant se.
300   haec tibi si mea imperia capesses, multa bona in pec-
          tore consident.

LYS   semper ego usque ad hanc aetatem ab ineunte adules-
          centia
      tuis seruiui seruitutem imperiis, [et] praeceptis, pater.
      pro ingenio ego me liberum esse ratus sum, pro impe-
          rio tuo
      meum animum tibi seruitutem seruire aequom censui.

305 PHIL qui homo cum animo inde ab ineunte aetate depugnat
          suo,
      utrum itane esse mauelit ut eum animus aequom cen-
          seat,
      an ita potius ut parentes eum esse et cognati uelint:
      si animus hominem pepulit, actum est: animo seruit,
          non sibi;
      si ipse animum pepulit, dum uiuit uictor uictorum
          cluet.
310   tu si animum uicisti potius quam animus te, est quod
          gaudeas.

148

their hands do they consider it right to keep their hands
away from; as for the rest: carry off, drag off, flee, hide—
when I see this, it makes me weep because I've lived to   290
see this type of men. Why did I not cross over to the
majority earlier? Yes, men now praise the ways of their
ancestors, but the very same men sully the ones they
praise. As for these arts, I renounce your cultivating   295
them or tainting your character with them. Live my way
and by the old standards, do what I teach you. I don't
care for those filthy and murky standards with which
they disgrace themselves. If you take these commands of   300
mine to heart, many good things will make their home
in your breast.

LYS I've always, from my earliest youth up to my present age,
lived in full obedience to your commands and teachings,
my father. With regard to my natural endowment I've
considered myself to be free; with regard to your author-
ity I've thought it right that my instinct should fully obey
you.

PHIL The man who pits himself against his desires from an   305
early age, struggling whether he should prefer to be the
way his instinct deems fair or the way his parents and
relatives want him to be—if his heart gets the better of
him, he's done for; he's obeying his heart and not himself.
If he himself gets the better of his heart, he's called the
winner of winners as long as he lives. If you have con-   310
quered your heart rather than your heart you, you have
reason to be happy. It's much better for you to be the way
you need to be than the way your heart likes it: those who

296 neu Ω, ne *Hermann*
302 et *del. Bothe*

nimio satiust ut opust ted ita esse quam ut animo lubet:
qui animum uincunt quam quos animus semper pro-
   biores cluent.

LYS   istaec ego mi semper habui aetati integumentum meae;
ne penetrarem me usquam ubi esset damni conciliabu-
   lum

315   neu noctu irem obambulatum neu suom adimerem al-
   teri

neu tibi aegritudinem, pater, parerem, parsi sedulo:
sarta tecta tua praecepta usque habui mea modestia.

PHIL   quid exprobras? bene quod fecisti tibi fecisti, non mihi;
mihi quidem aetas acta est ferme: tua istuc refert
   maxume.

320   is probus est quem paenitet quam probus sit et frugi
   bonae;

qui ipsus sibi satis placet nec probus est nec frugi bo-
   nae:

qui ipsus se contemnit, in eo est indoles industriae.
benefacta benefactis aliis pertegito, ne perpluant.

LYS   ob eam rem haec, pater, autumaui, quia res quaedam
   est quam uolo

325   ego me aps te exorare.

PHIL   quid id est? dare iam ueniam gestio.

LYS   adulescenti huic genere summo, amico atque aequali
   meo,

minus qui caute et cogitate suam rem tractauit, pater,
bene uolo ego illi facere, si tu non neuis.

PHIL   nemp' de tuo?

LYS   de meo: nam quod tuom est meum est, omne meum
   est autem tuom.

326 huic Ω, hinc *Vollbehr*

conquer their hearts are always known as more decent than those whom their hearts conquer.

LYS I've always considered this to be a shield for my youth; I've diligently refrained from entering any meeting where loss is sustained, from going around at night to 315 meet others, from taking another's possessions away from him, and from upsetting you, my father. I've always kept your teachings in good repair through my self-restraint.

PHIL Why are you blaming it on me? What you did well you did for yourself, not for me. My time is almost up; all this is of importance for yourself above all. That man is 320 decent who is dissatisfied with how decent and well-conducted he is; the man who is content with himself is neither decent nor well-conducted. The man who despises himself has the possibility for industry within him. Protect your good deeds with other good deeds so that they won't let the rain through.

LYS Father, I said this for the simple reason that there's a favor I want to obtain from you. 325

PHIL What is it? I'm already keen to grant permission.

LYS If you're not against it, father, I want to do a good turn to this young chap from a family of the highest standing, a friend and contemporary of mine, who hasn't handled his affairs very cautiously and thoughtfully.

PHIL You mean from your own funds, don't you?

LYS Yes, from my own funds: what belongs to you belongs to me, and everything that belongs to me belongs to you in turn.

330 PHIL quid is? egetne?

LYS   eget.

PHIL   habuitne rem?

LYS   habuit.

PHIL   qui eam perdidit?
    publicisne affinis fuit an maritumis negotiis?
    mercaturane, an uenalis habuit ubi rem perdidit?

LYS nihil istorum.

PHIL   quid igitur?

LYS   per comitatem edepol, pater;
    praeterea aliquantum animi causa in deliciis disperdi-
        dit.

335 PHIL edepol hominem praemandatum ferme familiariter,
    qui quidem nusquam per uirtutem rem confregit atque
        eget!
    nil moror eum tibi esse amicum cum eius modi uirtuti-
        bus.

LYS quia sine omni malitia est, tolerare eius egestatem
    uolo.

PHIL de mendico male meretur qui ei dat quod edit aut bi-
        bat;

340   nam et illud quod dat perdit et illi prodit uitam ad mi-
        seriam.
    non eo haec dico, quin quae tu uis ego uelim et faciam
        lubens:
    sed ego hoc uerbum quom illi quoidam dico, prae-
        monstro tibi,
    ut ita te aliorum miserescat, ne tis alios misereat.

LYS deserere illum et deiuuare in rebus aduorsis pudet.

PHIL What about him? Is he broke?   330

LYS Yes, he is.

PHIL Did he have money?

LYS Yes, he did.

PHIL How did he lose it? Was he engaged in business for the
state or on sea? In trade, or did he have slaves when he
lost his money?[10]

LYS None of that.

PHIL Well then?

LYS Through his generosity, father; moreover, he wasted
quite a sum on his own entertainment, indulging him-
self.

PHIL (*with irony*) Goodness, a man recommended in a very   335
friendly way! He ruined his wealth in no legitimate busi-
ness and is broke now. I don't care for you having him as
your friend with virtues of this kind.

LYS Because he's without any bad disposition, I want to sup-
port him in his poverty.

PHIL A man who gives a beggar something to eat or drink does
him bad service: what he gives him gets wasted and he   340
prolongs his life in misery. My saying this doesn't mean
that I don't want what you want or that I wouldn't do it
with pleasure; but when I'm saying this word against that
particular fellow, I'm advising you beforehand to have
pity on others only to the extent that others won't have
to have pity on you.

LYS I feel shame to desert him and to fail to act in his mis-
fortune.

---

[10] Slave trade was not considered dishonorable in itself.

345 PHIL   pol pudere quam pigere praestat totidem litteris.

   LYS   edepol, deum uirtute—dicam, pater—et maiorum et
          tua
      multa bona bene parta habemus, bene si amico feceris
      ne pigeat fecisse, ut potius pudeat si non feceris.

  PHIL   de magnis diuitiis si quid demas, plus fit an minus?

350 LYS   minus, pater; sed ciui immuni scin quid cantari solet?
      "quod habes ne habeas et illuc quod [nunc] non habes
          habeas [uelim], malum,
      quandoquidem nec tibi bene esse pote pati neque al-
          teri."

  PHIL   scio equidem istuc ita solere fieri; uerum, gnate mi,
      is est immunis quoi nihil est qui munus fungatur suom.

355 LYS   deum uirtute habemus et qui nosmet utamur, pater,
      et aliis qui comitati simus beneuolentibus.

  PHIL   non edepol tibi pernegare possum quicquam quod
          uelis.
      quoi egestatem tolerare uis? loquere audacter patri.

   LYS   Lesbonico huic adulescenti, Charmidei filio,

360   qui illic habitat.

  PHIL   quin comedit quod fuit, quod non fuit?

   LYS   ne opprobra, pater; multa eueniunt homini quae uolt,
      quae neuolt.

351 nunc *om. A*   uelim *om. P*

358 cuius Ω, quoi *Ritschl*   loquere audacter patri *P*, eloquere patri
audacter *A*

359 Charmidi *A*, Charmide *P*, Charmidei *Wackernagel*

PHIL Shame is better than upset by every letter of the   345
word.[11]

LYS Thanks to the gods—I may say so, father—and to our
ancestors and to you, we have much property, acquired
well, so that, if you've done a friend a good turn, you
shouldn't be upset to have done so, and so that you
should rather feel shame if you haven't done so.

PHIL If you take something away from great wealth, does it get
more or less?

LYS Less, father; but don't you know the ditty one usually has   350
for a citizen not doing his duty? "May you not have what
you have now, and may you have what you don't have
now, a thrashing, since you can't bear it that either you
yourself or someone else should have a good time."

PHIL I know that's what usually happens; but, my son, that
man isn't doing his duty who has no money with which
to carry out his duty.

LYS Father, thanks to the gods we have the means both to   355
sustain ourselves and to be kind to others who wish us
well.

PHIL I can't deny you anything you wish. Who do you want to
support in his poverty? Speak to your father boldly.

LYS Young Lesbonicus here, the son of Charmides, who lives   360
over there. (*points to it*)

PHIL You mean the one who ate up what he had and what he
didn't have?

LYS Don't cast it in his teeth, father; many things happen to
a man which he wants and which he doesn't want.

---

[11] A pun on *pudet*, "feel shame," and *piget*, "feel upset," which are
of identical length.

PHIL   mentire edepol, gnate, atque id nunc facis hau consue-
         tudine.

        nam sapiens quidem pol ipsus fingit fortunam sibi:

        eo non multa quae neuolt eueniunt, nisi fictor malust.

365   LYS   multa illi opera opust ficturae, qui se fictorem probum

        uitae agundae esse expetit: sed hic admodum adules-
         centulust.

PHIL   non aetate, uerum ingenio apiscitur sapientia;

        sapienti aetas condimentum est, sapiens aetati cibust.

        agedum eloquere, quid dare illi nunc uis?

LYS   nil quicquam, pater;

370   tu modo ne me prohibeas accipere si quid det mihi.

PHIL   an eo egestatem ei tolerabis, si quid ab illo acceperis?

LYS   eo, pater.

PHIL   pol ego istam uolo me rationem edoceas.

LYS   licet.

        scin tu illum quo genere natus sit?

PHIL   scio, apprime probo.

LYS   soror illi est adulta uirgo grandis: eam cupio, pater,

375   ducere uxorem sine dote.

PHIL   sine dote uxorem?

LYS   ita;

        tua re salua hoc pacto ab illo summam inibis gratiam

        nec commodius ullo pacto ei poteris auxiliarier.

PHIL   egone indotatam te uxorem ut patiar?

LYS   patiundum est, pater;

        et eo pacto addideris nostrae lepidam famam familiae.

---

12 In other words, the relationship between natural disposition and
age is that between food and seasoning; a good disposition is good even
without great age, but better with the accompanying age, whereas age
without a good disposition is of no worth.

PHIL You're lying, son, and you're not acting according to your habit now; the wise man devises his own fortune: that's why not many things happen to him which he doesn't want, unless he's a bad deviser.

LYS A man who is keen on being a decent deviser for leading 365
his life needs much practice in devising; but this chap is a mere youngster.

PHIL It's not through age, but through natural disposition that wisdom is obtained; for a wise nature age is a mere seasoning, but a wise nature is solid food for age.[12] Go on, tell me, what do you want to give him now?

LYS Absolutely nothing, father; it's simply that you shouldn't 370
prevent me from receiving something if he gives it to me.

PHIL You'll support him in his poverty by receiving something from him?

LYS Yes, father.

PHIL I want you to enlighten me about that.

LYS Yes. Do you know in what family he was born?

PHIL I do, in an outstanding one.

LYS He has a grown-up virgin sister; father, I'm keen on taking her as my wife without a dowry. 375

PHIL As your wife without a dowry?

LYS Yes. In this way you'll get his greatest gratitude with no expense to yourself, and you couldn't be able to help him more agreeably in any way.

PHIL Should I tolerate you taking a wife with no dowry?

LYS You should, father; and in this way you'll add a delightful reputation to our household.

380 PHIL   multa ego possum docta dicta et quamuis facunde lo-
           qui,
       historiam ueterem atque antiquam haec mea senectus
           sustinet;
       uerum ego quando te et amicitiam et gratiam in nos-
           tram domum
       uideo allicere, etsi aduorsatus tibi fui, istac iudico:
       tibi permitto; posce, duce.
    LYS   di te seruassint mihi!
385   sed adde ad istam gratiam unum.
    PHIL   quid id est autem unum?
    LYS   eloquar.
       tute ad eum adeas, tut' concilies, tute poscas.
    PHIL   eccere!
    LYS   nimio citius transiges: firmum omne erit quod tu ege-
           ris.
       grauius tuom erit unum uerbum ad eam rem quam
           centum mea.
    PHIL   ecce autem in benignitate hoc repperi, negotium!
390   dabitur opera.
    LYS   lepidus uiuis. haec sunt aedes, hic habet;
       Lesbonico est nomen. age, rem cura. ego te opperiam
           domi.

II. iii: PHILTO

    PHIL   non optuma haec sunt neque ut ego aequom censeo;
       uerum meliora sunt quam quae deterruma.
       sed hoc unum consolatur me atque animum meum,
395   quia qui nil aliud nisi quod sibi soli placet
       consulit aduorsum filium, nugas agit:
       miser ex animo fit, factius nihilo facit.

PHIL I could say many wise words, and that as eloquently as 380
you like; being old, I have the facts of old and ancient
history stored up in my head. But since I can see that
you're enticing friendship and goodwill into our house,
I'll judge the way you wish, even if I had opposed you: I
give you permission; ask for her, marry her.

LYS May the gods keep you for me! But add one thing to that 385
favor.

PHIL Well, what's this one thing?

LYS I'll tell you. *You* should approach him, *you* should win
him over, *you* should ask for her.

PHIL Look at that!

LYS You'll sort it out much more quickly; everything you do
will be firmly fixed. One word from you will have more
weight in this than one hundred from me.

PHIL Surely I've found this in my kindness, trouble! (*after a* 390
pause) I'll attend to it.

LYS You're very good. (*pointing*) This is the house, here is
where he lives; his name is Lesbonicus. Go on, take care
of it. I'll wait for you at home.

Exit LYSITELES *to the left.*

PHIL This isn't ideal or the way I consider it appropriate; yet
it's better than the worst would be. But this one fact
consoles me and my heart: the man who takes no mea- 395
sures with regard to his son except for what he alone
likes is badly mistaken. He becomes utterly wretched
and brings his designs no nearer accomplishment. He

---

391 opperiam *A*, operiar *P*
394 me unum consolatur *A*, unum consolaturum (-turu *CD*) me *P*

suae senectuti is acriorem hiemem parat,
quom illam importunam tempestatem conciet.
400 sed aperiuntur aedes quo ibam: commodum
ipse exit Lesbonicus cum seruo foras.

II. iv: LESBONICVS. STASIMVS. PHILTO

LES minus quindecim dies sunt quom pro hisce aedibus
minas quadraginta accepisti a Callicle.
estne hoc quod dico, Stasime?

STA   quom considero,
405 meminisse uideor fieri.

LES   quid factum est eo?

STA comesum, expotum, exunctum, elotum in balineis;
piscator, pistor apstulit, lanii, coqui,
holitores, myropolae, aucupes: confit cito;
non hercle minus diuorse distrahitur cito
410 quam si tu obicias formicis papauerem.

LES minus hercle in istis rebus sumptum est sex minis.

STA quid quod dedisti scortis?

LES   ibidem una traho.

STA [quid] quod ego defrudaui?

LES   em, istaec ratio maxuma est.

STA non tibi illud apparere, si sumas, potest;
415 nisi tu immortale rere esse argentum tibi.

PHIL sero atque stulte, prius quod cautum oportuit,
postquam comedit rem, post rationem putat.

LES nequaquam argenti ratio comparet tamen.

406 exussum *A*, exutum *P*, exunctum *Gulielmus*
413 quid *del. Fritzsche*

creates a harsher winter for his old age when he stirs up
that wild storm. But the house to which I was going is   400
opening up; Lesbonicus himself is coming out with his
slave at just the right time.

Enter LESBONICUS *from the annex, carrying a writing tablet
and accompanied by* STASIMUS; *they do not notice anyone.*

LES   It's less than two weeks that you got forty minas for this
      house from Callicles. Isn't it true what I'm saying, Stasi-
      mus?

STA   When I think about it, I seem to remember it happen-   405
      ing.

LES   What's happened with the money?

STA   It's been eaten up, drunk up, anointed away, washed
      away in the baths; the fisherman took it away, the miller,
      the butchers, the cooks, the vegetable-sellers, the per-
      fumers, the poultry-sellers. It gets used up quickly; it
      gets carried off just as quickly as if you throw poppy seed   410
      in front of ants.

LES   Less than six minas were spent on those things.

STA   What about the money you gave to prostitutes?

LES   I include that in the list.

STA   *(half aside)* And the money I tricked you out of?

LES   *(overhearing)* There, that's the main reason.

STA   Your money can't still be there if you spend it; unless you   415
      think it's immortal.

PHIL   *(aside)* He should have thought about this before, but
      he's keeping count too late and in a stupid way, after eat-
      ing up his possessions.

LES   *(examining the writing tablet)* Still, I can't make sense of
      the accounts at all.

161

	STA	ratio quidem hercle apparet: argentum οἴχεται.
420		minas quadraginta accepisti a Callicle,
		et ille aedis mancupio aps te accepit?
	LES	admodum.
	PHIL	pol opino affinis noster aedis uendidit;
		pater quom peregre ueniet, in porta est locus,
		nisi forte in uentrem filio correpserit.
425	STA	mille drachumarum tarpezitae Olympico,
426		quas de ratione dehibuisti, redditae?
426ᵃ	LES	nemp' quas spopondi.
	STA	immo "quas dependi" inquito,
		quia sponsionem nuper tute exactus es,
		pro illo adulescente quem tu esse aibas diuitem.
	LES	factum.
	STA	ut quidem illud perierit.
	LES	factum id quoque est.
430		nam nunc eum uidi miserum et me eius miseritum est.
	STA	miseret te aliorum, tui nec miseret nec pudet.
	PHIL	tempust adeundi.
	LES	estne hic Philto qui aduenit?
		is hercle est ipsus.
	STA	edepol ne ego istum uelim
		meum fieri seruom cum suo peculio.

---

425 trapezitae mille drachumarum Ω, *transp. et corr. Ritschl*
427 *ante* 426ᵃ *in* P   qua Ω, quia *Renkema*, quas *Ernout*   pronuper
Ω, nuper *Renkema*   tute *A*, tu *P*

---

[13] In the Latin, a pun between Lesbonicus' *nequaquam . . . comparet*, "it is not clear at all," and Stasimus' *apparet*, "it is visible (on a writing tablet)."

STA   You can easily sense the accounts:[13] it's the money that's
       gone. You got forty minas from Callicles, and he got the   420
       house from you by formal conveyance?[14]

LES   Quite.

PHIL   (*aside*) I believe our relation has sold the house. When
       his father comes from abroad, there's room at the door,[15]
       unless by chance he creeps into his son's belly.

STA   Has the banker Olympicus been paid the one thousand   425
       drachmas that you owed him according to the account?

LES   Yes, the ones I promised as a pledge.

STA   No, say "the ones I was forced to pay," because you were
       dunned for the pledged money recently for that young
       chap who you said was wealthy.[16]

LES   Yes, that happened.

STA   Namely that it got lost.

LES   Yes, that happened too. Well, I saw how wretched he was   430
       now and felt pity for him.

STA   You feel pity for others, but for yourself you feel neither
       pity nor shame.

PHIL   (*aside*) It's time to approach. (*does so*)

LES   (*to Stasimus*) Isn't this Philto who is coming here? It's
       him in person.

STA   (*half aside*) I'd really like him to become my slave, along
       with his personal fortune.

       [14] The formal conveyance is the so-called *mancipatio*, which was
       done in the presence of witnesses.   [15] As beggar.
       [16] Lesbonicus guaranteed a banker that his friend would repay the
       money if he got a loan and promised one thousand drachmas in case
       the friend would not do so; since the friend did not pay, Lesbonicus
       was forced to do so instead. Stasimus points out that making the pledge
       amounted to losing the money.

163

435	PHIL	erum atque seruom plurumum Philto iubet
		saluere, Lesbonicum et Stasimum.
	LES	di duint
		tibi, Philto, quaequomque optes. quid agit filius?
	PHIL	bene uolt tibi.
	LES	edepol mutuom mecum facit.
	STA	nequam illud uerbum est "bene uolt" nisi qui bene
		facit.
440		ego quoque uolo esse liber: nequiquam uolo;
		hic postulet frugi esse: nugas postulet.
	PHIL	meus gnatus me ad te misit, inter te atque nos
		affinitatem ut conciliarem et gratiam.
		tuam uolt sororem ducere uxorem; et mihi
445		sententia eadem est et uolo.
	LES	hau nosco tuom:
		bonis tuis [in] rebus meas res irrides malas.
	PHIL	homo ego sum, homo tu es: ita me amabit Iuppiter,
		nec te derisum aduenio nec dignum puto.
		uerum hoc quod dixi: meus me orauit filius
450		ut tuam sororem poscerem uxorem sibi.
	LES	mearum me rerum nouisse aequom est ordinem.
		cum uostra nostra non est aequa factio.
		affinitatem uobis aliam quaerite.
	STA	satin tu es sanus mentis aut animi tui
455		qui condicionem hanc repudies? nam illum tibi
		ferentarium esse amicum inuentum intellego.

446 rebus *P*, in rebus *A*

---

17 An etymological pun: a *ferentarius* is a light-armed skirmisher on horseback, but as the noun is derived from *ferre*, "bring," Plautus treats it as if it still had the meaning "someone who brings (help)." This fits

PHIL   Philto gives his best regards to master and slave, to Les-   435
      bonicus and Stasimus.

LES   May the gods grant you whatever you wish, Philto. What
      is your son up to?

PHIL   He wishes you well.

LES   He reciprocates with me.

STA   (*aside*) That phrase "he wishes well" is useless unless one
      acts well. I also want to be free; I want it in vain. This   440
      chap might want to be frugal; he'd want the impossi-
      ble.

PHIL   (*to Lesbonicus*) My son has sent me to you in order to
      obtain an alliance and friendship between you and us.
      He wants to marry your sister; and I have the same sen-   445
      timent and wish for it.

LES   This is very unlike you: in your good situation you're
      mocking my bad one.

PHIL   I am human, you are human; as truly as Jupiter will love
      me, I haven't come to laugh at you and I don't think that
      you deserve it. But as I said: my son has asked me to   450
      request your sister as his wife.

LES   It's right for me to understand the status that corre-
      sponds with my financial position. Our standing isn't
      equal to yours. Find another alliance for yourselves.

STA   (*quietly, to Lesbonicus*) Are you in your right mind, since   455
      you reject this match? I can see that a friend ready to
      assist[17] you has been found for you.

with the etymology in Paul. *Fest.* 75 L., while the ones in Varro and
Festus are slightly different (*ling.* 7.57: a soldier carrying weapons;
Fest. 506 L.: a servant bringing weapons and drink to soldiers). The
modern derivation from *ferire*, "to strike," is morphologically prob-
lematic.

LES   abin hinc dierecte?

STA   si hercle ire occipiam, uotes.

LES   nisi quid me aliud uis, Philto, respondi tibi.

PHIL   benigniorem, Lesbonice, te mihi

460   quam nunc experior esse confido fore;

            nam et stulte facere et stulte fabularier,

            utrumque, Lesbonice, in aetate hau bonum est.

STA   uerum hercle hic dicit.

LES   oculum ego effodiam tibi,

            si uerbum addideris.

STA   hercle qui dicam tamen;

465   nam si sic non licebit, luscus dixero.

PHIL   ita tu nunc dicis, non esse aequiperabilis

            uostras cum nostris factiones atque opes?

LES   dico.

PHIL   quid nunc? si in aedem ad cenam ueneris

            atque ibi opulentus tibi par forte obuenerit—

470   apposita cena sit popularem quam uocant—

            si illi congestae sint epulae a cluentibus:

            si quid tibi placeat quod illi congestum siet,

            edisne an incenatus cum opulento accubes?

LES   edim, nisi si ille uotet.

STA   at pol ego etsi uotet

475   edim atque ambabus malis expletis uorem,

            et quod illi placeat praeripiam potissumum

            neque illi concedam quicquam de uita mea.

            uerecundari neminem apud mensam decet,

            nam ibi de diuinis atque humanis cernitur.

---

[18] This reflects the Greek situation, where two people lie on a couch; in Rome it was three.

[19] A feast from the tithes sacrificed to Hercules.

[20] Jocular reference to a formula of the senate: *nulla uerecundia*

LES   Won't you go and hang yourself?

STA   If I did as much as begin to go, you'd forbid me.

LES   *(turning back to Philto)* Unless you want anything else from me, Philto, I've given you my reply.

PHIL   Lesbonicus, I trust that in the future you'll be more cor-   460
dial toward me than I'm finding you now; both talking stupidly and acting stupidly isn't good at any time of life, Lesbonicus.

STA   *(to Lesbonicus)* He's speaking the truth.

LES   I'll gouge your eye out if you add another word.

STA   I'll speak nonetheless; if I may not do so like this, I'll   465
speak one-eyed.

PHIL   Are you now saying that your connections and means are not comparable with ours?

LES   Yes.

PHIL   Well then? If you came into a temple for dinner and by chance a rich man turned up there as your dinner part-ner[18]—let what they call the "public dinner"[19] be served   470
—and if delicacies were brought to him by his clients: if you liked anything that's been brought to him, would you eat it or would you recline next to the rich man without dinner?

LES   I'd eat, unless he forbade it.

STA   But I would eat even if he did forbid it, I'd gulp it down   475
with both cheeks full, I'd snatch away especially what he likes, and I wouldn't make any concession to him from what means life to me. Nobody ought to be bashful at table: that's where one decides about divine and human affairs.[20]

---

nos debet demouere a sententia dicunda ubi de rebus diuinis et humanis agitur, "no bashfulness must prevent us from stating our opinion in a situation where one deals with divine and human affairs."

480	PHIL	rem fabulare.
	STA	non tibi dicam dolo:

decedam ego illi de uia, de semita,
de honore populi; uerum quod ad uentrem attinet,
non hercle hoc longe, nisi me pugnis uicerit.
cena hac annona est sine sacris hereditas.

485 PHIL semper tu hoc facito, Lesbonice, cogites,
id optumum esse tute uti sis optumus;
si id nequeas, saltem ut optumis sis proxumus.
nunc condicionem hanc, quam ego fero et quam aps te
    peto,
dare atque accipere, Lesbonice, te uolo.

490 di diuites sunt, deos decent opulentiae
et factiones, uerum nos homunculi,
satillum animai qui quom extemplo emisimus,
aequo mendicus atque ille opulentissumus
censetur censu ad Accheruntem mortuos.

495 STA mirum quin tu illo tecum diuitias feras.
ubi mortuos sis, ita sis ut nomen cluet.

    PHIL nunc ut scias hic factiones atque opes
non esse nec nos tuam neglegere gratiam,
sine dote posco tuam sororem filio,

500 quae res bene uortat—habeon pactam? quid taces?
    STA pro di immortales, condicionem quoius modi!
    PHIL quin fabulare, "di bene uortant, spondeo"?

492 satillum *A*, salillum *P*
502 di *P*, uin *A*   uortat Ω, uortant ς

---

[21] As a slave he is of course not eligible for public office.

PHIL You're talking to the point.   480

STA I'll tell you without guile: I'll step aside for him from the street, from the path, from public office;[21] but as far as my stomach is concerned, not this far (*indicates with his fingers*), unless he wins against me with his fists. With the present high prices a dinner is an inheritance without sacrifices.[22]

PHIL Lesbonicus, always make sure that you consider it to be   485
best to be the best yourself; if you can't be that, at least that you should be next to the best. Now, Lesbonicus, I want you to grant and accept this match which I'm bringing to you and seeking from you. Only the gods are rich,   490
and displays of power and connections are only appropriate for the gods; but we are mere men: as soon as we let go of the little seed of our soul, the beggar in his death is rated with an equal rating in the Underworld as the richest of men.

STA (*aside*) It's a wonder that you don't take your riches there   495
with you. When you're dead, you should be so in the full sense of the word.

PHIL (*to Lesbonicus*) Now so that you may know that connections and means don't count here and that it's your friendship that matters to us, I ask for your sister to marry my son without a dowry. May this turn out well—   500
have I got it settled? Why are you silent?

STA Immortal gods, what a match!

PHIL (*to Lesbonicus*) Why don't you say, "may the gods grant it success, I promise her to him"?

---

[22] People often got inheritances on condition that they would make regular sacrifices for the deceased. Such sacrifices were expensive and cumbersome.

169

STA eheu! ubi usus nil erat dicto, "spondeo"
dicebat; nunc hic, quom opus est, non quit dicere.

505 LES quom affinitate uostra me arbitramini
dignum, habeo uobis, Philto, magnam gratiam.
sed si haec res grauiter cecidit stultitia mea,
Philto, est ager sub urbe hic nobis: eum dabo
dotem sorori; nam is de diuitiis meis

510 solus superfit praeter uitam relicuos.

PHIL profecto dotem nil moror.

LES   certum est dare.

STA nostramne, ere, uis nutricem quae nos educat
abalienare a nobis? caue sis feceris.
quid edemus nosmet postea?

LES   etiam tu taces?

515 tibin ego rationem reddam?

STA   plane periimus
nisi quid ego comminiscor. Philto, te uolo.

PHIL si quid uis, Stasime.

STA   huc concede aliquantum.

PHIL   licet.

STA arcano tibi ego hoc dico, ne ille ex te sciat
neue alius quisquam.

PHIL   crede audacter quidlubet.

520 STA per deos atque homines dico, ne tu illunc agrum
tuom siris umquam fieri nec gnati tui.
ei rei argumenta dicam.

PHIL   audire edepol lubet.

STA primum omnium olim terra quom proscinditur,
in quinto quoque sulco moriuntur boues.

509 stultitia mea *P*, stultitiis meis *A*, diuitiis meis *Bergk*
515 tibin egon *A*, tibi ego *P*, tibin ego *Lindsay*

170

STA (*aside*) Dear me! When there was no need to speak, he
said "I promise"; now here, when there is a need, he can't
speak.

LES I'm very grateful to all of you, Philto, for considering me   505
worthy of a connection with you. But even if my situation
has turned out harshly through my own stupidity, Philto,
we still have a plot of land here below the city; this I'll
give to my sister as a dowry: this alone is the sole remain-
der of my wealth, apart from my life.   510

PHIL I honestly don't care about the dowry.

LES I'm resolved to give her one.

STA Master, do you want to take our nurse away from us, the
one who nurtures us? Please don't do that. What will we
ourselves eat afterward?

LES Be quiet, will you? Should I be accountable to you?   515

STA (*aside*) We're plainly dead unless I think up something.
(*aloud*) Philto, I want to speak to you.

PHIL If you want anything, Stasimus.

STA Walk over here a bit.

PHIL All right. (*they withdraw a little*)

STA I'm telling you this in secret; neither he nor anyone else
should know this from you.

PHIL Entrust me boldly with anything you wish.

STA I beg you by gods and men, don't ever let that land be-   520
come yours or your son's. I'll tell you the reasons for
this.

PHIL I'm keen to hear them.

STA First of all, at the time when the soil is plowed, the oxen
die in every fifth furrow.

525	PHIL	apage!
	STA	Accheruntis ostium in nostro est agro.
		tum uinum prius quam coctum est pendet putidum.
	LES	consuadet homini, credo. etsi scelestus est,
		at mi infidelis non est.
	STA	audi cetera.
		postid, frumenti quom alibi messis maxuma est,
530		tribus tantis illi minus re[d]dit quam opseueris.
	PHIL	em istic oportet opseri mores malos,
		si in opserendo possint interfieri.
	STA	neque umquam quisquam est quoius illic ager fuit
		quin pessume ei res uorterit: quorum fuit,
535		alii exsulatum abierunt, alii emortui,
		alii se suspendere. em nunc hic quoius est
		ut ad incitas redactust!
	PHIL	apage a me istum agrum!
	STA	magis "apage" dicas, si omnia ex me audiueris.
		nam fulguritae sunt alternae arbores;
540		sues moriuntur angina acerrume;
		oues scabrae sunt, tam glabrae, em, quam haec est manus.
		tum autem Syrorum, genus quod patientissumum est
		hominum, nemo exstat qui ibi sex menses uixerit:
		ita cuncti solstitiali morbo decidunt.
545	PHIL	credo ego istuc, Stasime, ita esse; sed Campans genus
		multo Syrorum iam antidit patientia.
		sed iste est ager profecto, ut te audiui loqui,

530 reddit Ω, redit *Lambinus*
533 ille ager fuit Ω, illic ager fuit *Leo*, ille fuit ager *Luchs*
534 quoium Ω, quorum *Brix*   538 a Ω, ex *Kampmann*
540 acerrume Ω, macerrumae *Onions*

PHIL Get away with you!   525

STA The gateway to the Underworld lies on our land. Next, before the grapes are ripe, they hang there rotten.

LES (*observing from a distance*) He's trying to persuade him, I believe. Even if he's a crook, he's not faithless toward me.

STA Listen to the rest. Later, when there's an enormous crop of wheat elsewhere, the return on our land there is three 530 times less than you've sown.

PHIL There! That's where one ought to sow moral laxity, if it could be destroyed during the sowing.

STA There's never been anyone who owned that land without things turning out very badly for him; of those who have owned it, some have gone into exile, some have died, 535 some have hanged themselves. Look how the present owner has been checkmated!

PHIL Away with that plot of land from me!

STA You'd say "away" even more if you heard everything from me: every other tree has been struck by lightning; the 540 pigs die of quinsy in the most frightful way; the sheep are as mangy and as hairless, look, as this hand is. And then there's none of the Syrians, the race which is the hardiest of all men, who has survived there for six months: that's how they all die from sunstroke.

PHIL I do believe that it's like that, Stasimus; but the Campanian[23] race now surpasses that of the Syrians in endur- 545 ance by far. But from what I've heard you say, that land

23 The Campanians, in southern Italy, were renowned for their luxurious lifestyle. During the Second Punic War, Capua, a major city in Campania, sided with Hannibal, and after Capua was conquered by Rome, its inhabitants were enslaved.

		malos in quem omnis publice mitti decet,
		sicut fortunatorum memorant insulas,
550		quo cuncti qui aetatem egerint caste suam
		conueniant; contra istoc detrudi maleficos
		aequom uidetur, qui quidem istius sit modi.
	STA	hospitium est calamitatis: quid uerbis opust?
		quamuis malam rem quaeras, illi reperias.
555	PHIL	at tu hercle et illi et alibi.
	STA	caue sis dixeris
		me tibi dixisse hoc.
	PHIL	dixisti arcano satis.
	STA	quin hicquidem cupit illum ab se abalienarier,
		si quem reperire possit quoi os sublinat.
	PHIL	meus quidem hercle numquam fiet.
	STA	si sapies quidem.
560		lepide hercle de agro ego hunc senem deterrui;
		nam qui uiuamus nihil est, si illum amiserit.
	PHIL	redeo ad te, Lesbonice.
	LES	dic sodes mihi,
		quid hic est locutus tecum?
	PHIL	quid censes? homo est:
		uolt fieri liber, uerum quod det non habet.
565	LES	et ego esse locuples, uerum nequiquam uolo.
	STA	licitum est, si uelles; nunc, quom nihil est, non licet.
	LES	quid tecum, Stasime?
	STA	de istoc quod dixti modo:
		si ante uoluisses, esses; nunc sero cupis.
	PHIL	de dote mecum conuenire nil potes‹t›:
570		quod tibi lubet tute agito cum nato meo.

569 potes‹t› *Acidalius*

is indeed such that all bad people ought to be sent onto
it by public decree, just as they speak of the Isles of the
Blessed, where all those come together who have lived   550
their lives morally; by contrast, it seems fair that wrong-
doers are thrust off onto that land, since it is like that.

STA   It's the home of disaster; what need is there for words?
      However bad the thing you're looking for, you can find
      it there.

PHIL (*half aside*) But *you* can find it there and elsewhere.   555

STA   Please make sure you don't say that I said this to you.

PHIL You've said it secretly enough.

STA   As a matter of fact, he wishes to get rid of it, if he can
      find someone to fool.

PHIL It'll never become mine.

STA   If you're smart. (*aside*) I've scared this old chap away   560
      from the plot of land delightfully; we have nothing to live
      on if he loses that. (*they go back to Lesbonicus*)

PHIL I'm returning to you, Lesbonicus.

LES   Please tell me, what did he speak to you about?

PHIL What do you expect? He's human; he wants to become
      free, but doesn't have anything to pay.

LES   And I want to be rich, but want it in vain.   565

STA   (*in a low voice*) It was possible, if you'd wanted it; now
      that you have nothing, it's impossible.

LES   What are you talking to yourself about, Stasimus?

STA   About what you've just said: if you'd wanted it before,
      you'd be rich; now you wish for it too late.

PHIL (*to Lesbonicus*) About the dowry you can't make any
      agreement with me: you yourself must discuss with my   570
      son what you want. Now I'm requesting your sister for

175

       nunc tuam sororem filio posco meo.

       quae res bene uortat! quid nunc? etiam consulis?

LES   quid istic? quando ita uis: di bene uortant! spondeo.

STA   numquam edepol quoiquam ⟨tam⟩ exspectatus filius

575   natus quam illuc est "spondeo" natum mihi.

       di fortunabunt uostra consilia.

PHIL   ita uolo.

LES   sed, Stasime, abi huc ad meam sororem ad Calliclem,

       dic hoc negoti quo modo actum est.

STA   ibitur.

LES   et gratulator meae sorori.

STA   scilicet.

580 PHIL   i hac, Lesbonice, mecum, ut coram nuptiis

       dies constituatur; eadem haec confirmabimus.

LES   tu istuc cura quod iussi. ego iam hic ero.

⟨STA   i modo.⟩

LES   dic Callicli, me ut conueniat.

STA   quin tu i modo.

LES   de dote ut uideat quid opus sit facto.

STA   i modo.

585 LES   nam certum est sine dote hau dare.

STA   quin tu i modo.

LES   neque enim illi damno umquam esse patiar—

STA   abi modo.

LES   —meam neglegentiam.

STA   i modo.

LES   ⟨nullo modo⟩

       aequom uidetur quin quod peccarim—

STA   i modo.

---

574 tam *add.* ς   582 STA i modo *add. Niemeyer*
587 nullo modo *add. Ritschl*

my son. May this turn out well! (*when there is no reaction*) What now? Are you still debating the matter?

LES Very well. Since you want it like this, may the gods bless it! I engage her.

STA Never has a son been born so eagerly awaited to anyone   575
as that "I engage her" was born to me. (*to both*) The gods will bless your plans.

PHIL That's what I wish.

LES But Stasimus, go over here to my sister to Callicles and say how things have been arranged.

STA Yes.

LES And congratulate my sister.

STA Of course.

PHIL Lesbonicus, come with me this way, so that we can settle   580
a date for the wedding in person; at the same time we'll ratify our agreement. (*moves to the left and waits*)

LES (*to Stasimus*) You take care of what I ordered you. I'll be back soon.

STA Just go.

LES Tell Callicles to meet me.

STA Just go.

LES He is to see what needs to be done about the dowry.

STA Just go.

LES Because I'm resolved not to give her in marriage without   585
a dowry.

STA Just go.

LES Yes, I won't ever let my carelessness—

STA (*interrupting*) Just go away!

LES —harm her.

STA Just go!

LES In no way does it seem right that my folly—

STA (*interrupting*) Just go!

LES —potissumum mi id opsit.

STA   i modo.

LES   o pater,

590   enumquam aspiciam te?

STA   i modo, i modo, i modo!
tandem impetraui abiret. di uostram fidem!
edepol re gesta pessume gestam probe,
si quidem ager nobis saluos est; etsi admodum
in ambiguo est etiam nunc quid ea re fuat.
595   sed id si alienatur, actum est de collo meo,
gestandust peregre clupeus, galea, sarcina:
effugiet ex urbe, ubi erunt factae nuptiae,
ibit istac, aliquo, in maxumam malam crucem,
latrocinatum, aut in Asiam aut in Ciliciam.
600   ibo huc quo mi imperatum est, etsi odi hanc domum,
postquam exturbauit hic nos [ex] nostris aedibus.

ACTVS III

III. i: CALLICLES. STASIMVS

CAL quo modo tu istuc, Stasime, dixti?

STA   nostrum erilem filium
Lesbonicum suam sororem despondisse. em hoc modo.

CAL quoi homini despondit?

601 ex *del. Guyet*

LES —should stand in anybody's way but mine.

STA Just go!

LES O father, will I ever see you again?   590

STA Just go, just go, just go!

Exeunt PHILTO and LESBONICUS to the left.

STA At last I succeeded in having him go away. Gods, your
     protection! Goodness, in the midst of disaster one suc-
     cess, if the plot of land is safe for us! Even if it's still
     highly doubtful what will happen with it. But if it's taken   595
     away, it's the end for my neck; I'll need to carry shield,
     helmet, and baggage abroad: he'll run away from the city
     when the wedding is over, he'll go that way (*points to the
     left*), to some place, either to Asia or to Cilicia,[24] to his
     own greatest ruin, in order to serve as a mercenary. I'll   600
     go here, where I've been told to, even if I've hated this
     house ever since this man threw us out of our house.

Exit STASIMUS into the house of Charmides.

ACT THREE

*Enter CALLICLES and STASIMUS from the house of Char-
mides.*

CAL How did you mean that, Stasimus?

STA That our master's son Lesbonicus has engaged his sister.
     There, like that.

CAL Who did he engage her to?

24 Cilicia is not a separate region from Asia (Minor), but its south-
eastern part; they became different provinces later.

STA   Lysiteli Philtonis filio,

605   sine dote.

CAL   sine dote ille illam in tantas diuitias dabit?
non credibile dicis.

STA   at tu edepol nullus creduas.
si hoc non credis, ego credidero—

CAL   quid?

STA   me nihili pendere.

CAL quam dudum istuc aut ubi actum est?

STA   ilico hic ante ostium,
"tam modo," inquit Praenestinus.

CAL   tanton in re perdita

610   quam in re salua Lesbonicus factus est frugalior?

STA atque equidem ipsus ultro uenit Philto oratum filio.

CAL flagitium quidem hercle fiet, nisi dos dabitur uirgini.
postremo edepol ego istam rem ad me attinere intel-
     lego.
ibo ad meum castigatorem atque ab eo consilium pe-
     tam.

615 STA propemodum quid illic festinet sentio et subolet mihi:
ut agro euortat Lesbonicum, quando euortit aedibus.
o ere Charmides, quom apsenti hic tua res distrahitur
     tibi,
utinam te rediisse saluom uideam, ut inimicos tuos
ulciscare et mihi, ut erga te fui et sum, referas gratiam!

620   nimium difficile est reperiri amicum ita ut nomen
     cluet,

606 dices *P*, dicis ς
619 ut mihi *P*, et mihi *Ritschl*

STA	To Lysiteles, the son of Philto, without a dowry.	605
CAL	Will he give her into such great wealth without a dowry? You can't make me believe that.	
STA	Then don't believe it. If you don't believe this, I'll believe—	
CAL	(*interrupting*) What?	
STA	That I don't care.	
CAL	How long ago and where did that happen?	
STA	In this very place, here in front of the door, "very now," says the man from Praeneste.[25]	
CAL	Has Lesbonicus become more frugal after the loss of such great wealth than when it was safe?	610
STA	What's more, Philto himself took the initiative to come and ask for his son.	
CAL	(*aside*) It'll be a disgrace if the girl isn't given a dowry. In short, I realize that this business concerns me. I'll go to the chap who reproved me and seek advice from him.	

Exit CALLICLES *to the right.*

STA	I have a pretty good idea and an inkling of why he's in a rush: in order to turn him out of his land after he's turned him out of his house. O master Charmides, now that your wealth is being torn apart in your absence, I wish I could see you back here safe and sound so as to take revenge on your enemies and to thank me as I have deserved and deserve still at your hands! A friend worthy of the name	615 620

25 In Praeneste (modern Palestrina), a different dialect of Latin was spoken. To a native of Rome the phrase *tam modo*, "very now" (= "just now") must have sounded wrong.

quoi tuam quom rem credideris, sine omni cura dor-
    mias.

sed generum nostrum ire eccillum uideo cum affini
    suo.

nescioquid non satis inter eos conuenit: celeri gradu
eunt uterque, ille reprehendit hunc priorem pallio.

625   haud ineuscheme astiterunt. huc aliquantum apsces-
    sero:

est lubido orationem audire duorum affinium.

III. ii: LYSITELES. LESBONICVS. STASIMVS

LYS   sta ilico, noli auorsari nec te occultassis mihi.

LES   potin ut me ire quo profectus sum sinas?

LYS   si in rem tuam,
Lesbonice, esse uideatur, gloriae aut famae, sinam.

630 LES quod est facillumum, facis.

LYS   quid id est?

LES   amico iniuriam.

LYS   nec meum est nec facere didici.

LES   indoctus quam docte facis!
quid faceres, si quis docuisset te, ut sic odio esses
    mihi?

[qui] bene quom simulas facere mihi te, male facis,
    male consulis.

LYS   egone?

LES   tune.

LYS   quid male facio?

LES   quod ego nolo, id quom facis.

635 LYS tuae rei bene consulere cupio.

633 qui *del. Hermann*
635 tu [mihi] es melior *Bergk*, tu melius *Renkema*

is terribly difficult to find, someone who lets you sleep without any worry when you entrust your possessions to him. (*after a pause*) But look, I can see our son-in-law walking with his relation. They're at odds over something; they're both walking at a fast pace, and that one is grabbing the one in front by his cloak. Now they've   625
stopped there quite gracefully. I'll walk a little over here: I'm keen to hear the conversation of the two relations. (*walks to a spot where he cannot be seen*)

Enter LESBONICUS *from the left, followed by* LYSITELES.

LYS Stand where you are, don't turn away or hide from me.
LES Can't you let me go where I'm bound?
LYS I would, Lesbonicus, if it seemed to be to your benefit, for your honor or reputation.
LES You're doing what's easiest.   630
LYS What's that?
LES An injustice to a friend.
LYS It's not my habit and I haven't learned to do so.
LES In what a well-taught way you do it without having been taught! What would you be doing if anyone had taught you to be so hateful to me? While pretending to do me a good turn, you do me a bad one and treat me badly.
LYS I?
LES Yes, you.
LYS In what respect am I doing you a bad turn?
LES In doing what I don't want.
LYS I wish to act in your best interest.   635

LES   tu [mihi] es melior quam egomet mihi?
        sat sapio, satis in rem quae sint meam ego conspicio
            mihi.

LYS   an id est sapere, ut qui beneficium a beneuolente repu-
            dies?

LES   nullum beneficium esse duco id quod quoi facias non
            placet.
        scio ego et sentio ipse quid agam, nec mens officio mi-
            grat

640   nec tuis depellar dictis quin rumori seruiam.

LYS   quid ais? nam retineri nequeo quin dicam ea quae pro-
            meres:
        itan tandem hanc maiores famam tradiderunt tibi tui,
        ut uirtute eorum anteparta per flagitium perderes
        atque honori posterorum tuorum ut uindex fieres?

645   tibi paterque auosque facilem fecit et planam uiam
        ad quaerundum honorem: tu fecisti ut difficilis foret
        culpa maxume et desidia tuisque stultis moribus.
        praeoptauisti amorem tuom uti uirtuti praeponeres.
        nunc te hoc facto credis posse optegere errata? aha!
            non ita est.

650   cape sis uirtutem animo et corde expelle desidiam tuo:
        in foro operam amicis da, ne in lecto amicae, ut solitus
            es.
        atque istum ego agrum tibi relinqui ob eam rem enixe
            expeto,
        ut tibi sit qui te corrigere possis, ne omnino inopiam
        ciues obiectare possint tibi quos tu inimicos habes.

655 LES   omnia ego istaec quae tu dixti scio, uel exsignauero,
        ut rem patriam et gloriam maiorum foedarim meum:

      652 istum ego *A*, ego istum *P*

184

LES   Are you better to me than I am myself? I'm intelligent
enough, I can see well enough for myself what's in my
best interest.

LYS   Is this being intelligent, to reject a good turn from some-
one wishing you well?

LES   I don't consider a good turn something that the person
for whom you do it doesn't like. I know and understand
myself what I'm doing, my mind doesn't evade its duty,
and I won't be deterred by your words from having re-   640
gard for public opinion.

LYS   What do you say? I can't be kept from saying what you
deserve: was it for this that your ancestors left you this
reputation, for you to ruin through your disgraceful be-
havior what they had acquired through their virtue, and
then suddenly to become a champion for the distinction
of your successors? Both your father and your grand-   645
father gave you an easy and plain way for finding dis-
tinction. You are the one who made it difficult, mostly
through your fault, laziness, and stupid habits. You opted
to prefer your love to your virtue. Do you believe you
can now cover up your mistakes through this deed? Ha!
It doesn't work like that. Do get hold of virtue and drive   650
your laziness from your heart. Apply yourself to your
male friends in the forum, not to your girlfriend in bed,
which is what you do at the moment. And I earnestly
desire that that land should remain with you, for the
simple reason that you should have the means to mend
your ways, so that the citizens you have as your enemies
can't cast your abject poverty in your teeth.

LES   I know all those things you've said, and I'd even put my   655
seal on your words when you say that I've squandered
my father's wealth and the reputation of my ancestors. I

scibam ut esse me deceret, facere non quibam miser;
ita ui Veneris uinctus, otio [c]aptus in fraudem incidi.
et tibi nunc, proinde ut merere, summas habeo gratias.

660   LYS   at operam perire meam sic et te haec [dicta] corde
         spernere
perpeti nequeo, simul me piget parum pudere te;
et postremo, nisi mi auscultas atque hoc ut dico facis,
tute pone te latebis facile, ne inueniat te Honor,
in occulto iacebis quom te maxume clarum uoles.

665   pernoui equidem, Lesbonice, ingenium tuom inge-
         nuom admodum;
scio te sponte non tuapte errasse, sed Amorem tibi
pectus opscurasse; atque ipse Amoris teneo omnis uias.
ita est Amor ballista ut iacitur: nil sic celere est nec uo-
         lat;
atque is mores hominum moros et morosos efficit:

670   minus placet magis quod suadetur, quod dissuadetur
         placet;
quom inopia est, cupias, quando eius copia est, tum
         non uelis;
ill' qui aspellit is compellit, ill' qui consuadet uotat.
insanum [et] malum est in hospitium deuorti ad Cupi-
         dinem.
sed te moneo hoc etiam atque etiam ut reputes quid
         facere expetas.

675   si istuc, ut conare, facis incendium, tuom incendes ge-
         nus;
tum igitur tibi aquai erit cupido genus qui restinguas
         tuom,
atque si eris nactus, proinde ut corde amantes sunt
         cati,

knew how I ought to be, but I couldn't do it, poor me;
that's how I fell into ruin, bound by the power of Venus
and idle by nature. And I'm very grateful to you now, the
way you deserve.

LYS But I can't bear it that my effort should come to nothing   660
in this way and that you should despise this in your heart;
at the same time I'm unhappy that you aren't ashamed
enough; and finally, if you don't listen to me and do this
the way I'm telling you, you'll easily stand in your own
light so that Esteem can't find you, and you'll lie in a
hidden place when what you want most is to be well
known. I know your noble character perfectly, Lesboni-   665
cus. I know that you didn't go wrong on purpose, but that
Love beclouded your breast; and I myself know all of
Love's ways. Love is like a hurled missile: nothing is as
quick, and nothing flies like it; and he makes people's
characters stupid and difficult. You like less what you're   670
more advised to do, you like what you're advised against;
you're keen when there's no possibility, you don't want
to when you have the possibility; the man who drives you
off forces you into it, the man who recommends it for-
bids it. It's a dreadful misfortune to put up at Cupid's
lodgings. But I urge you again and again to consider what
you're bent on doing. If you make that destructive fire,   675
as you're trying to, you'll set your family on fire; then
you'll have a desire for water in order to quench your
family again, and if you get hold of it, clever as lovers are

---

658 aptus *A*, captus *P*   660 dicta *A*, haec dicta *P*, haec
Bothe   673 insanum et malum (e)st *B*, insanumst et malum *CD*,
insanum malumst *Brix*   675 incidium (*i.e.* incendium) *T*, indi-
cium *BCD*, indigne *Niemeyer*   tuom *del. Trappes-Lomax*

ne scintillam quidem relinques genus qui congliscat
tuom.

LES facile est inuentu: datur ignis, tam etsi ab inimico pe-
tas.

680 sed tu obiurgans me a peccatis rapis deteriorem in
uiam.

meam ut sororem tibi dem suades sine dote. aha! non
conuenit

me, qui abusus sum tantam rem patriam, porro in ditiis
esse agrumque habere, egere illam autem, ut me me-
rito oderit.

numquam erit alienis grauis qui suis se concinnat
leuem.

685 sicut dixi faciam: nolo te iactari diutius.

LYS tanto meliust te sororis causa egestatem exsequi
atque eum agrum me habere quam te, tua qui toleres
moenia?

LES nolo ego mi te tam prospicere qui meam egestatem
leues,

sed ut inops infamis ne sim, ne mi hanc famam diffe-
rant,

690 me germanam meam sororem in concubinatum tibi,
si sine dote ⟨dem⟩, dedisse magis quam in matrimo-
nium.

quis me inprobior perhibeatur esse? haec famigeratio
te honestet, me collutulentet, si sine dote duxeris:
tibi sit emolumentum honoris, mihi quod obiectent
siet.

691 dem *add. Klotz*

in their hearts, you won't even leave a spark with which
your family could be rekindled.

LES   It's easy to find: you get fire even if you ask for it from
your enemy. But while you're chiding me, you're hurry-   680
ing me from my errors onto an even worse road. You
advise me to give you my sister without a dowry. Ah! It
isn't appropriate that I, who have squandered my father's
enormous wealth, should continue to live in riches and
have a plot of land, and that she, by contrast, should be
poor, so that she'd hate me deservedly. Someone who
forfeits respect among his own family will never possess
influence among strangers. I'll do as I told you; I don't   685
want you to trouble yourself any longer.

LYS   Is it so much better that you should live in poverty for
the sake of your sister and that I should have this land
rather than you, the land with which you could support
your responsibilities?

LES   I don't want you to look out so much for something with
which to alleviate my poverty, as rather to make sure that
I won't have a bad reputation in my poverty, so that
people won't spread the rumor against me that I've given   690
my own sister to you into concubinage rather than mar-
riage, if I were to give her to you without dowry. Who
would be considered to be more worthless than me? This
rumor would bring honor to you and disgrace to me, if
you were to marry her without dowry. You would have
an advantageous position of honor, I would have some-
thing they could cast in my teeth.

695	LYS	quid? te dictatorem censes fore, si aps te agrum acce- perim?
	LES	nec uolo nec postulo nec censeo, uerum tamen is est honos homini pudico, meminisse officium suom.
	LYS	scio equidem te animatus ut sis; uideo, subolet, sentio: id agis ut, ubi affinitatem inter nos nostram astrinxeris
700		atque eum agrum dederis nec quicquam hic tibi sit qui uitam colas,
		effugias ex urbe inanis; profugus patriam deseres, cognatos, affinitatem, amicos factis nuptiis:
		mea opera hinc proterritum te meaque auaritia autu- ment.
		id me commissurum ut patiar fieri ne animum induxe- ris.
705	STA	non enim possum quin exclamem: eugae, eugae, Lysi- teles, πάλιν!
		facile palmam habes: hic uictus⟨t⟩, uicit tua comoedia. hic agit magis ex argumento et uorsus meliores facit. etiam ob stultitiam tuam te auri multabo mina.
	LES	quid tibi interpellatio aut in consilium huc accessio est?
710	STA	eodem pacto quo huc accessi apscessero.
	LES	i hac mecum domum, Lysiteles, ibi de istis rebus plura fabulabimur.
	LYS	nil ego in occulto agere soleo. meus ut animust elo- quar:

701 profugiens *P*, profugus *Camerarius*
706 uictus⟨t⟩ *Ritschl*
708 curis *B*, turis *CD*, auri *Niemeyer*

LYS   What? Do you believe you'll be a dictator,[26] if I take the   695
land from you?

LES   I don't want to, I don't expect it, and I don't think so, but
still it is an honor for a decent man to remember his
duty.

LYS   I for one know what you're up to; I see it, I have an in-
kling, and I feel it: it's your intention that once you've
tied our bond between us, have given me this land, and   700
don't have anything here to live on, you should flee from
the city empty-handed. Once the wedding is over, you
will, as a runaway, desert your country, relatives, connec-
tions, and friends. People would say that you were driven
away by my doing and by my greed. Don't think for a
moment that I'd allow this to happen.

STA   (*approaching*) I really can't help shouting it out: bravo,   705
bravo, Lysiteles, encore! You easily have the palm:
(*pointing to Lesbonicus*) this chap is beaten, your com-
edy beat him. (*pointing to Lysiteles*) This chap here acts
more in accord with the plot and makes better lines.
Also, because of your stupidity I'll fine you one gold
mina.

LES   What do you mean by interrupting or walking here into
our assembly?

STA   I'll walk away in the same way in which I walked in.   710
(*moves away a little*)

LES   Come home with me this way, Lysiteles, there we'll talk
more about these matters.

LYS   I'm not used to doing anything in secret. I'll tell you what

---

[26] A Roman official appointed during political crises. Lysiteles takes
honos, "position of honor," in a more concrete sense than Lesbonicus
had intended.

   si mi tua soror, ut ego aequom censeo, ita nuptum
    datur,
   sine dote, neque tu hinc abituru's, quod meum erit id
    erit tuom;
715   sin aliter animatus es—bene quod agas eueniat tibi,
   ego amicus numquam tibi ero alio pacto. sic sententia
    est.
STA abiit [hercle] illequidem. ecquid audis, Lysiteles? ego
   te uolo.
   hic quoque hinc abiit. Stasime, restas solus. quid ego
    nunc agam,
   nisi uti sarcinam constringam et clupeum ad dorsum
    accommodem,
720   fulmentas iubeam suppingi soccis? non sisti potest.
   uideo caculam militarem me futurum hau longius:
   at aliquem ad regem in saginam erus sese coniciet
    meus,
   credo ad summos bellatores acrem . . . fugitorem fore
   et capturum spolia ibi illum qui . . . [meo] ero aduorsus
    uenerit.
725   egomet autem quom extemplo arcum [mihi] et phare-
    tram et sagittas sumpsero,
   cassidem in caput . . . dormibo placidule in taberna-
    culo.
   ad forum ibo: nudius sextus quoi talentum mutuom
   dedi, reposcam, ut habeam mecum quod feram uiati-
    cum.

716 si *P*, sic ς   717 hercle *del. Fleckeisen*
720 socios *B*, sotios *CD*, fico *uel* foco *Nonius*, soccis *Camerarius*
722 at *B*, aut *CD* coniecit *P*, coniciet *Leo*
724 meo *del. Bothe*   725 mihi *del. Müller*
726 placide *P*, placidule *Koch*

my intention is: if I'm given your sister in marriage in the way I consider fair, without a dowry, and if you aren't going to leave, what's mine will be yours; if you're differ- 715
ently inclined—may you have success in what you do, but I'll never be your friend in another way. That's my position.

Exit LYSITELES to the left.

STA He's gone. (*calling after him*) Can you hear me, Lysite-les? I want to speak to you!

Exit LESBONICUS into the annex.

STA He's gone, too. Stasimus, you are left alone. What should I do now, except for tying up a backpack, attaching a shield to my back, and having my footwear height- 720
ened?[27] It can't be stopped. I can see that I'll be a sol-dier's servant very soon; but my master will throw him-self at some king for fattening up, and I believe that in comparison with the greatest fighters he'll be a val-iant . . . flighter, and that the spoils will be taken there by the man who . . . meets my master. But as soon as I 725
have taken bow, quiver, arrows, and a helmet for my head . . . I'll sleep calmly in the tent. I'll go to the forum; I'll demand a talent[28] back from the chap to whom I loaned it five days ago, so as to have travel provisions to carry with me.

Exit STASIMUS to the right.

[27] Flat shoes are for comedy, shoes with built-up soles for tragedy; the situation is turning hopeless.

[28] An unrealistically large sum for a slave.

III. iii: MEGARONIDES. CALLICLES

MEG   ut mihi rem narras, Callicles, nullo modo
730   potest fieri prorsus quin dos detur uirgini.
CAL   namque hercle honeste fieri ferme non potest,
      ut eam perpetiar ire in matrimonium
      sine dote, quom eius rem penes me habeam domi.
MEG   parata dos domi est; nisi exspectare uis,
735   ut eam sine dote frater nuptum collocet.
      post adeas tute Philtonem et dotem dare
      te ei dicas, facere id eius ob amicitiam patris.
      uerum hoc ego uereor ne istaec pollicitatio
      te in crimen populo ponat atque infamiam;
740   non temere dicant te benignum uirgini:
      datam tibi dotem, ei quam dares, eius a patre,
      ex ea largiri te illi, neque ita ut sit data
      columem te sistere illi, et detraxe autument.
      nunc si opperiri uis aduentum Charmidi,
745   perlongum est: huic ducendi interea apscesserit
      lubido; atque ea condicio huic uel primaria est.
CAL   nam hercle omnia istaec ueniunt in mentem mihi.
      uide si hoc utibile magis atque in rem deputas,
      ut ipsum adeam Lesbonicum, edoceam ut res se habet.
750   sed ut ego nunc adulescenti thesaurum indicem
      indomito, pleno amoris ac lasciuiae?
      minime, minime hercle uero. nam certo scio,
      locum quoque illum omnem ubi situst comederit;
      quem fodere metuo, sonitum ne ille exaudiat
755   neu rem ipsam indaget, dotem dare si dixerim.
MEG   quo pacto ergo igitur clam dos depromi potest?

749 ut *P*, ipsum *A*, ut ipsum *Brix*

Enter MEGARONIDES and CALLICLES from the right.

MEG The way you tell me the story, Callicles, it's absolutely necessary that a dowry be given to the girl.   730

CAL Yes, it really cannot happen in any decent way that I should allow her to get married without dowry, when I have her father's money with me at home.

MEG The dowry is ready at home; unless you want to wait for   735 her brother to give her in marriage without dowry. You might go to Philto later and say that you'd give her a dowry and that you'd do this out of friendship with her father. But I'm afraid that that promise would expose you to accusation and ill repute with the people. They'd say   740 that it's not without good reason that you're generous toward the girl; that you were given a dowry by her father to pass on to her, that you were giving her only a part of it, and that you weren't handing it over to her intact, as it was given to you; and they'd say that you'd taken something away. Now if you want to wait for the arrival of Charmides, it'll be a very long time; in the meantime this   745 chap will lose interest in marrying her, and this match is absolutely first-rate for her.

CAL Yes, all your points come to my mind as well. See if you find it more useful and to the point that I should approach Lesbonicus himself and inform him what the situation is like. But should I now point out the treasure   750 to an untameable young man full of love and licentiousness? No, absolutely not: I know for sure, he'll even eat up that entire place where it's buried. I'm afraid to dig it up, in case he might hear the sound and ferret the matter   755 out, if I should say I'm providing a dowry.

MEG Then how can the dowry be taken out in secret?

CAL   dum occasio ei ‹rei› reperiatur, interim
       ab amico alicunde mutuom argentum rogem.
MEG   potin est ab amico alicunde exorari?
CAL   potest.
760   MEG   gerrae! ne tu illud uerbum actutum inueneris:
       "mihi quidem hercle non est quod dem mutuom."
CAL   malim hercle ut uerum dicas quam ut des mutuom.
MEG   sed uide consilium, si placet.
CAL   quid consili est?
MEG   scitum, ut ego opinor, consilium inueni.
CAL   quid est?
765   MEG   homo conducatur aliquis iam, quantum potest,
       quasi sit peregrinus.
CAL   quid is scit facere postea?
MEG   is homo exornetur graphice in peregrinum modum,
       ignota facies quae ‹hic› non uisitata sit;
       mendaciloquom aliquem—
CAL   quid is scit facere postea?
770   MEG   —falsidicum, confidentem—
CAL   quid tum postea?
MEG   —quasi ad adulescentem a patre ex Seleucia
       ueniat, salutem ei nuntiet uerbis patris:
       illum bene gerere rem et ualere et uiuere,
       et eum rediturum actutum; ferat epistulas
775   duas; eas nos consignemus, quasi sint a patre:
       det alteram illi, alteram dicat tibi
       dare sese uelle.
CAL   perge porro dicere.

757 rei *add. Camerarius*   758 roges Ω, rogem ς
768 hic *add. Ritschl*   769 *uersus fertur solum in* A   quid is
scit facere postea A, oportet hominem deligi *Leo*

CAL   Until an opportunity is found for this business, I could ask some friend for the money on loan.

MEG   Is it possible that some friend could be prevailed upon?

CAL   Yes.

MEG   Nonsense! Seriously, you'll instantly come across that   760
      saying: "I for one don't have anything that I could give on loan."

CAL   (*replying to the imaginary friend*) "I'd prefer you to speak the truth than to give money on loan."

MEG   But see if you like my plan.

CAL   What plan is that?

MEG   I've found a clever plan, I think.

CAL   What is it?

MEG   Let some fellow be hired as quickly as possible now,   765
      pretending to be a foreigner.

CAL   What does he know how to do next?

MEG   He should be dressed up realistically in foreign fashion, an unknown appearance that isn't normally seen here—

CAL   (*interrupting*) What does he know how to do next?

MEG   —who tells lies and speaks falsehoods, someone self-   770
      confident—

CAL   (*interrupting*) What next?

MEG   —professing to come to the young man from his father from Seleucia and to greet him in his father's name. He should say that his father is successful, well, and alive, and that he'll return soon. He should carry two letters;   775
      we should seal them as if they came from his father. He should give one to him and say that he wants to give the other to you.

CAL   Go on speaking.

197

	MEG	seque aurum ferre uirgini dotem a patre
		dicat patremque id iussisse aurum tibi dare.
780		tenes iam?
	CAL	propemodum atque ausculto perlubens.
	MEG	tum tu igitur demum adulescenti aurum dabis,
		ubi erit locata uirgo in matrimonium.
	CAL	scite hercle sane!
	MEG	hoc, ubi thesaurum effoderis,
		suspicionem ab adulescente amoueris:
785		censebit aurum esse a patre allatum tibi,
		tu de thesauro sumes.
	CAL	satis scite et probe!
		quamquam hoc me aetatis sycophantari pudet.
788		sed epistulas quando opsignatas afferet,
[788ª]		sed quom opsignatas attulerit epistulas]
		nonne arbitraris eum adulescentem anuli
790		paterni signum nosse?
	MEG	etiam tu taces?
		sescentae ad eam rem causae possunt colligi:
		illum quem ⟨ante⟩ habuit perdidit, [alium post] fecit
		nouom.
		iam si opsignatas non feret, dici hoc potest,
		apud portitores eas resignatas sibi
795		inspectasque esse. in huius modi negotio
		diem sermone terere segnities mera est:
		quamuis sermones possunt longi texier.
		abi ad thesaurum iam confestim clanculum,
		seruos, ancillas amoue. atque audin?
	CAL	quid est?

780 prope modo *BCD*, propemodum ς
788ª *uersum secl. Ritschl*

MEG   And he should say that he was bringing gold to the girl as
        a dowry from her father and that her father had told him
        to give this gold to you. Do you catch the idea now?   780

CAL   Almost, and I listen to you with great pleasure.

MEG   Then at last you'll give the gold to the young man, when
        the girl has been given in marriage.

CAL   Terrifically clever!

MEG   This way you'll remove all suspicions from the young
        man's mind when you've dug up the treasure; he'll think   785
        the gold was brought to you from his father, but you will
        take it from the treasure.

CAL   Quite clever and proper! Although I'm ashamed to deal
        in deceit at my time of life. But when he brings those
        letters all sealed, [but when he brings those letters all
        sealed,] don't you think that this young fellow knows the   790
        seal of his father's ring?

MEG   Won't you be quiet? Six hundred excuses can be pro-
        duced for this matter: he lost the one he had before and
        made a new one; furthermore, if he doesn't bring them
        sealed, it can be said that they were unsealed at the
        custom officers' and inspected. In business of this kind   795
        it's sheer waste of time to use up the day with chattering.
        Chattering of any length can be produced. Off with you
        to the treasure now in a hurry and in secret; send away
        your male and female slaves. (*as Callicles turns to go*)
        And can you hear me?

CAL   What is it?

---

792 ante *add. Ritschl*   alium post *del. Ritschl*
794 portitorem *P*, portitores *Valla*

800	MEG	uxorem quoque eampse hanc rem uti celes face.
		nam pol tacere numquam quicquam est quod queat.
		quid nunc stas? quin tu hinc amoues et te moues?
		aperi, deprome inde auri ad hanc rem quod sat est,
		continuo operito denuo; sed clanculum,
805		sicut praecepi; cunctos exturba aedibus.
	CAL	ita faciam.
	MEG	at enim nimis longo sermone utimur,
		diem conficimus quom iam properato est opus.
		nihil est de signo quod uereare; me uide:
		lepida illa est causa, ut commemoraui, dicere
810		apud portitores esse inspectas. denique
		diei tempus non uides? quid illum putas,
		natura illa atque ingenio? iam dudum ebriust.
		quiduis probare poterit; tum, quod maxumum est,
		afferre, non petere hic se dicet.
	CAL	iam sat est.
815	MEG	ego sycophantam iam conduco de foro
		epistulasque iam consignabo duas,
		eumque huc ⟨ad⟩ adulescentem meditatum probe
		mittam.
	CAL	eo ego igitur intro ad officium meum.
		tu istuc age.
	MEG	actum reddam nugacissume.

800 ipsam *P*, eampse *Ritschl*   ut *P*, uti *Bothe*
807 quod *P*, quom *Fleckeisen*
809 lepidast illa (ille *B*) *P*, lepida illast *Reiz*
813 maxumi *P*, maxumum *Brix*
817 ad *add. Camerarius*

MEG Make sure that you conceal this business also from your   800
wife herself: there's never anything she can keep silent
about. Why are you standing around now? Why don't you
remove yourself from here and get a move on? Open it,
take out a sufficient amount of gold for this business
from there, and close it again at once; but in secret, as   805
I've instructed you; throw everybody out of the house.

CAL Yes, I'll do so.

MEG But really, we're talking for far too long, we're wasting
the day when haste is needed now. There's no reason for
you to worry about the seal; trust me: as I told you, it's a
delightful excuse to say that the letters were inspected   810
at the custom officers'. Finally, can't you see the time of
day? What state do you think he's in, with that nature and
character? He's been drunk for a while now. Our man
will be able to make him believe anything. Then, some-
thing of the greatest importance, he'll say that he's bring-
ing money, not demanding any.

CAL That'll do now.

MEG I'll hire an impostor from the forum at once, I'll put a   815
seal on two letters at once, and I'll send him here to the
young chap well primed.

CAL I'll go inside to my duty then. You, carry this out.

MEG I'll make sure that the trick is carried out to perfection.

Exeunt CALLICLES *and* MEGARONIDES, *the former into the
house of Charmides, the latter to the right.*

ACTVS IV

IV. i: CHARMIDES

820 CHAR salsipotenti et multipotenti Iouis fratri et Nerei Nep-
tuno

laetus lubens laudis ago et gratis gratiasque habeo et
fluctibus salsis,

quos penes mei ‹fuit saepe› potestas, bonis meis quid
foret et meae uitae,

quom suis med ex locis in patriam urbem usqu' colu-
mem reducem faciunt.

atque ego, Neptune, tibi ante alios deos gratias ago at-
que habeo summas;

825 nam te omnes saeuomque seuerumque atque auidis
moribus commemorant,

spurcificum, immanem, intolerandum, uesanum: ‹ego›
contra opera expertus,

nam pol placido te et clementi meo usque modo, ut
uolui, usus sum in alto.

atque hanc tuam gloriam iam ante auribus acceperam
et nobilest apud homines,

pauperibus te parcere solitum, dites damnare atque
domare.

830– abi, laudo, scis ordine ut aequom est tractare homines;
31 hoc dis dignum est. [semper mendicis modesti sint.]

832 fidus fuisti: infidum esse iterant; nam apsque foret te,
sat scio in alto

distraxissent disque tulissent satellites tui me miserum
foede

820 neptuni *P*, Neptuno *Scaliger*   822 quom *B*, qm *CD*, quos
Camerarius   fuit saepe *add. Hermann*

ACT FOUR

Enter CHARMIDES from the left.

CHAR To Neptune, the brother of Jupiter and Nereus,[29] ruling   820
over the salty sea with might, I joyfully and happily offer
praise and thanksgiving, and to the salty waves, which
frequently had power over me, as to what would happen
to my goods and my life; I thank them for safely bringing
me back from their territory to my country and my city.
And yet, Neptune, I give and feel greatest thanks to you
above the other gods: all people call you wild and harsh   825
and having a greedy character, vile, monstrous, unbear-
able, mad; by actual experience I've found the opposite:
I've found you calm and mild to my liking throughout
while at sea, just as I wanted it. I'd heard of this reputa-
tion of yours already before, and it's well known among
men, that you usually spare the poor and punish and
tame the rich. Enough, I praise you, you know how to   830
treat people according to their station, as is fair; this is
worthy of the gods. [Let them always be restrained to-
ward the destitute.] You were faithful; people say you're
faithless. Had it not been for you, I know well enough
that your attendants would have torn me apart and

[29] Neptune, god of the sea, was indeed considered Jupiter's brother,
but Nereus, a sea Titan, was not; the transmitted text is dubious.

823 urbis cummam *B*, urbis cumam *CD*, urbem usque columem
Brix   826 ego *add. Hermann*
828 nobilis *B*, nobiles *CD*, nobilest *Leo*
830–31 semper mendicis modesti sint *del. Müller*

bonaque omnia ⟨mea⟩ item una mecum passim caeru-
    leos per campos:
835   ita iam quasi canes, hau secus, circum stabant nauem
    turbines uenti,
imbres fluctusque atque procellae ⟨ferri⟩ infensae
    frangere malum,
ruere antemnas, scindere uela, ni tua pax propitia foret
    praesto.
apage a me sis, dehinc iam certum est otio dare me;
    satis partum habeo
quibus aerumnis deluctaui, filio dum diuitias quaero.
840   sed quis hic est qui in plateam ingreditur
cum nouo ornatu specieque simul?
842   pol quamquam domi cupio, opperiar,
842ᵃ   quam hic rem agat [gerit] animum aduortam.

IV. ii: SYCOPHANTA. CHARMIDES

SYC   huic ego die nomen Trinummo facio; nam ego operam
    meam
tribus nummis hodie locaui ad artis nugatorias.
845   aduenio ex Seleucia, Macedonia, Asia, atque Arabia,
quas ego neque oculis nec pedibus umquam usurpaui
    meis.
uiden egestas quid negoti dat homini misero mali,
quin ego nunc subigor trium nummum causa ut hasce
    epistulas

834 mea *add. Leo*
836 ferri *add. Spengel*
842 domi *A*, domum *P*
842ᵃ gerit *del. Ritschl*

dragged me apart in the sea in a frightening way, wretch
that I am, and they'd also have dragged all my goods all
over the place throughout the azure plains, together with
me. Just like dogs, no differently, the whirlwinds sur-   835
rounded my ship, and the hostile showers, floods, and
storms would have dragged me around, broken the mast,
charged against the sail yards, and torn apart the sails, if
your peace hadn't graciously protected me. But get away
from me now, please, I'm resolved to dedicate myself to
leisure from now on. I've acquired enough through the
hardships I fought with while seeking riches for my son.
(*looking around*) But who is this who's coming onto the   840
street at the same time as me, in a strange outfit and
appearance? Even though I long for home, I'll wait and
pay attention to what he's up to. (*steps aside*)

Enter the SYCOPHANT *from the right, wearing a broad-brimmed hat and carrying two letters.*

SYC (*aside*) I call this day *Three-Dollar Day:* I've hired out
my labor for the arts of deception for three dollars[30] to-
day. I'm coming from Seleucia, Macedonia, Asia, and   845
Arabia,[31] which I've never set eye or foot on. Can you see
what bad trouble poverty gives to a wretch? Actually, for
the sake of three dollars I'm now forced to say that I re-
ceived these letters from someone whom I neither know

[30] Lit., "coins" (*nummi*), probably referring to sesterces.
[31] The list is not nonsensical; if he were coming from Seleucia,
where Charmides had gone, the natural route would be: Mesopotamia
called *Arabia*), Asia Minor, Thrace (not mentioned), Macedonia, and
Greece as final destination.

dicam ab eo homine me accepisse quem ego qui sit
homo nescio

850   nec noui, nec natus necne is fuerit id solide scio.

CHAR pol hic quidem fungino genere est: capite se totum te-
git.

Hilurica facies uidetur hominis, eo ornatu aduenit.

SYC ill' qui me conduxit, ubi conduxit, abduxit domum,
quae uoluit mihi dixit, docuit et praemonstrauit prius

855   quo modo quidque agerem; nunc adeo si quid ego ad-
didero amplius,

eo conductor melius de me nugas conciliauerit.

ut ille me exornauit, ita sum ornatus; argentum hoc
facit.

ipse ornamenta a chorago haec sumpsit suo periculo.

nunc ego si potero ornamentis hominem circumdu-
cere,

860   dabo operam ut me esse ipsum plane sycophantam
sentiat.

CHAR quam magis specto, minus placet mi haec hominis fa-
cies. mira sunt

ni illic homo est aut dormitator aut sector zonarius.

loca contemplat, circumspectat sese atque aedis nosci-
tat.

credo edepol, quo mox furatum ueniat speculatur loca.

865   magis lubido est opseruare quid agat: ei rei operam
dabo.

SYC   has regiones demonstrauit mi ille conductor meus;
apud illas aedis sistendae mihi sunt sycophantiae.
fores pultabo.

857 hoc *CD*, hac *AB*

nor am acquainted with, and of whom I don't know for   850
certain if he's been born or not.

CHAR *(aside)* This chap belongs to the mushroom variety: he's
completely covering himself with his own head. His ap-
pearance seems Illyrian,[32] that's the dress he's coming
in.

SYC *(aside)* When the man who hired me hired me, he took
me home, told me what he wanted, and taught and
showed me first how I should do everything; now then,   855
if I add anything more, my employer will get that much
more trickery for his money. I am dressed the way he
dressed me; the money does this. He himself borrowed
this costume from the stage manager at his own risk. If
I can now cheat him out of the costume, I'll bet that he   860
realizes that I'm an impostor through and through.

CHAR *(aside)* The more I look, the less I like his appearance. I
wouldn't be surprised if he's a night prowler[33] or a cut-
purse. He's examining the area, looking around himself,
and acquainting himself with the houses. I do believe
he's spying out places where he can soon come to steal.
I'm all the keener to observe what he's up to; that's what   865
I'll give my attention to.

SYC *(aside)* That employer of mine showed me this area; this
is the house at which my tricks must be set on foot. I'll
knock at the door.

[32] Illyria is the ancient name of a region in the western Balkan
Peninsula.

[33] A *dormitator* (Greek *hemerokoitos*) is someone who sleeps in
daytime and steals at night.

207

CHAR   ad nostras aedis hic quidem habet rectam uiam.
      hercle opinor mi aduenienti hac noctu agitandum est
      uigilias.

870   SYC   aperite hoc, aperite. heus, ecquis his foribus tutelam
      gerit?

CHAR   quid, adulescens, quaeris? quid uis? quid istas pultas?
      SYC heus senex,
      census quom ⟨sum⟩, iuratori recte rationem dedi.
      Lesbonicum hic adulescentem quaero in his regionibus
      ubi habitet, et item alterum ad istanc capitis albitudi-
      nem:

875   Calliclem aiebat uocari qui has dedit mi epistulas.

CHAR   meum gnatum hic quidem Lesbonicum quaerit et ami-
      cum meum
      quoi ego liberosque bonaque commendaui, Calliclem.

SYC   fac me, si scis, certiorem hisce homines ubi habitent,
      pater.

CHAR   quid eos quaeris? aut quis es? aut unde es? aut unde
      aduenis?

880   SYC   multa simul rogitas, nescio quid expediam potissumum.
      si unum quicquid singillatim et placide percontabere,
      et meum nomen et mea facta et itinera ego faxo scias.

CHAR   faciam ita ut uis. agedum nomen tuom primum me-
      mora mihi.

SYC   magnum facinus incipissis petere.

CHAR   quid ita?

872 sum *add. Acidalius*
878 hosce *BC*, eosce *D*, hisce ς

CHAR *(aside)* He's going straight to our house. I do believe that on my arrival I need to keep watch this night.

SYC *(knocking)* Open this up, open up! Hey, does anyone 870 have charge of this door?

CHAR *(approaching)* What are you looking for, young man? What do you want? Why are you knocking at that door?

SYC Hey, old chap, when I was registered in the census, I explained myself to the assessor.[34] I'm trying to find out where in this area young Lesbonicus lives, and also a chap with a head as white as yours. The fellow who gave 875 me these letters said he's called Callicles.

CHAR *(aside)* He's looking for my son Lesbonicus and my friend Callicles, to whom I entrusted my children and my possessions.

SYC If you know it, inform me where these people live, father.[35]

CHAR Why are you looking for them? Who are you? Where are you from? Where are you coming from?

SYC You ask many questions at the same time, I don't know 880 what I should tell you first. If you gently ask me one thing at a time, I'll let you know my name, my deeds, and my travels.

CHAR I'll do as you wish. Go on, tell me your name first.

SYC You're beginning to demand a major undertaking.

CHAR How so?

[34] The Roman census contained information about family background and wealth; the *iuratores*, "assessors," assisted the censor.

[35] A respectful term of address for an older man, but here unintentionally ironic, as Charmides is the father of Lesbonicus.

SYC   quia, pater,

885   si ante lucem ⟨hercle⟩ ire occipias a meo primo no-
           mine,
       concubium sit noctis prius quam ad postremum perue-
           neris.

CHAR opus facto est uiatico ad tuom nomen, ut tu praedicas.

SYC   est minusculum alterum, quasi uexillum uinarium.

CHAR quid est tibi nomen, adulescens?

SYC   "Pax," id est nomen mihi.

890   hoc cottidianum est.

CHAR   edepol nomen nugatorium!
       quasi dicas, si quid crediderim tibi, "pax"—periisse
           ilico.
       hic homo solide sycophanta est. quid ais tu, adules-
           cens? SYC quid est?

CHAR eloquere, isti tibi quid homines debent quos tu quaeri-
           tas?

SYC   pater istius adulescentis dedit has duas mi epistulas,

895   Lesbonici. is mi est amicus.

CHAR   teneo hunc manufestarium.
       me sibi epistulas dedisse dicit. ludam hominem probe.

SYC   ita ut occepi, si animum aduortas, dicam.

CHAR   dabo operam tibi.

SYC   hanc me iussit Lesbonico suo gnato dare epistulam,
       et item hanc alteram suo amico Callicli iussit dare.

900 CHAR mihi quoque edepol, quom hic nugatur, contra nugari
           lubet.
       ubi ipse erat?

885 hercle *add. Ritschl*
888 uixillum (iuxillum *B*) *P*, uasculum *Gronovius*

SYC   Because, father, if you started walking from my first   885
name before sunrise, it would be bedtime before you
reach the last.

CHAR From what you say, one needs to provide a travel fund
in the case of a name like yours.

SYC   There's a tiny other one, like a wine label.

CHAR What's your name, young man?

SYC   "Presto," that's my name. This is the one for everyday   890
use.

CHAR Goodness, an absurd name! As if you were saying that if
I were to entrust anything to you, "presto"—it would be
gone at once. (*aside*) This chap is an impostor through
and through. (*aloud*) What do you say, young man?

SYC   What is it?

CHAR Tell me, what do those people you're looking for owe
you?

SYC   The father of that young chap, Lesbonicus, has given me
these two letters. (*shows them*) He's a friend of mine.   895

CHAR (*aside*) I've got him cornered. He says that I have given
him the letters. I'll make fun of him in style.

SYC   If you give me your attention, I'll finish telling you in the
same way that I began.

CHAR Yes, I'm giving you my attention.

SYC   (*holding up the letters one by one*) He told me to give
this letter to his son Lesbonicus, and he also told me to
give this other one to his friend Callicles.

CHAR (*aside*) Since he's trying to deceive me, I too am keen to   900
try to deceive him in turn. (*aloud*) Where was he him-
self?

SYC	bene rem gerebat.
CHAR	ergo ubi?
SYC	in Seleucia.
CHAR	ab ipson istas accepisti?
SYC	e manibus dedit mi ipse in manus.
CHAR	qua facie est homo?
SYC	sesquipede quiddam est quam tu longior.
CHAR	haeret haec res, si quidem ego apsens sum quam praesens longior.

905   nouistin hominem?

SYC	ridicule rogitas, quocum una cibum capere soleo.
CHAR	quid est ei nomen?
SYC	quod edepol homini probo.
CHAR	lubet audire.
SYC	illi edepol—illi—illi—uae misero mihi!
CHAR	quid est negoti?
SYC	deuoraui nomen imprudens modo.
CHAR	non placet qui amicos intra dentes conclusos habet.

910 SYC   atque etiam modo uorsabatur mi in labris primoribus.

CHAR	temperi huic hodie anteueni.
SYC	teneor manufesto miser.
CHAR	iam recommentatu's nomen?
SYC	deum hercle me atque hominum pudet.
CHAR	uide modo ut hominem noueris!
SYC	tam quam me. fieri istuc solet, quod in manu teneas atque oculis uideas, id desideres.

915   litteris recomminiscar. <C> est principium nomini.

CHAR Callias?

915 C *add. Scaliger*

SYC He was having a success.

CHAR Yes, but where?

SYC In Seleucia.

CHAR Did you receive the letters from him in person?

SYC He himself put them from his hands into mine.

CHAR What does he look like?

SYC He's something like a foot and a half taller than you.

CHAR (*aside*) There's a problem here, if indeed I am taller in
my absence than in my presence. (*aloud*) Do you know   905
him?

SYC You're asking a silly question; I eat with him regularly.

CHAR What's he called?

SYC (*hesitating*) What a decent man is called.

CHAR I wish to hear it.

SYC Well, he—he—he—poor, wretched me!

CHAR What's the matter?

SYC I've just swallowed his name inadvertently.

CHAR I don't like a man who keeps his friends locked up inside
his teeth.

SYC But just now he was on the tip of my tongue.[36]   910

CHAR (*aside*) I've forestalled him just in time today.

SYC (*aside*) I'm caught in the act, poor me.

CHAR Have you thought up the name now?

SYC (*half aside*) I'm ashamed in front of gods and men.

CHAR Just see how well you know him!

SYC As well as myself. It tends to happen that you can't locate
what you hold in your hand and see with your eyes. I'll   915
think him up by the letters. His name has C as its begin-
ning.

CHAR Callias?

[36] Lit., "on the outside of my lips."

213

SYC	non est.
CHAR	Callippus?
SYC	non est.
CHAR	Callidemides?
SYC	non est.
CHAR	Callinicus?
SYC	non est.
CHAR	Callimarchus?
SYC	nil agis.

neque adeo edepol flocci facio, quando egomet memini
mihi.

CHAR at enim multi Lesbonici sunt hic: nisi nomen patris
920 dices, non monstrare istos possum homines quos tu
quaeritas.
quod ad exemplum est? coniectura si reperire possu-
mus.
SYC ad hoc exemplum est—
CHAR an Chares? an Charmides?
SYC enim Charmides.
em istic erit. qui istum di perdant!
CHAR dixi ego iam dudum tibi:
te potius bene dicere aequom est homini amico quam
male.
925 SYC satin inter labra atque dentes latuit uir minimi preti?
CHAR ne male loquere apsenti amico.
SYC quid ergo ille ignauissumus
mi latitabat?
CHAR si appellasses, respondisset nomini.
sed ipse ubi est?
SYC pol illum reliqui ad Rhadamantem in
Cercopio [insula].

SYC No.

CHAR Callippus?

SYC No.

CHAR Callidemides?

SYC No.

CHAR Callinicus?

SYC No.

CHAR Callimarchus?

SYC It's no use. And what's more, I don't care a straw, since I remember it for my own purposes.

CHAR But as a matter of fact there are many Lesbonicuses here. Unless you tell me his father's name, I can't show   920
you those people you're looking for. What's it like? On the chance that we can find it by guessing.

SYC Like this—

CHAR (*interrupting*) Chares? Or Charmides?

SYC Yes, Charmides! That'll be the fellow. May the gods ruin him!

CHAR I already told you a while ago: it's more appropriate for you to speak well of a friend than badly.

SYC Did the worthless chap really hide between my lips and   925
teeth?

CHAR Stop insulting a friend in his absence.

SYC Then why did that useless fellow hide from me?

CHAR If you'd called him, he'd have replied to his name. But where is he himself?

SYC I left him with Rhadamas in Monkeyland.

---

922 mim *B*, min *CD*, enim *Ribbeck*
927 nomine *P*, nomini *Ritschl*
928 in cecropia insula *P*, in Cercopio *Guyet*

CHAR quis homo est me insipientior, qui ipse egomet ubi sim
      quaeritem?
930   sed nil disconducit huic rei. quid ais? quid hoc quod te
      rogo?
      quos locos adiisti? SYC nimium mirimodis mirabilis.
CHAR lubet audire nisi molestum est.
SYC   quin discupio dicere.
      omnium primum in Pontum aduecti ad Arabiam ter-
      ram sumus.
CHAR eho an etiam Arabia est in Ponto?
SYC   est: non illa ubi tus gignitur,
935   sed ubi apsinthium fit ac cunila gallinacea.
CHAR nimium graphicum hunc nugatorem! sed ego sum insi-
      pientior
      qui egomet unde redeam hunc rogitem, quae ego
      sciam atque hic nesciat;
      nisi quia lubet experiri quo euasurust denique.
      sed quid ais? quo inde isti porro?
SYC   si animum aduortes, eloquar.
940   ad caput amnis, qui de caelo exoritur sub solio Iouis.
CHAR sub solio Iouis?
SYC   ita dico.
CHAR   e caelo?
SYC   atque ⟨e⟩ medio quidem.
CHAR eho an etiam in caelum escendisti?
SYC   immo horiola aduecti sumus
      usque aqua aduorsa per amnem.

933 a *P*, *del.* ꞅ, *ad Camerarius*
940 quod *P*, qui *Guyet*
941 ⟨e⟩ medio *Pareus*

CHAR (*aside*) Who could be more stupid than I am, seeing that
I myself am asking where I am? But nothing is too silly   930
for this business. (*aloud*) What do you say? What about
the thing I ask you? What places did you go to?

SYC Absolutely amazing ones.

CHAR I'd like to hear about it, if it isn't too much trouble.

SYC No, I'm only too glad to tell you. First of all, we traveled
to Pontus[37] to Arabia.

CHAR What! Is there also an Arabia in Pontus?

SYC Yes; not the one where incense comes from, but the one   935
where wormwood[38] is produced and wild marjoram.

CHAR (*aside*) This trickster is absolutely first-class! But I am
being rather silly, as I'm asking him where I'm returning
from, something that I know and he doesn't; except that
I'm keen to try out where he'll get to in the end. (*aloud*)
But what do you say? Where did you go next?

SYC If you pay attention, I'll tell you. To the source of the   940
river which rises from heaven under Jupiter's throne.

CHAR Under Jupiter's throne?

SYC That's what I'm saying.

CHAR From heaven?

SYC And right from its center at that.

CHAR Hey, did you also climb up to heaven?

SYC No, we got there in a small fishing boat on the river,
straight upstream.

---

[37] Region at the southern coast of the Black Sea. The correct geography which the impostor rehearsed in l. 845 (and which may come from Philemon) is forgotten and replaced by tall stories (which are likely to be Plautine inventions).

[38] Wormwood often came from Pontus, as Pliny tells us (*nat.* 27.45).

CHAR	eho an tu etiam uidisti Iouem?
SYC	alii di isse ad uillam aiebant seruis depromptum cibum.

945   deinde porro—

CHAR	deinde porro nolo quicquam praedices.
SYC	⟨sed—
CHAR	abe⟩o hercle, si es molestus. nam pudicum neminem,

       ⟨Pax, refer⟩re oportet, qui aps terra ad caelum per-
       uenerit.

SYC   ⟨facia⟩m ita ut te uelle uideo. sed monstra hosce homi-
       nes mihi

       quos ego quaero, quibus me oportet has deferre epis-
       tulas.

950 CHAR quid ais? tu nunc si forte eumpse Charmidem
       conspexeris,

       illum quem tibi istas dedisse commemoras epistulas,
       norisne hominem?

SYC   ne tu me edepol arbitrare beluam,

       qui quidem non nouisse possim quicum aetatem exege-
       rim.

       an ille tam esset stultus qui mi mille nummum crederet

955   Philippum, quod me aurum deferre iussit ad gnatum
       suom

       atque ad amicum Calliclem, quoi rem aibat mandasse
       hic suam?

       mihi concrederet, nisi me ille et ego illum nossem
       probe?

CHAR enim uero ego nunc sycophantae huic sycophantari
       uolo,

       si hunc possum illo mille nummum Philippum circum-
       ducere

946 SYC ⟨sed—CHAR abe⟩o *Leo*   947 ⟨Pax, refer⟩re *Leo*

CHAR Hey, did you also see Jupiter?

SYC The other gods said he'd gone to his country estate to
deal out rations to his slaves. After that—   945

CHAR (*interrupting*) After that I don't want you to say any-
thing.

SYC But—

CHAR (*interrupting*) I'm leaving, if you annoy me: Presto, no
decent man ought to tell how he got from earth to
heaven.[39]

SYC I'll do as I see you want me to. But show me the people
I'm looking for, to whom I should bring these letters.

CHAR What do you say? If by chance you were to spot Char-   950
mides in person now, the one who you say has given you
those letters, would you recognize him?

SYC You really think I'm such a fool that I couldn't recognize
the man who I've spent my life with. Would he be so
stupid as to entrust one thousand Philippics to me,   955
money which he told me to bring to his son and to his
friend Callicles, in whose charge he said he'd put his
affairs here? Would he have entrusted it to me if he
didn't know me properly and I him?

CHAR (*aside*) I really want to play the impostor for this impos-
tor now, on the chance that I can trick him out of those

---

[39] Perhaps in addition to the literal meaning also a reference to
Ganymede, abducted by Zeus, who assumed the form of an eagle; Zeus
kept Ganymede as cupbearer and lover. The early Latin form of the
name, borrowed via Etruscan, was *Catamitus*, a noun that had the
double meaning "Ganymede"/"catamite."

---

948 mit aut *P* (*praecedente spatio in CD*), ‹facia›m ita ut *Spengel*
949 hos *P*, quos ς

960   quod sibi me dedisse dixit, quem ego qui sit homo
          nescio

neque oculis ante hunc diem umquam uidi. eine
         aurum crederem,

quoi, si capitis res sit, nummum numquam credam
         plumbeum?

aggrediundust hic homo mi astu. heus, Pax, te tribus
         uerbis uolo.

SYC   uel trecentis.

CHAR   haben tu id aurum quod accepisti a Charmide?

965 SYC   atque etiam Philippum, numeratum illius in mensa
        manu,

      mille nummum.

CHAR   nempe ab ipso id accepisti Charmide?

SYC   mirum quin ab auo eius aut proauo acciperem qui sunt
        mortui.

CHAR adulescens, cedodum istuc aurum mi.

SYC   quod ego aurum dem tibi?

CHAR quod a me te accepisse fassu's.

SYC   aps te accepisse?

CHAR   ita loquor.

970 SYC   quis tu homo es?

CHAR   qui mille nummum tibi dedi ego sum Charmides.

SYC   neque edepol tu is es neque hodie is umquam eris,
        auro huic quidem.

      abi sis, nugator: nugari nugatori postulas.

CHAR Charmides ego sum.

SYC   nequiquam hercle es, nam nihil auri fero.

      nimis argute ‹me› obrepsisti in eapse occasiuncula:

962 siet *P* (*scriptio plena*)
974 me *add. Ritschl*

one thousand Philippics which he said I'd given to him,   960
a man whom I don't know and have never set eyes on
before this day. Would I have entrusted money to this
chap, when I'd never entrust a lead coin to him, even if
it were a matter of life and death? I have to approach
him with guile. (*aloud*) Hey, Presto, I want three words
with you.

SYC   Three hundred, if you wish.

CHAR   Do you have this money that you received from Char-
mides?

SYC   Yes, and what's more, it's one thousand Philippics,   965
counted out by his hand on the banker's table.

CHAR   You received it from Charmides in person, didn't you?

SYC   Odd that I didn't get it from his grandfather or great-
grandfather, who are dead.

CHAR   Young man, give me that money.

SYC   What money should I give you?

CHAR   That which you've admitted receiving from me.

SYC   Receiving from you?

CHAR   That's what I'm saying.

SYC   Who are you?   970

CHAR   I'm the man who gave you one thousand Philippics,
Charmides.

SYC   No, you aren't the man and you'll never be him today, so
far as this money is concerned. Go away, if you will,
trickster: you're trying to trick a trickster.

CHAR   I am Charmides.

SYC   It will do you no good to be him: I'm not carrying any
money. You've crept up on me very cleverly at just the

975   postquam ego me aurum ferre dixi, post tu factu's
      Charmides;
    prius tu non eras quam auri feci mentionem. nil agis;
    proin tu te, itidem ut charmidatus es, rursum rechar-
      mida.
CHAR quis ego sum igitur, siquidem is non sum qui sum?
SYC   quid id ad me attinet?
    dum ille ne sis quem ego esse nolo, sis mea causa qui
      lubet.
980   prius non is eras qui eras: nunc is factu's qui tum non
      eras.
CHAR age si quid agis.
SYC   quid ego agam?
CHAR   aurum redde.
SYC   dormitas, senex.
CHAR fassu's Charmidem dedisse aurum tibi.
SYC   scriptum quidem.
CHAR properas an non properas [ab]ire actutum ab his regio-
      nibus,
    dormitator, prius quam ego hic te iubeo mulcari male?
985 SYC quam ob rem?
CHAR   quia illum quem ementitus es, ego sum
     ipsus Charmides
    quem tibi epistulas dedisse aiebas.
SYC   eho, quaeso, an tu is es?
CHAR is enim uero sum.
SYC   ain tu tandem? is ipsusne es?
CHAR   aio.
SYC   ipsus es?
CHAR ipsus, inquam, Charmides sum.
SYC   ergo ipsusne es?
CHAR   ipsissumus.
    abin hinc ab oculis?

right moment; after I said I was carrying money, you 975
became Charmides. You weren't him until I mentioned
the money. You aren't getting anywhere; so just as you
Charmidized yourself, un-Charmidize yourself again.

CHAR Then who am I, if I'm not the one I am?

SYC What does that matter to me? So long as you're not the
one who I don't want you to be, you can be anyone you
like for all I care. First you weren't the one you were; 980
now you've become the one you weren't.

CHAR Do it if you're going to do anything.

SYC What should I do?

CHAR Return the money.

SYC You're dreaming, old chap.

CHAR You've admitted that Charmides has given you money.

SYC Yes, in writing.

CHAR Are you hurrying or not to leave this area at once, night
prowler, before I have you beaten here terribly?

SYC What for? 985

CHAR Because I'm the one you lied about, Charmides, who you
claimed had given you the letters.

SYC Hey, I ask you, are you the one?

CHAR Yes, I am the one.

SYC Do you really say so? Are you the one yourself?

CHAR Yes.

SYC Are you the one yourself?

CHAR I'm telling you, I am Charmides myself.

SYC Then are you him yourself?

CHAR My selfest self. Won't you get out of my sight?

---

977 tute . . . te echarmida *Ritschl*
983 [ab]ire *Guyet*
989 abhinc P *Priscianus*, abin hinc *Guyet*

SYC   enim uero serio, quoniam aduenis . . .
990   uapulabis meo arbitratu et nouorum aedilium.
CHAR at etiam maledicis?
SYC   immo, saluos quandoquidem aduenis . . .
        di te perdant, si te flocci facio an periisses prius.
        ego ob hanc operam argentum accepi, te macto infor-
           tunio:
        ceterum qui sis, qui non sis, floccum non interduim.
995   ibo ad illum, renuntiabo qui mihi tris nummos dedit,
        ut sciat se perdidisse. ego abeo. male uiue et uale!
        qui di te omnes aduenientem peregre perdant, Char-
           mides!
CHAR postquam illic hinc abiit, post loquendi libere
        uidetur tempus uenisse atque occasio.
1000   iam dudum meum ille pectus pungit aculeus,
        quid illi negoti fuerit ante aedis meas.
        nam epistula illa mihi concenturiat metum
        in corde et illud mille nummum quam rem agat.
        numquam edepol temere tinnit tintinnabulum:
1005   nisi qui illud tractat aut mouet, mutum est, tacet.
        sed quis hic est qui huc in plateam cursuram incipit?
        lubet opseruare quid agat: huc concessero.

IV. iii: STASIMVS. CHARMIDES

STA   Stasime, fac te propere celerem, recipe te ad dominum
        domum,

1005 mutus *P*, mutumst *Pareus*

224

SYC   Truly and honestly, since you've arrived . . . you'll get a   990
      thrashing on my orders and those of the new aediles.[40]

CHAR What, do you even abuse me?

SYC   No, since you've arrived safe and sound . . . may the gods
      destroy you, if I care one straw about whether you'd
      been killed earlier. I've received my money for this job
      and you can have my curse; as for everything else, I
      couldn't care less who you are and who you aren't. I'll go   995
      to the fellow who gave me the three dollars and report,
      so that he knows that he's lost them. I'm off. Live and
      fare badly! May all the gods ruin you on your arrival from
      abroad, Charmides!

Exit the SYCOPHANT *to the right.*

CHAR Now that he's left, the time and opportunity to speak
      freely seems to have come. That sting has been piercing   1000
      my breast for some time now, what business he had in
      front of my house: that letter and those one thousand
      Philippics marshal fear in my heart about what they're
      up to. A bell never rings without a cause; unless someone   1005
      pulls at it or moves it, it's silent and quiet. But who is this
      who is running into the street here? I'm keen to observe
      what he's up to; I'll go over here. (*does so*)

Enter STASIMUS *in great haste from the right, without noticing
his master.*

STA   Stasimus, make yourself really speedy and return home

---

   [40] Here and in what follows, jokes are made on the convention of
giving a dinner to someone who has returned from abroad. The aediles
are Roman magistrates responsible for public games and buildings.

ne subito metus exoriatur scapulis stultitia ⟨tua⟩.
1010 adde gradum, appropera. iam dudum factum est quom
abiisti domo.
caue sis tibi ne bubuli in te cottabi crebri crepent,
si aberis ab eri quaestione. ne destiteris currere.
ecce hominem te, Stasime, nihili! satin in thermopolio
condalium es oblitus, postquam thermopotasti guttu-
rem?
1015 recipe te et recurre petere ⟨re⟩ recenti.
CIIAR   huic, quisquis est,
gurgulio est exercitor; is hunc hominem cursuram do-
cet.
STA quid, homo nihili, non pudet te? tribusne te poteriis
memoriam esse oblitum? an uero, quia cum frugi ho-
minibus
ibi bibisti, qui ab alieno facile cohiberent manus?
1020 Struthus [fuit], Circonicus, Cremnus, Cercobulus, Col-
labus,
loculiripidae, cruricrepidae, ferriteri mastigiae:
inter eosne homines condalium te redipisci postulas?
coram eorum unus surrupuit currenti cursori solum.

1009 stultitiam *P*, stultitia tua *Camerarius*

1015 re *add. Camerarius*

1016 gurguliost *B*, gurgiliost *C*, gurgula *D^1*, gurgulast *D^2*, Curcu-
liost *Gratwick praecedente Lambino*

1018 memoria *P*, memoriam *Seyffert*, memoriae *Guyet*

1020 truthus *B*, truchus *C*, terruchus *D*, Struthus *Schoell*, Trochus
Spengel   fuit *del. Gratwick* Cerconicus *P*, Circonicus *Leo*   Crinnus
P, Crimnus *Scaliger*, Cremnus *Trappes-Lomax*

1021 oculicrepidae *P*, loculiripidae *Gratwick*

1023 quorum *P*, coram *Gratwick*

226

to your master, so that no fear will suddenly arise for your shoulder blades through your stupidity. Quicken your pace and hurry! It's a long time since you left home. Do make sure that cowhide blows[41] won't clatter on you constantly, if you're absent when your master looks for you. Don't stop running. (*pauses*) Look, Stasimus, you're a useless fellow! Did you really forget your ring in the wineshop after you'd warmed your throat with hot drinks? Return and run back to demand it while the matter is still fresh.

1010

1015

CHAR (*aside*) Whoever this fellow is, his gullet is his trainer; it teaches him to run.[42]

STA What, you useless chap? Don't you have any shame? Could you really forget your memory after three wine cups? Or is it because you were drinking there with decent men, who could easily keep their hands off another's possessions? Struthus, Circonicus, Cremnus, Cercobulus, and Collabus,[43] crooks who snatch purses, have chains clanking around their shins, and wear fetters smooth; do you expect to recover your ring from among these people? In my presence, one of them stole the sole of a runner's shoe from him while he was actually running.

1020

---

[41] The "blows" are *cottabi* in Latin. *Cottabos* was a popular Greek game in which remains of wine were thrown into a metal vessel with as much noise as possible, the aim being to make the metal vessel fall. Here the *cottabi* refer to the individual throws of wine/blows of the whip, not to several games. [42] I.e., after drinking so much he cannot walk straight. [43] Comical names. *Struthus* means "lascivious," and *Circonicus* "someone who beats hawks"; *Cremnus* means "cliff" and thus "dangerous"; *Cercobulus* refers to someone who "thinks of genitals"; and *Collabus* stands for *collops* "hermaphrodite."

CHAR ita me di ament, graphicum furem!

STA   quid ego quod periit petam?

1025   nisi etiam laborem ad damnum apponam epithecam in-
     super.

    quin tu quod periit periisse ducis? cape uorsoriam,
    recipe te ad erum.

CHAR   non fugitiuost hic homo, commeminit domi.

STA utinam ueteres homin‹um mor›es, ueteres parsimo-
     niae

    potius ‹in› maiore honore hic essent quam mores mali!

1030 CHAR di immortales, basilica hicquidem facinora inceptat lo-
     qui!

    uetera quaerit, uetera amare hunc more maiorum
     scias.

STA nam nunc mores nihili faciunt quod licet nisi quod lu-
     bet:

    ambitio iam more sancta est, libera est a legibus;

    scuta iacere fugereque hostis more habent licentiam:

1035   petere honorem pro flagitio more fit.

CHAR   morem improbum!

STA strenuiores praeterire more fit.

CHAR   nequam quidem!

STA mores leges perduxerunt iam in potestatem suam,

    magisque is sunt obnoxiosae quam . . . parentes liberis.

    eae miserae etiam ad parietem sunt fixae clauis ferreis,

1040   ubi malos mores affigi nimio fuerat aequius.

   1028 homin‹um mor›es *Lindemann*
   1029 maiori honori *P*, in maiore honore *Loman*
   1036 strenuos *P*, strenuiores *Leo*, strenuosos *Löwe*
   1038 magis qui sunt *P*, magisque is sunt *Spengel*
   1039 ea miserere *P*, eae miserae *Ritschl*

CHAR (*aside*) As truly as the gods may love me, a first-class thief!

STA Why should I look for what has perished? Unless I add 1025
my trouble to the loss as a bonus on top. Why don't you
consider lost what has been lost? Take the rope for turn-
ing sail, return to your master.

CHAR (*aside*) He isn't a runaway, he remembers home.

STA I wish people's old customs and their old thriftiness were
in greater honor here rather than bad customs!

CHAR (*aside*) Immortal gods, he's beginning to talk about mat- 1030
ters of state! He's looking for the old ways, you can see
that he loves the old ways according to our forefathers'
customs.

STA Yes, customs nowadays don't care for what's allowed,
only for what's pleasurable: bribery is now sanctioned by
custom and free from the laws; through custom people
think they have the freedom to throw their shields away
and flee from the enemy. Through custom, public office 1035
is sought as a reward for criminal behavior.

CHAR (*aside*) An indecent custom!

STA Through custom it happens that they don't elect their
betters.

CHAR (*aside*) Awful!

STA Customs have now brought the laws into their power,
and the laws are more under their thumb than . . . par-
ents are under that of their children. Those wretched
laws are even fastened to the walls with iron nails, where 1040
it would have been much fairer to fasten bad cus-
toms.[44]

---

[44] Laws are nailed onto walls so as to be visible; Stasimus pretends
that this is a punishment.

CHAR lubet adire atque appellare hunc; uerum ausculto per-
  lubens

  et metuo, si compellabo, ne aliam rem occipiat loqui.

STA neque istis quicquam lege sanctum est: leges mori ser-
  uiunt,

  mores autem rapere properant qua sacrum qua publi-
  cum.

1045 CHAR hercle istis malam rem magnam moribus dignum est
  dari.

STA nonne hoc publice animum aduorti? nam id genus ho-
  minum omnibus

  uniuorsis est aduorsum atque omni populo male facit:

  male fidem seruando illis quoque abrogant etiam fidem

  qui nil meriti; quippe eorum ex ingenio ingenium ho-
  rum probant.

1050   hoc qui in mentem uenerit mi? re ipsa modo commoni-
  tus sum.

  si quoi mutuom quid dederis, fit pro proprio perditum:

  quom repetas, inimicum amicum beneficio inuenias
  tuo.

  si mage exigere occupias, duarum rerum exoritur optio:

  uel illud quod credideris perdas, uel illum amicum
  amiseris.

1055 CHAR meus est hicquidem Stasimus seruos.

STA   nam ego talentum mutuom

  quoi dederam, talento inimicum mi emi, amicum uen-
  didi.

  sed ego sum insipientior qui rebus curem publicis

  potius quam, id quod proxumum est, meo tergo tute-
  lam geram.

  eo domum.

CHAR   heus tu, asta ilico! audi.

230

CHAR (*aside*) I wish to approach and address him; but I listen to him with great pleasure and I'm afraid that if I address him, he'll begin talking about something else.

STA Nothing is laid down as binding by law for them. The laws are slaves to custom, while customs hurry to carry off everything both sacred and profane.

CHAR (*aside*) Those customs really ought to be given a big thrashing.   1045

STA Is it possible that this shouldn't be punished by the state? People of this sort are opposed to each and all and harm the entire populace. By keeping faith badly they take away faith even from those who haven't done anything wrong; the reason is that people judge the character of one group from that of the other. You wonder how this has occurred to me? I've just been reminded by an actual instance. If you lend someone something, it's lost instead of being your own. When you claim it back, you find your friend is your enemy because of your good deed. If you begin to demand it more strongly, a choice between two alternatives arises: either you lose what you lent, or you lose that friend.   1050

CHAR (*aside*) This is actually my slave Stasimus!   1055

STA Well, I loaned a talent to someone; with that talent I bought myself an enemy and sold my friend. But it's rather stupid of me to look after public affairs instead of looking out for my back, which is of immediate concern. I'm going home.

CHAR Hey you! Stand where you are! Listen!

1042 sed *P*, et *Acidalius*

STA	heus tu! non sto.
CHAR	te uolo.
1060 STA quid si ego me te uelle nolo?

CHAR aha nimium, Stasime, saeuiter!

STA emere meliust quoi imperes.

CHAR pol ego emi atque argentum dedi;
sed si non dicto audiens est, quid ago?

STA da magnum malum.

CHAR bene mones, ita facere certum est.

STA nisi quidem es obnoxius.

CHAR si bonus es, obnoxius sum; sin secus es, faciam ut iu-
bes.

1065 STA quid id ad me attinet, bonisne seruis tu utare an malis?

CHAR quia boni malique in ea re pars tibi est.

STA partem alteram
tibi permitto; illam alteram apud me, quod boni est,
apponito.

CHAR si eris meritus, fiet. respice huc ad me. ego sum Char-
mides.

STA hem! quis est qui mentionem homo hominis fecit op-
tumi?

1070 CHAR ipsus homo optumus.

STA mare, terra, caelum, di uostram fidem!
satin ego oculis plane uideo? estne ipsus an non est? is
est,
certe is est, is est profecto. o mi ere exoptatissume,
salue.

CHAR salue, Stasime.

STA saluom te—

1064 ut mones *A*, uti iubes *P*

232

STA (*refusing to look back*) Hey you! I won't stand.

CHAR I want you.

STA What if I don't want you to want me?   1060

CHAR Ah, Stasimus, you're behaving too violently!

STA It's better to buy someone to order around.

CHAR I did buy someone and paid money; but if he doesn't obey me, what am I to do?

STA Give him a big thrashing.

CHAR You're giving me good advice, I'm resolved to act accordingly.

STA Unless of course you are under obligation to him.

CHAR If you're good, I'm under obligation to you; if you're otherwise, I'll do as you tell me to.

STA What does it have to do with me whether you have good   1065
slaves or bad ones?

CHAR Because you have a share of good and bad in this matter.

STA I leave the second share to you; that first one, the one of good, you must place with me.

CHAR If you deserve it, it will be done. Look here at me. I am Charmides.

STA Oh! Who is it who is mentioning the best of men?

CHAR The best of men himself.   1070

STA (*finally turning around*) Sea, earth, heaven, gods, your protection! Am I really seeing clearly with my eyes? Is it he himself or not? It's him, it's certainly him, it's him indeed! O my master, who I longed for so much, my greetings!

CHAR My greetings, Stasimus.

STA That you're safe and sound—

CHAR   scio et credo tibi.
     sed omitte alia, hoc mihi responde: liberi quid agunt
         mei,
1075   quos reliqui hic filium atque filiam?
STA   uiuont, ualent.
CHAR nempe uterque?
STA   uterque.
CHAR   di me saluom et seruatum uolunt.
     cetera intus otiose percontabor quae uolo.
     eamus intro, sequere.
STA   quo tu te agis?
CHAR   quonam nisi domum?
STA   hicin nos habitare censes?
CHAR   ubinam ego alibi censeam?
1080 STA   iam—
CHAR   quid iam?
STA   non sunt nostrae aedes istae.
CHAR   quid ego ex te audio?
STA   uendidit tuos natus aedis—
CHAR   perii!
STA   —praesentariis
     argenti minis numeratis—
CHAR   quot?
STA   quadraginta.
CHAR   occidi!
     quis eas emit?
STA   Callicles, quoi tuam rem commendaueras;
     is habitatum huc commigrauit nosque exturbauit foras.
1085 CHAR ubi nunc filius meus habitat?
STA   hic in hoc posticulo.
CHAR male disperii!
STA   credidi aegre tibi id, ubi audisses, fore.

234

CHAR (*interrupting*) I know and I believe you. But forget about
    the rest and answer me this: how are my children, my   1075
    son and daughter, whom I left here?

STA   Alive and well.

CHAR Both of them?

STA   Yes, both of them.

CHAR The gods want me safe and sound. The other things that
    I want I'll ask inside at my leisure. Let's go in, follow me.
    (*turns to the door of his house*)

STA   Where are you going?

CHAR Home, where else?

STA   Do you think we live here?

CHAR Where else should I think we live?

STA   Now—   1080

CHAR (*interrupting*) What now?

STA   Now that house doesn't belong to us any more.

CHAR What are you telling me?

STA   Your son has sold the house—

CHAR (*interrupting*) I'm dead!

STA   —for silver minas cash down, in number—

CHAR (*interrupting*) How many?

STA   Forty.

CHAR I'm done for! Who bought it?

STA   Callicles, to whom you'd entrusted your possessions; he
    moved here to live and drove us out.

CHAR Where does my son live now?   1085

STA   Here in this annex.

CHAR I've perished wretchedly!

STA   I believed this would upset you when you heard it.

CHAR ego miserrumis periclis sum per maria maxuma
uectus, capitali periclo per praedones plurumos
me seruaui, saluos redii: nunc hic disperii miser
1090 propter eosdem quorum causa fui hac aetate exercitus.
adimit animam mi aegritudo. Stasime, tene me.

STA   uisne aquam
tibi petam?

CHAR   res quom animam agebat, tum esse offusam oportuit.

IV. iv: CALLICLES. CHARMIDES. STASIMVS

CAL   quid hoc hic clamoris audio ante aedis meas?

CHAR o Callicles, o Callicles, o Callicles!
1095   qualine amico mea commendaui bona?

CAL   probo et fideli et fido et cum magna fide.
et salue et saluom te aduenisse gaudeo.

CHAR credo omnia istaec si ita est ut ⟨tu⟩ praedicas.
sed quis iste est tuos ornatus?

CAL   ego dicam tibi.
1100   thesaurum effodiebam intus, dotem filiae
tuae quae daretur. sed intus narrabo tibi
et hoc et alia. sequere.

CHAR   Stasime.

STA   hem!

CHAR   strenue
curre in Piraeum atque unum curriculum face.
uidebis iam illic nauem qua aduecti sumus.

1087 miserum meis *P*, miserrumeis *Leo*, miser summis *Kampmann*

1090 hac aetate *P*, hoc aetate *Nonius* (*qui* aetas *masculini esse generis putat; ex* hoc aetatis *corruptum esse cognouit Ritschl*)

1098 tu *add. Hermann*

236

CHAR Under the most wretched dangers I've traveled through the greatest seas, under danger to my life I've got safely through very many pirates, and I've returned safe and sound; now I'm utterly ruined here, wretch that I am, because of the same people for whose sake I underwent afflictions at my time of life. Anguish is taking my breath away! Stasimus, hold me! (*begins to faint*) 1090

STA (*grabbing him*) Do you want me to get you some water?

CHAR You should have poured water on my property when it was breathing its last.

Enter CALLICLES *from the house of Charmides, wearing work clothes.*

CAL What's this shouting that I hear in front of my house?

CHAR O Callicles, o Callicles, o Callicles! What sort of friend did I entrust my possessions to? 1095

CAL To a decent, reliable, trustworthy one of great reliability. My greetings to you, and I'm happy that you've arrived safe and sound.

CHAR I believe you in all this, if it is the way you say. But why are you dressed up like that?

CAL I'll tell you. I was digging up the treasure, to be given as a dowry to your daughter. But I'll tell you about this and the other news inside. Follow me. 1100

CHAR Stasimus!

STA Yes.

CHAR Run to the Piraeus[45] energetically and don't stop by the way. There you'll now see the ship on which we came.

---

[45] The Athenian harbor.

1105   iubeto Sangarionem quae imperauerim
      curare ut efferantur, et tu ito simul.
      solutum est portitori iam portorium:
      nihil est morae tibi, ambula, actutum redi.
STA   illic sum atque hic sum.
CAL   sequere tu hac me intro.
CHAR   sequor.
1110 STA   hic meo ero amicus solus firmus restitit
      nec demutauit animum de firma fide,
      quamquam labores multos ⟨ideo pertulit.⟩
      sed hic unus, ut ego suspicor, seruat fidem,
      ⟨quam⟩ ob rem laborem eum ego cepisse censeo.

ACTVS V

V. i: LYSITELES

1115 LYS   hic homo est omnium hominum praecipuos,
      uoluptatibus gaudiisque antepotens:
      ita commoda quae cupio eueniunt,
      quod ago assequitur, subest, supsequitur,
      ita gaudiis gaudium suppeditat.
1120   modo me Stasimus Lesbonici seruos conuenit ⟨domi⟩;
      is mihi dixit suom erum peregre huc aduenisse Char-
        midem.
      nunc mi is propere conueniundust, ut quae cum eius
        filio
      egi, ei rei fundus pater sit potior. eo ⟨quantum potest⟩.
      sed fores hae sonitu suo mi moram obiciunt incom-
        mode.

1108 moracii *BC*, moratii *D*, morae tibi *Müller*
1112 ideo pertulit *add. Naudet*   1114 quam *addidi*
1120 domi *add. Ritschl*   1123 quantum potest *add. Leo*

Tell Sangario to make sure that what I told him is un-   1105
loaded, and you must go back with him. The custom
officer has already been paid the harbor tax; there's no
delay for you, go and come back quickly.

STA I'm there and back already.

CAL (*to Charmides*) You follow me inside this way.

CHAR Yes.

Exeunt CALLICLES and CHARMIDES into the latter's house.

STA This man alone has remained a reliable friend to my   1110
master and hasn't changed his mind from reliable trust-
worthiness, even though he has borne many hardships
because of it. But I suspect this one man keeps faith,
which is why he's undertaken this toil, I think.

Exit STASIMUS to the left.

ACT FIVE

Enter LYSITELES from the left.

LYS (*pointing to himself*) This man is exceeding all men, sur-   1115
passing them in pleasures and joys: so opportunely do
the things I wish for happen, so opportunely does what
I'm doing follow, arrive, and occur, and so much does
one joy crowd on other joys. Just now Stasimus, the slave   1120
of Lesbonicus, met me at home; he told me that his
master Charmides has arrived from abroad. Now I need
to meet him quickly, so that the father may provide a
more reliable footing for the deal I made with his son.
I'm going as fast as possible. But this door is inconve-
niently throwing a delay in my way by its creaking.
(*moves away a little*)

V. ii: CHARMIDES. CALLICLES. LYSITELES.
LESBONICVS

1125   CHAR   nec fuit neque erit neque esse quemquam hominem in
        terra arbitror

        quoi fides fidelitasque amicum erga aequiperet tuam;

        nam exaedificauisset me ex his aedibus, apsque te
        foret.

     CAL   si quid amicum erga bene feci aut consului fideliter,

        non uideor meruisse laudem, culpa caruisse arbitror.

1130   nam beneficium, homini proprium quod datur, pror-
        sum perit,

        quod datum utendum est, id repetundi copia est
        quando uelis.

  CHAR   est ita ut tu dicis. sed ego hoc nequeo mirari satis,

        eum sororem despondisse suam in tam fortem fami-
        liam.

     CAL   Lysiteli quidem Philtonis filio.

     LYS   enim me nominat.

1135   CHAR   familiam optumam occupauit.

     LYS   quid ego cesso hos colloqui?

        sed maneam etiam opinor, namque hoc commodum or-
        ditur loqui.

  CHAR   uah!

     CAL   quid est?

  CHAR   oblitus intus dudum tibi sum dicere:

        modo mi aduenienti nugator quidam occessit obuiam,

        nimis pergraphicus sycophanta; is mille nummum se
        aureum

1140   meo datu tibi ferre et gnato Lesbonico aibat meo;

        quem ego nec qui esset noram neque eum ante us-
        quam conspexi prius.

        sed quid rides?

Enter CHARMIDES *and* CALLICLES *from the former's house.*

CHAR Never has there been nor will there be nor do I believe   1125
there to be anyone on earth whose reliability and trust-
worthiness toward his friend equals yours: had it not
been for you, he'd have dispossessed me of this house.

CAL If I did a good turn to a friend or looked after his in-
terests reliably, I don't think that I've deserved praise,
merely that I've remained free from reproach; a gift   1130
that's given to someone outright is lost at once, but what's
given as a loan you may demand back whenever you
wish.

CHAR It's as you say. But I can't wonder enough that he en-
gaged his sister into such a powerful family.

CAL Yes, to Lysiteles, the son of Philto.

LYS *(aside)* Well, he's mentioning me.

CHAR He's secured an excellent family.   1135

LYS *(aside)* Why am I hesitating to address them? But I'd
better keep waiting, I think, because he's beginning to
say such an agreeable thing.

CHAR Oh!

CAL What is it?

CHAR I forgot to tell you a while ago: just now, on my arrival,
some trickster crossed my way, an absolutely classic im-
postor; he said he was bringing one thousand gold Phi-   1140
lippics provided by me to you and my son Lesbonicus; I
didn't know who he is and I've never seen him before.
But why are you laughing?

1131 uelis *D*, uelit *BC*

CAL   meo allegatu uenit, quasi qui aurum mihi
      ferret aps te quod darem tuae gnatae dotem, ut filius
      tuos, quando illi a me darem, esse allatum id aps te
      crederet
1145   neu qui rem ipsam posset intellegere, [et] thesaurum
      tuom
      me esse penes, atque eum [a] me lege populi patrium
      posceret.
CHAR scite edepol!
CAL   Megaronides communis hoc meus et tuos
      beneuolens commentust.
CHAR   quin collaudo consilium et probo.
LYS   quid ego ineptus, dum sermonem uereor interrum-
      pere,
1150   solus sto nec quod conatus sum agere ago? homines
      colloquar.
CHAR quis hic est qui huc ad nos incedit?
LYS   Charmidem socerum suom
      Lysiteles salutat.
CHAR   di dent tibi, Lysiteles, quae uelis.
CAL   non ego sum salutis dignus?
LYS   immo salue, Callicles;
      hunc priorem aequom est me habere: tunica propior
      pallio est.
1155 CAL   deos uolo consilia uostra ‹uobis› recte uortere.
CHAR filiam meam tibi desponsam esse audio.
LYS   nisi tu neuis.

1145 et *del. Bothe*   1146 a *del. Müller*
1153 salute dignus *P*, dignus salutis *Nonius*, salutis dignus *Pius*
1155 uobis *add. Hermann*
1156 desponsam *B*, desponsatam *CD*

CAL He came at my instigation, pretending to bring me gold
from you, for me to give as a dowry to your daughter, so
that your son would believe, when I was giving it to her
from myself, that it was brought from you, and so that he 1145
couldn't realize the truth, that your treasure was with
me, and then demand his father's property in accordance
with the public law.

CHAR Clever indeed!

CAL Megaronides, my and your common friend, came up
with this idea.

CHAR Truly, I praise and approve of your scheme.

LYS (*aside*) Silly me, why am I standing here alone, while
being afraid to interrupt the conversation, and why aren't 1150
I doing what I've tried to do? I'll address them. (*approaches*)

CHAR Who is this who is coming here to us?

LYS Lysiteles gives his greetings to Charmides, his father-in-law.

CHAR May the gods grant you what you wish, Lysiteles.

CAL Don't I deserve a greeting?

LYS Yes, my greetings, Callicles; but it's only fair that I should
consider this man more important: the shirt is closer
than the overcoat.[46]

CAL (*to both*) I want the gods to bless your plans for you. 1155

CHAR (*to Lysiteles*) I hear that my daughter is engaged to
you.

LYS Unless you object.

---

[46] Lit., "the *tunica* is closer than the *pallium*"; the *tunica* is a type
of undergarment, the *pallium* a cloak.

CHAR immo hau nolo.

LYS   sponden ergo tuam gnatam uxorem mihi?

CHAR spondeo et mille auri Philippum dotis.

LYS   dotem nil moror.

CHAR si illa tibi placet, placenda dos quoque est quam dat
       tibi.

1160   postremo quod uis non duces, nisi illud quod non uis
       feres.

CAL ius hic orat.

LYS   impetrabit te aduocato atque arbitro.
       istac lege filiam tuam sponden mi uxorem dari?

CHAR spondeo.

CAL   et ego spondeo idem hoc.

LYS   oh saluete, affines mei!

CHAR atque edepol sunt res quas propter tibi tamen suscen-
       sui.

1165 LYS quid ego feci?

CHAR   meum corrumpi quia perpessu's filium.

LYS si id mea uoluntate factum est, <est> quod mihi sus-
       censeas.
       sed sine me hoc aps te impetrare quod uolo.

CHAR   quid id est?

LYS   scies.
       si quid stulte fecit, ut ea missa facias omnia.
       quid quassas caput?

CHAR   cruciatur cor mi et metuo.

LYS   quidnam id est?

1170 CHAR quom ille ita est ut esse nolo, id crucior; metuo, si tibi
       denegem quod me oras, ne te leuiorem erga me putes.
       non grauabor. faciam ita ut uis.

1166 est *add. Camerarius*

CHAR No, I don't object.

LYS Then do you promise your daughter in marriage to me?

CHAR I do, and one thousand gold Philippics in dowry.

LYS I don't care about the dowry.

CHAR If you like her, you must also like the dowry she gives you. In short, you won't get what you want unless you take what you don't want. 1160

CAL (*to Lysiteles*) What he says is right.

LYS (*to Callicles*) He'll succeed with you as advocate and judge. (*to Charmides*) Do you promise your daughter in marriage to me under that condition?

CHAR Yes, I promise her.

CAL And I promise the same.

LYS Oh, my greetings, my relations!

CHAR And yet there are things that have made me angry with you.

LYS What have I done? 1165

CHAR Because you allowed my son to be corrupted.

LYS If this happened according to my wish, you have reason to be angry with me. But let me achieve from you what I wish.

CHAR What's this?

LYS You'll find out. If he did anything stupid, you should forgive him for all that. Why are you shaking your head?

CHAR It pains my heart and I'm afraid.

LYS What's this?

CHAR It pains me that he is the way I don't want him to be; I'm afraid that if I deny you what you ask of me, you might believe yourself to be of little influence with me. I won't make a fuss. I'll do as you wish. 1170

LYS   probus es. eo, ut illum euocem.

CHAR miserum est, male promerita, ut merita sunt, si ulcisci
       non licet.

LYS aperite hoc, aperite propere et Lesbonicum, si domi
       est,

1175   [foras] euocate: ita subito est propere quod eum
       conuentum uolo.

LES quis homo tam tumultuoso sonitu me exciuit [subito]
       foras?

LYS beneuolens tuos atque amicust.

LES   satine salue? dic mihi.

LYS recte. tuom patrem rediisse saluom peregre gaudeo.

LES quis id ait?

LYS   ego.

LES   tun uidisti?

LYS   et tute item uideas licet.

1180 LES o pater, pater mi, salue.

CHAR   salue multum, gnate mi.

LES si quid tibi, pater, laboris—

CHAR   nihil euenit, ne time:
       bene re gesta saluos redeo, si tu modo frugi esse uis.
       haec tibi pacta est Calliclei filia.

LES   ego ducam, pater,
       et eam et si quam aliam iubebis.

CHAR   quamquam tibi suscensui,

1185   miseria ⟨una⟩ uni quidem homini est affatim.

1175 foras *del. Guyet*
1176 subito *del. Guyet*
1183 Callicl⟨e⟩i *Wackernagel*
1185 una *add. Lambinus*

LYS That's good of you. I'm going in order to call him out. (*walks to the annex*)

CHAR It's a sad state of affairs if you can't take revenge for bad deeds as they deserve.

LYS (*knocking at the door*) Open up, open up quickly and call out Lesbonicus, if he's at home, so pressing is the matter   1175 about which I want to meet him.

Enter LESBONICUS *from the annex.*

LES Who has called me out with such a racket?

LYS It's your well-wisher and friend.

LES Is all well? Tell me.

LYS Yes. I'm happy that your father has returned safely from abroad.

LES Who says so?

LYS I do.

LES Have you seen him?

LYS Yes, and you can also see him.

LES (*spotting him*) O father, my father, greetings!   1180

CHAR My best greetings, my son.

LES Father, if any distress—

CHAR (*interrupting*) I've had none, don't be afraid; after doing business successfully I'm returning safely, if only you want to behave sensibly. This daughter of Callicles is betrothed to you.

LES Father, I'll marry both her and anyone else, if you tell me to.

CHAR Even though I was angry with you, one affliction is   1185 enough for one man.

247

CAL   immo huic parum est,
      nam si pro peccatis centum ducat uxores, parum est.
LES   at iam posthac temperabo.
CHAR   dicis; si facies modo.
LYS   numquid causae est quin uxorem cras domum ducam?
CHAR   optumum est. [licet.]
      tu in perendinum paratus sis ut ducas.
GREX   plaudite.

1188 licet *del.* Guyet

CAL No, for him it's too little: even if he were to marry a hundred wives for his misbehavior, it would be too little.

LES But from now on I'll reform.

CHAR You say so; if only you'll do it.

LYS Is there any reason why I shouldn't marry tomorrow?

CHAR (*to Lysiteles*) It's perfect. (*to Lesbonicus*) You be ready to marry the day after tomorrow.

TROUPE Give us your applause.

TRUCULENTUS

INTRODUCTORY NOTE

The *Truculentus* is one of those Plautine plays that has attracted highly divergent judgments. As Cicero tells us (*Cato* 50), Plautus himself was very pleased with this comedy, which he had written in his old age, like the *Pseudolus;* this positive assessment, shared by many Renaissance scholars, also predominates today. Earlier, however, the play was held in much lower esteem, especially in the nineteenth century; thus Kiessling once remarked that Plautus' fondness for this play could only be explained by the fact that fathers are generally fond of their youngest and weakest children.

This negative attitude is not difficult to explain. There is not much action in the play and its main theme is the success of the clever, calculating prostitute Phronesium over her customers. They are so completely enthralled that they do not realize how she is taking advantage of them or that, despite being aware of her true character, they still cannot help being subservient to her. In Plautine comedy a girl intended for prostitution can triumph, but only if she has a good character and is revealed to be a freeborn virgin. The victory of an actual prostitute over her customers, treated as the main theme of a comedy, is unprecedented in Plautus. At the end of the play the nor-

mative happy ending does not occur; there is no reward
for love or virtue.

But before assessing the merits of the play or its lack
thereof, we must look at its structure. The prologue of the
Truculentus in its current form is only twenty-one lines
long and rather uninformative. Not all Plautine prologues
are primarily intended to set out the plot structure, but
there are clear indications that something has been lost
from this one. In its present form, all that the prologue
tells us about the contents of the comedy is that Phrone-
sium, who is said to have a character typical of the present
generation (l. 13), has fraudulently introduced a boy into
her family and claims to be his mother in order to get fi-
nancial support from the soldier Stratophanes, who is re-
turning from Babylon and who believes that he is the
child's father.

We glean more information from the ensuing mono-
logue of Diniarchus,[1] who used to be Phronesium's main
customer but was ousted by the wealthier Stratophanes.
Diniarchus, who returned from state business in Lemnos
two days before our comedy begins, is certainly aware that
Phronesium has always taken advantage of him financially,

---

[1] This name is unusual. Deinias is a common Greek name,
rendered as Dinia in Roman comedy, and Deinarchos is also at-
tested, but not Deiniarchos, the basis for Diniarchus. Gratwick
(1990) regards the name as a comic formation based on the
deinias, a type of shoe named after its inventor. Diniarchus would
then mean "commander of shoes," and Gratwick wants to see a
pun on this name in the references to shoes in ll. 363, 367, and
765.

but he admits that nevertheless he is too weak to resist her. He is also well informed of Phronesium's plan to swindle Stratophanes out of money; since he has never seen her pregnant, he himself knows the truth.

The next scene is a dialogue between Diniarchus and Astaphium, Phronesium's main servant. Astaphium is presented as a ruthless woman who is very unfriendly toward Diniarchus as long as she believes him to be bankrupt but who turns polite again as soon as he states that he still has money left. Diniarchus is further characterized as a sexually voracious man who had dealings not only with Phronesium, but also with Astaphium and with boys. When he mentions his money, he gets permission to go inside and see Phronesium, which makes him so happy that he is soon willing to play along and accept, in the face of all the evidence to the contrary, that Phronesium was pregnant and has now given birth.

Act divisions did not exist in Plautine comedy but did in the Greek models. Modern editors of Plautus follow the act divisions introduced during the Renaissance, which means that we have a lengthy second act (ll. 209–644); since the stage does not become empty after l. 208, this modern act division cannot correspond to the one in the Greek original. A more suitable end for the first act in the Greek play would be after l. 447. This division would give us a similar lack of balance because of a long first act and a short second act, but at least the stage is empty after l. 447.

If we follow the Renaissance act division, the second act starts with a monologue of Astaphium, who further expounds her philosophy of life and mentions a third lover of Phronesium, the young farmer Strabax. Strabax is uncouth and presumably ugly, as his Greek name means "squint-eyed," but he is held in high esteem because of his wealth. In addition to a country residence, his father owns the house next to Phronesium's. When Astaphium goes over to check if Strabax is in town, she is worried that she might meet Truculentus, a slave owned by the father of Strabax.

It is indeed Truculentus who answers the door, and he does credit to his name, which means "savage" or "uncivilized": he is rude and unfriendly toward Astaphium because he feels that Phronesium is damaging Strabax both morally and financially, his speech is full of rural imagery, and he cannot avoid a number of malapropisms. In short, he is a caricature of the character typical of previous generations and glorified in other literary genres. The irony is that he is a slave rather than a freeborn citizen. Yet despite all his blustering and verbal aggression, he cannot entirely hide his admiration for Astaphium's beauty (l. 290). Equally interesting is the fact that he mishears or misunderstands Astaphium several times, and that each time Astaphium's innocuous words are given an obscene twist by an apparently outraged Truculentus. In the end he says that he will go to the city center in order to meet the father of Strabax, whom he wants to inform of the goings-on; but as he comes out of the house in l. 669, it seems that he never made it to the center, and the father in fact never appears in the play at all.

Next, Diniarchus comes out of Phronesium's house without having met her because she is still having a bath. He sends Astaphium in and then launches into another lamentation about his financial situation and the loss of Phronesium's affections, while admitting again that he feels unable to change his behavior.

Finally Phronesium appears to an overjoyed Diniarchus; she confides to him that she has smuggled a boy into her family in order to make Stratophanes pay more, and she promises Diniarchus to continue her relationship with him at a later date. She also invites him to dinner to celebrate his safe return from abroad. Diniarchus feels honored by Phronesium's trust and duly vows to send her a gift.

As soon as he has left, Phronesium praises the wickedness of women and gets ready to play a weak new mother. After Astaphium has come out to support her mistress, Stratophanes appears on stage. Already his name, "one who makes an appearance like an army," leads us to expect the standard *miles gloriosus* or "boastful soldier"; but Stratophanes at first defies our expectations by inveighing against military men whose words outshine their actions. However, it does not take long for him to show his true colors and fully live up to the Plautine stereotype. Yet Stratophanes not only boasts but also presents expensive gifts to Phronesium. The prostitute finds fault with all of them, until Stratophanes wants to leave.

At this point we meet Cyamus,[2] a slave of Diniarchus.

---

[2] In l. 577 Cyamus is addressed as Geta in the manuscripts, a name that has found its way into some modern editions. This ethnonym is a common name for slaves in Roman comedy, but here it is unlikely to be more than a corruption that arose when manuscripts in capitals were copied: CHIAME → CHIA ME → CHIA → GETA.

He brings Phronesium five minas as a substantial gift from his master, and in addition there are food and wine for the dinner. The food and wine are also expensive; Cyamus had a budget of a whole mina for it, but tells us that he secretly took some of it aside, saying that it would be wasted one way or the other. Phronesium is very pleased with the gifts, much to the chagrin of Stratophanes, who has been watching from a distance and is now becoming aggressive. Phronesium, however, is unimpressed and rebukes him. Cyamus leaves and Phronesium goes inside, so that Stratophanes is at loss what to do. After an angry monologue he leaves as well.

The short third act (ll. 645–98) has only two scenes. In the first, Strabax arrives and is taken into the house by Astaphium in order to meet Phronesium. The money Strabax uses to pay was supposed to be given to his father, but Strabax prefers to keep it for himself to sustain his lifestyle. While such tricks are a stock motif of Roman comedy, Strabax is particularly crude and even speaks of exterminating both father and mother (ll. 660–61). In the second scene, Truculentus appears, now a changed man. He has money, which he wants to use to hire Astaphium, and he tries to be affable and witty, albeit with limited success. Only one minor outburst of indignation (ll. 694–95) shows that he has not yet completely managed to change his ways. Astaphium is happy to have a new customer, even though she gently mocks him for his linguistic peculiarities.

The subject of the fourth act (ll. 699–892) is the downfall of Diniarchus. When he appears on stage, he is still overjoyed because Cyamus has told him that his presents were welcome. But when he meets Astaphium, he has to

hear that he is not allowed inside and that the food he
bought is now being consumed by Phronesium and Stra-
bax. After Astaphium has gone back in, Diniarchus is pre-
pared to make a public scene, but suddenly the old man
Callicles appears together with one of his slave girls and
Syra, a hairdresser belonging to Phronesium; both women
are tied up and receive severe beatings from Callicles, who
relies on brute force rather than intelligent questioning to
get the information he needs. Diniarchus hides because
he is afraid that another of his indiscretions will now be
revealed. We hear that he was engaged to the daughter of
Callicles, but that there was an estrangement between the
two, resulting in a dissolution of the engagement. It turns
out that the daughter of Callicles had been raped and was
pregnant but wanted to conceal this. The boy she bore was
given to the slave girl belonging to Callicles, who passed
him on to Syra, who then gave him to Phronesium. Since
it becomes known that Diniarchus is the boy's father, he
comes forward to apologize. He promises to marry the girl
and to retrieve the boy. Callicles agrees and Diniarchus
goes to see Phronesium. As soon as they meet, however,
Phronesium persuades him without difficulty to let her
keep the boy for a while until she has got as much money
out of the soldier as possible. Diniarchus shows so little
self-control that he promises to continue his relationship
with Phronesium even after his marriage.

The final act presents us with the downfall of Strato-
phanes and Strabax. Stratophanes brings more money to
Phronesium to win her favor, and he and Strabax com-
pete for Phronesium's attention by paying and promising
money. Phronesium aptly remarks that an idiot and a mad-
man are trying to be worse off than one another, to her

own benefit (l. 950). The play ends with Phronesium's promise that she will treat the spectators in the same way.

It is unknown who wrote the Greek original of the *Truculentus*; Webster suggested Menander, Enk originally preferred a pupil of Menander, but later followed Webster, and Marx thought of Diphilus. What is beyond doubt is that Plautus must have reworked the original to a large extent. For instance, the scene in ll. 775–853 requires four speaking parts, while Greek comedy allows for only three. More important, the daughter of Callicles must know who raped her unless the rape happened at night, as in the *Aulularia*. If she knows her rapist, part of Callicles' investigation is superfluous; if the crime took place at night, a Greek playwright would certainly have mentioned this. But what is most significant is that the *Truculentus*, unlike the plays of Greek New Comedy, consists of loosely connected scenes without much of a plot and without a happy ending. *Drama* literally means "action," yet there is little of it; and not even the recognition of the baby boy as Diniarchus' child leads to a joyful resolution. What is it, then, that made Plautus so proud of this piece? The answer seems to be that this is Plautus' only satirical comedy, a play that foreshadows the work of Lucilius and Horace; one could even go so far as to say that the *Truculentus* is not just a comedy with satirical elements, but a satire dressed up as a comedy. The major theme is the way prostitutes exploit their customers, and Diniarchus, Stratophanes, and Strabax represent the lover in general at various stages of his unhappy relationship: Diniarchus, broken both mentally and financially, has already been discarded; Stratophanes, already tricked out of some money, but still rich, is in the process of being discarded; and Strabax, solvent and optimistic, is fresh enough to be exploited for some time to come.

Plautus named this play after a seemingly peripheral character; Truculentus does not do business with Phronesium herself, and if the two scenes in which he appears were cut, the piece would not lose its structure. And yet Truculentus has a more important function than merely providing comic relief. His character is emblematic of the societal changes Plautus witnessed in his own day, of the replacement of the old ways by the new ones exemplified by Phronesium. To many scholars this change has seemed so sudden that they assume the loss of some scenes. But this seems unlikely, as already Donatus must have known the play in its present form, since he too mentions the abruptness of the development (*Ad.* 986). Presumably Plautus was content with foreshadowing the change through Truculentus' lecherous behavior, and with indicating that the change was not completed fully by giving him a short angry outburst.

While the author of the Greek original of the *Truculentus* remains obscure, the time of its first performance can be established with relative certainty. As already mentioned, Cicero states that the *Truculentus* is a piece that Plautus, who died in 184 BC, wrote in his old age. This information is valuable, though somewhat vague. The musical structure of the play points in the same general direction: later comedies contain more song, and less than one-third of the *Truculentus* consists of spoken *senarii*, while the rest is made up of recited long verses and songs proper.

We can, however, date the play much more precisely

because the *Truculentus* contains three reasonably clear references to contemporary events. The most important of these is in l. 486, where *falsis de pugnis*, "about battles falsely fought," is an allusion to Cato's speech *In Q. Minucium Thermum de falsis pugnis*, "Against Quintus Minucius Thermus, about battles falsely fought"; cf. fr. 58 (Malcovati), which was delivered in 190 BC, our *terminus post quem*. In l. 75 we are told that the state is at peace. This could be a reference to the aftermath of the Battle of Magnesia, which was fought in December 190 or January 189; the peace treaty was ratified in 188. But the Aetolian War was not yet over, so we may have to assume an even later date. The third reference is found in l. 485, where a *Homeronida*, a "son of Homer," is mentioned in connection with the "battles falsely fought." The son of Homer must be Ennius, whose *Ambracia*, which celebrated the achievements of Fulvius Nobilior, was staged in December 187 on the occasion of his triumph; this triumph was preceded by some controversies (see Liv. 38.44.6). Thus the *Truculentus* was probably staged in 186 BC. If so, we can try to find an even more precise date. In l. 761 new magistrates are mentioned; magistrates were designated on January 26 and began office on March 15, so it is perhaps possible that our play was staged on March 5, 186, on the occasion of the triumph of Gnaeus Manilius (see Liv. 39.6).

Readers will notice the unusually large number of textual notes in this comedy. This is due to the particularly poor transmission of the play. Only three sections of the *Truculentus* are available in the Ambrosian palimpsest (ll. 111–44, 174–318, and 353–90), but here the text is as well preserved as elsewhere in the palimpsest. By contrast, the text presented in the Palatine manuscripts is highly corrupt. The best explanation for this situation is probably the one given by Lindsay (1896): the mistakes in the Palatine manuscripts are the characteristic reproduction errors that occur when the handwriting of a previous copyist using an early minuscule script is unfamiliar and his abbreviations are not understood properly. If manuscript B, the *Codex uetus Camerarii*, is not a direct copy of the Palatine archetype, which was written in capitals, but rather a copy of an intervening minuscule manuscript, like the other Palatine manuscripts, the mistakes can be easily explained. In B, the *Trinummus* and the *Truculentus* were copied by the same scribe, but if in the production of the intervening minuscule text a different scribe had been employed for the *Truculentus* than for the *Trinummus*, it would only be natural if the scribe copying the last two plays for manuscript B became confused and made a large number of errors when working on the *Truculentus*.

SELECT BIBLIOGRAPHY

Editions and Commentaries

Enk, P. J. (1953), *Plauti Truculentus cum prolegomenis, notis criticis, commentario exegetico* (Groningen).

Hofmann, W. (2001), *Plautus, Truculentus: Herausgegeben, übersetzt und kommentiert* (Darmstadt).

Kruse, K. H. W. (1974), *Kommentar zu Plautus Truculentus* (diss., Heidelberg).

Criticism

Dessen, C. S. (1977), "Plautus' Satiric Comedy: The *Truculentus*," *Philological Quarterly* 56: 145–68.

Enk, P. J. (1964), "Plautus' *Truculentus*," in C. Henderson Jr. (ed.), *Classical, Medieval and Renaissance Studies in Honor of Berthold Louis Ullman*, vol. 1 (Rome), 49–65.

Gratwick, A. S. (1990), "What's in a Name? The 'Diniarchus' of Plautus' *Truculentus*," in E. M. Craik (ed.), *'Owls to Athens': Essays on Classical Subjects Presented to Sir Kenneth Dover* (Oxford), 305–9.

Grimal, P. (1970–1974), "Le 'Truculentus' de Plaute et l'esthétique de la 'palliata,'" with a discussion by A. Barchiesi, *Dioniso* 45: 532–43, 544–48.

Khan, H. A. (1967), "Plautus, *Truculentus*, 525–27," *Latomus* 26: 1035–36.

Lefèvre, E. (1991), "*Truculentus* oder Der Triumph der Weisheit," in E. Lefèvre, E. Stärk, and G. Vogt-Spira (eds.), *Plautus barbarus: Sechs Kapitel zur Originalität des Plautus* (Tübingen), 175–200.

Lindsay, W. M. (1896), "On the Text of the Truculentus of Plautus," *American Journal of Philology* 17: 438–44.

Musso, O. (1969), "Sulla datazione del «Truculentus» di Plauto," *Studi Italiani di Filologia Classica* NS 41: 135–38.

Rau, P. (1985), "Textvorschläge zu Plautus' Truculentus," *Rheinisches Museum für Philologie* 128: 296–305.

TRVCVLENTVS

ARGVMENTVM

Tres unam pereunt adulescentes mulierem,
Rure unus, alter urbe, peregre tertius;
Vtque ista ingenti militem tangat bolo,
Clam sibi supposuit clandestino editum.
5 **V**i magna seruos est ac trucibus moribus,
Lupae ne rapiant domini parsimoniam.
Et is tamen mollitur. miles aduenit
Natique causa dat propensa munera.
Tandem compressae pater cognoscit omnia,
10 **V**tque illam ducat qui uitiarat conuenit,
Suomque is repetit a meretrice subditum.

arg. 9 tamen *P*, tandem ς

TRUCULENTUS

PLOT SUMMARY

Three young men are madly in love with one woman, one from the countryside, one from the city, and one from abroad. And in order to rob the soldier through a great trick, the woman stealthily pretended to have given birth to a boy born in secret. There's a slave of great brutality and savage character, trying to   5
prevent the prostitutes from getting hold of the goods his master acquired through his thriftiness. And yet he is softened up. The soldier arrives and gives enormous gifts for the sake of his supposed son. In the end the father of a girl who had been raped realizes everything and it is agreed that the man who had   10
done violence to her should marry her; the young man reclaims his son, who had been smuggled in by the prostitute.

PERSONAE

DINIARCHVS adulescens
ASTAPHIVM ancilla
TRVCVLENTVS seruos
PIIRONES1VM meretrix
STRATOPHANES miles
CYAMVS seruos
STRABAX adulescens rusticus
CALLICLES senex
ANCILLA CALLICLIS
SYRA tonstrix, ancilla Phronesii

SCAENA

Athenis

TRUCULENTUS

CHARACTERS

DINIARCHUS a young man; has been Phronesium's lover
   for longer than his rivals
ASTAPHIUM a slave girl; works for Phronesium
TRUCULENTUS a slave; belongs to the father of Strabax
PHRONESIUM a prostitute; clever and greedy
STRATOPHANES a soldier; has recently returned from
   Babylon
CYAMUS a slave; works for Diniarchus
STRABAX a young man from the countryside; wealthy, but
   uncouth
CALLICLES an old man; had once betrothed his daughter to
   Diniarchus
SERVANT GIRL OF CALLICLES has helped the daughter
   of Callicles to get rid of her baby boy, who had been born
   out of wedlock as a result of her rape by Diniarchus
SYRA a hairdresser, slave girl of Phronesium; involved in
   Phronesium's criminal activities

STAGING

The stage represents a street in Athens. To the left it leads to
the countryside and the harbor, to the right to the city center.
In the middle of the street we find two houses: the one on the
left belongs to Phronesium, the other is the city residence of
the father of Strabax. In front of the houses there is an altar.

PROLOGVS

PRO   perparuam partem postulat Plautus loci
de uostris magnis atque amoenis moenibus,
Athenas quo sine architectis conferat.
quid nunc? daturin estis an non? annuont.

5   miror quid de urbe me ablaturum sine mora;
quid si de uostro quippiam orem? abnuont.
eu hercle! in uobis resident mores pristini,
ad denegandum ut celeri lingua utamini.
sed hoc agamus quoia huc uentum est gratia.

10   Athenis traueho, ita ut hoc est, proscaenium,
tantisper dum transigimus hanc comoediam.
hic habitat mulier nomen quoi est Phronesium;
haec huius saecli mores in se possidet:
numquam ab amatore [suo] postulat . . . id quod datum
    est,

15   sed relicuom dat operam . . . ne sit relicuom,
poscendo atque auferendo, ut mos est mulierum;
nam omnes id faciunt, quom se amari intellegunt.
ea se peperisse puerum simulat militi,
quo citius rem ab eo auorrat cum puluisculo.

5 melior me quidem uobis *P*, fateor quid de urbe *Enk*, sciunt quid de urbe *Kruse*, miror quidem a uobis *Rau*, miror quid de urbe *scripsi* 10 Athenis tracto *P*, Atenis traueho *Enk*, Athenas tracto *Rau* 14 suo *del. Weise*

PROLOGUE

Enter the SPEAKER OF THE PROLOGUE.

PRO Plautus asks for a tiny piece of space from your great and
beautiful city, so that he may bring Athens there with-
out engineers. Well then? Are you going to give it to
me or not? (*looks around*) They nod in agreement. I'm   5
surprised that I can take something away from the city
without hindrance. What if I were to ask for something
from your personal possessions? (*looks around again*)
They shake their heads in disagreement. Goodness! Your
ancient habits remain in you, so that you have a quick
tongue for saying no.

But let's sort out what I've come here for. I'm moving   10
this stage, just as it is, from Athens over to here for as
long as we're staging this comedy. (*pointing to the house
on the left*) Here lives a woman whose name is Phrone-
sium; she has the habits of this generation within her:
she never asks a lover for . . . what has already been
given, but takes care that what remains . . . should not   15
remain, by demanding and by taking away, as is the habit
of women; yes, they all do that when they realize that
they're loved.

She is pretending to a soldier that she's born him a
son, so that she may sweep his property away from him

20 quid multa? *** †stuic superet muliere†
†hiscum anima ad eum habenti erce teritur.†

ACTVS I

I. i: DINIARCHVS

DIN non omnis aetas ad perdiscendum sat est
amanti, dum id perdiscat, quot pereat modis;
neque eam rationem eapse umquam educet Venus,
25 quam penes amantum summa summarum redit,
quot amans exemplis ludificetur, quot modis
pereat, quotque exoretur exorabulis:
quot illic blanditiae, quot illic iracundiae
sunt, quot supplicia danda, di uostram fidem, hui!
30 quid periurandum est etiam, praeter munera!
primumdum merces annua, is primus bolust,
ob eam tres noctes dantur; interea loci
aut aera aut uinum aut oleum aut triticum;
temptat benignusne an bonae frugi sies:
35 quasi in piscinam rete qui iaculum parat,
quando abiit rete pessum, adducit lineam;
si inierit rete piscis, ne effugiat cauet:
dum huc dum illuc rete uortit, impedit
piscis usque adeo donicum eduxit foras.
40 itidem est amator: si quod oratur dedit

20–21 *uersus et mutili et corrupti* quid multa? ⟨uita⟩ si huic su-
pererit mulieri/uiscum, hamum, laqueum habenti, hercle exercebitur
Lindsay 29 sui perclamanda *P*, supplicia danda *Bücheler*, su-
perba facta *Spengel*

all the more quickly, down to the last speck. What need   20
is there for many words? ***

Exit the SPEAKER OF THE PROLOGUE.

ACT ONE

Enter DINIARCHUS *from the right.*

DIN   For a lover not even an entire lifetime of learning is
enough to learn in how many ways he's being destroyed.
Not even Venus herself, in whose hands lie the sum and   25
substance of lovers, will be able to count up by how many
methods a lover is tricked, in how many ways he is de-
stroyed, and with how many entreaties he's entreated.
How many flattering words there are, how many out-
bursts of anger, how often one has to give satisfaction!
Gods, your protection! Oh! The false oaths one has to   30
give, in addition to the presents!

Firstly a year's pay, that's her first haul; for that three
nights are granted. In the meantime there's money or
wine or oil or wheat. She's testing whether you're indul-
gent or thrifty; just like the man who gets a casting net   35
ready for catching fish: when the net sinks to the bottom,
he pulls at the string; if a fish enters the net, he makes
sure it doesn't escape: he turns the net this way and that
and keeps the fish entangled until he's taken them out.
A lover is just the same: if he gives what he's asked for   40

---

30 perierandum *P*, pollicitandum *Enk*
37 siniecit *B*, sinietit *CD*, si inierit *Bücheler*
38 or *P*, uortit *Spengel*

atque est benignus potius quam frugi bonae,
adduntur noctes; interim ille hamum uorat;
si semel amoris poculum accepit meri
eaque intra pectus se penetrauit potio,
45   extemplo et ipsus periit et res et fides.
si iratum scortum forte est amatori suo,
bis perit amator, ab re atque ⟨ab⟩ animo simul;
sin alter alteri propitiust, fide perit.
si raras noctes ducit, ab animo perit;
50   sin increbrauit, ipsus gaudet, res perit.
50ᵃ   ita agitur tecum in aedibus lenoniis:
prius quam unum dederis, centum quae poscat parat:
aut periit aurum aut conscissa pallula est
aut empta ancilla aut aliquod uasum argenteum
aut uasum ahenum antiquom aut lectus sculptilis
55   aut armariola Graeca aut—aliquid semper ⟨est⟩
quod praestet debeatque amans scorto suo.
atque haec celamus nos clam magna industria,
quom rem fidemque nosque nosmet perdimus,
ne qui parentes neu cognati sentiant;
60   quos quom celamus si faximus conscios,
qui nostrae aetati tempestiuo temperent,
62   unde anteparta demus postpartoribus,
62ᵃ   faxim lenonum nec scortorum plus siet

47 ab² *add. Lambinus*   48 potius est *P*, propitiust *Bücheler* idem *P*, fide *Lindsay in apparatu*, itidem *Camerarius*

50 sin crebrauit *B*, si increbrauit *D¹*, si increpauit *CD²*, sin increbrauit *Camerarius*

50ᵃ ita et *CD*, iteca *B*, ita est *Enk*, ita agitur tecum *Leo* lenosis *P*, lenoniis ς, lenonis *Schoell uersum del. Schoell*

54 aliquod *P*, antiquom *Bücheler* laptiles *P*, sculptilis *Kiessling*

and is indulgent rather than thrifty, nights are added;
in the meantime he swallows the hook. Once he takes
the cup of undiluted love and this drink enters into his
breast, he himself, his fortune, and his reputation have 45
perished instantly. If by chance the prostitute is angry
with her lover, the lover perishes twice, with regard to
his fortune and to his mind; but if they are well-disposed
toward each other, he perishes in his reputation. If he
hires infrequent nights, he perishes with regard to his
mind; but if he increases them, he himself is happy and 50
his fortune perishes.

That's how you're treated in the houses of pimps:
before you give one thing, she finds a hundred things to
ask for: a piece of jewelry got lost or a mantle got torn, a
slave girl was bought or some silver vessel, or an old
bronze vessel or an engraved couch, or Greek jewelry 55
boxes or—there's always something which a lover should
get for his prostitute and which he owes her.

And when we're ruining our fortune, credibility, and
ourselves, we make a great effort to keep this secret and
under cover, so that our parents and relatives won't find
out somehow. If instead of concealing it from them we 60
informed them, the people who'd moderate our youth at
the right time, from whom we'd pass on property ac-
quired in the past to those acquiring it later, I'd bet
there would be fewer pimps and prostitutes and fewer

---

55 est *add. Camerarius*
56 petra *P*, praestet *Bücheler*
57 mina *P*, magna *Leo*, nimia *Brakman*
60 facimus *P*, faximus *Camerarius*, faciamus *Lindsay in apparatu*
62[a] et *P*, nec *Lindsay*   est *P*, siet *Lindsay*

et minus damnosorum hominum quam nunc sunt siet.
nam nunc lenonum et scortorum plus est fere
65 quam olim muscarum est quom caletur maxume.
nam nusquam alibi si sunt, circum argentarias
scorta et lenones quasi sedent cottidie.
ea nimia est ratio; quippe qui certo scio
fere plus scortorum esse iam quam ponderum.
70 quos equidem quam ad rem dicam in argentariis
referre habere, nisi pro tabulis, nescio,
ubi aera perscribantur usuraria:
accepta dico, expensa ne qui censeat.
postremo id magno in populo multis hominibus,
75 re placida atque otiosa, uictis hostibus:
amare oportet omnis qui quod dent habent.
nam mihi haec meretrix quae hic habet, Phronesium,
78 suom nomen omne ex pectore emouit meo,
78ᵃ Φρονῆσιν, nam φρόνησις est sapientia.
nam me fuisse huic fateor summum atque intumum,
80 quod amantis multo pessumum est pecuniae;
eadem postquam alium repperit qui plus daret,
damnosiorem meo exinde immouit loco,
quem antehac odiosum sibi esse memorabat mala,
Babyloniensem militem. is nunc dicitur
85 uenturus peregre; eo nunc commenta est dolum:

spendthrifts than there are now; now there are practi-
cally more pimps and prostitutes than there are flies at   65
the height of summer. Well, even if they're nowhere else,
the prostitutes and pimps sit around the banks virtually
every day. They make up an enormous total; yes, I know
for sure that there are practically more prostitutes than
weights. I don't know what the point is of having them   70
in the banks, except as tablets where loans are recorded;
I mean loans that people have received, in case anyone
thinks of loans people have made.[1]

In short, this happens in a great people with a large
population, when the political situation is peaceful and   75
calm and the enemy has been defeated: everybody who
has something to give ought to be in love.

Well, this prostitute who lives here, Phronesium, has
removed her name from my breast in its entirety, Phro-
nesis, for *phronesis* means "wisdom."[2] Yes, I admit that
I was her dearest and closest friend, which is by far the   80
worst thing for a lover's money. But after she found
someone else who could give her more, she ushered
the greater spendthrift into my place, even though the
crooked woman used to say before this that he was hate-
ful to her, the soldier from Babylon. Now he's said to be   85
coming from abroad. That's why she has come up with a

[1] I.e., what customers lend to pimps will not receive interest and
probably will not even be paid back, whereas loans that pimps give to
their customers are recorded carefully because they have to be paid
back with interest.

[2] *Phronesis* is a contracted form of the name *Phronesium.* The
name *Phronesis* and the common noun *phronesis* can be distinguished
by their accentuation in Greek.

86	peperisse simulat sese, ut me extrudat foras;
88	atque ut cum solo pergraecetur milite,
87	eum esse simulat militem puero patrem.
88ª	eo isti suppositum puerum opinor pessumae.
89	mihi uerba retur dare se? an me censuit
90	celare se potesse, grauida si foret?
	nam ego Lemno aduenio Athenas nudiustertius,
	legatus quo hinc cum publico imperio fui.
	sed haec quidem eius Astaphium est ancillula;
	cum ea quoque etiam mihi fuit commercium.

I. ii: ASTAPHIVM. DINIARCHVS

95	AST	ad fores auscultate atque asseruate aedis,
		nequis aduentor grauior abaetat quam adueniat,
		neu, qui manus attulerit sterilis intro ad nos,
		grauidas foras exportet. noui ego hominum mores;
		ita nunc adulescentes morati sunt: quini
100		aut seni adueniunt ad scorta congerrones;
		consulta sunt consilia: quando intro aduenerunt,
		unus eorum aliqui osculum amicae usque oggerit, dum illi agant ceteri cleptae;
		sin uident quempiam se asseruare, obludiant qui custodem oblectent
		per ioculum et ludum; de nostro saepe edunt: quod fartores, faciunt.
105		fit pol hoc, et pars spectatorum scitis pol haec uos me hau mentiri.

87 *post* 88 *pos. Kruse*
88ª eum *P*, eo ς   opus *P*, opinor *Dombart*
102 oculum *P*, osculum *Camerarius*, poculum *Wieland*
103 obludeant *P*, obludiant *Gronovius*, obludunt *Merula*

trick now: she's pretending to have given birth so as to throw me out; and in order to live in Greek style with the soldier alone, she pretends that this soldier is the boy's father. I think that's why this wicked woman had a boy smuggled into her household. Does she think she's fooling me? Did she believe she could conceal it from me if she'd been pregnant? I reached Athens from Lemnos the day before yesterday; I'd been sent there as an envoy with state authority. (*as the door of Phronesium's house opens*) But this is her servant girl Astaphium; I've also had dealings with her.

Enter ASTAPHIUM *from Phronesium's house.*

AST   (*into the house*) Listen at the door and watch over the house, so that no customer leaves more heavily laden than he was when he arrived and so that the man who brings barren hands inside to our place does not take them outside teeming. (*to the audience*) I know people's ways; this is what young men are like nowadays: five or six boon companions arrive at the prostitutes' at one time; their plans are settled. When they come in, one of them keeps kissing his girlfriend while the other thieves are doing their business. But if they see that someone's watching them, they play the fool in order to entertain the guardian through joke and jest; they often eat from what belongs to us: they do what sausage makers do.[3] This does happen, and some of you spectators know that I'm not lying to you in this. For them it's an exploit and

90

100

105

---

[3] Sausage makers eat part of the meat they receive and put other things into the casings.

ibi est ibus pugnae et uirtuti de praedonibus praedam
    capere.

107–
10   at ecastor nos rursum lepide referimus gratiam furibus
    nostris:

nam ipsi uident quom eorum aggerimus bona atque
    etiam ultro ipsi aggerunt ad nos.

DIN   me illis quidem haec uerberat uerbis,
nam ego huc bona mea degessi.

AST   commemini, iam pol ego eumpse ad nos, si domi erit,
    mecum adducam.

115 DIN heus! manedum, Astaphium, prius quam abis.

AST   qui reuocat?

DIN   scies: respice huc.

AST   quis est?

DIN   uobis qui multa bona esse uolt.

AST   dato,
si esse uis.

DIN   faxo erunt. respice huc modo.

AST   oh!
enicas me miseram, quisquis es.

120 DIN pessuma, mane.

AST   optume, odio es.
Diniarchusne illic est? atque is est.

DIN   salua sis.

AST   et tu.

DIN   fer contra manum et pariter gradere.

125 AST tuis seruio atque audiens sum imperiis.

DIN   quid agis?

AST   ualeo et ualidum teneo.
peregre quoniam aduenis, cena detur.

	an honor to rob the robbers of their booty there. But we return the favor to our thieves nicely: they themselves look on when we bring their possessions here, and they themselves carry them here to us of their own accord.	110
DIN	(*aside*) With those words she's scourging me because I brought all my possessions here.	
AST	(*into the house again, reacting to a noise from within*) I remember, I'll bring him along to us now if he's at home.	
DIN	Hey! Wait, Astaphium, before you leave.	115
AST	(*without looking*) Who's calling me back?	
DIN	You'll find out: look here.	
AST	Who is it?	
DIN	Someone who wants you to have lots of good things.	
AST	Give them to us if you want us to have them.	
DIN	I'll make sure that you have them. Just look here.	
AST	(*still not looking*) Oh! Poor me, you bore me to death, whoever you are.	
DIN	You worst of all creatures, wait!	120
AST	You best of all creatures, you're annoying me. (*looking at him*) Is that Diniarchus? Yes, it's him.	
DIN	My greetings to you.	
AST	And mine to you.	
DIN	(*solemnly*) Give me your hand and walk with me.	
AST	I serve and obey your commands.	125
DIN	(*clasping her hand*) What are you up to?	
AST	I'm healthy and holding a healthy man. Since you've arrived from abroad, you'll be given a dinner.	

---

106 ibi sibus *B*, ibi usibus *CD*, ibist ibus *Camerarius*

111 aggerimus Ω, agerimus *Goetz et Schoell*   127 cena detur *A*, centur *P*, cenetur *Lindsay*

DIN	bene dicis benigneque uocas, Astaphium.
AST	amabo,
	sine me ire era quo iussit.
DIN	eas. sed quid ais?
AST	quid uis?
DIN	dic quo iter inceptas; quis est? quem arcessis?
AST	Archilinem
	meretricem.
DIN	mala tu femina es, oles unde es disciplinam.
	manufesto mendaci, mala, teneo te.
AST	quid iam, amabo?
DIN	quia te adducturam huc dixeras eumpse, non eampse;
	nunc mulier facta est iam ex uiro: mala es praestrigia-
	trix.
	sed tandem eloquere, quis is homo est, Astaphium?
	nouos amator?
AST	nimis otiosum te arbitror hominem esse.
DIN	qui arbitrare?
AST	quia tuo uestimento et cibo alienis rebus curas.
DIN	uos mihi dedistis otium.
AST	qui, amabo?
DIN	ego expedibo.
	rem perdidi apud uos, uos meum negotium apstulistis.
	si rem seruassem, fuit ubi negotiosus essem.
AST	an tu te Veneris publicum aut Amoris alia lege
	habere posse postulas quin otiosus fias?
DIN	illa, haud ego, habuit publicum: peruorse interpretaris;

130 (at "dic quo iter inceptas")
135 (at "sed tandem eloquere")
140 (at "si rem seruassem")

128 bene dicis benigneque uocas *A*, benigne dicis *P*
131 meretricem *A*, obstetricem *P*

DIN   That's nice of you to say and it's kind of you to invite me, Astaphium.

AST   Please let me go where my mistress told me to.

DIN   Do go. But what do you say?

AST   What do you want?

DIN   Tell me where you're off to. Who is it? Who are you   130
fetching?

AST   The prostitute Archilis.

DIN   You're a bad woman, you smell of your home training.
I've caught you in the act of lying, you crook.

AST   How so, please?

DIN   Because you said that you'd bring "him" here, not "her."
Now the man has turned into a woman: you're a sly
trickster. But do tell me, who is this fellow, Astaphium?   135
A new lover?

AST   I think you have far too much free time.

DIN   Why do you think so?

AST   Because you care about other people's business while
providing your own clothing and food.[4]

DIN   You have given me free time.

AST   How, please?

DIN   I'll explain. I lost my possessions at your place, you've
taken my business away from me. If I'd saved my posses-   140
sions, I'd have somewhere to do business.

AST   Do you really expect to be able to occupy the public land
of Venus or Love except on the terms of becoming a man
of leisure?

DIN   She occupied the public land, not me. You're giving it a

---

[4] I.e., he works without pay.

nam aduorsum legem meam ob meam scripturam pe-
cudem cepit.

145 AST   plerique idem quod tu facis faciunt rei male gerentes:
ubi non est scripturam unde dent, incusant publicanos.

     DIN   male uortit res pecuaria mihi apud uos: nunc uicissim
uolo habere aratiunculam pro copia hic apud uos.

     AST   non aruos hic, sed pascuost ager: si arationes
150   habituris, qui arari solent, ad pueros ire meliust.
hunc nos habemus publicum, illi alii sunt publicani.

     DIN   utrosque pernoui probe.

     AST   em istoc pol tu otiosu's,
quom et illic et hic peruorsus es. sed utriscum rem
esse mauis?

     DIN   procaciores estis uos, sed illi periuriosi;
155   illis perit quicquid datur neque ipsis apparet quic-
quam:
uos saltem si quid quaeritis, ebibitis et comestis.
postremo illi sunt improbi, uos nequam et gloriosae.

     AST   male quae in nos dicis, ea omnia tibi dicis, Diniarche,
et nostram et illorum uicem.

     DIN   qui istuc?

     AST   rationem dicam:
160   quia qui alterum incusat probri, sumpse enitere opor-
tet.

149 rationes *P*, arationes *Valla*
154 periuriosi *P*, periuriores *Brix*
157 quam *P*, nequam *Merula*   gloriosi *P*, gloriosae *Valla*
158 illis *P*, dicis *Spengel*

[5] A tax collector may keep cattle only if the pasturage tax has not
been paid.

wrong twist: against the law she impounded my cattle in
lieu of pasturage tax.[5]

AST   Most people do the same as you do when they're unsuc-   145
cessful: when they don't have the means to pay the pas-
turage tax, they blame the tax collectors.

DIN   Your land for grazing cattle has turned out poorly for me;
now in turn I want to have a little plow land here at your
place, as far as circumstances allow.[6]

AST   This isn't land for plowing, but for grazing.[7] If you're
keen on having plow land, you'd better go to boys, who   150
are used to being plowed. We occupy this public land,
but over there there are other tax collectors.

DIN   I know both very well.

AST   There, that's why you're a man of leisure, because you're
misguided both there and here. But which of the two do
you prefer to have dealings with?

DIN   You are more licentious, while they are addicted to per-
jury. Whatever is given to boys is lost to those who give   155
it, and the boys themselves don't have anything to show
for it. You at least drink and eat it up when you get some-
thing. In short, they are shameless, you are wicked and
conceited.

AST   All the insults you utter against us you utter against your-
self instead of us and them, Diniarchus.

DIN   How so?

AST   I'll tell you the reason: because a man who accuses an-   160
other of an offense ought to be blameless himself. You,

[6] Ambiguous expression; he means both "as far as my means allow"
and "as far as you can provide it."

[7] *Plowing* is a metaphor for anal intercourse, while *grazing* refers
to regular sex.

tu a nobis sapiens nihil habes, nos nequam aps ted ha-
    bemus.

DIN o Astaphium, haud istoc modo solita es me ante appel-
    lare,

sed blande, quom illuc quod apud uos nunc est apud
    med habebam.

AST dum uiuit, hominem noueris: ubi mortuost, quiescat.

165 te dum uiuebas noueram.

DIN   an me mortuom arbitrare?

AST qui potis [est], amabo, planius? qui antehac amator
    summus

habitu's[t], nunc ad amicam uenis querimonias referre.

DIN uostra hercle factum iniuria, quae properauistis olim:

rapere otiose oportuit, diu ut essem incolumis uobis.

170 AST amator similest oppidi hostilis.

DIN   quo argumento[st]?

AST quam primum expugnari potis [est], tam id optumum
    est amicae.

DIN ego fateor, sed longe aliter est amicus atque amator:

certe hercle quam ueterrumus, tam homini
    optumus‹t› amicus.

non hercle ‹ego omnino› occidi, sunt mi etiam fundi
    et aedes.

175 AST quor, opsecro, ergo ante ostium pro ignoto alienoque
    astas?

‹i› intro, haud alienus tu quidem es; nam ecastor ne-
    minem hodie

---

161 te *CD*, ce *B*, ted *Bothe*   habeamus *BC*, abeamus *D*, habe-
mus ʂ   163 haberem *P*, habebam *Luebbert*   164 quiescas *P*,
quiescat *Bothe*   166 est *del. Bothe*   167 habitus si istunc *B*,
habitus est istunc *CD*, habitu's nunc *Spengel*   uerimonia *P*, querimo-
nias *Camerarius*

the wise man, have nothing from us, we, the bad women, have it from you.

DIN O Astaphium, that's not the way you used to address me before, but flatteringly, when I had the property at my place which is at yours now.

AST While he's alive, you should know a man; when he's dead, let him rest in peace. I knew you as long as you were   165 alive.

DIN Do you actually consider me dead?

AST Please, how could one be so more plainly? You, who were considered a first-rate lover before, are now coming to your girlfriend to bring her nothing but your complaints.

DIN It happened through your fault: you were in such a rush back then. You should have plundered me slowly, so that you'd have me intact for a long time.

AST A lover resembles an enemy town.   170

DIN On what account?

AST The sooner he can be conquered, the better it is for the girlfriend.

DIN I admit it, but there's a big difference between a friend and a lover. Surely the older a friend is, the better he is for a man. I haven't died completely, I still have land and houses.

AST Then please, why are you standing in front of the door   175 like a stranger and outsider? Go in, you for one aren't an

170 argumento[st] ς
171 est *del. Kiessling*
173 a momini *P*, tam homini *Spengel*   optimus‹t› *Camerarius*
174 ego omnino *add. Brix*
176 i *add.* ς

		mage amat corde atque animo suo, si quidem habes
		fundum atque aedis.
	DIN	in melle sunt linguae sitae uostrae atque orationes,
		facta atque corda in felle sunt sita atque acerbo aceto:
180		eo dicta lingua dulcia datis, corde amara facitis.
[181	AST	amantes si qui non danunt—non didici fabulari.
181ᵃ	DIN	†amantis si cui quod dabo non est†—non didici fabu-
		lari.]
	AST	non istaec, mea benignitas, decuit te fabulari,
		sed istos qui cum geniis suis belligerant parcepromi.
	DIN	mala es atque eadem quae soles illecebra.
	AST	ut exspectatus
185		peregre aduenisti! quam, opsecro, cupiebat te era ui-
		dere!
	DIN	quid tandem?
	AST	te unum ex omnibus amat.
	DIN	eugae! fundi et aedes,
		per tempus subuenistis. sed quid ais, Astaphium?
	AST	quid uis?
	DIN	estne intus nunc Phronesium?
	AST	utut aliis, tibi quidem intus.
	DIN	ualetne?
	AST	immo edepol melius iam fore spero, ubi te uidebit.
190	DIN	hoc nobis uitium maxumum est: quom amamus tum
		perimus;
		si illud quod uolumus dicitur, palam quom mentiuntur,
		uerum esse insciti credimus, ne ut iusta utamur ira.

181 *uersum om.* A   181ᵃ *uersum qui nihil est nisi uitiosa lectio uersus praecedentis om.* P   185 *nam* Ω, *quam* Seyffert

192 *uias utamur* A, *uti nestu mutuamur (mutuantur D)* P, *ut iusta utamur* Bücheler

286

outsider: she doesn't love anyone more in her heart and mind today, (*aside*) if indeed you have land and houses.

DIN   Your tongues and talks are soaked in honey, but your actions and hearts are soaked in gall and biting vinegar. That's why you give us sweet words with your tongues,   180
but do bitter things with your hearts.

[AST   If any lovers aren't giving anything—I haven't learned to speak.

DIN   ***—I haven't learned to speak.]

AST   It wasn't appropriate for you to say that, my generous friend, but for those niggards who wage war against their own well-being.

DIN   You're sly and the same temptress as usual.

AST   How we longed for you to come back from abroad!   185
Please, how keen my mistress was to see you!

DIN   Really? Why?

AST   You alone she loves out of all men.

DIN   (*aside*) Hurray! Land and houses, you've come to my assistance just in time. (*aloud*) But what do you say, Astaphium?

AST   What do you want?

DIN   Is Phronesium at home now?

AST   However she treats others, as far as you are concerned she is at home.

DIN   Is she well?

AST   Yes, and I hope she'll be even better now when she sees you.

DIN   (*half aside*) This is our greatest problem: when we're in   190
love, we perish; if the things we want to hear are said, when they're lying openly, we dimwits believe them to be true, let alone that we should have righteous anger.

	AST	heia! haud ita est res.
	DIN	ain tu eam me amare?
	AST	immo unice unum.
	DIN	peperisse audiui.
	AST	ah, opsecro, tace, Diniarche!
	DIN	quid iam?

195 AST horresco misera, mentio quotiens fit partionis,
ita paene nulla tibi fuit Phronesium. i intro, amabo,
uise illam. atque opperimino: iam exibit; nam lauabat.

DIN quid ais tu? quae numquam fuit praegnas qui parere
potuit?
nam equidem illi uterum, quod sciam, numquam extu-
mere sensi.

200 AST celabat metuebatque te, ne tu sibi persuaderes
ut abortioni operam daret puerumque ut enicaret.

DIN tum pol istic est puero pater Babyloniensis miles,
quoius nunc ista aduentum expetit.

AST immo ab eo ut nuntiatum est,
iam hic affuturum aiunt eum. nondum aduenisse mi-
ror.

205 DIN ibo igitur intro?

AST quippini? tam audacter quam domum ad te;
nam tu quidem edepol noster es etiam nunc, Diniar-
che.

DIN quam mox te huc recipis?

AST iam hic ero: prope est profecta quo sum.

DIN redi uero actutum. ego interim hic apud uos opperibor.

199 *uel* illic

288

AST   (*overhearing*) Goodness! It's not like that.

DIN   Do you say that she's in love with me?

AST   Yes, with you alone.

DIN   I've heard that she's given birth.

AST   Ah, please, be quiet, Diniarchus!

DIN   Why?

AST   Poor me, I shudder every time there's a mention of birth,   195
that's how close your Phronesium came to dying. Please
go in and see her. Or rather, wait: she'll come out in a
moment; she was having a bath.

DIN   What do you say? How could a woman who was never
pregnant give birth? Well, as far as I know, I never no-
ticed her womb swell up.

AST   She hid it and was afraid that you'd urge her to have an   200
abortion and kill the child.

DIN   Then that boy's father is the soldier from Babylon, whose
arrival she's awaiting eagerly now.

AST   Yes. According to a message from him, they say he'll be
here soon. I'm surprised he hasn't arrived yet.

DIN   Shall I go in then?   205

AST   Why not? As boldly as into your own house; you're still
one of us, even now, Diniarchus.

DIN   How soon are you returning here?

AST   I'll be back soon; the place I'm bound for is close by.

DIN   Do return at once. In the meantime I'll wait here at your
place.

Exit DINIARCHUS into the house of Phronesium.

ACTVS II

II. i: ASTAPHIVM

AST hahahae! requieui,

210 quia intro abit odium meum.

tandem sola sum. nunc quidem meo arbitratu

loquar libere quae uolam et quae lubebit.

huic homini amanti mea era apud nos naeniam dixit
   domi,

nam fundi et aedes obligatae sunt ob Amoris praedium.

215 uerum apud hunc mea era sua consilia summa eloqui-
   tur libere,

magisque adeo ei consiliarius hic amicust quam auxilia-
   rius.

dum fuit, dedit; nunc nihil habet: quod habebat nos
   habemus,

iste id habet quod nos habuimus. humanum facinus
   factum est.

actutum fortunae solent mutari, uaria uita est:

220 nos diuitem istum meminimus atque iste pauperes nos:

uorterunt sese memoriae; stultus sit qui id miretur.

si eget, necesse est nos pati: amauit, aequom ei factum
   est.

piaculum est miserere nos hominum rei male geren-
   tum.

[bonis esse oportet dentibus lenam probam, ar—

225 ridere ut quisque ueniat blandeque alloqui,

male corde consultare, bene lingua loqui.]

meretricem similem sentis esse condecet,

quemquem hominem attigerit, profecto ei aut malum
   aut damnum dare.

ACT TWO

ASTAPHIUM slowly walks over to the house of Strabax.

AST Ha, ha, ha! I'm relieved that my nuisance has gone in-   210
side. At long last I'm alone. Now I'll say freely at my own
discretion what I want and what I like. My mistress sang
the funeral dirge for this lover at our place at home be-
cause his land and houses are mortgaged for payments
on Love's estate. But my mistress confides her most im-   215
portant plans to him freely, and to her he's more of a
friend to give advice than one to give aid. As long as he
had, he gave; now he has nothing: we have what he used
to have, and he has what we had. It's the way the world
goes. Fortunes tend to change in an instant, life is in-
constant. We remember him rich and he remembers us   220
poor; the situations remembered have changed. It would
take a fool to be surprised about it. If he's poor, we must
bear it; he was in love, justice was done to him. It would
be a sin for us to take pity on those who mismanage their
affairs.

[A decent procuress should have good teeth; when-   225
ever someone comes, she should smile at him and ad-
dress him flatteringly, make crooked plans in her heart,
and speak nicely with her tongue.] A prostitute should
be similar to a briar; she should indeed cause damage or

---

213 domi *Festus*, de bonis Ω, bonis *Spengel*   224–26 *del.*
Fleckeisen   224–25 adridere Ω, adripere *Bücheler cui systema*
iambicum displicet   225 quisque *A*, quisquis *P*   227 sentis
similem esse *A*, esse similem sentis *P*, similem sentis esse *Fleck-*
eisen   condecet *P*, addecet *A*   228 dari Ω, dare *Bothe*

	numquam amatoris meretricem oportet causam nos- cere,
230	quin, ubi nil det, pro infrequente eum mittat militia domum.
231	neque umquam erit probus quisquam amator nisi qui rei inimicust suae.
234	nugae sunt nisi [qui], modo quom dederit, dare iam lubeat denuo;
235	is amatur hic apud nos, qui quod dedit id oblitust da- tum.
236	probust amator, qui relictis rebus rem perdit suam.
232	dum habeat, tum amet; ubi nil habeat, alium quaestum coepiat.
233	aequo animo, ipse si nil habeat, aliis qui habent det locum.
237	at nos male agere praedicant uiri solere secum
	nosque esse auaras. qui sumus? quid est quod male agimus tandem?
	nam ecastor numquam satis dedit suae quisquam ami- cae amator,
240	nec pol nos satis accepimus neque umquam ulla satis poposcit.
	nam quando sterilis est amator ab datis,
	si negat se habere quod det, soli credimus,
	nec satis accipimus, satis quom quod det non habet:
	semper datores nouos oportet quaerere,
245	qui de thesauris integris demus danunt.
	uelut hic agrestis est adulescens qui hic habet,

232–33 *post* 235 *A, post* 236 *Thierfelder*
234 qui modo *A,* quodomodo *B,* quod amodo *CD,* modo *Bothe*
235 is amatur hic Ω, is hic amatur *Müller*

loss to whoever she touches. A prostitute ought never to take notice of a lover's circumstances; rather, when he doesn't give anything, she should send him back home as a deserter from military service. No one will ever be a decent lover unless he's an enemy of his own possessions. It's a waste of time unless he wants to give again immediately when he's just given something. That man is loved here at our place who forgets that he's given what he's given. It's a decent lover who drops everything else and then drops his money too. As long as he has something, he should be in love. When he has nothing, he should begin another occupation. If he has nothing himself, he should calmly give his place to those who do. But men say that we usually treat them badly and that we're greedy. In what way are we greedy? How is it actually that we treat them badly? No lover has ever given enough security[8] to his girlfriend, we have never received enough of it, and no girl has ever demanded enough: when a lover is barren with his gifts, if he says he doesn't have anything to give, we believe him on his own, and we don't receive security when he doesn't have any to give.

One should always look for new givers, who give from treasures still untouched. For instance there's this country lad who lives here, a very delightful mortal and a very

230

235

240

245

---

[8] A deliberate ambiguity: *satis* means "enough," but if combined with verbs of giving or receiving it takes on the legal meaning of "guarantee, security." Astaphium says that prostitutes are greedy because they cannot get enough and that they do not lead secure lives.

---

245 demus danunt *P*, demum oggerunt *A*, demunt danunt *Pistoris*

nimis pol mortalis lepidus nimisque probus dator.
[sed is clam patrem etiam hac nocte illac per hortum
transiluit ad nos. eum uolo conuenire.]
250   sed est huic unus seruos uiolentissumus,
qui ubi quamque nostrarum uidet prope hasce aedis
     aggrediri,
item ut de frumento anseres, clamore apsterret, abigit;
ita est agrestis. sed fores, quicquid est futurum, feriam.
254–   ecquis huic tutelam ianuae gerit? ecquis intus exit?
55

II. ii: TRVCVLENTVS. ASTAPHIVM

TRVC   quis illic est qui tam proterue nostras aedis arietat?
AST   ego sum, respice ad me.
TRVC   quid "ego"?
AST   nonne "ego" uideor tibi?
TRVC   quid tibi ad hasce accessio aedis est prope aut pultatio?
AST   salue.
TRVC   sat mi est tuae salutis. nil moror. non salueo.
260   aegrotare malim quam esse tua salute sanior.
sed uolo scire, quid debetur hic tibi nostrae domi?
AST   comprime sis eiram.
TRVC   eam quidem hercle tu, quae solita es, comprime,
impudens, quae per ridiculum rustico suades stuprum.

248–49 *del.* Leo   257 nonne "ego" uideor tibi? *Astaphio dedit*
Schoell   262 eam *P,* meam *A,* eram *Spengel*

---

9 Sacerdos (*gramm.* 6.433.7–8) remarks that because *saluere*, "be
well," is a defective verb, the first-person statement employed by Truc-
ulentus is unidiomatic.

10 The word *ira*, "anger, distress," originally contained the diph-
thong *ei* in its first syllable; in Plautus' day the diphthong was still
written and possibly still pronounced, though it is more likely that in
pronunciation it had already developed into a closed *ē*. Truculentus

decent giver. [But he leaped over to us that way through the garden last night, behind even his father's back. It's him I want to meet.] But he has one most savage slave; every time he sees one of us coming close to this house, he frightens us and drives us away with his shouting, like geese from the corn; he's such a country bumpkin. But I'll knock at the door, whatever's going to happen. (*does so*) Is anyone guarding this door? Is anyone coming out? 250

255

Enter TRUCULENTUS *from the house of Strabax.*

TRUC Who is it who's battering our house so recklessly?

AST I am the one, look at me.

TRUC What do you mean, "I"?

AST Don't I seem an "I" to you?

TRUC Why have you come to this house or knocked thereon?

AST Be well.

TRUC I have enough of your well-being. I don't care for it. I'm diswell.[9] I'd rather be ill than healthy through your well-being. But I want to know, what are you owed here in our house? 260

AST Do keep your distress in check.

TRUC No, you, who are used to doing it, keep your mistress in check,[10] you shameless creature! You jokingly advise a country lad to have sex.

(probably deliberately) misunderstands the word as *ĕra*, "mistress," which leads to a different interpretation of *comprimere:* Astaphium had intended the meaning "keep in check, control," whereas Truculentus interprets it as "keep in check, rape." In the Latin, Astaphium goes on to say that Truculentus removed one letter (*eira* → *era*); in the translation this is rendered as "changing one letter" (*distress* → *mistress*).

AST		"eiram" dixi: ut decepisti! dempsisti unam litteram.
265		nimis quidem hic truculentust.
TRVC		pergin male loqui, mulier, mihi?
AST		quid [tibi] ego male dico?
TRVC		quia enim me truncum lentum nominas.

nunc adeo, nisi abis actutum aut dicis quid quaeras
    cito,
    iam hercle ego hic te, mulier, quasi sus catulos pedibus
        proteram.

AST		rus merum hoc quidem est.
TRVC		pudendum est uero clurinum pecus.
270		aduenisti huc te ostentatum cum exornatis ossibus,

quia tibi suaso infecisti propudiosa pallulam?
an eo bella es, quia accepisti armillas aeneas?

AST		nunc places, quom mi inclementer dicis.
TRVC		quid hoc quod te rogo?

mancupion qui accipias, gestas tecum ahenos anulos?

275		pignus da ni ligneae haec sint quas habes Victorias.
AST		ne attigas me.
TRVC		egon te tangam? ita me amabit sarculum,

ut ego me ruri amplexari mauelim patulam bouem

---

264 ut decepisti *A*, ut esse cepisti (i.e., ut excepisti) *P*, ut tu accepisti
Müller   266 tibi *del. Enk*   truncum lentum *A*, truculentum *P*
272 qui accepistibi armilias aeneas *A*, quiaccepisti arme (arma *CD*)
aduenias *P*

---

[11] In the Latin, Astaphium says that he is *truculentus,* "wild, rude."
Truculentus (probably on purpose) mishears this as *truncus lentus;*
truncus means "tree trunk," but can also be a euphemism for the penis,
and *lentus,* when modifying the *membrum virile,* means "limp" (cf.
Petron. 132.11).

AST   I said "distress": how you've tricked me! You've changed one letter. (*half aside*) He's such a rude chappy.   265

TRUC (*overhearing her*) Are you continuing to insult me, woman?

AST   How am I insulting you?

TRUC By calling me a lewd chopper.[11] Now unless you leave this instant or say quickly what you want, I'll stamp on you with my feet here, woman, like a sow does on its litter.

AST   This is plain farmyard!

TRUC What you really need to be ashamed of is your troop of monkeys. Have you come here to present yourself with 270 your decorated bones, because you've dyed your little cloak with gray color, you shameless creature? Are you pretty just because you've got bronze bracelets?

AST   Now that you talk rough to me, I like you.

TRUC What about the question I'm asking you? Are you carrying bronze rings with you so that you can make formal purchases?[12] Make a bet that those Victories[13] you have 275 aren't made of wood. (*tries to grab them*)

AST   Don't touch me!

TRUC I should touch you? As truly as my hoe will love me, I'd prefer embracing a cow in heat[14] on our farm and spend-

---

[12] A double insult: bronze rings were cheap and thus less desirable, and slaves were not allowed to make formal purchases through the process called *mancupatio*, for which bronze weights were required.

[13] Earrings in the shape of Victoria, the goddess of military success.

[14] This is how Spengel interprets *patula* here; Paul. Fest. 246 L. believes that the adjective means that the horns point in different directions and stand far apart from each other.

cumque ea noctem in stramentis pernoctare perpetim
quam tuas centum cenatas noctes mihi dono dari.
280   rus tu mi opprobras? ut nancta es hominem quem pu-
deat probri!
sed quid apud nostras negoti, mulier, est aedis tibi?
quid tu huc occursas, in urbem quotiensquomque
aduenimus?
AST   mulieres uolo conuenire uostras.
TRVC   quas tu mulieres
mihi narras, ubi musca nulla femina est in aedibus?
285 AST   nullan istic mulier habitat?
TRVC   rus, inquam, abierunt. abi.
AST   quid clamas, insane?
TRVC   abire hinc ni properas grandi gradu,
iam hercle ego istos fictos, compositos, crispos cincin-
nos tuos,
unguentatos usque ex cerebro euellam.
AST   quanam gratia?
TRVC   quia ad fores nostras unguentis uncta es ausa accedere
290   quiaque bucculas tam belle purpurissatas habes.
AST   erubui mecastor misera propter clamorem tuom.
TRVC   itane? erubuisti? quasi uero corpori reliqueris
tuo potestatem coloris ulli capiendi, mala!
buccas rubrica, creta omne corpus intinxti tibi.
295   pessumae estis.
AST   quid est quod uobis pessumae haec male fecerint?
TRVC   scio ego plus quam tu arbitrare scire me.
AST   quid id opsecro est
quod scias?
TRVC   erilis noster filius apud uos Strabax

285 inquam abierunt *P*, abierunt inquam *A*

298

ing an entire night with her in the straw to being given a
hundred nights with you as a gift, dinner included. Are   280
you reproaching me because of my rusticity? You really
have met someone who's ashamed of that reproach! But
what business do you have at our house, woman? Why do
you keep running here every time we come into town?

AST   I want to meet your womenfolk.

TRUC   What women are you talking about, when there isn't
even a female fly in the house?

AST   Doesn't any woman live there?   285

TRUC   They've gone to our farm, I'm telling you. Go away!

AST   Why are you shouting, you madman?

TRUC   If you don't hurry to get away from here with big steps,
I'll instantly tear those nicely arranged, fixed-up, curly,
perfumed locks of yours right out of your brains.

AST   What for?

TRUC   Because you've dared to come to our door perfumed
with perfumes and because your little cheeks are so pret-   290
tily painted with purple.

AST   Poor me, I've blushed because of your shouting!

TRUC   Really? You've blushed? As if you'd left your body the
chance to take on any color, you crook! You've painted
your cheeks with rouge and your entire body with clay.
You're absolutely vile creatures.   295

AST   What's the harm these absolutely vile creatures have
done you?

TRUC   I know more than you think I do.

AST   Please, what is it that you know?

TRUC   How our master's son Strabax is being destroyed at your

ut pereat, ut eum illiciatis in malam fraudem et pro-
brum.

AST   sanus si uideare, dicam: "dicis contumeliam."

300   nemo homo hic solet perire apud nos: res perdunt
suas;

ubi res perdidere, abire hinc si uolunt saluis licet.

ego istunc non noui adulescentem uostrum.

TRVC   ueron serio?

quid maceria illa ait in horto quae est, quae in noctes
singulas

latere fit minor, qua isto ad uos damni permensust
uiam?

305 AST   nil mirum—uetus est maceria—lateres si ueteres
ruont.

TRVC ain tu uero ueteres lateres ruere? numquam edepol
mihi

quisquam homo mortalis posthac duarum rerum cre-
duit,

ni ego ero maiori uostra facta denarrauero.

AST   estne item uiolentus ut tu?

TRVC   non enim ill' meretriculis

310   munerandis rem coegit, uerum parsimonia

duritiaque: quae nunc ad uos clam exportatur, pessu-
mae;

eam uos estis, exunguimini, ebibitis. egone haec mussi-
tem?

iam quidem hercle ibo ad forum atque haec facta nar-
rabo seni;

neque istuc insegesti tergo coget examen mali.

304 qua is hoc ad uos *Priscianus*, quaisaputuos *A*, qua isti uos *P*,
qua is ad uos ς, qua isto ad uos *Seyffert*

place and how you lure him into wicked deceit and dis-
grace.

AST If you seemed sane, I'd say: "you're insulting us." No- 300
body is ever destroyed here at our place. People waste
their money; when they've wasted it, they're free to leave
safe and sound if they so wish. I don't know that young
chap of yours.

TRUC Really and truly? What does that wall say which is in our
garden and which night by night becomes one brick
lower where he's traveled on the road to ruin over to your
place?

AST It's not surprising—the wall is old—if old bricks tumble 305
down.

TRUC Do you really say that it's old bricks tumbling down? May
no mortal ever believe me hereafter in the two things,[15]
unless I inform my older master of your deeds.

AST Is he as savage as you?

TRUC Yes, he didn't acquire his wealth by making gifts to pros- 310
titutes, but through frugality and austerity; that wealth
is now being secretly carried over to your place, you
crooks. You eat it up, anoint it up, drink it up. Should
I keep quiet about this? This instant I'll go to the fo-
rum and tell the old man about these deeds; and that
will prevent my back from getting a mass of unsown
trouble.

[15] The human and the divine.

---

311 exportatur *P*, exportantur *A*
312 ea *A*, em *BD*, hem *C*, eam *Kiessling*
314 istuc Ω, is huic *Leo*

315 AST si ecastor hic homo sinapi uictitet, non censeam
tam esse tristem posse. at pol ero beneuolens uisust
suo.
uerum ego illum, quamquam uiolentust, spero immu-
tari pote
blandimentis, hortamentis, ceteris meretriciis;
uidi equom ex indomito domitum fieri atque alias be-
luas.
320 nunc ad eram reuidebo. ‹sed› eccum odium progredi-
tur meum.
tristis exit. hau conuenit etiam hic dum Phronesium.

II. iii: DINIARCHVS. ASTAPHIVM

DIN piscis ego credo, qui usque dum uiuont lauant,
minus diu lauare quam haec lauat Phronesium.
si proinde amentur, mulieres diu quam lauant,
325 omnes amantes balneatores sient.
AST non quis parumper durare opperirier?
DIN quin hercle lassus iam sum durando miser:
mi quoque prae lassitudine opus est ‹ut› lauem.
sed opsecro hercle, Astaphium, ‹i› intro ac nuntia
330 me adesse, ut properet suade, iam ut satis lauerit.
AST licet.
DIN   audin etiam?
AST   quid uis?
DIN   di me perduint
qui te reuocaui! non tibi dicebam "i" modo?

317 potest Ω, pote *Kampmann*
318 hortamentis *A*, ornamentis *P*, oramentis *Meursius*
319 equidem exinem intu domito *B*, equidem exinen intum domito
BC, equom ex indomito domitum *Weise*
320 et cum *P*, sed eccum *Camerarius*

302

TRUCULENTUS turns toward the right exit, but then goes back into the house of Strabax.

AST   Even if this man lived on mustard, I wouldn't think that   315
he could be so fierce. Yet he seemed well-disposed to-
ward his master. But even though he's savage, I hope
he can be changed with flattering, enticements, and the
other arts of prostitutes. I've seen a horse and other
animals turning from untamed to tame. Now I'll check   320
on my mistress again. (*turns toward Phronesium's house*)
But look, my nuisance is appearing. He's coming out,
looking glum. He still hasn't met Phronesium.

Enter DINIARCHUS from Phronesium's house.

DIN   I believe that fish, which bathe as long as they live,
don't bathe for as long as Phronesium here is bathing. If
women could be loved for as long as they bathe, all lovers   325
would be bath keepers.
AST   Can't you endure waiting for a short while?
DIN   No, I'm already exhausted from enduring it, poor me:
because of my exhaustion I too need to bathe. But please,
Astaphium, go in and announce that I'm here; advise her   330
that she should hurry up and that she's bathed enough
now.
AST   All right. (*turns to go*)
DIN   Can you still hear me?
AST   (*turning around*) What do you want?
DIN   May the gods ruin me for calling you back! Didn't I just
say "go" to you?

---

328 laue *P*, ut lauem *Camerarius*   329 i *add.* ς

AST   quid iam reuocabas, improbe nihilique homo?
      tute tibi mille passum peperisti morae.
335 DIN   sed quid haec hic autem tam diu ante aedis stetit?
      nescioquem praestolata est; credo, militem.
      illum student iam; quasi uolturii triduo
      prius praediuinant quo die esuri sient:
      illum inhiant omnes, illi est animus omnibus;
340   me nemo magis respiciet, ubi is [est] huc uenerit,
      quasi abhinc ducentos annos fuerim mortuos.
      ut rem seruare suaue est! uae misero mihi!
      post factum flector, qui antepartum perdidi.
      uerum nunc si qua mi optigerit hereditas
345   magna atque luculenta, nunc postquam scio
346   dulce atque amarum quid sit ex pecunia,
349   ego istos qui nunc me culpant confutauerim:
347   ita ego illam edepol seruem itaque parce uictitem,
348   ut . . . nulla faxim cis dies paucos siet.
350   sed aestuosas sentio aperiri fores,
      quae opsorbent quicquid uenit intra pessulos.

II. iv: PHRONESIVM. DINIARCHVS

PHRO num tibi nam, amabo, ianua est mordax mea,
      quo intro ire metuas, mea uoluptas?
DIN   uer uide:
      ut tota floret, ut olet, ut nitide nitet!

    340 is est *P*, is ς
    341 quam si hinc *P*, quasi abhinc *Fleckeisen*
    349 *post 346 pos. Göller*

AST   Why did you call me back now, you worthless good-for-nothing? You've created a mile of delay for yourself.

Exit ASTAPHIUM *into Phronesium's house.*

DIN   But why did she stand here in front of the house for so   335
long? She was waiting for someone; the soldier, I believe.
Now it's him they're keen on; like vultures they have
foreknowledge three days in advance as to what day
they'll be eating on. They're all gaping at him, that's
where all their minds are. When he comes here, nobody   340
will pay any more attention to me than if I'd been dead
for two hundred years. How pleasant it is to hold on to
one's money! Poor, wretched me! I'm changing course
after the event, now that I've lost the property acquired
in the past. But if I now got hold of a big and splendid in-   345
heritance, now that I know what sweet and bitter things
money brings you, I'd silence those who are criticizing
me now: I'd hold on to it so tightly and I'd live so frugally
that . . . I'd bet it would be gone within a few days. But   350
I notice that that seething door is opening up, which
gulps down anything that comes within its bolts.[16]

Enter PHRONESIUM *from her house, accompanied by two servants.*

PHRO   Please, my darling, you don't think my door will bite you,
do you, so that you should be afraid to go in?
DIN   Look, it's springtime: how she's all in bloom, all fragrant,
all aglow!

---

[16] An allusion to Charybdis, a sea monster in the Strait of Messina
which creates whirlpools and swallows everything that comes near it.

355 PHRO quid tam inficetu's Lemno adueniens qui tuae
       non des amicae, Diniarche, sauium?
  DIN uah! uapulo hercle ego nunc, atque adeo male.
  PHRO quo te auortisti?
  DIN   salua sis, Phronesium.
  PHRO salue. hicine hodie cenas, saluos quom aduenis?
360 DIN promisi.
  PHRO   ubi cenabis?
  DIN   ubi tu iusseris.
  PHRO hic; me lubente facies.
  DIN   edepol me magis.
       nemp' tu eris hodie mecum, mea Phronesium?
  PHRO uelim, si fieri possit.
  DIN   cedo soleas mihi,
       properate, auferte mensam.
  PHRO   amabo, sanun es?
365 DIN non edepol bibere possum iam, ita animo male est.
  PHRO mane, aliquid fiet, ne abi.
  DIN   ah! aspersisti aquam.
       iam rediit animus. deme soleas, cedo bibam.
  PHRO idem es mecastor qui soles. sed dic mihi,
       benene ambulatum est?
  DIN   huc quidem hercle ad te bene,
370   quia tui uidendi copia est.
  PHRO   complectere.
  DIN lubens. heia! hoc est melle dulci dulcius.
       hoc tuis fortunis, Iuppiter, praestant meae.

    363 mihi *P*, puer *A*

PHRO	Why are you so unmannered that on your arrival from 355 Lemnos you won't give your girlfriend a kiss, Diniar- chus?
DIN	(*aside*) Bah! I'm getting a thrashing now, and a bad one at that.
PHRO	Where have you turned to?
DIN	My greetings, Phronesium.
PHRO	And mine to you. Won't you have dinner here today, since you've arrived safely?
DIN	I have a prior engagement. 360
PHRO	Where are you going to have dinner?
DIN	Where you tell me to.
PHRO	Here; you'll do me a pleasure.
DIN	Myself even more. You'll be with me today, won't you, my dear Phronesium?
PHRO	I'd love to, if it were possible.
DIN	(*as if to dinner attendants, pretending to leave the table*) Give me my sandals! Hurry up, remove the table!
PHRO	Please, are you in your right mind?
DIN	I can't drink any more, I feel so faint. 365
PHRO	Wait, we'll find a way, don't go away!
DIN	Ah! You've sprinkled water onto me. Now my mind has returned. (*as if to a dinner attendant*) Take my sandals off and give me something to drink.
PHRO	You're your usual self. But tell me, did you have a good trip?
DIN	Yes, here to you, because I have the opportunity to see 370 you.
PHRO	Embrace me.
DIN	(*doing so*) With pleasure. Ah! This is sweeter than sweet honey. In this respect my fortunes are better than yours, Jupiter.

PHRO dan sauium?

DIN   immo uel decem.

PHRO   em istoc pauper es:
    plus pollicere quam ego aps te posco aut postulo.

375   DIN   utinam a principio rei item repersisses meae
    ut nunc repercis sauiis.

PHRO   si quid tibi
    compendi facere possim, factum edepol uelim.

DIN   iam lauta es?

PHRO   iam pol mihi quidem atque oculis meis.
    num tibi sordere uideor?

DIN   non pol mi quidem;

380   uerum tempestas quondam, dum uixi, fuit
    quom inter nos sordebamus alter de altero.
    sed quod ego facinus audiui adueniens tuom
    quod tu hic me apsente noui negoti gesseris?

PHRO quid id est?

DIN   primumdum, quom tu es aucta liberis

385   quomque bene prouenisti salua, gaudeo.

PHRO concedite hinc uos intro atque operite ostium.
    tu nunc superstes solus sermoni meo es.
    tibi mea consilia semper summa credidi.
    equidem nec peperi puerum nec praegnas fui;

390   uerum assimulaui me esse praegnatem: hau nego.

DIN   quem propter, o mea uita?

PHRO   propter militem
    Babyloniensem, qui quasi uxorem sibi
    me habebat annum dum hic fuit.

---

  373 da *A*, dant *P*, dan *Camerarius*   374 posco aut *A*, *om. P*
  375 a principio rei item *P*, item a principio *A*   pepercisses *A*, par-
sissi *P*, repersisses *Spengel*   381 alter de altero *A*, alteri *P*, alter
alteri *Gruterus*   385 gaudeo *P*, gratulor *A*

PHRO Won't you give me a kiss?

DIN Even ten. (*kisses her enthusiastically*)

PHRO There, that's why you're poor: you promise more than I ask or demand from you.

DIN I wish you'd been as sparing of my finances from the 375 beginning as you're now sparing of kisses.

PHRO If I could save you anything, I'd really want it done.

DIN Are you washed now?

PHRO Yes, at least to myself and my own eyes.[17] I don't seem dirty to you, do I?

DIN No, not to me; but there was a period once while I was 380 alive when we were soiled from one another.[18] But what's this deed of yours I heard about on my arrival, that you've done new business here in my absence?

PHRO What's that?

DIN First of all, I'm happy that you've been blessed with a 385 child and that you've pulled through safe and sound.

PHRO (*to her servants*) You, go inside and shut the door. (*they obey*) You are the only witness to my speech now. I've always confided my greatest plans to you. I for one have neither given birth to a boy, nor have I been pregnant. But 390 I pretended to be pregnant, I don't deny it.

DIN Because of whom, o my life?

PHRO Because of the soldier from Babylon, who kept me like a wife during the year he was here.

---

[17] Diniarchus wants to know if she has finally finished her bath, but Phronesium thinks that he wants to know if she is clean and tidy.

[18] The verb *sordere* refers to the "defilement" suffered by sexual partners during the act.

---

390 adsimulaui *P*, adsimulasse *A*
391 que *B*, quae *CD*, quem *Bugge*

DIN   ego senseram.
        sed quid istuc? quoi rei te assimulare retulit?
395 PHRO ut esset aliquis laqueus et redimiculum,
        reuorsionem ut ad me faceret denuo.
        nunc huc remisit nuper ad me epistulam
        sese experturum quanti sese penderem:
        si quod peperissem id ⟨non n⟩ecarem ac tollerem,
400   bona sua me habiturum omnia [esse].
DIN   ausculto lubens.
        quid denique agitis?
PHRO   mater ancillas iubet,
        quoniam iam decumus mensis aduentat prope,
        aliam aliorsum ire, praemandare et quaerere
        puerum aut puellam qui supponatur mihi.
405   quid multa uerba faciam? tonstricem Syram
        nouisti nostram?
DIN   quaen erga aedis hasce habet?
        noui.
PHRO   haec, ut opera est, circumit per familias,
        puerum uestigat; clanculum ad me detulit,
        datum sibi esse dixit.
DIN   o mercis malae!
410   eum nunc non illa peperit quae peperit prior,
        sed tu posterior.
PHRO   ordine omnem rem tenes.
        nunc ut praemisit nuntium miles mihi,
        non multo post hic aderit.

399 ide carem *P*, id non necarem *Schoell*
400 esse *del. Camerarius*
406 quem *P*, quaen *Bergk*   aedem sese *P*, aedis hasce *Enk*
407 ut opera *P*, ut operast *Schoell*, data opera *Koch*

TRUCULENTUS

DIN I'd guessed as much. But what's that? Why was it impor-
     tant for you to pretend?

PHRO In order that there'd be some tie and band,[19] to make 395
     him return to me again. Now recently he sent a letter to
     me here saying that he was going to test how much I
     value him; if I didn't kill the child I'd given birth to and
     if I took it up, I'd have all his possessions. 400

DIN I hear it with pleasure. What did you do in the end?

PHRO Since the tenth month[20] was getting close already, my
     mother told each of her slave girls to go to a different
     place, to procure and look beforehand for a boy or a
     girl that could be smuggled into my household. Why 405
     should I use a lot of words? Do you know our hairdresser
     Syra?

DIN The one who lives opposite this house? I do.

PHRO She went round the households, as her job demands, and
     found a boy. She brought him to me in secret and said
     that he was given to her.

DIN What a bad piece of work! Now not the woman who gave 410
     birth to him gave birth to him, that earlier one, but you,
     the later one.

PHRO You understand the whole business to a tee. Now accord-
     ing to the message the soldier sent me, he'll be here
     shortly.

[19] Strictly speaking, a decorative band that women attach to the
back of headdresses (cf. Fest. 336 L.).

[20] Pregnancy is said to last for ten rather than nine months because
these are lunar months, which are shorter.

311

DIN   nunc tu te interim
      quasi pro puerpera hic procuras?

PHRO   quippini,

415   ubi sine labore res geri pulchre potest?
      ad suom quaestum aequom est esse quemque calli-
        dum.

DIN   quid me futurum est quando miles uenerit?
      relictusne aps te uiuam?

PHRO   ubi illud quod uolo
      habebo ab illo, facile inueniam quo modo

420   diuortium et discordiam inter nos parem:
      postid ego [totum] tecum, mea uoluptas, usque ero
      assiduo.

DIN   immo hercle uero accubuo mauelim.

PHRO [quin] dis hodie sacruficare pro puero uolo,
      quinto die quod fieri oportet.

DIN   censeo.

425 PHRO non audes aliquid dare mihi munusculum?

DIN   lucrum hercle uideor facere mi, uoluptas mea,
      ubi quippiam me poscis.

PHRO   at ego, ubi apstuli.

DIN   iam faxo hic aderit. seruolum huc mittam meum.

PHRO sic facito.

DIN   quicquid attulerit, boni consulas.

430 PHRO ecastor munus te curaturum scio,
      ut quoius me non paeniteat mittatur mihi.

416 quemque aequum est quaestum esse P, *transp. Enk*
419 inueniam CD, inuenio B   421 totum *del. Bothe*
423 quin his P, dis *Spengel*   424 optet P, oportet ς
425 mihi dare P, *transp. Camerarius*
431 mitta B, mitte CD, mittatur *Bücheler*, mittas *Camerarius*

DIN Now in the meantime you're looking after yourself like a woman who's just delivered?

PHRO Why not, when success can be had without having to   415
work for it? Everybody ought to know the tricks of his trade.

DIN What's going to happen to me when the soldier comes? Will I have to live deserted by you?

PHRO As soon as I have what I want from him, I'll easily find a means of creating divorce and disharmony among us.   420
After this, my darling, I'll be beside you permanently.

DIN But I'd prefer you to be bedside me.[21]

PHRO Today I want to sacrifice to the gods for the boy, which ought to be done on the fifth day.[22]

DIN You're right.

PHRO Don't you want to give me some tiny present?   425

DIN I feel I'm making a profit, my darling, whenever you ask me for something.

PHRO (aside) But I, when I carry it off.

DIN I'll make sure that it'll be here in a moment. I'll send my slave here.

PHRO Do.

DIN Whatever he brings here you should think well of.

PHRO I know that you'll get me such a present that I won't be   430
dissatisfied with what I'm sent.

[21] *Accubuo*, "bedside, reclining," is a nonce-formation based on Phronesium's *assiduo*, "permanently," which Diniarchus interprets as if it came from *assidere*, "sit next to someone."

[22] Reference to the *Amphidromia*, a Greek festival celebrating the introduction of a newly born child into the family.

DIN num quippiam aliud me uis?

PHRO   ut quando otium
    tibi sit ad me reuisas, et ualeas.

DIN   uale.

    pro di immortales! non amantis mulieris,

435   sed sociai unanimantis, fidentis fuit
    officium facere quod modo haec fecit mihi,
    suppositionem pueri quae mihi credidit,
    germanae quod sorori non credit soror.
    ostendit sese iam mihi medullitus:

440   se mi infidelem numquam, dum uiuat, fore.
    egone illam ut non amem? egone illi ut non bene
        uelim?
    me potius non amabo quam huic desit amor.
    ego isti non munus mittam? immo ex hoc loco
    iubebo ad istam quinque perferri minas,

445   praeterea opsonari ‹una› dumtaxat mina.
    multo illi potius bene erit quae bene uolt mihi
    quam mihi, qui mihimet omnia facio mala.

II. v: PHRONESIVM

PHRO puero isti date mammam. ut miserae
    matres sollicitaeque ex animo

450   sunt cruciantur-
451   que! edepol commentum male, quomque eam
451ᵃ   rem in corde agito,
    nimio . . . minus perhibemur malae quam

---

433 t (*sequente* u) *P*, tu *Camerarius*, et *Geppert*, nunc *Bugge*
445 una *add. Bergk*
447 mihimet omnia qui (quae *D*) mihi *P*, mihi qui mihimet omnia *Fleckeisen*
450–51 uni cruciant quae *P*, sunt crucianturque *Merula*

DIN   Do you want anything else from me?

PHRO Yes: when you have free time, visit me again; and be
well.

DIN   You too.

Exit PHRONESIUM *into her house.*

DIN   Immortal gods! It wasn't the duty of a woman in love,   435
but of a trusting soul mate, to do what she just did to me:
she confided the smuggling in of the boy to me, some-
thing which a true sister doesn't confide to her sister. She
revealed herself to me from the depths of her heart: that   440
she'll never be unfaithful to me for as long as she lives.
Should I not love her? Should I not wish her well? I'd
rather not love myself than that she should be lacking in
love. Should I not send her a present? No, this very in-
stant I'll have five minas brought over to her, and in ad-   445
dition I'll have food bought for at least one mina. I'd
rather she, who wishes me well, has a good time than I,
who do all bad things to myself.

Exit DINIARCHUS *to the right.*
Enter PHRONESIUM *from her house, wearing a nightgown; she
is followed by servants carrying out a couch and coverlets.*

PHRO *(to those inside)* Give the breast to that boy! *(to the au-
dience)* How wretched and worried mothers are in their
hearts and how they torture themselves! Really, a sly   450
trick, and when I think it through in my heart, we're
considered far . . . less crooked than we are by nature. I

sumus ingenio.
ego prima de me, domo docta, dico.
455   quanta est cura in animo, quantum corde capio
dolorem . . . dolus ne occidat morte pueri:
mater dicta quod sum, eo magis studeo uitae;
quae ausa hunc sum, tantundem dolum <nunc> aggre-
    diar.
lucri causa auara probrum sum exsecuta,
460   alienos dolores mihi supposiui.
    <sed> nullam rem oportet dolose aggrediri
nisi astute <eam> accurateque exsequare.
uosmet iam uidetis ut ornata incedo:
puerperio ego nunc med esse aegram assimulo.
465   male quod mulier facere incepit, nisi <id> efficere per-
        petrat,
id illi morbo, id illi senio est, ea illi miserae miseria est;
bene si facere incepit, eius rei nimis cito odium perci-
    pit.
nimis quam paucae sunt defessae male quae facere oc-
    ceperunt,
nimisque paucae efficiunt si quid facere occeperunt
    bene:
470   mulieri nimio male facere leuius onus est quam bene.
ego quod mala sum, matris opera mala sum et meapte
    malitia,
quae me grauidam esse assimulaui militi Babylonio:
eam nunc malitiam accuratam miles inueniat uolo.

454 modo *P*, domo *Goeller*
458 huc ausa *BD*, ausa *C*, hunc ausa ς, ausa hunc *Leo*   nunc *add.*
Leo
461 sed *add. Geppert*

speak about myself first, taught by my own experience.
What great worry is on my mind, what great pain do I   455
feel in my heart, for fear that . . . my trick might come to
nothing through the boy's death. I'm all the keener on
his survival because I've been called his mother; I, who
have dared to do this trick, am now taking on an equally
great one. Greedy as I am, I've carried out an offense for   460
the sake of profit, I've taken on another's pangs as my
own. But you shouldn't approach any business guilefully
unless you also execute it cleverly and meticulously. You
can see yourselves now in what outfit I'm walking: I'm
pretending to be unwell from giving birth now. Unless a   465
woman completes carrying out the bad deed that she's
begun, it's an illness for her, it's an affliction for her, it's
wretchedness for the wretched woman. If she's begun to
do a good deed, aversion to it seizes her all too quickly.
Very few women who have begun to do a bad deed have
grown tired of it, and very few women succeed if they've
begun to do a good deed. For a woman doing a bad deed   470
is a far lighter burden than doing a good one. As for the
fact that I'm bad, I'm bad through my mother's training
and my own badness, since I pretended to the soldier
from Babylon that I was pregnant. Now I want the sol-
dier to find this wickedness performed painstakingly.

---

462 eam *add. Geppert*
465 id *add. Camerarius*
470 melius onus est *B*, melius est onus *CD*, leuius est onus ς, leuius
onus est *Leo*, melius opus est *Scaliger*

is hic hau multo post, credo, aderit; nunc prius prae-
caueo sciens

475 sumque ornata ita ut aegra uidear quasi puerperio cu-
bem.

date mi huc stactam atque ignem in aram, ut uenerem
Lucinam meam.

hic apponite atque abite ab oculis. eho, Pithecium!

face ut accumbam, accede, adiuta. em sic decet puer-
peram.

soleas mihi deduce, pallium inice in me huc, Archilis.

480 ubi es, Astaphium? fer huc uerbenam mi intus et bella-
ria.

date aquam manibus. nunc ecastor adueniat miles ue-
lim.

II. vi: STRATOPHANES. PHRONESIVM. ASTAPHIVM

STRAT ne exspectetis, spectatores, meas pugnas dum praedi-
cem:

manibus duella praedicare soleo, haud in sermonibus.

scio ego multos memorauisse milites mendacium:

485 et Homeronida[m] et postilla mille memorari pote[st],

475 eumque ornatum ut grauida *P*, sumque ornata ita ut aegra
uidear *Bücheler*   479 duce *P*, deduce *Geppert*
481 um ueniret *P*, adueniat *Müller*
485 Homeronida[m] *Leo*   pote[st] *Leo*

---

[23] An alternative name for Juno used to indicate her function as
goddess of childbirth (lit., "the one who brings to light").

[24] An aromatic shrub commonly used in religious ceremonies.

[25] Homer was the father of Greek epic; his greatest imitator at the
time of Plautus was Ennius.

He'll be here presently, I believe; now I'm deliber-
ately taking precautions and am fitted out in such a way   475
that I appear unwell as if I were confined to bed after
childbirth. (*into the house*) Bring me some myrrh here
and put some fire onto the altar, so that I can do homage
to my Lucina![23] Put it here and get out of my sight. (*as
they obey, into the house*) Hey, Pithecium! Let me lie
down, come here, help me! (*a servant girl appears and
assists Phronesium*) There, that's how it should be for
a new mother. (*into the house again*) Take my sandals
off and put the cloak here over me, Archilis! (*a servant
appears and obeys; into the house*) Where are you,   480
Astaphium? Bring me some verbena[24] and dainties from
inside.

*Enter ASTAPHIUM from Phronesium's house, with the things
requested.*

PHRO (*into the house*) Give me water for my hands. (*servants
appear with a bowl of water; after Phronesium has
washed her hands, all servants except for Astaphium and
one other girl go back in*) Now I'd like the soldier to
come.

*Enter STRATOPHANES from the left, followed by two women in
exotic dress and a servant carrying a purple cloak and some
boxes.*

STRAT Spectators, don't wait for me to tell you of my battles.
It's my custom to tell of my fights with my hands, not my
speeches. I know that many soldiers have lied: both the   485
son of Homer[25] and a thousand others after him can be

319

qui et conuicti et condemnati falsis de pugnis sient.
[non laudandust quoi plus credit qui audit quam ⟨ille⟩
    qui uidet.]
non placet quem illi plus laudant qui audiunt quam qui
    uident.
pluris est oculatus testis unus quam auriti decem;
490 qui audiunt audita dicunt, qui uident plane sciunt.
non placet quem scurrae laudant, manipulares mussi-
    tant,
neque illi quorum lingua gladiorum aciem praestringit
    domi.
strenui nimio plus prosunt populo quam arguti et cati:
facile sibi facunditatem uirtus argutam inuenit,
495 sine uirtute argutum ciuem mihi habeam pro praefica,
quae alios collaudat, eapse sese uero non potest.
nunc ad amicam decumo mense post Athenas Atticas
uiso, quam grauidam hic reliqui meo compressu, quid
    ea agat.

PHRO uide quis loquitur tam propinque.
AST   miles, mea Phronesium,
500 tibi adest Stratophanes. nunc tibi opust aegram ut te
    assimules.
PHRO   tace.
quoi adhuc ego tam mala eram monetrix, me maleficio
    uinceres?
STRAT peperit mulier, ut ego opinor.
AST   uin adeam ad hominem?
PHRO   uolo.

487 ille *add. Leo*   *uersum del. Brix*
493 arguit eccati *P*, arguti et cati *Merula*, argute cati *Seyffert*

mentioned who have been convicted and condemned
for false battles. [A man who is believed more by the
one who hears him than by the one who sees him does
not deserve praise.] I don't like a man who is praised
more by those who hear him than by those who see him.
One witness furnished with eyes is worth more than ten
witnesses furnished with ears. People who hear recount   490
what they've heard, but those who see know it plainly. I
don't like a fellow whom the men about town praise, but
whom his comrades in arms keep silent about, nor do I
like those whose tongues outdazzle the edge of swords
while they're at home. Energetic men benefit the people
far more than eloquent, clever ones. Bravery easily finds
eloquent fluency for itself, but I'd consider an eloquent   495
citizen without bravery to be like a woman hired to
mourn, who praises others, but cannot truthfully praise
herself. Now I'm visiting my girlfriend in Attic Athens
after ten months, to see how she's doing; I left her behind
pregnant as a result of our relationship.

PHRO *(to Astaphium)* Check who is talking so close by.

AST My dear Phronesium, the soldier Stratophanes is here   500
for you. *(quietly)* Now you need to pretend to be un-
well.

PHRO *(quietly)* Be quiet. You, to whom I've been such a wicked
adviser till now, would beat me in acting wickedly?

STRAT *(to himself)* The woman has given birth, I think.

AST *(to Phronesium)* Do you want me to approach him?

PHRO Yes.

---

496 apsa *B*, abse *CD*, a se *Nonius*, eapse *Scioppius*   se *P*, sese
Camerarius

STRAT eugae! Astaphium eccam it mi aduorsum.

AST salue ecastor, Stratophanes.
[uenire] saluom ⟨te⟩—

STRAT scio. sed peperitne, opsecro, Phronesium?

505 AST peperit puerum nimium lepidum.

STRAT ehem, ecquid mei similest?

AST rogas?
quin ubi natust machaeram et clupeum poscebat sibi?

STRAT meus est, scio iam de argumentis.

AST nimium tui similest.

STRAT papae!
iam magnust? iamne iit ad legionem? ecquae spolia
rettulit?

AST gerrae! nudiusquintus natus illequidem est.

STRAT quid postea?

510 inter tot dies quidem hercle iam aliquid actum opor-
tuit.
quid illi ex utero exitio est prius quam poterat ire in
proelium?

AST consequere atque illam saluta et gratulare illi.

STRAT sequor.

PHRO ubi illa, opsecro, est quae me hic reliquit, eapse abiit?
ubi est?

AST assum, adduco tibi exoptatum Stratophanem.

PHRO ubi is est, opsecro?

515 STRAT Mars peregre adueniens salutat Nerienem uxorem
suam.

504 uenire saluum *P*, saluom te *Kampmann*
508 quae *P*, ecquae *Kiessling*   509 ere *P*, gerrae *Palmer*

---

[26] Nerio (whose name means "strength") was, according to Roman

STRAT Hurray! Look, Astaphium is coming toward me.

AST My greetings, Stratophanes. That you've come safe and sound—

STRAT (*interrupting*) I know. But please, has Phronesium given birth?

AST She's given birth to an absolutely delightful boy. 505

STRAT Hey, does he resemble me at all?

AST Do you ask? As soon as he was born, he demanded sword and shield for himself!

STRAT He's mine, I already know it from the evidence.

AST He resembles you absolutely.

STRAT Goodness! Is he already big? Has he already joined the army? Has he brought back any spoils?

AST Nonsense! He was born only four days ago.

STRAT So what? Within so many days he ought to have per- 510
formed some deed already. Why did he leave the womb before he could go into battle?

AST Follow me, greet her, and congratulate her.

STRAT Yes.

PHRO (*weakly*) Please, where's the girl who left me here and went away herself? Where is she?

AST I'm here, I'm bringing you your longed-for Stratophanes.

PHRO Where is he, please?

STRAT (*stepping forward*) On his arrival from abroad, Mars 515
greets his wife Nerio.[26] I congratulate you on pulling

tradition, the wife of Mars, the god of war. In a discussion of this name, Gellius (13.23) also proffers (and subsequently rejects) the alternative view that *nerio* was simply an attribute of Mars and that Plautus made Stratophanes refer to *nerio* as the wife of Mars in order to characterize him as stupid.

      quom tu recte prouenisti quomque es aucta liberis,
      gratulor, quom mihi tibique magnum peperisti decus.

PHRO salue, qui me interfecisti paene uita et lumine
      uimque mihi magni doloris per uoluptatem tuam
520   condidisti in corpus, quo nunc etiam morbo misera
         sum.

STRAT heia! haud ab re, mea uoluptas, tibi istic obuenit la-
        bos:
      filium peperisti, qui aedis spoliis opplebit tuas.

PHRO multo ecastor magis oppletis tritici opust granariis,
      ne, ille prius quam spolia capiat, hic nos extinxit fames.
525 STRAT habe bonum animum.

PHRO   sauium pete hinc sis. ah! nequeo caput
      tollere, ita dolet itaque aegre moueo, neque etiam
         queo
      pedibus mea sponte ambulare.

STRAT   si hercle me ex medio mari
      sauium petere tuom iubeas, petere hau pigeat [me],
         mel meum.
      id ita esse experta es: nunc experiere, mea Phronesium,
530   me te amare. adduxi ancillas tibi eccas ex Syria duas,
      is te dono. adduce huc tu istas. sed istae reginae domi
      suae fuere ambae, uerum ⟨earum⟩ patriam ego excidi
         manu.
      his te dono.

PHRO   paenitetne te quot ancillas alam,
      quin etiam insuper mi adducas quae mihi comedint ci-
        bum?

519 quiquem ibi *P*, uimque mihi *Bücheler*   524 hinc *P*, hic
Angelius   525 sis pete hinc *P*, pete hinc sis *Bothe*   526 ego
medulo *B*, ego medolo *CD*, aegre moueo *Seyffert*   528 me *del.*
Bothe   532 earum *add. Seyffert*   534 etiam men super *P*,

through well and being blessed with a child, and on hav-
ing given birth to a great distinction for myself and
you.

PHRO And my greetings to you, who have almost deprived me
of life and light, and who, for the sake of your own plea-
sure, have put an enormous amount of great pain into   520
my body, an illness because of which I'm wretched even
now.

STRAT Goodness! That labor hasn't fallen onto you to your
disadvantage, my darling: you've given birth to a son
who'll fill your house with spoils.

PHRO I have a much greater need for wheat-filled granaries so
that starvation won't wipe us out here before he can get
any spoils.

STRAT Have no fear.   525

PHRO Take a kiss from me, please. Ah! I can't lift up my head,
that's how much pain I'm in and how difficult it is to
move, and I still can't walk on my feet alone.

STRAT (*bowing down to her couch and kissing her*) If you told
me to come and get a kiss from you from the middle of
the sea, I'd gladly get it, my honey. You know by experi-
ence that this is the case; now, my dear Phronesium,
you'll learn by experience that I love you. Look, I've   530
brought you two slave girls from Syria; I present you with
them. (*to his servant*) You, bring them here. (*to Phrone-
sium*) Mind you, they were both queens in their home,
but I destroyed their country with my hand. I present
you with them.

PHRO Aren't you satisfied with the amount of slave girls I have
to feed, without bringing me girls in addition to eat up
my food?

---

etiam insuper mi *Müller*, examen super *Haupt*

535 STRAT hoc quidem hercle ingratum est donum. cedo tu mi
istam purpuram.

mea uoluptas, attuli eccam pallulam ex Phrygia tibi.
tene tibi.

PHRO hoccin mi ob labores tantos tantillum dari?

STRAT perii hercle ⟨ego⟩ miser! iam ⟨mi⟩ auro contra constat
filius:

etiam nihili pendit addi purpuram. ex Arabia tibi

540 attuli tus, Ponto amomum. tene tibi, uoluptas mea.

PHRO accipe hoc, ⟨Astaphium,⟩ abduce hasce hinc e con-
spectu Syras.

STRAT ecquid amas me?

PHRO nihil ecastor nec meres.

STRAT nilne huic sat est?

ne bonum uerbum quidem unum dixit. uiginti minis

uenire illaec posse credo dona quae ei dono dedi.

545 uehementer nunc mi est irata, sentio atque intellego;

uerum abibo. quid ais? nunc tu num neuis me, uolup-
tas mea,

quo uocatus sum ire ad cenam? mox huc cubitum ue-
nero.

quid taces? planissume edepol perii. sed quid illuc noui
est?

quis ⟨hic⟩ homo est qui inducit pompam tantam? cer-
tum est quo ferant

550 opseruare. huic credo fertur. uerum iam scibo magis.

535 puere per uiam *P*, purpuram *Bücheler*, puere perulam *Gruterus*
(*quam lectionem si defendimus, cum Bothe* donum *delendum est*)
538 ego *add. Bothe* mi *add. Camerarius*
541 accepi *P*, accipe ς Astaphium *add. Bach*
546 abdibo *B*, adibo *CD*, abibo *Bothe*

STRAT (*aside*) This present is unwelcome. (*to his servant*) You,   535
       give me that purple cloak. (*hands it over*) My darling,
       look, I brought you a mantle from Phrygia. Take it.
PHRO   Is only such a little thing given to me in return for such
       great labors?
STRAT (*aside*) Poor me, I'm dead! My son already costs me his
       weight in gold. She doesn't even consider the addition of
       a purple cloak worth anything. (*to Phronesium*) From
       Arabia I've brought you incense, from the Black Sea   540
       balsam. Take it, my darling. (*the servant steps forward
       again*)
PHRO   Take this stuff, Astaphium, and take these Syrians out of
       my sight. (*Astaphium takes the girls and gifts into the
       house and returns*)
STRAT Don't you love me at all?
PHRO   No, not at all, and you don't deserve my love. (*turns
       away*)
STRAT (*aside*) Isn't anything enough for this woman? She
       didn't even say one single kind word to me. I believe
       those gifts I presented her with could be sold for twenty
       minas. Now she's terribly angry with me, I feel and real-   545
       ize it; but I'll leave. (*to Phronesium*) What do you say?
       My darling, you wouldn't mind now if I went for dinner
       where I've been invited? I'll come back soon to lie with
       you. Why are you silent? (*aside*) I'm dead, it's absolutely
       obvious. But what novelty is that? Who is this man who's
       bringing such a procession? I'm resolved to watch where   550
       they're carrying it all. It's being carried to this woman
       here, I believe. But I'll know more in a moment.

---

547 mox *P*, nox *Fleckeisen*
549 hic *add. Seyffert*

II. vii: CYAMVS. PHRONESIVM. STRATOPHANES

CYA   ite, ite hac simul, mulieri damnigeruli,

     foras egerones, bonorum exagogae.

     satin, siquis amat, nequit quin nihili sit, atque improbis
       se artibus exspoliat?

     nam hoc qui sciam, ne quis id quaerat ex me,

555   domi est qui facit improba facta amator,

556   qui bona sua pro stercore habet,

556[a]   foras iubet ferri: metuit

     pulices: mundissumus fit;

     puras esse sibi uolt aedis: domi quicquid habet eicitur
       ἔξω.

     quandoquidem ipsus perditum se it, secreto hercle
       equidem eum adiutabo

560   nec mea quidem opera umquam hilo minus propere
       quam pote[st] peribit.

     nam iam de hoc opsonio de mina una deminui modo

     quinque nummos: mihi detraxi partem . . . Hercula-
       neam.

     nam hoc assimile est quasi de fluuio qui aquam deriuat
       sibi:

     nisi deriuetur, tamen ea aqua omnis abeat in mare;

565   nam hoc in mare abit misereque perit sine bona omni
       gratia.

     haec quom uideo fieri, suffuror, suppilo,

     de praeda praedam capio.

     meretricem ego item esse reor, mare ut est:

555 inproba *P*, inprobe *Lindsay*

557 publicos *P*, pulices *Seyffert*

560 nihili omnibus *P*, hilo minus *Lambinus*   potest *P*, pote
Schoell

Enter CYAMUS *from the right, with a wallet around his neck and followed by several slaves carrying food and cooking utensils.*

CYA Come, come along this way together, you porters of loss
for the benefit of a woman, you carriers-out, you export-
ers of goods. If someone's in love, can he really not avoid
being worthless and plundering himself with shameless
arts? Well, to stop anybody asking me how I know about
this, we have a lover at home who acts in a shameless   555
manner, who treats his possessions like dung and has
them taken out. He's afraid of fleas: he becomes abso-
lutely clean; he wants his house to be pure: whatever he
has at home is thrown outside. Since he's keen on ruin-
ing himself, I'll secretly help him, and with my help he   560
won't fail to perish as quickly as possible: now out of this
one mina from the catering account I just deducted ten
drachmas; I took for myself the part of . . . Hercules.[27]
Well, this is similar to someone who diverts water from
a river for himself; if it weren't diverted, all this water
would nevertheless go into the sea. For all this goes into   565
the sea and perishes wretchedly without any benefit in
return. When I see this happening, I filch, steal, and take
booty from the booty. I think a prostitute is like the sea:

[27] In the Latin, he takes five coins. Since Hercules was offered
tithes of successful business ventures and since one mina is worth one
hundred drachmas, the coins in question must be didrachms.

---

564 tamen omnis ea aqua *P, transp. Leo*

	quod des deuorat ‹nec dat›is umquam abundat.
570	hoc saltem: ‹rem› seruat neque ulli ubi sit apparet:
	des quantumuis, nusquam apparet nec datori neque
	acceptrici.
572–73	uelut haec meretrix meum erum miserum sua blanditia
	implicat pauperie:
	priuabit bonis, luce, honore, atque amicis.
575	attat! eccam adest propinque. credo audisse haec me
	loqui.
	pallida est, ut peperit puerum. alloquar quasi nesciam.
	iubeo uos saluere.

PHRO   noster Cyame, quid agis? ut uales?

CYA   ualeo et uenio ad minus ualentem et melius qui ualeat
       fero.

erus meus, ocellus tuos, ad te ferre me haec iussit tibi

580   dona quae uides illos ferre et has quinque argenti mi-
       nas.

PHRO pol hau perit quod illum tantum amo.

CYA   iussit orare ut haec grata haberes tibi.

PHRO grata acceptaque ecastor habeo. iube auferri intro, i
       Cyame.

CYA   ecquid auditis haec, quae ‹uobis› iam imperat?

585   uasa nolo auferant: desiccari iube.

569 deuoratis *P*, deuorat ‹nec dat›is *Camerarius*
570 rem *add. Leo*   mecum sub este *P*, nec ulli ubi sit *Leo*
572–73 intulit in pauperiem *P*, implicat pauperie *O. Skutsch*
576 ut peperit *P*, quasi pepererit *Kruse*
577 geta *P*, Cyame *Seyffert*
584 uobis *add. Enk*   tam *P*, iam *Leo*
585 iubet *P*, iube *Bücheler*, lubet *Camerarius*

330

she gulps down what you give her and never overflows
as a result of your gifts. Anyhow: she keeps her posses- 570
sions and no one can see where they are; you can give
her as much as you like, nowhere is it visible to giver or
receiver. For instance, the prostitute here entangles my
wretched master in poverty through her flattery; she'll
deprive him of possessions, light, reputation, and friends.
Goodness! Look, she's close by. I believe she's heard me 575
say this. She's pale from giving birth. I'll address her as
if I didn't know. (*aloud*) My greetings to you two!

PHRO Our dear Cyamus, what are you up to? How are you
feeling?

CYA I'm feeling well and I'm coming to someone feeling less
well and bringing her something because of which she'll
feel better. My master, the apple of your eye, told me to
bring you these gifts which you can see those men are 580
carrying, and these five silver minas. (*hands over the
money*)

PHRO My great love for him isn't coming to nothing.

CYA He told me to ask you to regard these gifts as welcome
to you.

PHRO I do regard them as welcome and accepted. Have them
brought in, go, Cyamus.

CYA (*to the servants*) Do you hear what orders she's giving
now? (*to Phronesium, after the servants have come out* 585
again) I don't want them to take the vessels away; have
them drunk dry.[28]

---

[28] He is worried that Phronesium wants to keep the vessels, and he
accuses prostitutes of drinking too much, which was a common stereo-
type in antiquity.

AST   impudens mecastor, Cyame, es.

CYA   egone?

AST   tu.

CYA   bona fide?

      tune ais me impudentem esse, ipsa quae sis stabulum
          flagiti?

PHRO dic, amabo te, ubi est Diniarchus?

CYA   domi.

PHRO dic ob haec dona quae ad me miserit

590   me illum amare plurumum omnium hominum ***
          ergo,

      meque honorem illi habere omnium maxumum,

      atque ut huc ueniat opsecra.

CYA   ilicet.

      sed quisnam illic homo est qui ipsus se comest, tristis,
          oculis malis?

      animo hercle homo est suo miser,

595   quisquis est.

PHRO   dignust mecastor. nequam est. non nosti, opsecro,

      militem, hic apud me ⟨qui⟩ erat? huius pater pueri illic
          est.

      usque adicit oculum, uisit, adit,

      mansit: auscultat, opseruat quem perdam.

CYA   noui hominem nihili.

      illicine est?

PHRO   illic est.

CYA   me intuetur gemens;

600   traxit ex intumo uentre suspiritum.

      hoc uide! dentibus frendit, icit femur;

      587 a(n)sin pudentem me *P*, ais me impudentem *Seyffert*
      590 ergo *P*, merito *Ussing*

332

AST   You really have no shame, Cyamus.

CYA   I?

AST   Yes, you.

CYA   Seriously? Are you saying that I have no shame, you, who are a store of vice yourself?

PHRO   Please tell me, where's Diniarchus?

CYA   At home.

PHRO   Tell him that on account of these gifts he's sent to me I   590
love him most of all men, because of ***, and that I have
the highest regard of all for him, and ask him to come
here.

CYA   At once. But who is that chap who's eating his own heart
out, glum, with unpleasant eyes? The man is wretched
in his heart, whoever he is.   595

PHRO   He really deserves it. He's worthless. Please, don't you
know the soldier who was here at my place? He's the
father of this boy. He's constantly eyeing us, checking
on us, coming to us, and he's stayed: he's listening and
watching who I'm ruining.

CYA   I know the no-good fellow. Is that him?

PHRO   That's him.

CYA   He's watching me, moaning; he's heaved a sigh from far   600
down in his belly. Look at this! He's gnashing his teeth

---

591 meumque honorem illum *BC*, meumque honorem meumque
C, meque honorem illi *Bothe*

596 qui *add. Schoell*

597 adecta culem *B*, ad iectaculum *C*, ad iectaculem *D*, adicit ocu-
lum *Lindsay*   iussit alii *P*, uisit adit *Lindsay*

598 mansi auscultaui obseruaui *P*, mansit auscultat obseruat
Leo   quempnam *B*, quem pnam *D*, quem per nam *C*, quem perdam
Lindsay

       num opsecro nam hariolust qui ipsus se uerberat?

STRAT nunc ego meos animos uiolentos meamque iram ex pec-
       tore iam promam.

604–5   loquere: unde es? quoius es? quor ausu's mi inclemen-
       ter dicere?

CYA   lubitum est.

STRAT istuc ne[c] mi responsis.

CYA   hoc: non ego te flocci facio.

STRAT quid tu? quor ausa es alium te dicere amare homi-
       nem?

PHRO   lubitum est.

STRAT ain tandem? istuc primum experiar. tun tantilli doni
       causa,

609–
10   holerum atque escarum et poscarum, moechum mala-
       cum, cincinnatum,

       umbraticulum, tympanotribam amas, hominem non
       nauci?

CYA   quae haec res?

       meon [ero] tu, improbe, ero male dicere ⟨nunc⟩ audes,
       fons uiti et periuri?

STRAT uerbum unum adde istoc: iam hercle ego te hic hac
       offatim conficiam.

CYA tange modo, iam ego ⟨te⟩ hic agnum faciam et me-
       dium distruncabo.

615   si tu in legioni bellator clues, at ego in culina clueo.

   606 ne[c] *Merula*
   612 ero[1] *del. Lindsay*   nunc *add. Lindsay*
   614 te *add.* ς
   615 sit uellegionem *P*, si tu in legione *Merula*

and beating his thigh. Please, is he a soothsayer who's beating himself?[29]

STRAT (*to Cyamus*) Now I'll emit my violent anger and my wrath from my chest. Speak: where are you from? Who do you belong to? Why did you dare to insult me? 605

CYA I felt like it.

STRAT Don't give me that reply.

CYA Oh yes, I do: I don't care a straw about you.

STRAT (*to Phronesium*) What about you? Why did you dare to say that you love another man?

PHRO I felt like it.

STRAT Do you say so? I'll test that first. For the sake of such a tiny gift, vegetables and food and vinegar water,[30] you 610 love a soft, curly-haired, shade-dwelling, tambourine-beating[31] adulterer, a man of no value?

CYA What's this? You crook, do you dare to insult my master now, you fount of vice and perjury?

STRAT Add one word to that: I'll chop you up into morsels here with this at once. (*grabs the hilt of his sword*)

CYA Just touch me and I'll turn you into a lamb here at once and cleave you through in the middle.[32] If you are fa- 615 mous in the army as a warrior, I am famous in the kitchen.

---

[29] Priests of orgiastic cults, especially those of the *Magna Mater*, "Great Mother," flagellated themselves. [30] A cheap drink for slaves. Diniarchus had of course sent proper wine.

[31] Priests of Cybele, the *Magna Mater* ("Great Mother"), usually had a *tympanum*, a kind of small drum; the term used by Stratophanes is insulting because the more radical followers of this deity castrated themselves. [32] Double entendre: "cleaving someone through" can also refer to anal intercourse.

PHRO si aequom facias, aduentores meos ⟨non⟩ incuses, quo-
      rum
    mihi dona accepta et grata habeo, tuaque ingrata, aps
      te quae accepi.
STRAT tum pol ego et donis priuatus sum et perii.
PHRO   plane istuc est.
CYA quid nunc ergo hic, odiose, sedes, confectis omnibus
    rebus?
620 STRAT perii hercle hodie, nisi hunc a te abigo.
CYA   accede huc modo, adi huc modo.
STRAT etiam, scelus uiri, minitare? quem ego [offatim] iam
    iam concipilabo.
    quid tibi huc uentio est? quid tibi hanc aditio est?
    quid tibi hanc notio est, inquam, amicam meam?
    emoriere ocius, ni manu uiceris.
625 CYA quid? manu uicerim?
STRAT   fac quod iussi, mane.
    iam ego te hic offatim conficiam; ⟨offatim⟩ occidi op-
    tumum est.
CYA captio est: istam machaeram longiorem ⟨tu⟩ habes
    quam haec est.
    sed uerum ⟨me⟩ sine dum petere: siquidem belligeran-
    dum est tecum,
    abero dum ego tecum, bellator, arbitrum aequom ce-
    perim.
630   sed ego cesso hinc me amoliri, uentre dum saluo licet?

---

616 non *add.* ς   617 quae aps te *P, transp. Kiessling*
   619 odies sees *B*, odiosees *C*, odiose es *D*, odiose sedes *Lind-*
say   confessus omnibus teus *P*, confectis omnibus rebus *Spengel*
   621 offatim *del. Bücheler*   626 offatim[2] *add. Lindsay*
   627 tu *add. Spengel*

PHRO (*to Stratophanes*) If you were behaving appropriately, you wouldn't criticize those of my visitors whose gifts I regard as accepted and welcome; the gifts I received from you I regard as unwelcome.

STRAT Then I've been deprived of gifts and I'm utterly ruined.

PHRO That's obvious.

CYA (*to Stratophanes*) Then why are you sitting around here now, you tedious creature, when your position has been ruined?

STRAT (*to Phronesium*) I really am ruined today unless I drive   620
this man away from you!

CYA Just step over here, just come here.

STRAT Are you even threatening me, you rascal? I'll chop you up this instant! Why are you coming here? Why are you approaching her? Why, I insist, do you know this girlfriend of mine? You'll die quickly unless you win fighting!

CYA What? I should win fighting? (*turns to go*)   625

STRAT Do what I've told you, stay! Now I'll chop you up into morsels here; it's best if you're cut up into morsels.

CYA It's a trap: that sword you have is longer than this here (*pulls out his kitchen knife*) is. But do let me get a spit; if I have to wage war with you, I'll be off till I've got hold of an appropriate referee for my fight with you, warrior. (*aside*) But why am I wasting time here while I can still   630
get away with my belly intact?

Exit CYAMUS to the right, followed by the servants.

---

628 me *add. Goeller*
629 abo *B*, ibo *CD*, abero *Enk*   domum *P*, dum *Geppert*

II. viii: PHRONESIVM. STRATOPHANES

PHRO datin soleas? atque me intro actutum ducite,
nam mihi de uento miserae condoluit caput.
STRAT quid mihi futurum est, quoi duae ancillae dolent,
quibus te donaui? iamne abiisti? em sic datur!
635   quo pacto excludi, quaeso, potui planius
quam exclusus nunc sum? pulchre ludificor. sine.
quantillo mi opere nunc persuaderi potest
ut ego hisc' suffringam talos totis aedibus!
num quippiam harum mutat mores mulierum?
640   postquam filiolum peperit, animos sustulit.
nunc quasi mi dicat: "nec te iubeo nec uoto
intro ire in aedis." at ego nolo, non eo.
ego faxo dicat me in diebus pauculis
crudum uirum esse. sequere me hac. uerbum sat est.

ACTVS III

III. i: STRABAX. ASTAPHIVM

645 STRAB   rus mane dudum hinc ire me iussit pater,
ut bubus glandem prandio depromerem.
post illoc quam ueni, aduenit, si dis placet,
ad uillam argentum meo qui debebat patri,
qui ouis Tarentinas erat mercatus de patre.

639 auarum ut at *P*, harum mutat *Lindsay*
647 aduenis ideis *P*, aduenit si dis *Merula*

---

[33] Wool from Apulia, especially from around Tarentum, was considered the best (Plin. *nat.* 8.48.190).

PHRO Aren't you giving me my sandals? (*as Astaphium obeys, to her and the other slave girl*) And take me inside immediately: poor me, I've got a headache from the wind.

Exeunt PHRONESIUM *and* ASTAPHIUM *into their house, followed by the remaining servant girl.*

STRAT (*calling after them*) What will happen to me? The two slave girls I presented you with are giving me an ache. Have you left already? (*to the audience*) There, that's how she receives presents! Please, how could I have 635 been shut out more plainly than I'm shut out now? I'm being ridiculed beautifully. Enough of that! How little it would take now to persuade me to break the ankles of this entire house! Does anything change the ways of these women? After giving birth to my boy she became 640 haughty. Now it's as if she were to tell me: "I neither order nor forbid you to come into the house." But I don't want to, I won't go. I'll see to it that she says within a few days that I'm an unfeeling man. (*to his servant*) Follow me this way. That's enough words.

Exit STRATOPHANES *to the right, followed by his servant.*

ACT THREE

Enter STRABAX *from the left, a wallet round his neck.*

STRAB A while ago in the morning my father told me to go 645 to the farm so as to fetch acorns for the cattle for their fodder. After I got there—would you believe it?—a man who owed my father money and who'd bought Tarentine sheep[33] from him came to the farmhouse.

339

650   quaerit patrem. dico esse in urbe. interrogo
               quid eum uelit. ***
               homo cruminam sibi de collo detrahit,
               minas uiginti mihi dat. accipio lubens,
               condo in cruminam. ille abiit. ego propere minas
655   ouis in crumina hac in urbem detuli.
               fuit edepol Mars meo periratus patri,
               nam oues illius hau longe apsunt a lupis.
               ne ego urbanos istos mundulos amasios
               hoc ictu exponam atque omnis eiciam foras.
660   eradicare est certum cumprimis patrem,
               post id locorum matrem. nunc hoc deferam
               argentum ad hanc, quam mage amo quam matrem
                   meam.
               tat! ecquis intust? ecquis hoc aperit ostium?
664–   AST   quid istuc? alienun es, amabo, mi Strabax,
65   qui non extemplo ‹intro› ieris?
    STRAB   anne oportuit?
    AST   ita te quidem, qui es familiaris.
    STRAB   ibitur,
               ne me morari censeas.
    AST   lepide facis.

          III. ii: TRVCVLENTVS. ASTAPHIVM
    TRVC mirum uidetur rure erilem filium
670   Strabacem non rediisse; nisi si clanculum

     651 concredat mihi si quid uelit *in lacuna add. Schoell*
     654 perpera *CD, om. B,* propere ς
     655 hac ‹huc› Geppert
     666 ire si *P,* intro ieris *Brix*

340

He was looking for my father. I told him he was in town. 650
I asked him what he wanted of him. *** He took a wallet
off his neck and gave me twenty minas. I took them with
pleasure and put them in my wallet. He left. I quickly
brought the bare-bellied[34] sheep into town in this wallet. 655
Mars was really very angry with my father: his sheep
aren't far away from the wolves.[35] Yes, I'll knock out
those neat little city lovers with this blow and throw them
all out. I'm resolved to root out my father first and then 660
my mother. Now I'll bring this money to the girl I love
more than my own mother. (*knocks at the door*) Rat-a-
tat! Is anyone inside? Is anyone opening this door?

Enter ASTAPHIUM *from inside.*

AST What's that? Please, are you a stranger, my dear Strabax, 665
that you didn't come straight in?
STRAB Should I have?
AST Yes, of course, since you're an intimate friend.
STRAB I'll go, so you won't think I'm wasting time.
AST That's charming of you.

Exit STRABAX *into Phronesium's house.*
Enter TRUCULENTUS *from the house of Strabax, a wallet round his neck.*

TRUC It seems odd that master's son Strabax hasn't returned 670

---

[34] A pun; *mina* as a noun refers to the monetary unit, but as an
adjective it means "bare-bellied."   [35] Wolves are sacred to Mars.
In order to punish the father of Strabax, Mars lets the wolves have his
sheep; the sheep are the money and the wolves are the prostitutes
(*lupa*, "she-wolf," is in fact a common word for a prostitute).

collapsus est hic in corruptelam suam.

AST iam pol illic inclamabit me si aspexerit.

TRVC nimio minus saeuos iam sum, Astaphium, quam fui,
iam non ⟨ego⟩ sum truculentus, noli metuere.

675   ⟨quid ais?⟩

AST   quid uis?

TRVC   quin tuam exspecto osculentiam.
dic, impera mi quid lubet quo uis modo.
nouos omnis mores habeo, ueteres perdidi.
uel amare possum uel iam scortum ducere.

AST lepide mecastor nuntias. sed dic mihi,

680 haben—

TRVC   parasitum te fortasse dicere?

AST intellexisti lepide quid ego dicerem.

TRVC heus tu! iam postquam in urbem crebro commeo,
dicax sum factus. iam sum caullator probus.

AST quid id est, amabo? mitte ridicularia;

685 cauillationes uis opinor dicere?

TRVC ita, at pauxillum differt a cauillibus.

AST sequere intro [me], amabo, mea uoluptas.

TRVC   tene hoc tibi:
rabonem habeto, uti mecum hanc noctem sies.

674 ego *add. Leo*
675 quid ais *add. Schoell*
680 parasitum *P*, marsipum *Leo*
684 istec *P*, mitte *Spengel*
686 ita ut *P*, ita at *Bothe*, istud *Leo*
687 me *del. Bothe*

---

[36] *Osculentia*, "kissery," is a nonce-formation based on *opsequentia*, "compliance, deference."

from the farm yet; unless he's secretly slipped into his moral corruption here.

AST   (*half aside*) Now that fellow will shout at me if he sees me.

TRUC   (*overhearing her*) I'm far less wild now than I used to be, Astaphium; I'm no longer savage, don't be afraid. What   675 do you say?

AST   What do you want?

TRUC   I'm waiting for your kissery.[36] Speak, command me what you like in any way you like. All my ways are new now, I've lost the old ones. I can make love or hire a prostitute.

AST   You're bringing me pleasant news. But tell me, do you   680 have—

TRUC   (*interrupting*) Perhaps you're saying a hanger-on?

AST   You've understood perfectly what I wanted to say.

TRUC   Hey you! Now that I come into town often, I've become witty. Now I'm a decent stalker.[37]

AST   What's that, please? Stop your jokes; I believe you want   685 to say "talks"?

TRUC   Yes, but there's little difference from "stalks."

AST   Please follow me in, my darling.

TRUC   (*handing over his wallet*) Take this: have it as a posit,[38] so that you'll spend the night with me.

---

[37] Truculentus means *cauillator*, "jester," but pronounces it as *caullator*, as if it came from *caulis*, "stalk." When Astaphium corrects him and says that he must mean *cauillationes*, "jests," he says that this word does not differ much from *cauilles*, a hypercorrect form of *caules*, "stalks." "Stalk" is also a euphemism for the penis.

[38] *Arrabo*, "deposit," a loanword from Greek (and ultimately from a Semitic language), is mutilated to *rabo* by Truculentus.

AST perii! "rabonem"? quam esse dicam hanc beluam?
690   quin tu "arrabonem" dicis?
TRVC   "a" facio lucri,
    ut Praenestinis "conea" est ciconia.
AST sequere, opsecro.
TRVC   Strabacem hic opperiar modo,
    si rure ueniat.
AST   is quidem hic apud nos est Strabax,
    modo rure uenit.
TRVC   priusne quam ad matrem suam?
695   eu edepol hominem nihili!
AST   iamne autem ut soles?
TRVC iamne—nihil dico.
AST   i intro, amabo, cedo manum.
TRVC tene. in tabernam ducor deuorsoriam,
    ubi male accipiar mea mihi pecunia.

ACTVS IV

IV. i: DINIARCHVS

DIN nec gnatust nec progignetur nec potest reperirier
700   quoi ego nunc ⟨aut⟩ dictum aut factum melius quam
        Veneri uelim.
    di magni, ut ego ⟨laete⟩ laetus sum et laetitia differor!
    ita ad me magna nuntiauit Cyamus hodie gaudia:

693 apud nos est hic *P, transp. Schoell*
700 nunc ⟨aut⟩ *Bothe*
701 laete *add. Spengel*   et laetitia *P, ut l. Bothe*

AST   I'm dead! "Posit"? What beast should I say this is? Why   690
don't you say "deposit"?

TRUC   I'm saving the "de," just as a woodpecker is a "pecker"
for the people of Praeneste.[39]

AST   Please follow me.

TRUC   I'll just wait for Strabax here in case he comes from the
farm.

AST   Strabax is here with us, he's just come from the farm.

TRUC   Before he went to his mother? Goodness, a worthless   695
fellow!

AST   Now your usual behavior?

TRUC   Now—I won't say anything.

AST   Please go in; give me your hand.

TRUC   Take it. (*aside*) I'm being led into an inn where I'll get a
bad reception from my own money.

Exeunt ASTAPHIUM *and* TRUCULENTUS *into Phronesium's
house.*

ACT FOUR

Enter DINIARCHUS *from the right.*

DIN   No one's been born, will be born, or can be found who   700
I'd like to be better spoken of or done by now than Venus. Great gods, how very happy I am and how I'm bursting with happiness! So great are the joys that Cyamus has

---

[39] The Latin word used is *ciconia*, "stork," which was *conea* in the
neighboring town of Praeneste. Truculentus points out the loss of the
initial syllable, but not the different vocalism, which, as far as we can
tell from inscriptions, was not made up by Plautus.

mea dona deamata acceptaque habita esse apud Phro-
nesium:

quom hoc iam uolup est, tum illuc nimium magnae
mellinae mihi,

705   militis odiosa ingrataque habita. totus gaudeo.

mea pila est: si repudiatur miles, mulier mecum erit.

saluos sum, quia pereo; si non peream, plane perierim.

nunc speculabor quid ibi agatur, quis eat intro, qui fo-
ras

ueniat; procul hinc opseruabo meis quid fortunis fuat.

710   quia nil habeo, nam amoui mi hic omnia, agam pre-
cario.

IV. ii: ASTAPHIVM. DINIARCHVS

AST   lepide efficiam meum ego officium: uide intus modo ut
tu tuom item efficias.

ama, id quod decet, rem tuam: istum exinani.

nunc dum isti lubet, dum habet, tempus ei rei secun-
dum est,

prome uenustatem tuam amanti, ut gaudeat quom
pereat.

715   ego hic interim restitans praesidebo,

istic dum sic faciat domum ad te exagogam;

nec quemquam interim istoc ad uos qui sit odio

intro mittam: tu perge ut lubet ludere istum.

DIN   quis iste est, Astaphium, indica, qui perit?

AST   amabo, hicin tu eras?

704 nimio *P*, nimium *Langen*

707 uriem *BD*, urient *C*, perierim *Goeller*

710 *uersum del. uel post 729 pos. Kruse*

714 pereis *P*, pereat *Müller*, perdis *Leo*   715 resti tricis *B*,
restitricis *CD*, restitans *Bücheler*, restitrix *Turnebus*

announced to me today: my gifts are considered loved and accepted by Phronesium. While this is already plea- 705
surable, the other news is absolutely sweet for me: the soldier's gifts were considered hateful and unwelcome. I'm completely joyful. The ball is mine:[40] if the soldier is rejected, the woman will be with me. I'm safe because I'm perishing. If I weren't perishing, I'd have plainly perished. Now I'll spy on what's going on there, who is going in, and who is coming out. From here from a distance I'll observe what's happening to my fate. As I don't 710
have anything—well, I've removed all my property here —I'll be at her mercy.

Enter ASTAPHIUM *from Phronesium's house.*

AST   (*into the house*) I'll carry out my job nicely; just see to it inside that you carry out yours in the same way. Love, as you ought to, your money; empty him. Now while he's eager, while he has something, it's an opportune time for this activity; produce your charm for your lover, so that he enjoys being ruined. Meanwhile I'll stay behind and 715
protect you, while he's exporting his property to your place like this. In the meantime I won't let anyone in to you who'd be tedious. You must continue to trick him as you like.

DIN   Tell me, Astaphium, who is that who's perishing?

AST   Please, were you here?

---

[40] I.e., "I have won."

---

718 ludinistos *P*, ludere istum *Bugge*
719 est iste ea *P*, est iste *W*, istest *Bach*

720	DIN	molestusne sum?
	AST	nunc magis quam fuisti,
		nam si quid nobis usust, nobis molestu's.
		sed opsecro, da mi operam ut narrem quae uolo.
	DIN	nam quid est? num mea refert?
	AST	non mussito.
		intus bolos quos dat!
	DIN	quid? amator nouos quispiam?
725	AST	integrum et plenum adorta est thesaurum.
	DIN	quis est?
	AST	eloquar, sed tu taceto. nostin tu hunc Strabacem?
	DIN	quidni?
	AST	solus summam habet hic apud nos, nunc is est fundus
		nouos.
		animo bono male ‹rem› gerit.
	DIN	perit hercle; ego idem
		bona perdidi, mala repperi, [factus] sum extumus a uo-
		bis.
730	AST	stultus es qui facta infecta facere uerbis postules.
		Thetis quoque etiam lamentando pausam fecit filio.
	DIN	non ego nunc intro ad uos mittar?
	AST	qui tu quam miles magis?
	DIN	quia enim plus dedi.
	AST	plus enim es intro missus quom dabas:
		sine uicissim qui dant [operam] ob illud quod dant
		operis utier.
735		litteras didicisti: quando scis, sine alios discere.

728 rem *add. Camerarius*   729 *uersum ab uno Prisciano ser-*
uatum hic posuit Langen   factus *del. Lindsay*
732 quidum *B*, quid um *CD*, qui tu *Kiessling*
734 operam *del. Lambinus*   oblit *P*, ob illud *Loman*

| DIN | Am I annoying you? | 720 |

AST   Now more than before, because if anything helps us, you're annoying us. But please, give me your attention so that I can tell you what I want.

DIN   What is it? Is it important for me?

AST   I won't keep quiet. What hauls she's making inside!

DIN   What? Some new lover?

| AST | She's come upon an intact new treasure. | 725 |

DIN   Who is it?

AST   I'll tell you, but you must be quiet. Do you know Strabax here?

DIN   Why not?

AST   He alone has the first rank here with us, now he's our new plot of land. He's doing bad business with good cheer.

DIN   He really is being ruined; I too lost my goods, found my ills, and am out of the picture for you.

| AST | It's silly of you to want to make undone with your words | 730 |

what's done. Even Thetis stopped lamenting for her son.[41]

DIN   Won't I be sent in to you now?

AST   Why you more than the soldier?

DIN   Well, because I gave more.

AST   Well, you were also sent in more when you were giving. Let in turn those who give use our services because of what they give. You've learned the alphabet; now that you know it, let others learn it.

| | | 735 |

---

[41] Thetis, a sea goddess, was the mother of Achilles, the greatest hero in Homer's *Iliad*.

DIN discant, dum mihi commentari liceat, ne oblitus siem.
AST quid erit interea magistrae, dum tu commentabere?
     uolt [interim] illa itidem commentari.
DIN   quid?
AST   rem accipere identidem.
DIN dedi equidem hodie: ⟨iussi⟩ ei quinque argenti deferri
     minas,
740   praeterea unam in opsonatum.
AST   idem istoc delatum scio.
     de eo nunc bene sunt tua uirtute.
DIN   ei! meane ut inimici mei
     bona istic caedant? mortuom hercle me quam ut id pa-
     tiar mauelim.
AST stultu's.
DIN   quid est? aperi re⟨m⟩. quid iam, ⟨Astaphium⟩?
AST   quia pol mauelim
     mihi inimicos inuidere quam med inimicis meis;
745   nam inuidere alii bene esse, tibi male esse, miseria est.
     qui inuident egent; illis quibus inuidetur, i rem habent.
DIN non licet donati opsoni me participem fieri?
AST si uolebas participari, auferres dimidium domum.
     nam item ut Accherunti hic ⟨apud nos⟩ ratio accepti
     scribitur:
750   intro accipitur; quando acceptum est, non potest ferri
     foras.
     bene uale.

736 argentarilliceam *B*, argentari illic eam *CD*, commentari liceat
Acidalius, adcentare liceat *Lindsay*   738 interim *del. Bothe*
    739 iussi *add. Brix*   742 cedent *P*, caedant *Goetz*
    743 aperire *P*, aperi rem *Lindsay*   Astaphium *add. Lindsay uer-*
sus in codicibus post 746 *inuenitur, hic posuit Weise*

DIN   Let them learn it, so long as I may practice it so as not to forget.

AST   What will become of your teacher in the meantime, while you practice? She wants to practice in the same way.

DIN   Practice what?

AST   Receiving tuition fees again and again.

DIN   I for one have given her mine today: I had five silver minas brought to her, and in addition one for provi-   740
sions.

AST   I know that this was brought there. They're now having a good time from it thanks to you.

DIN   Ah! Should my enemies slaughter my goods in there? I'd rather be dead than bear this.

AST   You're being stupid.

DIN   How so? Explain. Well then, Astaphium?

AST   Because I'd prefer my enemies envying me to me envy-   745
ing my enemies: it's wretchedness to envy another having a good time, having a bad time yourself. Those who envy are in need; those who are envied have money.

DIN   May I not have my share of the provisions I gave as a gift?

AST   If you wanted to have your share, you should have taken half home: just as in the Underworld, here at our place an account is kept of goods received. One receives de-   750
posits inside; once received, there are no withdrawals. Goodbye.

---

747 do *P*, donati *Spengel*, dimidio *Lindsay*
749 apud nos *add. Schoell*
750 accipiamur *P*, accipitur *Spengel*, accipimus *Camerarius*

351

DIN	resiste.
AST	omitte.
DIN	sine eam intro.
AST	ad te quidem.
DIN	immo istoc ad uos ⟨uolo⟩ ire.
AST	non potest, nimium petis.
DIN	sine experiri—
AST	immo opperire. uis est experirier.
DIN	dic me adesse.
AST	abi, occupata est. res ita est, ne frustra sis.
755 DIN	redin an non redis?
AST	[si] uocat me quae in me potest plus quam potes.
DIN	uno uerbo—
AST	eloquere.
DIN	mittin me intro?
AST	mendax es, abi.
	unum aiebas, tria iam dixti uerba atque ⟨ea⟩ mendacia.
DIN	abiit intro, exclusit. egon ut haec mi patiar fieri?
	iam hercle ego tibi, illecebra, ludos faciam clamore in uia,
760	quae aduorsum legem accepisti a plurumis pecuniam;
	iam hercle apud nouos omnis magistratus faxo erit nomen tuom,
	postid ego te manum iniciam quadrupuli, uenefica,
	suppostrix puerum. ego edepol iam tua probra aperibo omnia.

752 uolo *add. Bücheler*   753 experire *P*, experirier *Camerarius*
755 si *del. Geppert*   que *B*, quae *CD*, qui *Schoell* (*qui* si *non delet*)   quam potest *P*, quam potes *Lambinus*   *fortasse* si uocat me qui in me plus quam tu potest   757 ea *add. Gulielmus*
761 omnis *del. Bergk*   763 itua *P*, iam tua *Camerarius*

DIN   Stop! (*grabs her*)

AST   Let go!

DIN   Let me go in.

AST   Yes, to your place.

DIN   No, I want to go in there to your place.

AST   It's impossible, you demand too much.

DIN   Let me try—

AST   (*interrupting*) No, wait. Trying is violence.

DIN   Say that I'm here.

AST   Go away, she's busy. That's how it is, don't fool yourself.

DIN   Are you coming back or not?   755

AST   A woman's calling me who has more power over me than you do.

DIN   In one word—

AST   (*interrupting*) Speak.

DIN   Are you letting me in?

AST   You're a liar, go away. You said "one word," but you've uttered five[42] now, and false ones at that.

Exit ASTAPHIUM into Phronesium's house.

DIN   She's gone in and locked me out. (*angrily*) Should I tolerate being treated this way? Now, you temptress, I'll shame you by my shouting in the street: you've received 760 money from a lot of men, against the law. I'll make sure that your name will be with all the new magistrates in an instant, and then I'll bring you to court to pay fourfold damages, you poisoner and smuggler-in of supposititious

---

[42] Three words in the Latin (*mittin me intro?*).

nil me ⟨prohibet⟩, perdidi omne quod fuit: fio impu-
dens
765   nec mi adeo est tantillum pensi iam quos capiam cal-
ceos.
sed quid ego hic clamo? quid si me iubeat intro mit-
tier?
conceptis me non facturum uerbis iurem, si uelit.
nugae sunt. si stimulos pugnis caedis, manibus plus do-
let.
de nihilo nihil est irasci, quae te non flocci facit.
770   sed quid hoc est? pro di immortales! Calliclem uideo
senem,
meus qui affinis fuit, ancillas duas constrictas ducere,
alteram tonstricem illius, alteram ancillam suam.
pertimui: postquam una cura cor meum mouit modo,
timeo ne [me] male facta antiqua mea sint inuenta om-
nia.

IV. iii: CALLICLES. ANCILLA CALLICLIS.
DINIARCHVS. SYRA

775   CAL   egon tibi male dicam aut tibi atque male uelim? ut ani-
mus meust,
propemodum expertae estis quam ego sim mitis
tranquillusque homo.
rogitaui ego uos uerberatas ambas pendentis simul;

764 prohibet *add. Leo*   fio impudens *P*, fugio, impudens *Grat-
wick*   772 huius *P*, illius *Enk*   774 me *del. Camerarius*
775 adte *P*, atque *Ussing*
776 similes *P*, sim mitis *Camerarius*, sim lenis *Lindsay*

---

43 The "new magistrates" are the *tresuiri capitales*, the "Board of
Three" responsible for prisons and executions. The fourfold amount

children![43] Now I'll reveal all your misdeeds. Nothing prevents me, I've lost everything I had. I'm becoming shameless and I haven't the slightest bit of concern now   765 which shoes I put on.[44]

(*after calming down*) But why am I shouting here? What if she had me sent in? I'd swear in solemn terms that I wouldn't go, even if she wanted it. (*pauses*) That's nonsense! If you beat cattle prods with your fists, your hands hurt more. There's no point in getting angry for nothing about a girl who doesn't care a straw about you.

(*looks around*) But what's this? Immortal gods! I can   770 see old Callicles, who was a relation of mine, bringing two tied-up slave girls, one the hairdresser of that woman, the other his own servant. I've got scared: just after one worry has moved my heart, I'm afraid that my old misdeeds have all been discovered. (*hides against a wall*)

Enter CALLICLES *from the right, followed by his* SERVANT GIRL *and* SYRA, *both tied up and watched over by slaves.*

CAL   (*to the women*) I should speak hard words to you or to   775 you, and hold hard wishes against you? To my mind you've pretty much experienced what a mild and calm man I am. I've questioned both of you together while you were hung up and being beaten. I remember, I

was normally demanded for theft but is here used as punishment for the fraudulent introduction of children into a family.

[44] The soft, refined shoes of the city dweller or the work shoes of the farmer or soldier.

commemini, quo quicque pacto sitis confessae scio;
hic nunc uolo scire eodem pacto‹n› sine malo fatea-
     mini.
780 quamquam uos colubrino ingenio ambae estis, edico
     prius
ne duplicis habeatis linguas, ne ego bilinguis uos ne-
     cem,
nisi si ad tintinnaculos uoltis uos educi uiros.

ANC uis subigit uerum fateri, ita lora laedunt bracchia.

CAL at si uerum mi eritis fassae, uinclis exsoluemini.

785 DIN etiamnum quid sit negoti falsus incertusque sum,
nisi quia timeo tamen, egomet ‹quia› quod peccaui
     scio.

CAL omnium primum diuorsae state—em sic, istuc uolo;
neue inter uos significetis, ego ero paries. loquere tu.

ANC quid loquar?

CAL   quid puero factum est, mea quem peperit filia,
790 meo nepote? capita rerum expedite.

ANC   istae dedi.

CAL iam tace. accepistin puerum tu ab hac?

SYRA   accepi.

CAL   tace.
nil moror praeterea. satis es fassa.

SYRA   infitias non eo.

---

778 quicquam *P*, quicque *Camerarius*, quicquid *Lindsay*
779 pacto‹n› *Studemund*
786 ego net quid *B*, ego nec quid *CD*, egomet quia quod *Leo*

know how you admitted everything. I want to know now whether you admit it here in the same way without a beating. Although you both have the character of ser-   780 pents, I'm telling you in advance not to have double tongues, so that I won't kill you two-tongued creatures, unless you want to be taken out to the clanging men.[45]

SERVANT Your brutal treatment forces us to admit the truth, that's how the straps hurt our arms.

CAL But if you admit the truth to me, you'll be set free from your bonds.

DIN (*aside*) Even now I'm in the dark and uncertain as to   785 what business this is, except that I'm afraid nevertheless because I know what wrong I've done.

CAL First of all, stand apart from each other—there, like this, that's what I want; and so that you won't make signs to each other, I'll be a wall. (*positions himself in the middle; to his servant girl*) You, speak.

SERVANT What should I speak?

CAL What happened to the boy my daughter gave birth to, my grandchild? The main points, quickly.   790

SERVANT I gave him to her. (*points to Syra*)

CAL Be quiet now. (*to Syra*) Did you receive the boy from her?

SYRA Yes.

CAL Be quiet. I want nothing more. You've admitted enough.

SYRA I'm not denying anything.

---

[45] The "clanging men" are executioners, who carried clanging chains and fetters; they had to live outside the Esquiline Gate in Rome.

CAL   iam liuorem tute scapulis istoc concinnas tuis.
      conueniunt adhuc utriusque uerba.

DIN   uae misero mihi!

795   mea nunc facinora aperiuntur clam quae speraui fore.

CAL   loquere tu. qui dare te huic puerum iussit?

ANC   era maior mea.

[CAL   quid tu, quor eum accepisti?

SYRA   era med orauit minor,
      puer uti ⟨af⟩ferretur eaque ut celarentur omnia.]

CAL   loquere tu. quid eo fecisti puero?

SYRA   ad meam eram detuli.

800 CAL   quid eo puero tua era fecit?

SYRA   erae meae extemplo dedit.

CAL   quoi, malum, erae?

ANC   duae sunt istae.

CAL   caue tu nisi quod te rogo.
      ex te exquiro.

SYRA   mater, inquam, filiae dono dedit.

CAL   plus quam dudum [inqua] loquere.

SYRA   plus tu rogitas.

CAL   responde ocius:
      quid illa quoi ⟨dono⟩ donatust?

SYRA   supposiuit.

CAL   quoi?

797–98 *del.* Langen   798 ⟨af⟩ferretur *Camerarius*
800 facit *P*, fecit s   803 inqua *del. Bothe*
804 dono *add. Kampmann*

---

[46] From the beatings.

[47] Her older mistress is the wife of Callicles; her younger one would be his daughter.

CAL   With that you're now giving your shoulder blades a darker color.[46] So far the words of the two agree.

DIN   (*aside*) Poor, wretched me! Now my misdeeds are being   795
revealed, which I hoped would be secret.

CAL   (*to his servant girl*) You, speak. Who told you to give the boy to this woman?

SERVANT   My older mistress.[47]

[CAL   (*to Syra*) Well then? Why did you receive him?

SYRA   My younger mistress[48] asked me that a boy should be brought to her and that all this should be kept secret.]

CAL   (*to Syra*) You, speak. What did you do with that boy?

SYRA   I brought him to my mistress.[49]

CAL   What did your mistress do with that boy?   800

SYRA   She gave him to my mistress[50] at once.

CAL   What mistress, damn it?

SERVANT   There are two of them.

CAL   (*to his servant girl*) You, watch out, unless I ask you for something! (*to Syra*) I'm asking you.

SYRA   I'm telling you, the mother gave him to her daughter as a present.

CAL   You're talking more than before.

SYRA   You are asking more.

CAL   Answer quickly: what about the woman who got him as a gift?

SYRA   She smuggled him into the family.

CAL   Whose?

---

[48] Her younger mistress is Phronesium; her older one would be Phronesium's mother.

[49] Phronesium's mother.

[50] Phronesium herself.

	SYRA	sibi.
805	CAL	pro filiolon?
	SYRA	pro filiolo.
	CAL	di, opsecro uostram fidem!

CAL ut facilius alia quam alia eundem puerum unum parit!
haec labore alieno puerum peperit sine doloribus.
puer quidem beatust: matres duas habet et auias duas:
iam metuo patres quot fuerint. uide sis facinus mulie-
bre.

810 ANC magis pol haec malitia pertinet ad uiros quam ad mu-
lieres:
uir illam, non mulier praegnatem fecit.

CAL   [et] idem ego istuc scio.
tu bona ei custos fuisti.

ANC   plus potest qui plus ualet.
uir erat, plus ualebat: uicit, quod petebat apstulit.

CAL et tibi quidem hercle idem ⟨uir⟩ attulit magnum ma-
lum.

815 ANC idem istuc ipsa, etsi tu taceas, reapse experta intellego.

CAL numquam te facere hodie quiui ut is quis esset diceres.

ANC tacui ad⟨huc⟩: nunc ⟨non⟩ tacebo, quando adest nec
se indicat.

DIN lapideus sum, commouere me miser non audeo.
res palam omnis est, meo illic nunc sunt capiti comitia.

820 meum illuc facinus, mea stultitia est. timeo quam mox
nominer.

CAL loquere filiam meam quis integram stuprauerit.

811 et *del. Camerarius*
814 uir *add. Guyet*
815 de *P*, idem *Kiessling*   istoc *P*, istuc *Geppert*
817 ad nunc nunc *B*, at nunc nunc *CD*, adhuc nunc non *Seyffert*

SYRA Her own.

CAL As her son?   805

SYRA Yes, as her son.

CAL Gods, I implore your protection! How much easier it
was for one woman than for the other to give birth to
one and the same boy! This one gave birth to a boy
through another's labor and without pains. The boy at
least got lucky: he has two mothers and two maternal
grandmothers. Now I'm concerned about how many
fathers there have been. Do look at a woman's crime!

SERVANT This wickedness has more to do with men than with   810
women: a man got her pregnant, not a woman.

CAL I know that too. You've been a good guardian for her.

SERVANT The one who is stronger can do more. He was a man,
he was stronger. He overpowered her and took away
what he was after.

CAL And to you that same man brought a great thrashing.

SERVANT I'm well aware of that, even if you keep silent, be-   815
cause I've experienced it in reality.

CAL I've never managed today to make you say who it was.

SERVANT I've been silent till now; now I won't be silent be-
cause he's present and doesn't show himself.

DIN (*aside*) I'm petrified! Poor me, I don't dare to move. The
whole business is out and there the assembly deciding
over my life is taking place now. That's my misdeed,   820
my stupidity. I'm scared to think how soon I'll be men-
tioned.

CAL (*to his servant girl*) Tell me who violated my innocent
daughter.

ANC   uideo ego te, propter male facta qui es patronus pa-
          rieti.

DIN   nec uiuos nec mortuos sum nec quid nunc faciam scio
     neque ut hinc abeam neque ut hunc adeam scio, ti-
         more torpeo.

825 CAL   dicin an non?

ANC   Diniarchus, quoi illam prius desponderas.

CAL   ubi is homo est quem dicis?

DIN   assum, Callicles. per tua opsecro
     genua ut tu istuc insipienter factum sapienter feras
     mihique ignoscas quod animi impos uini uitio fecerim.

CAL   non placet: in mutum culpam confers ⟨qui non⟩ quit
         loqui.

830   nam uinum si fabulari possit se defenderet.
     non uinum ⟨uiris⟩ moderari, sed uiri uino solent,
     qui quidem probi sunt; uerum qui improbust si quasi
         bibit
     siue adeo caret temeto, tamen ab ingenio improbust.

DIN   scio equidem quae nolo multa mi audienda ob noxiam.

835   ego tibi me obnoxium esse fateor culpae compotem.

ANC   Callicles, uide quaeso magnam ne facias iniuriam:
     reus solutus causam dicit, testis uinctos attines.

CAL   soluite istas. agite, abite tu domum et tu autem do-
         mum.
     eloquere haec erae tu: puerum reddat, si quis eum pe-
         tat.

829 qui non *add. Luchs*
830 possit *P*, posset *Camerarius*
831 uiris *add. Schoell*
836 quaesomnem *P*, quaeso magnam ne *Schoell*, in quaestione
ne *Leo*

SERVANT (*calling to Diniarchus*) I can see you, you who are
      shielding the wall because of your misdeeds.

DIN   (*aside*) I'm neither alive nor dead, and I don't know what
      I should do now; I don't know how to get away from here
      or how to approach him. I'm paralyzed with fear.

CAL   (*to his servant girl*) Are you telling me or not?   825

SERVANT Diniarchus, to whom you'd once betrothed her.

CAL   Where is the man you name?

DIN   (*coming forward*) Here I am, Callicles. I implore you by
      your knees to accept my unwise deed wisely and to for-
      give me for what I did bereft of reason, through the fault
      of wine.

CAL   I don't like that; you're laying the blame on someone
      dumb who can't speak: if the wine could speak, it would   830
      defend itself. Wine is not in the habit of controlling men,
      but men are in the habit of controlling wine, at least
      those who are decent. But an indecent man, whether he
      drinks a little or whether he abstains from alcohol, is
      nonetheless indecent in his nature.

DIN   I know that because of my offense I'll have to listen to a
      lot of things I don't want to hear. I admit that I'm guilty   835
      and at your mercy.

SERVANT Callicles, please watch out that you don't commit a
      great injustice: the defendant is pleading his cause un-
      bound, but the witnesses you keep bound.

CAL   (*to his slaves*) Release them. (*to the women*) Come on,
      go away, you to your home and you to yours. (*to Syra*)
      You, tell your mistress: she is to return the boy if anyone
      demands him.

Exeunt the SERVANT GIRL OF CALLICLES *and* SYRA *to the
right.*

840   eamus tu in ius.

DIN   quid uis in ius me ire? tu es praetor mihi.
        uerum te opsecro ut tuam gnatam des mi uxorem, Cal-
           licles.

CAL   eundem pol te iudicasse pridem istam rem intellego.
        nam hau mansisti, dum ego darem illam: tute sumpsisti
           tibi.
        nunc habeas ut nactu's. uerum hoc ego te multabo
           bolo:

845   sex talenta magna dotis demam pro ista inscitia.

DIN   bene agis mecum.

CAL   filium istinc tuom te meliust repetere.
        ceterum uxorem quam primum potest abduce ex aedi-
           bus.
        ego abeo. iam illi remittam nuntium affini meo,
        dicam ut aliam condicionem filio inueniat suo.

850 DIN at ego ab hac puerum reposcam, ne mox infitias eat;
        nihil est, nam eapse ultro ut factum est fecit omnem
           rem palam.
        sed nimium pol opportune eccam eapse egreditur fo-
           ras.
        ne ista stimulum longum habet quae usque illinc cor
           pungit meum.

      IV. iv: PHRONESIVM. DINIARCHVS. ASTAPHIVM
PHRO blitea et lutea est meretrix nisi quae sapit in uino ad
      rem suam;

    842 eundem *P*, eam dem? *Palmer*
    852 oportuna *P*, opportune ς

CAL (*to Diniarchus*) You, let's go to court.   840

DIN Why do you want me to go to court? You are my prae-
     tor.[51] But I entreat you to give me your daughter in mar-
     riage, Callicles.

CAL I know that you yourself have already pronounced judg-
     ment on that matter: you didn't wait for me to give her
     to you, you took her yourself. Now keep her in accor-
     dance with that possession of her which you have already
     taken. But I'll punish you with this fine: I'll deduct six   845
     great talents from your dowry for your indiscretion.

DIN You're treating me kindly.

CAL You'd better demand your son back from there. As for
     the rest, take your wife out of my house as quickly as
     possible. I'm off. I'll send a message to my relative now
     and tell him that he should find another match for his
     son.

Exit CALLICLES *to the right.*

DIN But I shall demand my son back from this woman, so that   850
     she won't deny it later; it won't help her: she herself has
     revealed how the entire business was done. But look, just
     in the nick of time she's coming out herself. Goodness,
     she does have a long goad; even from all that distance
     she's piercing my heart.

Enter PHRONESIUM *from her house, followed by* ASTAPHIUM,
who stops in the doorway.

PHRO (*to the audience*) A prostitute is silly and worthless, un-
      less she's smart with regard to her business even while

---

[51] Roman official with mainly judicial functions.

855		si alia membra uino madeant, cor sit saltem sobrium.
		nam mihi diuidiae est, [in] tonstricem meam ⟨quae⟩ simulabam male
		edixe et meum Diniarchi puerum inuentum filium.
858		ubi id audiui, quam ***
858ᵃ	DIN	*** quam penes est mea omnis res et liberi.
	PHRO	uideo eccum qui amans tutorem med optauit suis bonis.
860	DIN	mulier, ad ⟨te⟩ sum profectus.
	PHRO	quid agitur, uoluptas mea?
	DIN	non "uoluptas," aufer nugas, nil ego nunc de istac re ago.
	PHRO	scio mecastor quid uelis et quid postules et quid petas:
		me uidere uis, [et me] te a me ire postulas, puerum petis.
	DIN	di immortales! ut planiloqua est, paucis ut rem ipsam attigit!
865	PHRO	scio equidem sponsam tibi esse et filium ex sponsa tua,
		et tibi uxorem ducendam iam, esse alibi iam animum tuom,
		ut ⟨me⟩ quasi pro derelicta sis habiturus. sed tamen
		cogitato mus pusillus quam sit sapiens bestia,
		aetatem qui non cubili ⟨uni⟩ umquam committit suam,
870		quin, si unum [odium] opsideatur, aliud ⟨iam⟩ perfugium ⟨ele⟩gerit.

856 in *del. Camerarius*   sicut multam *P*, ⟨quae⟩ simulabam *Ussing*, sic mulcatam *Camerarius*

857 ea dixit *P*, edixe et *Ussing*   eum *P*, meum *Bothe*

858–58ᵃ *unus uersus in P, sed aliquid uidetur deesse*

860 adsum profectust *P*, ad te sum profectus *Acidalius*

862 uis *P*, uelis *Camerarius*

having wine. Even if the other limbs are drunk from   855
wine, at least her heart should be sober. Well, I'm un-
happy that my hairdresser let out what I was concealing
slyly and that my boy was discovered to be the son of
Diniarchus. When I heard this, how ***.

DIN   (*aside*) *** with whom all my possessions and my son
are.

PHRO   (*aside*) Look, I can see the lover who chose me as guard-
ian for his goods.

DIN   Woman, I was on my way to you.   860

PHRO   How are you, my darling?

DIN   None of your "darling," stop the nonsense, I'm not con-
cerned with that sort of thing now.

PHRO   I do know what you want, what you demand, and what
you seek; you want to see me, you demand to leave me,
and you seek your boy.

DIN   Immortal gods! How direct she is, in how few words she
hit the nail on the head!

PHRO   I know that you have a betrothed and a son from your   865
betrothed, that you need to marry her now, and that
your mind is already elsewhere, so that you'll treat me as
an abandoned girl. But still, think what a clever animal
the little mouse is; it never entrusts its life to a single hole
without already having chosen another shelter if one is   870
being besieged.

---

863 et me *del. Bothe*   amare *P*, a me ire *Leo*
867 et *BC*, e *D*, ut me *Lambinus*
869 uni *add. Bücheler*
870 quia si *B*, quasi *CD*, quin si *Bothe*   odium *B*, *om. CD*, ostium
Camerarius   perfugium gerit *P*, iam perfugium elegerit *Leo*

DIN   otium ubi erit, de istis rebus tum amplius tecum lo-
        quar.
       nunc puerum redde.

PHRO   immo amabo ut hos dies aliquos sinas
       eum esse apud me.

DIN   minime.

PHRO   amabo.

DIN   quid ⟨eo⟩ opust?

PHRO   in rem meam ⟨est⟩.
       triduom hoc saltem, dum miles aliqua circumducitur,

875   sine me habere: siquidem habebo, tibi quoque etiam
         proderit;
       si auferes [puerum], a milite omnis [tum] mihi spes
         animam efflauerit.

DIN   factum cupio, nam refacere si uelim, non est locus;
       nunc puero utere et procura, quando quor cures habes.

PHRO multum amo te ob istam rem mecastor. ubi domi me-
       tues malum,

880   fugito huc ad me: saltem amicus mi esto momentarius.

DIN   bene uale, Phronesium.

PHRO   iam ⟨me⟩ tuom oculum ⟨non⟩ uocas?

DIN   id quoque interatim furtim nomen commemorabitur.
       numquid uis?

PHRO   fac ualeas.

DIN   operae ubi mi erit, ad te uenero.

---

873 eo *add. Studemund*   opus *P*, opust *Camerarius*   iure mea *P*,
in rem meam *Bothe*   est *add. Lambinus*
   874 aliquo milis *P, transp. Bothe*   aliquo *P*, aliqua *Lindsay*
   875 in eam rem siquid *P*, sine me habere siquidem *Bücheler*
   876 puerum *del. Guyet*   tum *del. Mueller*
   877 refacere *P*, nefacere ⸑

DIN When I have spare time, I'll talk about those things with you in more detail. Now return my boy.

PHRO No, I kindly ask you to let him be with me for the next few days.

DIN Absolutely not.

PHRO Please!

DIN What's that necessary for?

PHRO It's for my benefit. At least let me have him for these three days while the soldier is being tricked somehow; if I have him, it'll also benefit you. If you take him away, all hope from the soldier will have breathed its last. 875

DIN I want it done: even if I wanted to undo it, there isn't an opportunity; now use the boy and take good care of him, since you have reason to be careful.

PHRO I really love you a great deal because of this. When you're afraid of trouble at home, flee here to me; you must at least be my temporary friend. 880

DIN Goodbye, Phronesium.

PHRO Are you no longer calling me the apple of your eye?

DIN That name will also be secretly mentioned on occasion. Do you want anything?

PHRO Make sure you're well.

DIN When I have leisure, I'll come to you.

Exit DINIARCHUS to the right.

---

878 procures *P*, quor cures *Leo*, pro cura aes *Schoell*

880 manubinarius *P*, manubiarius *Camerarius*, momentarius *Enk in commentario*

881 me *et* non *add. Camerarius*

882 interim futatim *P*, interatim furtim *Lindsay*, interim furatim *Lipsius*

PHRO ille quidem hinc abiit, apscessit. dicere hic quiduis licet.

885 uerum est uerbum quod memoratur: "ubi amici, ibidem opes."

propter hunc spes etiam est hodie tactuiri militem;

quem ego ecastor mage amo quam me, dum id quod cupio inde aufero.

quae quom multum apstulimus, hau multum ⟨eius⟩ apparet quod datum est:

ita sunt gloriae meretricum.

AST   aha tace!

PHRO   quid est, opsecro?

890 AST ⟨pater⟩ adest pueri.

PHRO   sine eumpse adire huc. sine, si is est modo.

AST ⟨ipsus est.⟩

PHRO   sine eumpse adire, ut cupit, ad me.

AST   rectam tenet.

PHRO ne istum ecastor hodie aspiciam confectum fallaciis.

ACTVS V

V. i: STRATOPHANES. PHRONESIVM.
STRABAX. ASTAPHIVM

STRAT ego minam auri fero supplicium damnas ad amicam meam.

ut illud acceptum sit prius quod perdidi, hoc addam insuper.

895 sed quid uideo? eram atque ancillam ante aedis. adeundae haec mihi.

quid hic uos agitis?

---

886 tantum rimlitem *P*, tactum iri militem *Petit*
888 eius *add. Leo*   890 pater *add. Guyet*

PHRO He's left, he's gone away. I can say here whatever I like.
The saying they quote is true: "where your friends are, 885
there your resources are." Because of him I still have
hope that the soldier will be tricked today; I love that
soldier more than myself as long as I carry off from him
what I want. When we've taken away a lot, not much of
what we've been given can be seen: that's what the glori-
ous deeds of prostitutes are like.

AST Ah, be quiet!

PHRO What's the matter, please?

AST The boy's father is here. 890

PHRO Let him come here. Do let him, if only it's him.

AST It's him in person.

PHRO Let him come to me as he wishes.

AST He's headed straight here.

PHRO Seriously, I'll see him destroyed by my tricks today.

ACT FIVE

Enter STRATOPHANES *from the right, with a money belt on.*

STRAT *(to the audience)* Obliged to pay, I'm bringing a gold
mina to my girlfriend as amends. I'll add this on top in
order that what I lost earlier should be accepted. But 895
what do I see? Mistress and slave girl in front of the
house. I need to approach them. *(to the women)* What
are you two doing here?

---

891 ipsus est *add. Leo*
892 hastis *P,* aspiciam *Leo*
893 damnis *B,* dampnis *CD,* damnas *Dousa*

PHRO	ne me appella.
STRAT	nimium saeuis.
PHRO	sic datur.

potine ut mihi molestus ne si[e]s?

STRAT   ‹ec›quid, Astaphium, litium est?

AST   merito ecastor tibi suscenset.

PHRO   egon, atque isti etiam parum
    male uolo.

STRAT   ego, mea uoluptas, si quid peccaui prius,

900   supplicium hanc minam fero auri. si minus credis, re-
      spice.

PHRO manus uotat prius quam penes sese habeat quicquam
    credere.

    puero opust cibo, opus est matri autem, quae puerum
    lauit,

    opus nutrici, lacte ut habeat, ueteris uini largiter

    ut dies noctesque potet, opust ligno, opust carbonibus,

905   fasciis opus est, puluinis, cunis, incunabulis,

    oleo ‹opust›, opus est farina; porro opus est totum
    diem:

    numquam hoc uno die efficiatur opus quin opus sem-
    per siet;

    non enim possunt militares pueri ut auium educier.

STRAT respice ergo: accipe hoc ‹sis› qui istuc efficias opus.

910 PHRO cedo, quamquam parum est.

STRAT   addam etiam unam minam istuc post.

896 nimius eui sic *P*, nimium saeuis. PHRO sic datur *Spengel*
897 sies *P* (*scriptio plena*)   quid *P*, ecquid *Bücheler*
902 cibum *P*, cibo *Spengel*
906 oleum *P*, oleo *Spengel*   opust *add. Bücheler*   purus *P*, porro
opus *Bücheler*

PHRO (*without looking at him*) Stop addressing me.

STRAT You're too cruel.

PHRO That's my way. Can't you stop annoying me?

STRAT Is there any ill-feeling, Astaphium?

AST She's angry with you, and deservedly so.

PHRO Yes, and even so I'm still too well-disposed toward him.

STRAT My darling, if I did something wrong before, I'm bring- 900
ing you this gold mina as amends. If you distrust me, look
around here.

PHRO My hand forbids me trusting anything before it has it in-
side it. The boy needs food, and my mother, who washes
the boy, needs it too; in order to have milk, the nurse
needs a lot of old wine to drink day and night; we need
wood, we need charcoal, we need swaddling clothes, 905
cushions, a cradle, and cradle straps;[52] we need oil, we
need flour; further, we are in need the whole day. The
needs can never be met in one day without there being
needs all the time: sons of soldiers cannot be brought up
like the young of birds.[53]

STRAT Then look around here: please take this, so that you can
meet those needs with it.

PHRO Give it to me, although it's too little. 910

STRAT (*handing over some money*) I'll add yet another mina to
it later.

---

[52] "Cradle straps" (*incunabula*) prevent the baby from falling out.
[53] I.e., with very little.

---

908 et auio *P*, ut auium *Palmer*

909 sis *add. Spengel*

910 ad omnae manuc istic poste *P*, addam etiam unam minam istuc
post *Leo*

PHRO   parum est.
STRAT   tuo arbitratu quod iubebis dabitur. da nunc sauium.
PHRO   mitte me, inquam, odiosu's.
STRAT   nil fit, non amor, teritur dies.
       plus decem pondo . . . amoris pauxillisper perdidi.
PHRO   accipe hoc atque auferto intro.
STRAB   ubi mea amica est gentium?
915   nec ruri neque hic operis quicquam facio, corrumpor
           situ,
       ita mıser cubando in lecto hic exspectando obdurui.
       sed eccam uideo. heus amica, quid agis [mille]?
STRAT   quis illic ‹est› homo?
PHRO   quem ego ecastor mage amo quam te.
STRAT   quam me?
‹PHRO   quam te.
STRAT›   quo modo?
PHRO   hoc modo ut molestus ne sis.
STRAT   iam‹ne› abis, postquam aurum habes?
920 PHRO   condidi intro quod dedisti.
STRAB   ades, amica, te alloquor.
PHRO   at ego ad te ibam, mea delicia.

     917 mille *del.* ꕿ   est *add. Weise*
     918 ‹PHRO quam te. STRAT› *add. Bothe*
     919 iam *P*, iamne *Guyet*

    [54] Financially he has lost far more than ten pounds of silver.
    [55] The *opus*, "work," he does in the country is farm work, whereas
the "work" at Phronesium's place is a euphemism for intercourse.

PHRO It's still too little.

STRAT You'll get what you command, as you see fit. Now give me a kiss. (*grabs her*)

PHRO Let go of me, I'm telling you, you're annoying me.

STRAT Nothing comes out of it, I'm not loved, the day is being wasted. Bit by bit I've lost over ten pounds . . . of love.[54]

PHRO (*handing the money over to Astaphium*) Take this and bring it inside.

Exit ASTAPHIUM *into Phronesium's house. Enter* STRABAX *from there.*

STRAB Where on earth is my girlfriend? I'm not doing any   915
work in the country or here[55] and I'm going bad from sitting around: that's how stiff I got from lying on the couch and waiting here, wretch that I am. But look, I can see her. Hey, girlfriend, what are you doing?

STRAT (*to Phronesium*) Who is that person?

PHRO Someone I love more than you.

STRAT Than me?

PHRO Yes, than you.

STRAT How?

PHRO This is how, so that you won't be a nuisance. (*turns toward the door*)

STRAT Are you leaving already, now that you've got the money?

PHRO I've put inside what you gave me.   920

STRAB Come here, girlfriend, I'm talking to you.

PHRO But I was on my way to you, my darling.

STRAB   hercle uero serio,

     quamquam ego tibi uideor stultus, gaudere aliqui me
       uolo;

     nam quamquam tu es bella, malo tuo, nisi ego aliqui
       gaudeo.

PHRO uin te amplectar, sauium dem?

STRAB   quiduis face ‹qui› gaudeam.

925 STRAT meosne ante oculos ego illam patiar alios amplexa-
       rier?

     mortuom hercle me hodie satiust. apstine hoc, mulier,
       manum,

     nisi si te mea [manu ui in] machaera uis et hunc ‹una›
       mori.

PHRO philippiari satiust, miles, si te amari postulas;

     auro, hau ferro deterrere potes ‹hunc› ne amem, Stra-
       tophanes.

930 STRAT qui, malum, bella aut faceta es, quae ames hominem
       isti modi?

PHRO uenitne in mentem tibi quod uerbum in cauea dixit
       histrio?

     "omnes homines ad suom quaestum callent et fasti-
       diunt."

STRAT huncine hominem te amplexari tam horridum ac tam
       squalidum?

PHRO quamquam hic squalust, quam‹quam› hic horridus,
       scitus, bellust mihi.

923 es bella, malo tu *P, transp. Leo*
924 qui *add. Ussing*
926 medio satius *P*, me hodie satiust *Brix*
927 manu ui in *del. Schoell*   et hunc uis *P*, uis et hunc una
Bücheler

STRAB Really and truly, even though I may seem stupid to you, I want to enjoy myself somehow: even though you're pretty, you'll pay for it, unless I enjoy myself somehow.

PHRO Do you want me to embrace you and give you a kiss?

STRAB Do anything you like that makes me enjoy myself.

STRAT Should I tolerate it that she's embracing other men in   925
front of my eyes? It would be better for me to be dead today. Woman, take your hand away from him, unless you want you and him to die together by my sword!

PHRO It's better to cough up Philippics, soldier, if you expect to be loved; it's with gold, not with the sword[56] that you can deter me from loving him, Stratophanes.

STRAT How the deuce can you be pretty or charming when you   930
love a person like that?

PHRO Doesn't the saying that an actor spoke in the theater come to your mind? "All men are insensitive and squeamish according to the demands of their profession."

STRAT Is it possible that you embrace such an unkempt and filthy person?

PHRO Even though he's filthy, even though he's unkempt, he's smart and pretty to me.

[56] Ridicule of the famous words of Pyrrhus (Enn. *ann.* 184–85 Skutsch) that one needs to fight with the sword, not with gold.

928 nihiliphiari *P*, philippiari *Spengel*
929 hunc *add. Seyffert*
932 et *P*, nec *Bothe*
934 quali est *B*, qualis est *CD*, squalust *Lipsius*   quam *P*, quamquam *Merula*   citus bellum hi *P*, scitus bellust mihi *Lipsius*

935 STRAT dedin ego aurum—
PHRO   mihi? dedisti filio cibaria.
       nunc, si hanc tecum esse speras, alia opust auri mina.
STRAB malam rem is et magnam magno opere, serua tibi uia-
          ticum.
STRAT quid isti debes?
PHRO   tria.
STRAT   quae tria nam?
PHRO   unguenta, noctem, sauium.
STRAT par pari respondet. uerum nunc saltem, ⟨et⟩si
       ⟨istunc⟩ amas,
940   dan tu mihi de tuis deliciis [sum] quicquid ⟨est⟩
       pauxillulum?
PHRO quid id, amabo, est quod dem? dic tu.
⟨STRAB   ne id quidem, si quid⟩ supererit.
STRAT Campans, dico tibi, acceptaui; i consultum istuc, mi
          homo.
STRAB caue faxis uolnus tibi iam quoi sunt dentes ferrei.
STRAT uolgo ad se omnis intro mittit: apstine istac tu ma-
          num.
945 STRAB iam hercle cum magno ⟨malo⟩ tu uapula uir stre-
          nuos.

      939 si *P*, ⟨et⟩si ⟨istunc⟩ *Leo*

      940 sum *del. Geppert* est *add. Geppert*

      941 dictum super feri *B*, dictum super fert *CD*, dic tu. ⟨STRAB ne
id quidem, si quid⟩ supererit *Enk*

      942 capas *B*, campas *CD*, Campans *Schoell* dicit *P*, dico tibi
Kruse auaui *B*, ab aui *CD*, acceptaui *Lindsay* consultam *P*, i con-
sultum *Kruse*

      945 iam magno *P*, cum magno malo *Bothe*

STRAT Didn't I give gold— 935

PHRO (*interrupting*) To me? You gave food to your son. Now if you hope that this lady (*points to herself*) will be with you, another gold mina is needed.

STRAB (*to Stratophanes*) You're walking into your ruin, and a particularly big one at that; save some travel money for yourself.

STRAT (*to Phronesium*) What do you owe that person?

PHRO Three things.

STRAT Which three things?

PHRO Perfumes, the night, kissing.

STRAT She's quick at repartee. But even though you love that person, won't you give me at least the tiniest bit of your 940 delights now?

PHRO (*to Strabax*) Please, what is it that I should give him? You, tell me.

STRAB Not even this (*makes a gesture to indicate a small amount*), even if anything is left over.

STRAT Campanian,[57] I'm telling you, I've accepted your challenge; go over to your house to save yourself, my dear man.

STRAB Make sure you don't wound yourself now, since you have iron teeth.[58]

STRAT She lets everybody in to her promiscuously: you, keep your hand off her.

STRAB Now get a proper, thorough beating, you man of ac- 945 tion.

[57] An insult; the inhabitants of Campania were considered effeminate.

[58] His mouth is more dangerous than his sword; he only knows how to talk, not how to fight.

STRAT dedi ego huic aurum.

STRAB   at ego argentum.

STRAT   at ego pallam et purpuram.

STRAB   at ego ouis et lanam; et alia multa quae poscet dabo.
        meliust te minis certare mecum quam minaciis.

PHRO lepidu's ecastor mortalis, mi Strabax, perge opsecro.

950   stultus atque insanus damnis certant: nos saluae sumus.

STRAT age prior perde aliquid.

STRAB   immo tu prior perde et peri.

STRAT em tibi talentum argenti. Philippeum est, ⟨em⟩ tene
        tibi.

PHRO tanto melior: noster esto . . . sed de uostro uiuito.

STRAT ubi est quod tu das? solue zonas, prouocator. quid ti-
        mes?

955 STRAB tu peregrinu's, hic ⟨ego⟩ habito: non cum zona ego
        ambulo:
        pecua ad hanc collo in crumina ego obligata defero.
        quid dedi! ut discinxi hominem!

STRAT   immo ego uero qui dedi.

PHRO i intro, amabo, i, tu eris mecum; ⟨tum⟩ tu eris mecum
        quidem.

STRAT quid tu? quid ais? cum hocin ⟨eris⟩? ego ⟨ero⟩ poste-
        rior ⟨qui⟩ dedi?

946 eat apale puram *P*, at ego pallam et purpuram *Camerarius*
952 philippices est *P*, Philippeumst *Enk*   em² *add. Schoell*
954 xonas *P*, zonas *Ussing*, zonam *Bothe*
955 ego *add. Angelius*
958 tum *add. Ribbeck*
959 eris *et* ero *add. Ussing*   qui *add. Studemund*

STRAT I've given her gold.

STRAB But I've given silver.

STRAT But I, a mantle and a purple cloak.

STRAB But I, sheep and wool; and I'll give her many other things she asks for. It's better if you fight with me with cash than with brash.

PHRO You really are a charming man, my dear Strabax, please continue. An idiot and a madman are competing in 950 losses: we are safe.

STRAT Go on, lose something first.

STRAB No, you should lose something first and get lost.

STRAT Here's a silver talent for you. It's Philippic,[59] here, take it.

PHRO All the better of you: be one of us . . . but live of your own.

STRAT Where's what you are giving? Unfasten your belts, challenger. What are you afraid of?

STRAB You are a foreigner, I live here; I don't walk around with 955 my money belt on. I'm bringing sheep to her, tied to my neck in a wallet. What have I given! How I've removed this chap's belt!

STRAT No, what have I given!

PHRO (to Strabax) Go in, please, go, you'll be with me; (to Stratophanes) then you will be with me, too.

STRAT What are you doing? What do you say? Will you be with him? Will I, who have given you something, come second?

[59] The text is problematic: normally the adjective "Philippic" is only applied to gold.

960 PHRO tu dedisti iam, ⟨hic⟩ daturust: istuc habeo, hoc expeto.
　　　　uerum utrique mos geratur amborum ex sententia.
　STRAT fiat. ut rem gnatam uideo, hoc accipiundum est quod
　　　　　datur.
　STRAB　meum quidem te lectum certe occupare non sinam.
　PHRO lepide ecastor aucupaui atque ex mea sententia,
965　　　meamque ut rem uideo bene gestam, uostram rursum
　　　　　bene geram:
　　　　rem bonam si quis animatust facere, faciat ut sciam.
　　　　Veneris causa applaudite: eius haec in tutela est fabula.
　　　　[spectatores, bene ualete, plaudite atque exsurgite.]

　　　960 hic *add. Bücheler*
　　　965 debere negestam *P*, uideo bene gestam *Bothe*
　　　966 romabo *P*, rem bonam *Bücheler*　quid *P*, quis *Schoell*
　　　968 *uersum del. Geppert*

PHRO You have already given, he will still give: yours I have,   960
    his I'm seeking. But each of you will be gratified accord-
    ing to your wishes.

STRAT Yes. The way I see the situation, one has to accept what
    one's given.

STRAB I certainly won't let you occupy my bed.

PHRO (*to the audience*) I've netted them cleverly and according
    to my wish, and now that I've handled my affairs well,   965
    I'll handle yours well in turn: if anyone fancies having a
    good time, he should let me know. Applaud for the sake
    of Venus: this play is under her protection. [Spectators,
    farewell; applaud and rise.]

VIDULARIA

INTRODUCTORY NOTE

Of all the plays of the Varronian canon, the *Vidularia*, or "Tale of a Traveling-Bag," is the one that has been transmitted most poorly. We do not have the ending of the *Aulularia* or the beginning of the *Bacchides*, and some verses have been lost from the middle of the *Amphitruo*; but in none of these cases are we unable to understand the plot fully. By contrast, we have so little of the *Vidularia* that parts of the plot cannot even be reconstructed.

The text of the *Vidularia* is in such a bad state because, apart from a number of fragments quoted by ancient grammarians, it is only transmitted in the Ambrosian palimpsest, from which many leaves have been lost. A distant ancestor of the Palatine manuscripts must also still have had the play, as after the *Truculentus* the *Codex uetus Camerarii* contains the words *incipit Vidularia*, "here begins the *Vidularia*"; but since none of the Palatine manuscripts has preserved any of the text of the comedy, it is likely that the immediate ancestor of our extant manuscripts no longer had it, probably because the final pages of the codex were lost.

In the Ambrosian palimpsest the *Vidularia* is not the final play; it is preceded by the *Truculentus* and followed by the *Poenulus*. Because the palimpsest has an almost identical number of lines per page, and because its quaternions are numbered, we can say with reasonable certainty that the *Vidularia* was a fairly short play with roughly 800 to 830 verses.

Some more information on the relevant pages of the palimpsest may be helpful. A quaternion consists of four bifolios, yielding eight folios, or sixteen pages of text. The bifolios, consisting of animal skin, were put together in a systematic way, so that the first, fourth, fifth, eighth, ninth, twelfth, thirteenth, and sixteenth pages were the inside part of the skin ("int."), while the other pages were the outside part of the skin, originally covered by the animal's hair ("ext.").

Many folios of the *Truculentus* have been lost in the palimpsest; the last verse that we can read in its entirety is l. 390 on the last folio of quaternion lx. The remaining verses of this play, transmitted complete in the Palatine manuscripts, must have occupied two more quaternions and another folio in the palimpsest. The first folio of quaternion lxiii thus contains the ending of the *Truculentus*, which can be read with some difficulty. As this folio is part of a bifolio, containing also the eighth folio of the quaternion, the few letters that can be deciphered on folio eight, though by and large unclear in content, can be assigned to a definite position within the *Vidularia*. In modern editions the highly fragmentary verses on folio eight are referred to as ll. 17^a–17^g, even though a substantially larger number of verses than seventeen must have preceded; modern line numbering is continuous and does not take the obvious lacunae into account.

What is less clear is whether the beginning of the *Vidularia*, which has been preserved, was on the second or the third folio of this same quaternion. The folio containing the beginning of our play is now empty on the recto side and has the prologue on the verso side. The recto side probably contained a stage record in red ink, which was washed off more easily than black. As the folio has the structure int.–ext., it should be the third folio, which would mean that the second folio was left empty, an unusual procedure; but if the beginning stood on the second folio, the quaternion would have an irregular structure, which would also be unusual. The issue must remain unresolved.

Another bifolio exists. The absence of a quaternion number means that we are not dealing with folios one and eight. The fact that the text is not continuous indicates that it is not on folios four and five either. Given that the structure is ext.–int./int.–ext., we must be dealing with folios two (ll. 18–55) and seven (ll. 56–91). As the content of these verses seems to be situated early in the play, the bifolio must form part of quaternion lxiv.

The ending of the *Vidularia*, though lost, is easy to locate. Quaternion lxvi contains the beginning of the *Poenulus* on its second folio. The preceding folio, now lost, must have been the ending of the *Vidularia*.

A number of fragments have been transmitted indirectly through grammarians and lexicographers, namely Priscian, Nonius, Porphyry, Fulgentius, Philargyrius, Sacerdos, and the *Glossarium Plautinum*. Among these sources, only Fulgentius appears to have gathered his material by reading our comedy directly; the others seem to have copied their examples from earlier works, most notably by the grammarian Flavius Caper.

The text of the palimpsest and the fragments allow us to reconstruct a rough outline of the plot, though its de-

389

tails must remain unclear. After a shipwreck, a young girl called Soteris and her lover Nicodemus reach an unfamiliar shore separately, each believing that the other has drowned. Soteris finds shelter in the sanctuary of Venus, while Nicodemus stays with the fisherman Gorgines. Nicodemus overhears that Dinia needs a laborer on his farm and asks him if he can take up the job. Immediately realizing that Nicodemus, pale-skinned and with soft hands, is not used to hard work, Dinia is not very keen, but is persuaded by Nicodemus' promise to do his best.

As fr. xvi (xiii)[1] shows, Nicodemus turns out to be Dinia's son, whereas Soteris is the daughter of Gorgines. Thus the play ends with a double recognition and presumably a wedding between Nicodemus and Soteris. Given that Nicodemus does not recognize his father or his surroundings at once, he must have been kidnapped when young. Plautus, or rather Diphilus, seems to have kept Soteris offstage till the very end of the play, which could be explained if she would otherwise have recognized her father too early. This means that she was possibly abducted as an adult, although Roman comedy contains no parallels for abducted adults. Since she does not recognize the shore either, it is possible that Gorgines moved there after the abduction. It is an irony of fate that Dinia and Nicodemus are brought together, even though they cannot recognize each other, so that Nicodemus ends up as his father's servant, while Gorgines and Soteris are kept apart, even though each of these two would immediately know who the other is.

---

[1] Where my numbering of the fragments deviates from Calderan, I give his numbers in brackets.

Crucial for the recognition is the *uidulus*, or "traveling-bag," after which the comedy is named. It is found by the appropriately named Cacistus, meaning "the worst." His status is unclear; many scholars have assumed that he is a slave, but since in the conflict that is to follow he is advised to find a patron rather than his master to defend him, he is more likely to be free. The reason why he was at the seashore and found the bag is presumably that, like Gorgines, he is a poor fisherman.

Gorgines has a slave who observes from within the myrtle grove adjacent to the temple of Venus how Cacistus finds the bag. In most editions this slave is called Aspasius, "the welcome one," but it has to be said that only a few letters of his name are preserved in a scene heading, so that there can be no certainty in this matter. Aspasius, who has found out who owns the bag, wants it to be returned to the owner, but Cacistus intends to keep it for himself. The two of them fight; when Cacistus suggests Gorgines as umpire, Aspasius agrees, but when Cacistus finds out that Gorgines is the master of Aspasius, he despairs. He tries to find someone who is willing to support him and brings along Dinia. At the arbitration scene, at which Dinia and Gorgines are present together with Cacistus and Aspasius as well as Nicodemus and probably Soteris, the double recognition takes place, leading to a happy ending, presumably with a marriage between Nicodemus and Soteris and with the manumission of Aspasius. However Diphilus may have handled this final scene, it seems unlikely that he had five or six actors onstage.

It is not immediately obvious to whom the bag belongs; it is equally unclear at first sight to whom the ring belongs, a token also involved in the recognition, as we can see from

391

fr. xiv–xv (xi–xii). Here the scenario suggested by Dér is the most likely: she points out that the ring cannot be a recognition token to be found inside the bag, as the bag is sealed with the ring. The ring probably does not belong to Nicodemus at all, as in that case he would wear it; that he does not wear it is clear for two reasons. First, in l. 33 Dinia is examining the hands of Nicodemus, and if he were wearing the ring, the recognition would take place immediately, which it does not. And second, during the arbitration Nicodemus describes the seal (fr. xi) in order to demonstrate that he rather than Cacistus has a claim to the bag; this description would not be necessary if he had the ring on his finger. Thus the most natural assumption is that the ring belongs to Soteris and that Nicodemus believes it to have perished together with her. The recognition tokens of Nicodemus ought to be in the bag, which may belong to him, to Soteris, or to both together. If it is correct that Soteris was kidnapped as a young adult and would have recognized her father without tokens, we have to ask ourselves what the function of her ring is. It seems likely that both the ring and Aspasius, who could have met her in the grove, play a role in her recognition. In the arbitration Aspasius says that he compared the seal, presumably with his master's ring. Given that he did not know Soteris when he saw her, he must have been bought recently by his master.

While this much can be reconstructed with a fair degree of probability, one further fragment (xvii) is baffling. It is transmitted by Nonius and mentions a slave trying to trick a father out of his money. In Roman comedy such goings-on are always associated with a young man trying to get hold of his stingy father's money in order to free a girl owned by a pimp. For this reason Leo assigned to the *Vidularia* another fragment (fr. dub. iii) which mentions a pimp but was ascribed to the *Aulularia* by Nonius. Since the *Aulularia* has no pimp, Nonius cannot have been right, but Leo's theory remains no more than an assumption, as plays outside the Varronian canon were not devoid of pimps; the *Lenones Gemini*, "The Twin Pimps," must even have contained two.

The young man in question can hardly be Nicodemus. He has no slave, as he himself says (l. 26), he is only discovered to be Dinia's son at the end of the play, and given the mutual affection between Nicodemus and Dinia, it would be inconceivable in a Roman comedy that Nicodemus should trick his father. In his excellent commentary, Calderan suggests that the young man, to whose role he attaches great importance, could be a rival of Nicodemus, and that Soteris was at the time owned by a pimp. While I do not wish to exclude this possibility absolutely, an altogether different scenario seems not unlikely to me: even without a young man's intrigue and a pimp, the play contains more than enough action for 800 to 830 verses; Nonius wrongly assigned fr. dub. iii to the *Aulularia*; it is not impossible that Nonius also made a mistake when he assigned the fragment mentioning the slave's intrigue to the *Vidularia*.

Even though the *Vidularia* has been transmitted in such a poor state, we know who the author of the Greek original was and we are not without indications regarding the first performance of the Latin play. If the restoration of the title in l. 6 is correct, and there can be little doubt that it is, the Greek original was called *Schedia*, "The Raft," named after the means of rescue by which at

393

PLAUTUS

least one of the young people reached the shore. We know
of a play with this name written by Diphilus, who is thus
likely to be the author of the Greek original of the *Vidu-
laria*. As for the first performance, the reference to the
culleus in fr. xii (xiv) provides a *terminus post quem*. The
culleus is a sack into which a parricide was sewn before
being thrown into the Tiber. This punishment was first
used in 201 BC for Lucius Hostius, the first parricide.
Though this *terminus post quem* does not allow us to nar-
row down the timeline very much, it does at least prove
that the *Vidularia* does not belong to Plautus' earliest pe-
riod of literary activity.

SELECT BIBLIOGRAPHY

Editions and Commentaries

Calderan, R. (2004), *Vidularia: Introduzione, testo critico
e commento; edizione riveduta* (Urbino).
Monda, S. (2004), *Titus Maccius Plautus: Vidularia et de-
perditarum fabularum fragmenta* (Urbino).

Criticism

Birt, T. (1916), "Laus und Entlausung: Ein Beitrag zu Lu-
cilius und Martial," *Rheinisches Museum für Philologie*
71: 270–77.
Dér, K. (1987), "*Vidularia*: Outlines of a Reconstruction,"
Classical Quarterly 37: 432–43.
Lefèvre, E. (1984), *Diphilos und Plautus: Der* Rudens *und
sein Original* (Stuttgart).

VIDULARIA

Leo, F. (1894–1895), *De Plauti Vidularia commentatio* (Göttingen).

Marcos Celestino, M. (1997), "Étude lexicologique du terme myrtus et de son dérivé myrteta chez Plaute," *Estudios Humanísticos* 19: 201–9.

Schenk, R. (1899–1900), *O Plautove Vidularii* (Prague).

VIDVLARIA

PERSONAE

ASPASIVS seruos
NICODEMVS adulescens
GORGINES senex piscator
DINIA senex
CACISTVS piscator
SOTERIS uirgo
? seruos ?
? adulescens ?
? leno ?

SCAENA

incerta

THE TALE OF A TRAVELING-BAG

CHARACTERS

ASPASIUS a slave
NICODEMUS a young man
GORGINES an old fisherman
DINIA an old man
CACISTUS a fisherman
SOTERIS a young woman
? a slave ?
? a young man ?
? a pimp ?

STAGING

The stage represents a street in a coastal town. On it are the houses of Gorgines, to the left, and of Dinia, to the right. Between them there is a myrtle grove with a temple of Venus, which may be hidden behind the bushes. On the right, the street leads into the town center, and on the left, to the countryside and the coast.

PROLOGVS

PRO   *** hanc rem uetere nomine
      *** g *** ‹d›estitit
      potentiam inime *** rum s *** tisitio
      laudatus ia*** s *** gra‹ti›as
5   *** ius sc *** g *** f *** fero.
      Sc‹h›edi‹a haec› uo‹catur a› G‹r›ae‹cis›
        c‹omoedia›;
      ‹p›oeta ha‹nc› noster f‹ecit› V‹idularia›m,
      isqu‹e› *** t *** r *** o *** ciuntm ego fa‹x›o
        s‹cibi›tis.
      prius noscite ‹alia: sane› scitis, ipsus ‹e›s‹t›.
10   credo argumentum uelle uos ‹pern›os‹cer›e;
      int‹elle›g‹etis poti›us q‹uid a›g‹an›t q‹ua›nd‹o
        a›gent.
      a *** uos in loco; monitum ‹im›petro
      di *** q *** s *** commodiu‹s› *** tas
      ina *** ‹o›b meam
15   magis qu *** abeo *** ortis nunciam.
      uos ill‹um a›udite *** nox pro hoc ***.

2 ‹d›estitit *uel* ‹r›estitit *Studemund*
4 gra‹ti›as *Leo*
6 *suppl. Mariotti*
7 *suppl. Studemund*
8 *suppl. Leo*
9 alia: sane *add. Leo*   ‹e›s‹t› *Studemund*

PROLOGUE

Enter the SPEAKER OF THE PROLOGUE from the left.

PRO   *** this matter by an old name *** he ceased *** power
*** praised *** thanks *** I bring ***. This comedy is   5
called *Schedia*[1] by the Greeks; our poet made it *The Tale
of a Traveling-Bag*, and he ***. I'll make sure that you
know ***. First get to know other things: you do know,
it is he himself. I believe you want to get to know the   10
plot; you will instead understand what the actors are do-
ing when they're doing it. *** you in place. I achieve
my request *** more appropriately *** because of my
*** more *** I'm going away *** now. You must listen to   15
that man *** for him ***.

Exit the SPEAKER OF THE PROLOGUE *to the left.*

[1] "The Raft."

10–11 *suppl. Studemund*
12 ‹im›petro *Leo*
14 ‹o›b *Leo*
16 *suppl. Goetz*

PLAUTUS

ACTVS I

I. i: ASPASIVS

17 ASP   hominem, semel quem u⟨i⟩ sur⟨r⟩up⟨u⟩it Seruitus
***

FRAGMENTA

i   NIC   eiusdem Bacchae fecerunt nostram nauem Pentheum.

ii   NIC   inopiam, luctum, maerorem, paupertatem, algum, fa-
       mem.

iii   GOR   paupera haec res est.

iv   GOR   haec myrtus Veneris est.

17^a *** d ***
17^b *** q ***

17 *corr. Mariotti*   *post hunc uersum aut centum quinquaginta duo aut centum nonaginta uersus perierunt in* A

17^a–17^g *inter a et b spatium trium uersuum est, inter c et d spatium unius uersus, inter e et f spatium sex uersuum, inter f et g quattuor uersuum; post g deficiunt quinquaginta sex uersus in* A

---

2 Fr. i: Prisc. *gramm.* 2.300, Greek nouns in *-eus*, like *Pentheus*, normally take a Greek accusative form in Latin, though Plautus prefers the Latin ending. Fr. ii: Prisc. *gramm.* 2.235, the noun "cold" is either *algor* (third declension) or *algus* (fourth declension). Fr. iii: Prisc. *gramm.* 2.152, *pauper* (poor) belongs to the third declension, but can also have a feminine form in *-a*. Fr. iv: Porph. *ad Hor. carm.* 1.38.7, Plautus uses feminine *myrtus*, "myrtle (grove)."

3 When Pentheus banned the Bacchanalian worship of Dionysus, this god made Pentheus' mother and other Bacchants tear him to pieces. Here Neptune, the god of the sea, rather than Dionysus, must be the deity referred to obliquely.

VIDULARIA

ACT ONE

As the scene heading shows, what followed the prologue was a monologue by Aspasius. Of this prologue only the first line has been preserved.

ASP A man whom Slavery has snatched once ***   17

Between ll. 17 and 17ᵃ either 152 or 190 lines have been lost. Probably immediately after the monologue by Aspasius there was a dialogue between Nicodemus and Gorgines, in which the former told the latter about his fate; possibly the dialogue was overheard by Aspasius. Fr. i–iv² seem to be part of the dialogue. In fr. i Nicodemus tells Gorgines about the shipwreck and in fr. ii about his wretched situation and grief for his lost girlfriend. Leo, who compares fr. iii with Rud. 282, demonstrates that fr. iii was probably spoken by Gorgines, who invites Nicodemus to stay, despite being poor himself. In fr. iv Gorgines shows Nicodemus the surroundings.

NIC It was his Bacchants that have turned our ship into Pen- i
     theus.[3]
NIC Destitution, lamentation, grief, poverty, cold, hunger.   ii
GOR My circumstances are poor.   iii
GOR This myrtle grove belongs to Venus.   iv

The fragmentary ll. 17ᵃ–17ᵍ are incomprehensible. Intelligible text begins 56 verses later. Somewhere in this lost piece there must have been a scene in which Cacistus finds out about Nicodemus' lot and another scene in which Nicodemus overhears that Dinia is looking for a worker.

***   17ᵃ–
                                                               17ᵍ

17^c   in ***
17^d   qu ***
17^e   ser ***
17^f   *** q ***
17^g   *** ico
       ***

DINIA. NICODEMVS
       ***

18 DIN   est quo * nec ‹tem›pus censeo.
    NIC   quid ais? licet‹ne?
    DIN   m›axum‹e, si›quid est opus.
20   sed quid est negoti?
    NIC   te ego audi‹ui di›cere
          operarium te uelle ru‹s cond›uc‹ere›.
    DIN   re‹ct›e audiuisti.
    NIC   quid uis operis ‹fie›ri?
    DIN   qu‹id t›u istuc curas? an mihi tutor additu's?
    NIC   dare possum, opinor, satis bonum operarium.
25 DIN   est tibi [in] mercede seruos quem des quispia‹m›?
    NIC   inopia seruom ‹est›. i‹ta fit ut› e‹g› o me loc‹em›.
    DIN   quid tu? locastin q‹uaeso te umquam quoipiam›?
          nam equidem te m‹ercennarium haud esse arb›itror.
    NIC   non sum, si quidem tu no‹n uis mercedem dare›.
30   uerum, si pretium das, du‹c me te›cum simul.
    DIN   laboriosa, adulescens, uita est rustica.
    NIC   urbana egestas edepol aliquanto magis.
    DIN   talis iactandis tuae sunt consuetae manus.

18–23 *suppl. Studemund*   25 in *del. Goetz*
26 est *add. Bücheler, cetera add. Leo*
27 *suppl. Studemund*   28–29 *suppl. Leo*
30 *suppl. Brugman*

The following scene shows us Nicodemus asking Dinia for work.
Not much seems to have been lost at its beginning.

***

DIN It is *** nor do I think it's time.

NIC What do you say? May I?

DIN By all means, if you need anything. But what's the mat- 20
ter?

NIC I've heard you say that you want to hire a laborer for your
country estate.

DIN You've heard correctly.

NIC What sort of work do you want done?

DIN Why do you care about that? Have you been assigned to
me as my guardian?

NIC I think I can give you a sufficiently good laborer.

DIN Do you have any slave that you can let out for a wage? 25

NIC I have no slaves. This is how it comes about that I'm hir-
ing myself out to you.

DIN (*looking him over*) What about you? Please, have you
ever hired yourself out to anyone? Well, I for one don't
think you're a paid worker.

NIC I'm not, at least if you don't want to give me any pay. But 30
if you are prepared to give me wages, take me along with
you.

DIN Young man, life in the country is hard.

NIC Poverty in the city is quite a bit more so.

DIN Your hands are used to throwing dice.

403

	NIC	at qualis exercendas nunc intellego.
35	DIN	mollitia urbana atque umbra corpus candidum est.
	NIC	Sol est ad eam rem pictor: atrum fecerit.
	DIN	heus cunil *** illic estur *** so ***.
	NIC	misero male ess‹e fuerit› con‹senta›ne‹um›.
	DIN	quod aps te *** cp *** t quaeso ut m‹ih›i impertias.
40	NIC	si tibi pudico ‹homine› est opus et non malo,
		qui tibi ‹fid›elior sit quam serui tui
		cibique minimi maxumaque industria,
		minimo mendace, em me licet conducere.
	DIN	non edepol equidem credo mercennarium
45		te esse.
	‹NIC	an› non credis? non *** ‹c›ondu‹ci› arbit‹ror›
		n *** st dicat simul
		*** operarium.
	DIN	iam *** unde conducam mihi
		multum labor‹et, p›aullum mereat, paullum edi‹t›.
50	NIC	minus operis nihilo faciam quam qui plurumum,
		nec mihi nisi unum prandium quicquam duis
		praeter mercedem.
	DIN	quid merendam?
	NIC	ne duis
		nec cenam.
	DIN	non cenabis?
	NIC	immo ibo domum.
	DIN	ubi habitas?
	NIC	hic apud piscatorem Gorginem.

38 *suppl. Leo*   40 homine *add. Studemund*
41 ‹fid›elior *Studemund*
45 ‹NIC an› *add. Studemund*   ‹c›ondu‹ci› arbit‹ror› *Leo*
49 *suppl. Studemund*

NIC   But I understand that they now need to be trained with wicker baskets.[4]

DIN   From urban luxury and shade your body is white.   35

NIC   Sun is the painter for this: he'll make me black.

DIN   Hey, *** is eaten there.

NIC   It'll be appropriate for a wretch to eat poorly.

DIN   What *** from you, I ask you to confide it to me.

NIC   If you need a decent man and not a bad one, someone   40 who is more loyal to you than your own slaves, a man of very little food and very great industry, and someone who is absolutely no liar, then here you are, you can hire me.

DIN   I really don't believe that you're a paid worker.   45

NIC   You don't believe me? I don't think *** can be hired *** he should say at the same time *** a laborer.

DIN   Now from where I can hire *** for myself, he should work much, earn little, eat little.

NIC   I'll do no less work than the one who does most, and you   50 needn't give me anything besides a single lunch, apart from my pay.

DIN   What about an afternoon snack?

NIC   You needn't give me one, nor a dinner.

DIN   You won't dine?

NIC   No, I'll go home.

DIN   Where do you live?

NIC   Here, with the fisherman Gorgines.

---

[4] By making and repairing them.

55 DIN uicinus igitur es mihi, ut tu praedicas.
***

GORGINES. CACISTVS. ASPASIVS
***

FRAGMENTA

v GOR animum aduortite ambo sultis. uidulum hic apponite;
ego seruabo, quasi sequestro detis; neutri reddibo,
donicum res iudicata erit haec.

vi ASP hau fugio sequestrum.

56 CAC ibo et quaeram, si quem possim sociorum nanciscier
seu quem norim, qui aduocatus assit. iam hunc noui lo-
cum.
hicin uos habitatis?

55 *post hunc uersum centum quinquaginta uersus perierunt in A*

DIN   Then you're my neighbor, from what you say.   55
***

Around 150 verses have been lost in A after l. 55. Dinia and Nicodemus leave for the countryside. The Greek original is likely to have had an act break at this point.

***

Fr. v–vi[5] fall within this gap. Cacistus went fishing, found the traveling-bag, and encountered Aspasius on his way back. Aspasius, who knows the owner of the bag, wants it to be returned, but Cacistus opposes him. Cacistus suggests arbitration. In fr. v we meet Gorgines, who is willing to be an arbitrator. In fr. vi Aspasius agrees.

GOR   Please pay attention, both of you. Put the traveling-bag v
       here. I'll watch over it as if you were depositing it with
       me; I won't return it to either of you until this issue has
       been settled.

ASP   I'm not refusing to deposit it.   vi

Cacistus, who seems new to the area, is now looking for legal assistance. He has found out that Gorgines is the master of Aspasius and believes that he will lose the argument and his booty.

CAC   I'll go and look to see if I can get hold of any comrade or 56
       if I know anyone who could assist me as advocate. I know
       this place now. Do you two live here?

---

[5] Fr. v and vi: Prisc. *gramm.* 2.224, we find both *sequestre* (third declension) and *sequestrum* (second declension), meaning "deposit."

GOR   hisce in aedibus: huc adducito.

      at ego uidulum intro condam in arcam atque occludam
         probe.

60   tu si quem uis inuenire tibi patronum, quaerita;
      perfidiose numquam quicquam hic agere decretum est
         mihi.

CAC   quor, malum, patronum quaeram, postquam litem per-
         didi?

      ne ⟨ego⟩ homo miser e⟨s⟩t scelestus dudum at⟨que⟩
         infelix fui,

      uidulum q⟨ui⟩ ubi u⟨id⟩i, non me circumspexi cen-
         tiens;

65   uerbero illic, inter mu⟨rtos⟩ locust, in⟨de⟩ insidias
         dedit.

      tam scio quam med hic stare: captam praedam perdidi,
      nisi quid ego mei simile aliquid contra consilium paro.
      hic astabo atque opseruabo, si quem amicum conspi-
         cer.

              DINIA. NICODEMVS. CACISTVS

DIN   ne tu edepol hodie miserias multas tuas

70   mihi narrauisti, eoque ab opere maxume
      te abire iussi, quia me miserebat tui.

CAC   illic est adulescens quem tempe⟨st⟩as e mari
      eiecit *** t *** s atque arg *** en *** m *** rom
      et iam ego audiui *** d *** mr *** mmut ***.

75   in opus ut sese collocauit quam ⟨cit⟩o!
      ⟨po⟩l hau cessauit, postquam t⟨erra⟩m attigi⟨t⟩.

63 *suppl. Leo*   64 *suppl. Studemund*
65 *suppl. F. Skutsch*
73 –fic- A, eiecit *Marx*
75–76 *suppl. Studemund*

GOR (*pointing*) Yes, in this house; bring him here. But I shall put the traveling-bag inside in a chest and close it properly. (*to Cacistus*) You must look around if you want to   60 find yourself a patron; I'm resolved never to do anything treacherously in this matter.

Exeunt GORGINES *and* ASPASIUS *into their house.*

CAC (*going toward the left exit*) Why the deuce should I look for a patron after losing the dispute? Really, I was a wretched, cursed, and unlucky fellow a while ago, since I didn't look around myself a hundred times when I saw it. As for that crook, there's a place among the myrtle   65 trees, from there he ambushed me. I know it as surely as I know that I'm standing here: I've lost the booty I caught, unless I prepare some countercounsel similar to myself.[6] I'll stand here and watch if I can see any friend. (*steps aside*)

Enter DINIA *and* NICODEMUS *from the left, without noticing* CACISTUS.

DIN Really, you've told me your many misfortunes today, and   70 so I told you strongly to leave your work behind because I felt pity for you.
CAC (*aside*) That's the young man whom the storm cast ashore from the sea *** and *** and I've heard already ***. How   75 quickly he hired himself out to work! He didn't hang back after touching dry land.

---

[6] A pun; his name *Cacistus* (*kakistos* in Greek) means "worst, most objectionable."

DIN mirum est ni a⟨udiui⟩ tuam u⟨ocem u⟩squa⟨m gen-
         tium⟩.
       nos uos parenti *** dare possu *** tus fu ***.
       rem mihi na⟨rrauit⟩; ede⟨po⟩l i simul ***
80   puer isishi *** isp *** ⟨ma⟩gis.
NIC egentiorem ⟨ho⟩minem ⟨quam ego su⟩m neminem
       neque esse credo nec fuisse nec fore.
DIN caue tu istuc dixis. immo etiam argenti minam,
       quam med orauisti ut darem tibi faenori,
85   iam ego afferam ad te. faenus mihi nullum duis.
NIC di tibi illum faxint filium saluom tuom,
       quom mihi qui uiuam copiam inopi facis.
       sed quin accedat faenus, id non postulo.
DIN defaenerare hominem egentem hau decet.
90   quam ad redditurum te mihi dicis diem
       caue demutassis.
NIC   usque donec soluero
***

77 si *A*, ni *Studemund* (*qui hunc uersum suppleuit*)
79 *suppl. Studemund*   81 *suppl. Studemund*
82 atque *A ut uidetur*, neque *Studemund*, aeque *Lindsay*
89 ⟨con⟩decet *Studemund*

---

7 Fr. vii: Non. 178 L., *icere* means "to hit." Fr. viii: Porph. *ad Hor. carm.* 1.38.7: Plautus uses feminine *myrteta* (myrtle grove). Fr. ix: Non. 751 L., the deponent *luctari* (grapple) can also take active endings. Fr. x: Prisc. *gramm.* 2.528, the perfect of *pono* (I place) is *posui*, but Plautus still has *posiui*. Fr. xi: Prisc. *gramm.* 2.165, *claxendix*, a shell used to cover a seal, is feminine. Fr. xii: Non. 395 L., *contendere* can mean "to compare." Fr. xiii: Prisc. gramm. 2.317, the genitive of *Soteris* is *Soterinis*. Fr. xiv: Fulg. *serm. ant.* 53, a *culleus* is a sack that criminals were sewn into before being thrown into the sea. Fr. xv: Fulg. *serm.*

DIN   I'm sure I must have heard your voice somewhere be-
fore. We *** you *** parent *** be able to give ***. He
told me the story. Do go along ***. A boy *** more.   80

NIC   I don't think that there's any man poorer than I am, or
ever has been, or ever will be.

DIN   Take care you don't say that. No, I'll also bring you the
silver mina now which you've asked me to give you on   85
interest. But you needn't give me any interest.

NIC   May the gods save that son of yours for you, since in my
need you give me the means to live. But I don't expect
that no interest should be added.

DIN   One ought not to ruin a poor man by demanding inter-
est. (*pretending to be stern*) Make sure you don't change   90
the date by which you say you'll repay me.

NIC   Until I've paid you ***

*The rest of the play is lost in the palimpsest, but a number of
grammarians quote passages of the remaining sections because
of grammatical peculiarities.*[7] *Fr. vii could be spoken by Dinia,
reminiscing about his lost son. He prefers his son being dead to
him having to beg. Fr. viii–xi are probably spoken by Cacistus,
either in a monologue or when he asks Dinia to assist him. Fr.
xii and xiii are to be assigned to the arbitration; Aspasius and
Cacistus are fighting against each other. Fr. xiv–xvi come from
the recognition scene. Nicodemus describes the seal made with*

ant. 15, a *horia* is a small fishing boat. Fr. xvi: Non. 201 L., *mendicarier*
(deponent) is an alternative form of *mendicare* (active), "beg." Fr. xvii:
Non. 148/764 L., *expalpare* or *expalpari* means "to wheedle out." Fr.
xviii: Philarg. *ad Verg. ecl.* 2.63, *leo*, "lion," can also refer to the female
of the species. Fr. xix: Non. 326 L., *pedis*, "louse," is mostly masculine,
but can be feminine in Plautus.

FRAGMENTA

vII (xvi)	DIN	malim moriri meos quam mendicarier:
		boni miserantur illum, hunc irrident mali.
viii (vii)	CAC	ibi ut piscabar, fuscina ici uidulum.
ix (viii)	CAC	nescioqui seruos e myrteta prosil[u]it.
x (ix)	CAC	quid multa uerba? plurumum luctauimus.
xi (x)	CAC	nunc apud sequestrum uidulum posiuimus.
xii (xiv)	ASP	iube hunc in culleo insui
		atque in altum deportari, si uis annonam bonam.
xiii (xv)	CAC	malo hunc alligari ad horiam,
		ut semper piscetur, etsi sit tempestas maxuma.
xiv (xi)		opposita est claxendix.
	NIC	at ego signi dicam quid siet.
xv (xii)	ASP	signum recte comparebat; huius contendi anulum.
xvi (xiii)	NIC	immo id quod haec est nostra patria, et quod hic meus
		⟨est⟩ pater,
		illic autem Soterinis est pater.
xvii		nunc seruos argentum a patre expalpabitur.

fr. ix (viii) prosil[u]it *Bothe*
fr. xvi (xiii) nostra est *codices, transp. Calderan* est *add. Bothe*

412

the ring of Soteris, Aspasius recognizes the seal, and Dinia and Gorgines are discovered to be the fathers of Nicodemus and Soteris, respectively. Fr. xvii–xix are difficult to situate within the play. Fr. xvii describes a slave who will steal from his master in order to support his master's son. Fr. xviii is too general to be located with any certainty. And all that can be said about fr. xix is that the person who removes lice is not identical with the person having lice, but again the absence of context makes it problematic.

DIN	I'd prefer my family members to die rather than beg: good men have pity on the former, bad men ridicule the latter.	vii (xvi)
CAC	As I was fishing there, I hit the traveling-bag with my trident.	viii (vii)
CAC	Some slave leaped out from the myrtle grove.	ix (viii)
CAC	Why should I use many words? We grappled a lot.	x (ix)
CAC	Now we've placed the traveling-bag with a depositary.	xi (x)
ASP	Have him sewn into a sack and taken out into deep sea, if you want a good supply of corn.[8]	xii (xiv)
CAC	I'd prefer him to be tied to a fishing boat, so that he's always fishing, even when there's an enormous storm.	xiii (xv)
	A purple shell[9] is placed against it.	xiv (xi)
NIC	But I shall tell you what the seal looks like.	
ASP	The seal was perfectly clear; I've compared her ring with it.	xv (xii)
NIC	Rather, because this is our country and because this man is my father, while that man is the father of Soteris.	xvi (xiii)
	Now the slave will wheedle money out of the father.	xvii

---

[8] At Rome, parricides were sewn into sacks and thrown into the Tiber.   [9] The shell of the purple-dye sea snail.

xviii   nam audiui feminam ego leonem semel parire.
xix   ubi quamque pedem uiderat, suffurabatur omnis.

FRAGMENTA DVBIA

i   myrtum
ii   acm ***
            *** quod rogo
            *** n‹ec› fu***
iii   sed leno egreditur foras,
            hinc ex occulto sermonatus sublegam.

fr. dub. ii *inter* acm *et* quod rogo *spatium est duodeuiginti uersuum*

fr. dub. iii sermone atus *codices*, sermonatus *Lindsay*, sermonem eius *Mercerus*

Well, I've heard that a lioness gives birth only once.[10]   xviii

Whenever he saw a louse, he secretly removed them   xix
all.

Three more fragments are attested, but it is unclear if they belong to our play and if so, where they fit. In fr. i, Porphyry (ad Hor. carm. 1.38.7) attests a neuter form of the noun for "myrtle tree," but without giving any context; as he also quotes from the Vidularia in this passage, the neuter form could come from here as well. Fr. ii comes from the palimpsest (folio 485–86, part of a bifolio), and even though it cannot be excluded that the letters belong to a lost part of the Cistellaria, they are more likely to be part of our play. Fr. iii is ascribed to the Aulularia by Nonius (523 L.), but that play contains no pimp. Leo assigned the fragment to the Vidularia, although it could also come from a play outside the Varronian canon or from a different writer altogether.

a myrtle tree   i

*** what I ask *** nor was ***   ii

But the pimp's coming out; I'll take in his conversation   iii
from here from a hidden spot.

---

[10] Gellius (13.7.1–2) quotes Herodotus (3.108), who claims that a lioness gives birth only once in her life, and to only one cub. This ancient belief is obviously false, otherwise the species would become extinct. A lioness can give birth several times during her lifespan, and normally produces between one and four cubs per birth.

FRAGMENTS OF LOST PLAYS

INTRODUCTORY NOTE

In addition to the twenty-one comedies of the Varronian canon, which were the only ones unanimously considered to be genuinely Plautine by scholars in antiquity, fragments from other plays have come down to us as quotations by grammarians, lexicographers, and men of letters. Since Plautus was the most prolific writer of comedy in Rome, even plays not stemming from his hand were commonly ascribed to him; unfortunately, this means that none of the fragments can be regarded as belonging to Plautus with absolute certainty. Even though absolute certainty can no longer be reached, there are varying degrees of likelihood. I follow Monda's arrangement of the fragments[1] because it shows most clearly what these degrees of likelihood are.

In the first category of fragments (ll. 1–119), we find all those not only ascribed to Plautus but also transmitted together with the names of their plays; since each of these plays was believed to go back to Plautus by at least one

---

[1] As I do not follow Monda's spelling conventions, I have placed the *Phago* after the *Parasitus piger*, retaining, however, Monda's line numbers because they have become standard. (In Monda's edition the *Phago* is written *Pago* and hence precedes the *Parasitus medicus* as well as the *Parasitus piger*.)

ancient scholar, our chances of reading genuine Plautus
are highest in this section.[2] The second category (ll. 120–
206) comprises fragments assigned to Plautus but trans-
mitted without the names of the plays; in theory the likeli-
hood of reading true Plautine material ought not to be
lower here than in the first category, but in practice the
failure of the grammarians in question to mention a spe-
cific comedy may reflect the tendency for unusual words
or grammatical phenomena to be randomly ascribed to
Plautus as a major representative of archaic diction. The
last category (ll. 207–48) contains three main types of frag-
ments: those which have been transmitted under the name
of Plautus, but where serious doubts about their genuine-
ness exist; those which have been transmitted under the
name of Plautus by one author and under someone else's
name by another; and those which have been transmitted
not only without the names of the plays they come from,
but also without the name of Plautus. All the fragments of
this third type have on various grounds been associated
with Plautus by modern scholars, sometimes convincingly
and sometimes not. A brief discussion of both types be-
longing to the third category is found at the beginning of
that section.

None of our fragments come from the Ambrosian pa-

---

[2] Among these fragments I have not included the two plays of
which we have titles, but no text; they are the *Anus* ("The Old
Woman") and the *Bis compressa* ("The Twice-Raped Woman").
Gellius (3.3.9) tells us that Varro began his book on Plautine
comedies with the statement of Accius that they were not the
work of Plautus; but the fact that Accius had to make such a state-
ment indicates that it was not uncontroversial.

limpsest or the Palatine manuscripts, which are dedicated specifically to Plautus; rather, they are quotations by ancient scholars made in the context of discussions of grammar, lexicography, or literature. Since the manuscripts of these authors have not been discussed in the general introduction in volume 1, I have added a brief list of sigla after the bibliography (otherwise the textual notes would be incomprehensible); for a fuller list of sigla I refer to Monda's critical edition. It should also be noted that Festus, Paul the Deacon, and Nonius are cited according to Lindsay and that Charisius is cited according to Barwick.

So far nothing has been said about the content of these fragments. Many of them are only one word long and thus do not allow for literary analysis, while the longer ones often reflect stock themes of Roman comedy, for instance the hungry hanger-on or the extravagant lover. But not even in the case of plays for which several fragments exist can we reliably reconstruct plots. Many fragments were cited because they exhibit unusual linguistic features; if these fragments were all we had of Plautus, our picture of his language would be even more unreliable than our literary assessment.

SELECT BIBLIOGRAPHY

Editions and Commentaries

Monda, S. (2004), *Vidularia et deperditarum fabularum fragmenta* (Sarsina and Urbino).

Winter, F. (1885), *M. Acci Plauti fabularum deperditarum fragmenta* (Bonn).

PLAUTUS

Criticism

Ehrman, R. K. (1987), "Polybadiscus and the *Astraba* of Plautus: New Observations on a Plautine Fragment," *Illinois Classical Studies* 12: 85–91.

—— (1992), "Observations on the *Frivolaria* of Plautus," *Mnemosyne* NS 45: 78–83.

—— (1993), "The *Cornicula* Ascribed to Plautus," *Rheinisches Museum für Philologie* 136. 268–81.

Gratwick, A. S. (1979), "Sundials, Parasites, and Girls from Boeotia," *Classical Quarterly* 73: 308–23.

Jarcho, V. (1992), "Über die Bruchstücke des plautinischen *Kolax*," in M. Capasso (ed.), *Papiri letterari greci e latini* (Galatina), 325–30.

Lentano, M. (1995), "*Nupta verba—Praetextata verba*: Considerazioni sul frammento 68 Lindsay di Plauto," *Aufidus* 25: 7–17.

Lucas, H. (1938), "Zum Fretum des Plautus," *Rheinisches Museum für Philologie* 87: 188–90.

Reitzenstein, R. (1887), *Verrianische Forschungen* (Breslau).

Rowell, H. T. (1952), "Accius and the *Faeneratrix* of Plautus," *American Journal of Philology* 73: 268–80.

Thielmann, P. (1880), "Zu Cornificius II," *Hermes* 15: 331–36.

FRAGMENTS

SIGLA

Festus

F   Naples, Bibl. Nazionale, IV A 3 (Farnesianus);
11th century

Fronto

A   Milan, Bibl. Ambrosiana, E 147 super.; 5th century
V   Vatican, Bibl. Apostolica, Vat. lat. 5750; 5th century

Fulgentius

P   Vatican, Bibl. Apostolica, Pal. lat. 1578; 9th century
R   Vatican, Bibl. Apostolica, Reg. lat. 1462; 11th century

Isidore of Seville

B   Bern, Burgerbibliothek, 101; 9th/10th century
C   Leiden, Bibl. der Rijksuniversiteit, Vossianus lat. F 74; 9th/10th century
D   Basel, Öffentliche Bibl. der Universität, F. III. 15; 8th century
E   Paris, Bibl. Nationale, lat. 13028; 8th century
F   Weilburg, Gymnasialbibl., 3; 9th century
K   Wolfenbüttel, Herzog August Bibl., Weissenburg 64; 8th century
M   Cava dei Tirreni, Bibl. dell'Abbazia della SS. Trinità, 23; 8th century

N Karlsruhe, Badische Landesbibl., Aug. 57; 8th century

P St. Gallen, Stiftsbibl., 235; 9th century

T Madrid, Bibl. Nacional, 10008; 11th century

U El Escorial, Real Bibl. del Monasterio, T. II. 24; 9th century

V El Escorial, Real Bibl. del Monasterio, Et. I. 14; 9th century

Macrobius

A Cambridge, University Library, 260; 13th century

B Bamberg, Staatsbibl., class. 9 (M. V. 5); 9th century

F Florence, Bibl. Medicea Laurenziana, Plut. 90 sup. 25; 12th century

M Montpellier, Bibl. Universitaire, Section de médecine, 225; 9th century

N Naples, Bibl. Nazionale, V B 10; 9th century

P Paris, Bibl. Nationale, lat. 6371; 11th century

R Vatican, Bibl. Apostolica, Reg. lat. 2043; 10th century

T El Escorial, Real Bibl. del Monasterio, Q. I. 1; 15th century

V Vatican, Bibl. Apostolica, Reg. lat. 1650; 10th century

Nonius

L Leiden, Bibl. der Rijksuniversiteit, Vossianus lat. F 73; 9th century

FRAGMENTS

Priscian

G   St. Gallen, Stiftsbibl., 904; 9th century
K   Karlsruhe, Badische Landesbibl., Aug. 132; 9th century
L   Leiden, Bibl. der Rijksuniversiteit, BPL 67; 9th century

Varro

F   Florence, Bibl. Medicea Laurenziana, Plut. 51. 10; 11th century

FRAGMENTA

FRAGMENTA FABULARVM VNA CVM NOMINIBVS TRADITARVM

ACHARISTIO

1 quam ego tanta pauperaui per dolum pecunia

2 panem et polentam, uinum, murrinam

ADDICTVS

opus facere nimio quam dormire mauolo:
ueternum metuo. ***

FRAGMENTS

FRAGMENTS OF PLAYS
TRANSMITTED WITH THEIR NAMES

ACHARISTIO

1 whom I despoiled of so much money through a trick

Non. 230: *pauperare* means "to make poor."

2 bread and barley groats, wine, liqueur wine

Plin. *nat.* 14.92: *murrina,* "wine scented with myrrh," was highly appreciated among the ancients.[1]

[1] Despite this assertion by Pliny, *murrina* is probably to be derived differently and seems to have been made from boiled-down must and grapes.

THE BONDMAN

I much prefer doing work to sleeping; I'm afraid of torpor.
***

Serv. Dan. *georg.* 1.124: *ueternus* means "torpor."

PLAUTUS

AGROECVS

5   quasi lupus ab armis ualeo, clunes infractos fero.

ARTEMO

1 nunc mihi licet quiduis loqui, nemo hic adest superstes.

2 ‹mu›lionum nauteam fecisset.

     ‹mu›lionum *Ursinus*

8   **3** rauim

8[a]   **4** Plautus in *Artemone* carnificem dicebat se illectare.

ASTRABA

1 sequere assecue, Polybadisce, meam spem cupio consequi.

FRAGMENTS

THE RUSTIC

I'm as healthy as a wolf as far as my shoulders are concerned;
it's broken haunches that I carry around.

Non. 289: *clunes*, "haunches," can be masculine.

ARTEMO

1 Now I may say anything, there's no witness here.

Fest. 394–96: *superstes* means "standing by as witness."

2 He would have made the tanning liquid of mule-drivers.

Fest. 164, Paul. Fest. 165: *nautea* is a type of plant used by tanners; it
causes nausea.

3 hoarseness

Fest. 340, Paul. Fest. 341: *rauis* means "hoarseness."

4 Plautus said in the *Artemo* that an executioner was luring
him on.

Nonliteral citation of Plautus from a letter in the Codex Bambergensis
Class. 18 f. 117v; the point of citing Plautus is to show that he is distinct
from Plato; the quotation goes back to a part of Festus that is now
lost.

THE PACK-SADDLE

1 Follow me closely, Polybadiscus, I'm keen to pursue the
one I hope for.

10 POL sequor hercle equidem; nam lubenter meam speratam
         consequor.

2 axitiosae annonam caram e uili concinnant uiris.

3 quasi tolleno aut pilum Graecum reciprocas plana uia.

4 terebratus multum sit, [et] supscudes addite.
   et del. Ritschl

5 apluda(m)

15 6 terebra tu quidem pertundis.

   430

POL   Yes, I am following you; I'm pursuing the bride I hope
      for with pleasure.

Varro *ling.* 6.73: *spes*, "hope," and *spons*, "will," are probably etymo-
logically related.[1]

   [1] To the modern etymologist such a connection must seem impos-
sible.

2 Women extravagant in their use of toiletries turn market
prices from cheap to dear to the disadvantage of their hus-
bands.

Varro *ling.* 7.66: *axitiosae* are "women acting together," from *agere*,
"act."[1]

   [1] A false etymology. A woman is *axitiosa* if she uses too much *axitia*,
a toiletry article of unclear meaning.

3 Like a swing beam or a Greek pile driver[1] you move back-
ward and forward on a regular course.

Fest. 342: *reciprocare* means "move backward and forward."

   [1] The *tolleno* is a device for lifting objects; the *pilum Graecum* is a
mechanical pestle.

4 It should have many holes drilled into it; add pegs.

Fest. 398–400: *subscudes* are pegs used to connect timbers.

5 chaff

Gell. 11.7.5: *apluda* means "chaff."

6 You're perforating me with a drill.

7 dare pedibus protinam sese ab his regionibus

BACARIA

PAR   quis est mortalis tanta
fortuna affectus umquam
quanta nunc ego sum, quoius haec uentri portatur
    pompa?
20   uel nunc qui mi in mari acipenser latuit antehac, cuius
    ego
latus in latebras reddam meis dentibus et manibus.

19 quanta *T*, quam *MR*, qua *ABFNPV*

BOEOTIA

1 PAR ut illum di perdant, primus qui horas repperit
quique adeo primus statuit hic solarium;
qui mihi comminuit misero articulatim Diem!
25   nam ⟨unum⟩ me puero Venter erat solarium,
multo omnium istorum optumum et uerissumum.
ubi is te monebat, esses, nisi quom nil erat.
nunc etiam quom est non estur, nisi Soli lubet.
itaque adeo iam oppletum oppidum est solariis,
30   maior pars populi aridi reptant fame.

25 unum *add. Hertz*

28 quod *VPC*, quid *R*, quom *Bothe*

Non. 87: *exterebrare* means "get something out with a drill," both literally and metaphorically. Plautus jocularly uses *terebra*, "drill," in a metaphorical sense as well, in a phrase that means "to try to get information."

7 that he is taking flight from this area directly

Non. 598–99: *protinam*, "directly," is a by-form of *protinus*.

BACARIA

What mortal has ever had as great luck as I do, for whose belly this array of dishes is carried in a procession? Now for instance the sturgeon, which was hidden from me in the sea before, and whose side part I'll return to the darkness with my teeth and hands.

Macr. *Sat.* 3.16.1–2: the sturgeon used to be a delicacy.

THE WOMAN FROM BOEOTIA

1 May the gods ruin the fellow who first invented hours, and moreover the one who first set up a sundial here; poor me, he tore Day to pieces for me, limb by limb! When I was a boy, Belly was your only sundial, and by far the best and truest of them all. When he reminded you, you'd eat, unless there was nothing there. Now even when there is something there one doesn't eat, unless Sun sees fit. What's more, the town is now so full of sundials, the majority of the population creep around dry from hunger.

Gell. 3.3.3–5: the style of this fragment proves that the *Boeotia* was written by Plautus.

2 ubi primum accensus clamarat meridiem

CAECVS uel PRAEDONES

1 nil quicquam factum nisi fabre nec quicquam positum sine
   loco,
auro, ebore, argento, purpura, picturis, spoliis, ***,
tum statuis ***

33 *lacunam indicat Winter*

35 **2** neque eam inuito a me umquam abduces.

3 spectaui ludos magnifice atque opulenter.

4 plure altero tanto quanto eius fundust uelim.

5 ita sunt praedones: prorsum parcunt nemini.

434

2 as soon as the orderly had announced midday

Varro *ling.* 6.89: *accensus*, "orderly," can also be used like *praeco*, "herald."

THE BLIND MAN or THE BRIGANDS

1 Nothing has been made unless it was made skilfully, nothing was set up without its place, gold, ivory, silver, purple, paintings, spoils, ***, and then statues ***

Char. *gramm.* 259: *fabre*, "skilfully," is the adverb of *faber*, "skillful."

2 You'll never take her away from me against my will.

Char. *gramm.* 263: *inuito*, "against someone's will," is an adverb like *falso*, "wrongly."

3 I've watched the games in splendid and sumptuous fashion.

Char. *gramm.* 271: *opulenter*, "sumptuously," is an adverb in *-ter* where we would expect one in *-e*.

4 I'd like it sold at a price that's twice as high as the price of his estate is.

Char. *gramm.* 274: Plautus uses the adverb *plure*, "at a higher price."

5 That's what brigands are like: they spare absolutely no one.

Char. *gramm.* 274: Plautus uses *prorsum*, "absolutely."

6 in[1] peregre [est]?

> est *del. Leo* (in = isne)

> [1] Plautus does not combine *peregre* with prepositions, so *in* must be the same as *isne*.

40 **7** A uelim te arbitrari factum. B sedulo est.
summouentur hostes,
remouentur lapides.

> 40 sedulum *codd.*, sedulo *Leo*

8 *** si non strenue fatetur ubi sit aurum,
membra exsecemus serra. ***

45 **9** nil feci secus quam me decet.

10 A quis tu es qui ducis me? B mu. A perii hercle! Afer est.

6 Won't you go abroad?

Char. *gramm.* 275: *peregre*, "abroad," is a form used for direction (rather than location).

7 A I'd like you to think that it has been done. B There's no guile in it. The enemy is driven off, the stones are removed.

Char. *gramm.* 283: Plautus uses the adverb *sedulum*.[1]

  [1] This should probably be *sedulo*, "without guile, sincerely."

8 *** If he doesn't confess promptly where the gold is, let's cut his limbs off with a saw. ***

Char. *gramm.* 283: Plautus uses the adverb *strenue*, "promptly."

9 I haven't done anything differently from how I ought to.

Char. *gramm.* 285: Plautus uses the adverb *secus*, "differently."

10 A Who are you, who are leading me?

B Mu.

A I'm ruined! He's a Carthaginian.

Char. *gramm.* 313: Plautus uses the interjection *mu*.[1]

  [1] Perhaps *mu* should be interpreted as Punic *MH*, "what?" *Afer* can refer to any African, but is often used of the Carthaginians, who spoke Punic.

PLAUTUS

CALCEOLVS

*** molluscam nucem
super eius dixit impendere tegulas.

CARBONARIA

1 *** ego pernam, sumen, sueres, spetile, callum, glandia

50 **2** patibulum ferat per urbem, deinde affigatur cruci.

3 *** secundum eampse aram aurum apscondidi.

    ipsam *codd.*, eampse *Fleckeisen*

FRAGMENTS

THE SLIPPER

*** He said that a soft-shelled nut tree overhung his roof tiles.

Macr. *Sat.* 3.18.9–11: *nux mollusca* refers to a nut with soft shells; the tree does not grow in Italy because the climate is unsuitable.[1]

1 According to Pliny (*nat.* 15.24.91), we are dealing with a type of almond. Macrobius, however, seems to confuse the nut with the peach.

THE CHARCOAL PLAY

1 I *** ham, sow's udder, chops, belly meat, crust, sweet-breads

Fest. 444–46: *spetile* is a cut of pork from below the navel.

2 Let him carry the gibbet through the city and then let him be put on the cross.

Non. 327: *patibulum*, "gibbet," is neuter, even though some authors (but not Plautus) have a masculine by-form in *-us*.

3 *** I hid the gold next to the altar itself.

Prisc. *gramm.* 2.516: *apscondere* can have *apscondidi* as perfect.[1]

1 The classical form *apscondi* has lost its reduplication.

†CESISTIO†

di‹s› stribula ‹a›ut de lumbo opscena uiscera

distribula *F*, dis stribula *Buecheler*   ut *F*, aut *Schoppius*

COLAX

1 batiolam auream octo pondo habebam, accipere noluit.

2 qui data fide firmata fidentem fefellerint,
55   subdoli supsentatores, regi qui sunt proxumi,
qui aliter regi dictis dicunt, aliter in animis habent

56 animis *Anon. RecFr. apud van den Hout*, animo *A*

3 si me tu hodie irritaueris, numquam quicquam ***.

inuitaueris *cod.*, inritaueris *Leo*

4 nexum

FRAGMENTS

†CESISTIO†[1]

the ox's haunch for the gods, or the unclean organs from the loins

Varro *ling.* 7.67: *stribula*, "ox's haunch," refers to the meat around the hip.

[1] The title of the play is corrupt.

THE FLATTERER

1 I had a golden drinking vessel of eight pounds, but he didn't want to take it.

Non. 874: *batiola*, "drinking vessel," is attested in the *Colax*.

2 who have deceived the man who trusted them, after giving him their word and vouching for it, the tricky flatterers, who are closest to the king, and who speak words to the king in one sense, but have different intentions on their minds

M. Caes. ad Front. 28.7–16 van den Hout: Plautus describes the giving of bad advice neatly.

3 If you provoke me today, there will never be anything ***.

Schol. Verg. Veron. *Aen.* 2.670: the line is somewhat parallel to what Virgil wrote: *numquam omnes hodie moriemur inulti*, "never shall we all die without revenge today."

4 binding obligation

Varro *ling.* 7.105: *nexum* refers to a binding obligation between creditor and debtor.

COMMORIENTES

saliam in puteum praecipes

CONDALIVM

60   tam crepusculo, ferae ut amant, lampades accendite.

     fere *F*, ferae *Buecheler*

COPHINVS[1]

pro!

  [1] The name of the play is uncertain.

CORNICVLA

1 quid cessamus ludos facere? circus noster ecce adest.

MEN DYING TOGETHER

I'd jump into the well head first

Prisc. *gramm.* 2.280: *praecipes*, "head first," is an older form of *praeceps*.

THE RING

In such dusk as the wild animals like, put on the torches.

Varro *ling.* 7.77: *crepusculum*, "dusk," is a Sabellic word.[1] It refers to the time when there is doubt whether it is night or day.

> [1] The origin of the word remains obscure, despite Varro's assertion.

THE BASKET

Wow!

Fest. 256, Paul. Fest. 257: *pro* (adverb rather than preposition) expresses admiration.

THE LITTLE CROW

1 Why are we hesitating to have our games? Look, our entertainment is here.

Varro *ling.* 5.153: *circus* here refers to a soldier because those mocking him surround (*circum-ire*) him.[1]

> [1] A labored explanation. The soldier is the circus because the circus is the place for entertainment, and he is about to provide entertainment by being ridiculed.

2 qui regi latrocinatu's decem annos Demetrio

    decem annos *Varro*, annos decem *Nonius*

3 pulchrum et luculentum hoc nobis hodie euenit proelium.

65 **4** mihi Lauerna in furtis celerassit manus.

    celerassit *L*, celebrassit *codices ceteri*

5 qui amant ancillam meam Phidyllium oculitus

    fedulium *codd.*, Phidyllium *Winter*

6 *** em te opsecro,
Lyde, pilleum meum, mi sodalis, mea salubritas.

7 fac, ere, olant aedes Arabice.

DYSCOLVS

70 *** uirgo sum, ⟨si⟩ nondum didici nupta uerba dicere?

    si *add. Welsh*

2 you who have served King Demetrius as a soldier for ten years

Varro *ling.* 7.52: ancient poets called soldiers *latrones;* Non. 195: *latrocinari* means "get a soldier's pay."

3 This battle has turned out beautiful and bright for us today.

Non. 87–88: *luculentus* means "beautiful, good, clear."

4 May Laverna accelerate my hands during my thefts.

Non. 196: Laverna is the goddess of thieves.

5 who are passionately in love with my slave girl Phidyllium

Non. 215: *oculitus* means "from the heart, passionately."

6 *** Look, I entreat you, Lydus, my felt cap, my comrade, my salvation.

Non. 325: we find both *pilleus* and *pilleum*, "felt cap," worn as a sign of manumission.

7 Master, see to it that the house smells in Arabian fashion.[1]

Diom. *gramm.* 1.383: *olere*, "smell," belongs to the second conjugation, but in earlier texts also to the third conjugation.

[1] Incense was produced in Arabia.

THE GRUMPY MAN

Am I a virgin if I haven't learned to say married words yet?

Fest. 174: *nupta uerba*, "married words," are those words an unmarried girl is not supposed to say.

FAENERATRIX

1 heus tu, in barbaria quod dixisse dicitur
   libertus suae patronae, id ego dico ‹tibi›:
   "Libertas salue, uapula Papiria."

   72 tibi *add. Scaliger*

2 quae ego populabo probe

FRETVM

75 nunc [illud] est quod Arreti[ni] responsum ludis magnis dici-
   tur:
   "peribo si non fecero, si faxo uapulabo."

   75 illud *del. Fleckeisen*   Arretini *codd.*, Arreti *Hertz*

FRAGMENTS

THE MONEY-LENDRESS

1 Hey you, I'm saying to you what a freedman is said to have said to his patroness in barbarian lands: "Greetings, Freedom; get a thrashing, Papiria."

Fest. 512: *barbaria*, "barbarian lands," refers to Italy, and *uapula Papiria*, "get a thrashing, Papiria,"[1] was proverbial; former slaves who said this wanted to show that they did not care about being threatened because they were now free.

[1] The *gens Papiria* was a family of high standing; a woman of that family would be called *Papiria*.

2 which I'll plunder properly

Diom. *gramm.* 1.401: *populari*, "plunder," can also have active endings.

THE STRAIT[1]

Now comes the reply that is made in Arretium at the Great Games: "I'll perish if I don't do it; if I do do it, I'll get a thrashing."[2]

Gell. 3.3.7–8: the style of the *Fretum* shows that it was written by Plautus.

[1] Possibly the nickname of a prostitute who gulps down her lovers' possessions like the sea monster Charybdis.

[2] *Arretium* is modern Arezzo; the "Great Games" are votive games here, not the *ludi Romani* otherwise designated with this term.

FRIVOLARIA

1 commodo dictitemus

2 is mihi erat bilis, querquera, aqua intercus, tussis, febris.

querquera *om. Priscianus* aqua intercus *om. Paulus*

3 ‹nunc› sequimini med hac sultis, legiones omnes Lauernae.

nunc *add. Monda*

80 **4** A ubi rorarii estis? B assunt. A ubi sunt accensi? C ecce ‹nos›.

nos *add. Bothe*

5 agite nunc, supsidite omnes, quasi solent triarii.

448

THE TRIFLE PLAY

1 let's speak suitably

Char. *gramm.* 251: *commodo* is the same as *commode*, "suitably."

2 To me he was a bilious attack, shivering fit, dropsy, coughing, fever.

Fest. 308, Paul. Fest. 309: *querquera* means "shivering fit"; Prisc. *gramm.* 2.271: Plautus uses *intercus*, "subcutaneous."

3 Now follow me this way, please, all you legions of Laverna.

Fest. 388: *sultis*, "please," is the same as *si uoltis*, "if you wish."

4 A Where are you, skirmishers?

B They're here.

A Where are the supernumeraries?

C Look at us.

Varro *ling.* 7.58: *rorarii*, "skirmishers," begin a battle, and *accensi* are "attendants."[1]

[1] Varro's connection of the *rorarii* with *ros*, "dew," is untenable, and here the *accensi* are "supernumeraries" rather than "attendants."

5 Come on now, crouch down, all of you, the way third-row fighters do.

Varro *ling.* 5.89: *pilani*, "javelin throwers," were called *triarii*, "third-row fighters," because they formed the third row of military formations; they used to crouch down (*supsidere*) in battle.

6 naue agere oportet quod agas, non ductarier.

7 superaboque omnis argutando praeficas.

8 d*** tunc papillae primulum
85   fraterculabant—illud uolui dicere,
"sororiabant." ‹quid› opus est uerbi‹s mihi›?

    86 quid *add. Ursinus*   uerbi‹s mihi› *Monda in apparatu*

9 *** agnina tenen*** ‹stre›bulis

10 *** o amice ex multis mi une, Cephalio!

FVGITIVI

A age age, specta, uide uibices quantas! B iam inspexi. quid
est?

    agerge *F*, age age *Scaliger*

6 You ought to do what you do energetically, not be dragged along.

Fest. 168: *nauos* means "quick, energetic."

7 I'll surpass all mourning women in chattering.

Non. 92: *praeficae* are women hired for mourning.

8 *** Then for the first time her breasts swelled up like two little brothers—I meant to say "like two little sisters." What need is there for words?

Fest. 380, Paul. Fest. 381: when girls' breasts swell in puberty, the term is *sororiare* (from *soror*, "sister"), while for boys the term is *fraterculare* (from *fraterculus*, "little brother").

9 *** of lambs *** with thigh meat

Fest. 410: *strebula* is an Umbrian word[1] referring to the hips of sacrificial animals.

  [1] The origin of the word is far from certain.

10 *** O Cephalio, my one and only friend out of so many!

Prisc. *gramm.* 2.188–89: *unus*, "one, only," can have a vocative.

THE RUNAWAYS

A Come on, come on, look, see what enormous weals!
B I've looked at them. What is it?

Varro *ling.* 7.63: *uibex* means "weal."

PLAUTUS

GEMINI LENONES

90 dolet huic puello sese uenum ducier.

HORTVLVS

praeco ibi assit; cum corona quiqui liceat ueneat.

cuique *F*, quique *Scaliger*, quiqui *Trappes-Lomax per litteras*

LIPARGVS

nil moror mihi fucum in alueo, apibus qui peredit cibum.

NERVOLARIA

1 scobina ego illum actutum arrasi senem.

2 prohibentque moenia alia. unde ego fungar mea?

THE TWIN PIMPS

This boy is distressed at being led away for sale.

Fest. 290–92: *puer*, "boy," has a diminutive *puellus*.

THE LITTLE GARDEN

An auctioneer should be present; he should be sold with a garland for any price he fetches.

Fest. 400: a garland was worn by prisoners of war when they were auctioned; the garland thus came to indicate low value.

LIPARGUS[1]

I don't care for a drone in the hive to eat up the bees' food.

Prisc. *gramm.* 2.522: *edere*, "eat," mostly has *es* and *est* as second and third persons, but *edis* and *edit* (with short initial vowel) occur as well.[2]

[1] The meaning of this title is obscure.

[2] In our quotation, *peredit* is almost certainly a subjunctive rather than an indicative.

THE FETTER COMEDY

1 I forthwith fleeced that old man with a rasp.

Varro *ling.* 7.68: *scobina*, "rasp," is derived from *scobis*, "sawdust."

2 And other duties prevent me. From what means should I fulfill my own?

Fest. 128–30: *moenia* means "duties."

95 **3** ocissume nos liberi possimus fieri

4 producte prodigum esse amatorem addecet.

5 uinum sublestissimum

6 insanum ualde uterque deamat ***

7 scrattae, scrupipedae, strittabillae, sordidae

scrupedae *Gellius et Nonius in lemmate* (crupede *in uersu*), scruppidam *Varro in lemmate* (ruppe.ides *in uersu*), scrupipedae *Mueller*

PARASITVS MEDICVS

101 **1** in conspicillo asseruabam pallium,
opseruabam ***

FRAGMENTS

3 we could become free very swiftly

Fest. 192: the adverb *ocius*, "more swiftly," has a comparative and a superlative, but not an unmarked positive form.

4 A lover ought to be wasteful over a long period.

Fest. 254: *prodigere* (from which the adjective *prodigus* is derived) means "use up, waste."

5 very weak wine

Fest. 378: *sublestus* means "weak" or "causing weakness."

6 each of the two is crazily much in love with ***

Non. 185: *insanum* can be an adverb like the regular *insane*, "crazily."

7 wretched, bony, tottering, filthy women

Gell. 3.3.6: Favorinus assigned the *Nervolaria* to Plautus on the basis of this verse; Varro *ling.* 7.65 quotes the line as belonging to the *Cistellaria*; and Non. 248 quotes it as belonging to the *Aulularia*.

DOCTOR HANGER-ON

1 I looked at the mantle from a watching place, I observed it ***

Non. 118: a *conspicillum* is a "watching place."

103   **2** *** cum uirgis caseum radi potest

104   **3** addite lopadas, echinos, ostreas

105   **4** domi reliqui exoletam uirginem

PARASITVS PIGER

106   **1** inde hic bene potus prim<ul>o crepusculo

      primo *F*, primulo *Scaliger*

107   **2** domum ire coepi tramite dextra uia

2 *** the cheese can be scraped off together with the rods[1]

Non. 294: *caseus*, "cheese," has a neuter by-form, *caseum*.[2]

[1] Rods were used to make forms for pressing cheese and baskets for keeping it in.

[2] Actually, *caseus* refers to a piece of cheese, while *caseum* refers to cheese as a substance.

3 add limpets, sea urchins, and oysters

Non. 884: *lopades* are a type of mussel ("limpets").

4 I left a grown-up girl at home

Prisc. *gramm.* 2.489–90: *exoletus* (participle of *exolere*) means "big, grown up."

THE LAZY HANGER-ON

1 From there he *** at the first dusk, having had a good share of drink

Varro *ling.* 7.77: *crepusculum*, "dusk," is a Sabellic word.[1] It refers to the time when there is doubt whether it is night or day.

[1] The origin of the word is actually unclear.

2 I began to go home on the footpath on the right-hand street

Varro *ling.* 7.62: *trames*, "path," is derived from *transuersum*, "cross-wise."[1]

[1] The etymology contains a true part: *trames* is indeed derived from *trans-*, "through," but the second element has nothing to do with *uersum*, "turned."

108   **3** ambo magna laude lauti, postremo ambo sumus non nauci.

PHAGO

100   honos syncerasto periit, pernis, glandio.

      perit *F*, periit *Spengel*

PLOCINVS

109   nam coloratilem frontem habet, petilust, habrus

      petilis habris *codd.*, petilust habrus *Goetz*

SATVRIO

110   **1** catulinam carnem esitauisse

FRAGMENTS

3 We both have an air of respectability because of great praise bestowed on us, but, lastly, we're both worthless.

Fest. 166: *naucum*, "thing of little worth," is of unclear etymology.

THE EATER

The high esteem for hotchpotch, ham, and sweetbread has been lost.

Varro *ling.* 7.61: *syncerastum* is a Greek word referring to a "hotchpotch."

PLOCINUS[1]

he has a sunburned forehead and is thin and delicate

Non. 217: *petilus* means "thin, fine."

[1] The meaning of the title is obscure, and as it is transmitted in the ablative, it could equally well be *Plocinum*. If the latter, this could be a corruption of *Plocium*; Menander wrote a play called *Plocion*, "The Necklace," which was adapted by Caecilius.

SATURIO[1]

1 that they used to eat dog meat

Paul. Fest. 39: Plautus says that the Romans "used to eat" (*esitauisse*) dog meat; the form *esitauisse* has the same meaning as *comedisse*.[2]

[1] A personal name; the hanger-on in the *Persa* is called Saturio, too.

[2] The citation is probably not literal.

2 retrahi nequitur quoquo progressa est semel

3 male tibi euenisse uideo. glaber erat tamquam rien.

4 succenturiatum require qui te delectet domi.

SCHEMATICVS

nam pater tuos numquam cum illa etiam limauit caput

2 she can't be dragged back once she's gone somewhere

Fest. 160: Plautus uses passive forms of *nequire*, "be able."

3 I can see that you had bad luck. He was as smooth as a kidney.

Fest. 342–44: the *rienes*, "kidneys," used to be called *nefrundines*.

4 Find some replacement to entertain you at home.

Fest. 400: *succenturiare* means "to supply in order to fill up a century, to supply as a reinforcement."

SCHEMATICUS[1]

for your father has never rubbed heads with her

Non. 525: *limare*, "rub, file off," also means "join."[2]

---

[1] Another obscure title, if it is a title at all; Ritschl conjectured σχηματικῶς, "in a figure of speech," which would refer to the Plautine metaphor (which, however, Nonius appears not to have understood properly).

[2] *Limare* does not mean "join." Nonius does not understand the metaphor ("rub heads" = "kiss").

SITELLITERGVS

115 **1** A mulier es‹t›, uxorculauit. B ego noui, scio axitiosa
quam sit. ***

    115 mulieres *F*, mulier est *Seyffert*

2 A ‹quid› fit? B ea mihi insignitos pueros pariat postea
aut uarum aut ualgum aut compernem aut paetum aut
brocchum filium.

    fit ea *F*, sit ea *W*, A ‹quid› fit? B ea *Monda*

TRIGEMINI

nisi fugissem [inquit] ‹in› medium, credo, praemorsisset ***

    inquit *Gellii uidetur esse*   in *add. Winter*

FRAGMENTS

THE BUCKET-CLEANER

1 A She's a woman, she's played the part of a wife.

B I understand, I know how she overdoes it with toiletries.

***

Varro *ling.* 7.66: *axitiosae* are "women acting together," from *agere*, "act."[1]

---

[1] Wrong etymology. A woman is *axitiosa* if she excessively uses *axitia*, an unidentified toiletry article.

2A What's going on?

B She'd bear me distinctive children afterward, a bowlegged son or a knock-kneed one or one with his thighs too close together or one with a squint or one with prominent teeth.

Fest. 514: *ualgus*, "knock-kneed," is the term given to people whose calves are not identical.

THE TRIPLETS

If I hadn't fled into the middle, I believe he'd have bitten off

***

Gell. 6.9.7: *mordere*, "bite," has a reduplicated perfect, but in compounds the reduplication is absent.

FABVLARVM INCERTARVM FRAGMENTA

120   **1** Epeum fumificum, qui legioni nostrae habet coctum cibum

     2 quod uolt densum, ciccum non interduo

     3 gannit odiosus omni totae familiae

     4 prosis lectis

     5 penitissuma(e)

125   **6** aerumnula(s)

FRAGMENTS FROM PLAYS OF
UNCERTAIN NAME

1 Epeus the smoke maker, who has cooked food ready for our legion

Varro *ling.* 7.38: Epeus the smoke maker (*fumificus*) means Epeus the cook, named after the man who built the Trojan horse and cooked food for the Argives.

2 as for the fact that he wants it thick, I don't care a straw

Varro *ling.* 7.91: *ciccum*, "thing of little worth," refers to the membrane in a pomegranate.

3 the tedious fellow snarls at our entire household

Varro *ling.* 7.103: some words are properly said of animals, but can be used metaphorically of humans, e.g., *gannire*, "snarl," which is properly used of dogs.

4 with couches in a straight line

Isid. *orig.* 1.38.1: *prosus* means *rectus*, "straight."

5 inmost

Non. 320–21: Plautus would call a house that is *postica*, "back," *penitissuma*.

6 little toils

Paul. Fest. 22: Plautus refers to little forks for carrying backpacks as *aerumnulae*, "little toils."

7 licet uos abire curriculo

8 iam tibi tuis meritis crassus corius redditust

9 di bene uortant! tene cruminam. inerunt triginta minae.

10 nullam ego rem citiorem apud homines esse quam famam
reor.

130 **11** coquitare

12 stultus est aduorsum aetatem et capitis canitudinem.

13 corruspare tua consilia in pectore.

466

7 you may leave by running

Paul. Fest. 42: *curriculo* is another word for *cursim*, "by running."

8 now your hide has been thickened[1] as you deserve

Paul. Fest. 53: *corius* is a masculine by-form of *corium*, "hide."

[1] I.e., it is swollen from being beaten.

9 May the gods give it a good outcome! Take the wallet. There will be thirty minas inside.

Paul. Fest. 53: *crumina*, "wallet," is a type of bag.

10 I don't believe that there is anything faster among men than rumor.

Paul. Fest. 54: *citior* is the comparative of *citus*, "fast."

11 to cook frequently

Paul. Fest. 54: the frequentative of *coquere* in Plautus is *coquitare,* not *coctitare.*

12 He's stupid despite his age and the grayness of his head.

Paul. Fest. 54: *canitudo* is an alternative word for *canities* "gray(ness of the) hair."

13 Seek out your plans in your breast.

Paul. Fest. 54: *corruspari* means "seek out."

14 numnam mihi oculi caecultant? estne hic noster Hermio?

15 dirigere

135 **16** eiurauit militiam

17 *** sic me subes cottidie
quasi fiber salicem

18 herbam do

19 init te umquam febris?

140 **20** nec muneralem legem nec lenoniam,
rogata fuerit necne, flocci existumo.

14 My eyes aren't failing me, are they? Isn't this our Hermio?

Paul. Fest. 54: *caecultare* means "be almost blind."

15 to separate

Paul. Fest. 61: *dirigere* is found in Plautus in the meaning *discidere*, "cut apart, separate."

16 he swore an oath that he couldn't perform military service

Paul. Fest. 68: an *eiuratio* is a sworn declaration that one is unable to provide a service.

17 *** every day you eat away at me from below like a beaver at a willow

Paul. Fest. 80: a *fiber*, "beaver," is a quadruped.

18 I'm giving grass

Paul. Fest. 88: *herbam do*, "I'm giving grass," means "I admit defeat"; someone who lost a sports competition would pluck grass from the place where the competition had been held and give it to the winner.

19 Does a fever ever come upon you?

Paul. Fest. 98: *inire* can stand for *introire*, "enter."

20 I don't care at all about the law concerning gifts or the one concerning pimps, whether it was passed or not.

Paul. Fest. 127: the *muneralis lex*, "law concerning gifts," goes back to Cincius, who prevented people from taking bribes.

21 perfidiose captus edepol neruo ceruices probat.

22 muriatica autem uideo in uasis stagneis,
naritam bonam et canutam, et tagenia,
145   echinos fartos, conchas piscinarias

    143 muriaticam *F*, muriatica *Scaliger*

    144 naricam *F*, naritam *Scaliger*   taguma *F*, tagenia *Scaliger*

    145 quinas fartas *F*, echinos fartos *Scaliger*

23 non ego te noui, naualis scriba, columbare impudens?

    columbari *F*, columbare *apogr.*

24 nil deconciliare sibu's, nisi qui persibus sapis.

    persicus *F*, persibus *Scaliger*

25 sacrum an profanum habeas, parui penditur.

21 The man caught by treachery puts his neck to the test with the fetter.

Fest. 160–62: a *neruos* is a foot fetter, but in Plautus it is used to fasten a prisoner's neck.

22 but I can see pickled fish in metal jars, a good, gray sea snail, and fish for frying, stuffed sea urchins, and molluscs from fishponds

Fest. 166: *narita*, "sea snail," is a species of small fish.

23 Don't I know you, you ship scribe, you shameless pillory?

Fest. 168: among clerks, those on ships (*nauales scribae*) were looked down upon because of the dangers inherent in maritime travel; the reference to *columbar(e)*, "compartment for pigeons/pillory," or *columbarium*, "compartment for pigeons/hole for an oar in a ship," or *columbarius*, "pigeon keeper," is unclear.

24 You aren't clever enough to get out of trouble, unless it's as a particularly clever person that you show sense.

Fest. 238: *persibus* means "very clever."[1]

[1] *Sibus*, "clever," is probably a loanword from Oscan (*sipus*). Syntactically one would expect an adverb instead of the adjective *persibus*; interestingly, Varro (*ling.* 7.107) glosses *persibus* with the adverbs *perite*, "with experience," and *callide*, "cleverly."

25 One cares little whether you regard it as sacred or profane.

Fest. 256, Paul. Fest. 257: *profanum*, "profane," is what is not sacred.

26 pullaria(m)

150   **27** uix super *** ⟨regliscit. *** ua⟩e misero mihi!

     uae *add. Mueller*

  28 *** ⟨surus⟩ *** non est tibi

  29 nam qui *** ⟨f⟩icus surculis
     *** ⟨su⟩rum, tum poli***
     *** aut a⟨s⟩sulae

    152 ⟨f⟩icus *Monda in apparatu*

    153 ⟨su⟩rum *Monda*

    154 a⟨s⟩sulae *Lindsay*

155   **30** ulcerosam, compeditam, subuerbustam, sordidam

26 the one for boys[1]

Paul. Fest. 279: *pullaria* is what Plautus calls the right hand.

[1] A *pullus* is a chick or a foal. The term is also used for young male favorites; the right hand is the one for caressing such boys. (By contrast, the left hand is often called the one for thieving.)

27 barely above *** it grows. *** Poor, wretched me!

Fest. 348, Paul. Fest. 349: *regliscit* means "grows."

28 *** you don't have a stake

Fest. 382, Paul. Fest. 383: *surus*, "post, stake," is the noun from which *surculus*, "twig, rod," is derived.

29 a man who *** a fig tree with rods *** a stake, then *** or splinters

Context as in xxviii.

30 a woman full of sores, wearing shackles, laden with beatings, and filthy

Fest. 402: *subuerbustus* means "burned" (*ustus*) "by blows" (*uerberibus*).[1]

[1] An untenable etymology. This nonce-formation consists of *sub* ("somewhat"), *uerbera* ("beatings"), and an ending probably taken from *onustus* ("laden with").

473

31 uenter su‹i›llus. di b***
in illum. ego me hodie e***
esa farte. biberem ir

156 su‹i›llus *Ursinus*

157 inillum *F*, in illum *Leo*, scrutillum *Ursinus*

32 thocum

160　**33** uesperna

34 cancrum imitaris

162　**35** mittebam pulchrum uinum, murrinam

162ᵃ　**36** . . . quamquam hortos tutelae Veneris assignante Plauto

474

31 *** pork belly. The gods *** against him. Today I *** myself with stuffing; I would drink ***

Fest. 448, Paul. Fest. 449: *scrutillus* refers to stuffed pork belly.[1]

1 The item for which the verse has been cited has been lost, and it remains unclear where it should be supplemented.

32 chair

Paul. Fest. 504: *thocum* in Plautus refers to a type of chair.

33 evening meal

Paul. Fest. 505: *uesperna* in Plautus refers to dinner.

34 you're imitating a crab

Letter in the Codex Bambergensis Class. 18 f. 117v; the quotation goes back to a part of Festus that is now lost. The letter writer had requested a manuscript of Plautus, but received one of Plato instead; by quoting bits of Plato and bits of Plautus he tries to show his addressees the difference between the two.

35 I sent beautiful wine and liqueur wine[1]

Plin. *nat.* 14.92: the ancients had a high regard for wine scented with myrrh.

1 *Murrina* is probably to be derived differently and seems to have been made from boiled-down must and grapes.

36 . . . despite Plautus speaking of gardens being under the guardianship of Venus

Plin. *nat.* 19.50: gardens are often, though not universally, placed under the guardianship of the Satyrs.

37 quid est? hoc rugat pallium: amictus non sum commode.

38 exi tu Daue, age, sparge, mundum hoc esse uestibulum
    uolo.
165   Venus uentura est nostra, nolo hoc pulueret.

    164 esse hoc *codd.*, *transp. Ritschl*

39 *** Amoris imber guttis grandibus
167   non uestem modo permanauit, sed in medullam ultro
    fluit.

    166 grandibus guttis *V*, *transp. Schoell*

167[a] **40** dulcia Plautus ait grandi minus apta lieni.

41 glirium examina

37 What's this? This cloak is wrinkling: I'm not dressed suitably.

Gell. 18.12.1–3: some verbs which are commonly used as passives are active in early writers.[1]

[1] To be more precise, some verbs can have an active with an agent subject and a patient object (type *Jack is closing the door*) and a passive with the patient as subject (type *the door is being closed*); sometimes such verbs also have active forms with patient subjects (type *the door is closing*), and this is what Gellius finds surprising.

38 You, Davus, come out and sprinkle it; I want this hallway to be neat. Our Venus is coming, I don't want this to be full of dust.

Gell. 18.12.4: *puluerare* means not only "fill with dust," but also "be full of dust."

39 *** with its big drops Love's rainstorm not only soaked through my clothes, but flowed on deep into my heart.

M. Caes. ad Front. 26.4–7 van den Hout: the writer will have to compete with *Gratia*, "Grace," who acts as outlined in the quotation.

40 Plautus says that sweet things are less suitable for a big spleen.

Ser. Samm. 425, nonliteral quotation embedded in a dactylic hexameter.

41 multitudes of dormice

Non. 172: the genitive plural of *glis*, "dormouse," is *glirium*.

42 quid murmurillas tecum et te discrucias?

170 **43** leuior es quam tippula

44 nec, machaera, audes dentes frendere

45 in pellibus periculum portenditur

46 Cilix, Lycisce, Sosio, Stiche, Parmeno,
exite et ferte fustes priuos in manu.

175 **47** inimicus esto, donicum ego reuenero

478

42 Why are you muttering to yourself and tormenting yourself?

Non. 207: *murmurillum* means "muttering."

43 you're lighter than a water boatman

Non. 264: the *tippula*, "water boatman," is such a light animal that it can walk over the water.

44 and, my sword, you don't want to gnash your teeth

Non. 717: *frendere* means "to make a wretched or threatening sound" or "to crush."[1]

   [1] The second meaning, "to crush" (*frangere*), is an emendation, but a likely one, especially when one compares Varro *rust.* 2.4.7.

45 a danger is indicated in the fleeces

Porph. Hor. *sat.* 1.6.22: the ancients used to sleep in fleeces; in our passage Plautus jokes about a drunken old woman.

46 Cilix, Lyciscus, Sosio, Stichus, Parmeno, come out and bring one club each in your hands.

Ps. Acro Hor. *sat.* 2.5.11: *priuos*, "peculiar to one person, individual," refers to what belongs to a single man.

47 be my enemy until I return

Char. *gramm.* 256: *donicum*, "until," is an alternative form of *donec*.

48 *** si qua forte contio est, ubi eum hietare nondum
in mentem uenit

49 ego illi uenear

50 Vinum precemur, nam hic deus praesens adest.

180 **51** fortasse ted amare suspicarier

52 argentum hinc facite

53 corpus tuom uirgis ulmeis inscribam

480

48 *** if by chance there's any public meeting, where it hasn't occurred to anyone yet that he gapes a lot

Diom. *gramm.* 1.345: the ancients used both *hiare*, "gape," and its iterative *hietare*.

49 I would be sold there

Diom. *gramm.* 1.368: instead of a passive of *uendere*, "sell," one uses *uenire*, "go for sale, be sold"; in Plautus this verb has passive endings.

50 Let's pray to Wine: this god is present here.

Diom. *gramm.* 1.458: *uinum* can stand for *Bacchus,* the god of wine, which is a metonymy.

51 perhaps he suspects that you're in love

Don. Ter. *Hec.* 313: *fortasse*, "perhaps," can introduce the accusative and infinitive.

52 get money away from here

Don. Ter. *Phorm.* 635: *facere* means either "do" or "go" (= *facessere*).

53 I'll write on your body with elm rods

Serv. Dan. *Aen.* 1.478: *inscribere*, "write on," can mean "tear to pieces."[1]

[1] *Inscribere* simply means "to write on"; the marks left behind by the beating resemble writing.

54 numquam ad ciuitatem uenio nisi quom infertur peplum

55 neque ego ad mensam publicas res clamo nec leges crepo

185 **56** et ego te conculcabo ut sus catulos suos

57 scelerare

58 hunc sermonem institi

59 ipsa sibi auis mortem creat

482

54 I never come to town except when the robe is brought in in the procession

Serv. *Aen.* 1.480: *peplum* refers to the embroidered robe dedicated to Minerva.[1]

[1] This robe was displayed during the festival of the Panathenaea at Athens.

55 I don't blare about politics at table and I don't bellow about the laws

Serv. Dan. *Aen.* 1.738: an exhortation is better understood in a loud voice.

56 and I'll trample you underfoot like a sow does her litter

Serv. Dan. *Aen.* 2.357: *catuli*, "pups," are not just young dogs, but also young snakes and other animals.[1]

[1] Perhaps this line is an imprecise quotation of *Truc.* 268.

57 to defile

Serv. *Aen.* 3.42: *scelerare* means "defile."

58 I set about this talk

Serv. Dan. *Aen.* 4.533: *insistere*, "set about, proceed with," can be used with the accusative.

59 the bird creates death for itself

Serv. *Aen.* 6.205: mistletoe, from which birdlime was made, grows out of the seeds that have passed through the digestive tract of thrushes.

60 pro laruato te circumferam

61 castrum Poenorum

62 te dissupabo tamquam folia farfari

dissipabo te *codd.*, *transp. Winter*

63 faciles oculos habet

64 properate prandium

65 ego hunc hominem hodie texam pallio

60 I'll purify you as a madman

Serv. *Aen.* 6.229: *circumferre*, "carry around (sc. a torch or sulfur)," means to "purify."

61 a settlement of the Carthaginians

Serv. *Aen.* 6.775: *castrum* (singular) means "settlement," but the noun is normally in the plural.

62 I'll scatter you like coltsfoot leaves

Serv. *Aen.* 7.715: the river Fabaris is identical with the Sabine Farfarus.[1]

  [1] But in our quotation *farfarum* means "coltsfoot."

63 He has easy-moving eyes

Serv. *Aen.* 8.310: wine makes the eyes shifting.

64 get lunch ready in a hurry

Serv. Dan. *Aen.* 9.399: *properare*, "hurry (toward)," with plain accusative rather than with *ad* + accusative is archaic.

65 today I'll strip this fellow of his cloak

Serv. *Aen.* 10.424: *texit* in the passage from Virgil is the present of *texere* (glossed as *spoliare*, "despoil") and not the perfect of *tegere*, "cover."[1]

  [1] Plautus uses *texere* rather than *tegere* in the quoted passage, and the gloss fits; but in the passage from Virgil we are dealing with the perfect of *tegere*, and the meaning has to be "cover" rather than "despoil."

195 **66** paupera est haec mulier

67 me‹di›cum habet patagus morbus aes

me‹di›cum *Buecheler*

68 qui talis est de gnatabus suis

quintalis *K*, quin talis *GL*, qui talis *ceteri codices*, Quietalis *Monda*

69 acieris

70 glos

200 **71** interluere mare

486

66 this woman is poor

Serv. *Aen.* 12.519: *pauper*, "poor," is a third-declension adjective, even though Plautus used it as a first/second-declension adjective.

67 the clattering disease has bronze as its doctor

Macr. *Sat.* 5.19.11–12: bronze used to have many ritual uses; it was even employed to get rid of illnesses.[1]

[1] It remains unclear what the clattering disease is. It could conceivably be a euphemism for a beating, to be stopped by paying for one's debts. If this is the case, there is no point in looking for ritual or medicinal uses of bronze—it would simply stand for "bronze money."

68 who is like this about his daughters

Prisc. *gramm.* 2.293: animate nouns of the type *filius*, "son"/*filia*, "daughter," have a dative and ablative feminine plural in *-abus* because the expected *-is* would be ambiguous between masculine and feminine.

69 bronze ax

CGL 2.13.9/Paul. Fest. 9: an *acieris* is a priest's bronze ax.

70 sister-in-law

CGL 2.34.29: *glos* refers to the husband's sister.

71 wash away the seawater

Isid. *orig.* 5.26.17: the preposition *inter* can be used instead of *e*, "out," as in *interluere* for *eluere*, "wash away."

72 probus quidem antea iaculator eras

73 linna coopertust ‹e› textrina Gallica

coopertus *KMNP*, cooperta *BCEFTUV* testrino *BDEFT*, testino
UV, textrinam *N* gallea *C¹*, galliae *B*, gallio *P*, galliam *NDE* e tex-
trina Gallica *uiri docti apud Leonem*

74 *** si quid facturus es, appende in umeris pallium,
     et pergat quantum ‹plus› ualet tuorum pedum pernicitas

204 plus *add. Monda*

205 **75** aeneis coculis mi excocta est omnis misericordia

76 quid tu, o momar[sicule] homo, praesumis?

sicule *del. Monda, quia fragmentum ex Festi parte nunc amissa or-
tum esse uidetur* (Paul. Fest. 123: *"momar" Siculi stultum appellant*)

72 before you used to be a decent javelin thrower

Isid. *orig.* 19.5.2: *iaculum*, "javelin," and *iaculator*, "javelin thrower," are connected with *iactare*, "throw."

73 he's covered with a cloak from the Gaulish weaving-place

Isid. *orig.* 19.23.3: a *linna* is a square, soft cloak.

74 *** if you're going to do anything, bundle up your cloak on your shoulders, and the swiftness of your feet should move on as quickly as possible

Isid. *orig.* 19.24.1: the *pallium*, "cloak," covers servants' shoulders so that they can run around unhindered while serving.

75 all my pity has been boiled away in bronze cooking vessels

Isid. *orig.* 20.8.1: *coculum* means "cooking vessel."

76 What do you presume, you idiot?

Osb. M.ii.10B.: a *momarsiculus* is an idiot prone to anger.[1]

[1] Osbern must have misunderstood his source text because the word *momarsiculus* does not exist. Osbern's source text could have been the same as that of Paul. Fest. 123, where *momar* is referred to as a Sicilian word (with the meaning "idiot"). The word *momar* is also found in Greek (Lycophron 1134) in the meaning "reproach, blemish."

FRAGMENTA DVBIA

Fr. i was assigned to Plautus by Thielmann because it is similar to *Mil.* 439; but the similarity may be purely accidental. Fr. ii has the name of Plautus after the definition of the word, which could indicate that Plautus used it; alternatively, the Plautine quotation could have been lost in the transmission process. Fr. iii–xviii, assigned to Plautus by Reitzenstein, come from Paul the Deacon but ultimately derive from Verrius Flaccus. They come from those parts of the original dictionary that were not ordered alphabetically (beyond the first letter) or thematically but according to the author of the quotations; since in each case a Plautine quote precedes, fr. iii–xviii are likely to be Plautine. Fr. xix mentions pronunciations of both Plautus and Ennius, which could indicate that they were common in the early period rather than that Plautus used these words in his plays. Fr. xx and xxi are quoted by Nonius, who assigns them to the *Captiui* and the *Aulularia*, respectively; since they do not occur there, one wonders whether Nonius got only the names of the plays wrong or the author as well. Fr. xxii comes from Ammianus Marcellinus, who quotes a *comicus*, "writer of comedy"; Ribbeck identified this author as Plautus, but without good reason. Fr. xxiii and xxiv, both attributed to Plautus by Servius, could be imprecise quotations of *Amph.* 640 and *Most.* 767, respectively.[1] Fr. xxv is given to Plautus by Servius, but to Laevius by Priscian. Fr. xxvi could be an imprecise citation of

---

[1] But in fr. xxiii the speaker is a man, whereas in *Amph.* 640 it is a woman.

DOUBTFUL FRAGMENTS

Truc. 93. Fr. xxvii could be loosely based on *Curc.* 228. Fr. xxviii could have arisen by a misunderstanding: Sacerdos (*gramm.* 6.491) states that the Plautine *boo*, "call," is a Greek loanword and that *reboo*, "call back," is a derivative thereof; the text in Probus could have been based on this passage and could by accident have assigned *reboo* to Plautus. Fr. xxix, attributed to the *Caecus* of Titinius, was regarded as belonging to the Plautine *Caecus* by Winter. Fr. xxx is considered Plautine by Charisius, but ascribed to Naevius by Paul the Deacon. Fr. xxxi is said to be something that Plautus never said, but this denial points to a controversy among grammarians and perhaps someone else assigned the form to Plautus. Fr. xxxii, illustrating the combination of *cette*, "give" (imperative plural), with the dative, seems to be made up because the dative after *cette* in Plautus is always a first-person singular pronoun. Fr. xxxiii and xxxiv violate regular Plautine usage. Fr. xxxv and xxxvi are ascribed to Plautus by Priscian, but his account is based on Nonius, who ascribes the forms to Pacuvius and Sueius, respectively. Fr. xxxvii contradicts the regular usage of Plautus, who says *flocci facio*, "care a straw," rather than *flocci pendo*. Fr. xxxviii might be based on *Cist.* 709 or 655–56. Fr. xxxix contains a type of hyperbaton not attested in Plautus (noun + preposition + adjective). Fr. xl seems to be a conflation of *Cas.* 493 and *Rud.* 1325.

1 Athenis Megaram uesperi aduenit Simo;
  ubi aduenit Megaram, insidias fecit uirgini;
  insidias postquam fecit, uim in loco attulit.

210 **2** amussis

3 addues

4 aristophorum

5 ad exitam aetatem

6 angina(m) uinaria(m)

215 **7** affabrum

492

1 In the evening Simo reached Megara[1] from Athens; when he reached Megara, he set a trap for a virgin; after he set the trap, he did violence to her in that place.

Rhet. Her. 1.9.14: repetition is bad style.

[1] A city which is about twenty-five miles from Athens.

2 a mason's ruler

Varro *ling.* fr. 49 Goetz-Schoell: an *amussis* is an instrument for leveling; it is a board for joining stones.

3 you will have added

Paul. Fest. 25: *adduues* means *addideris*, "you will have added."

4 lunch basket

Paul. Fest. 25: an *aristophorum* is a discuslike vessel for carrying breakfast or lunch.

5 till the end of one's life

Paul. Fest. 25: *ad exitam aetatem* means *ad ultimam aetatem*, "up until the end of one's life."

6 wine quinsy

Paul. Fest. 25: *angina uinaria* is what those people have who are choked with wine.

7 skilfully made

Paul. Fest. 25: *adfabrum* means "wrought by a craftsman."

8 alimodi

9 aeneolo

10 aenulum

11 bitienses

220 **12** blandicella

13 bellitudinem

14 botulus

8 of a different type

Paul. Fest. 25: *alimodi* means *alius modi*, "of a different type."

9 made of bronze

Paul. Fest. 25: *aeneolus* refers to what is made of bronze.

10 bronze vessel

Paul. Fest. 25: an *aenulum* is a small bronze vessel.

11 travelers

Paul. Fest. 31: *bitienses* are those who often travel abroad.

12 little flatteries

Paul. Fest. 32: *blandicella* are "little flattering words."

13 prettiness

Paul. Fest. 32: according to Verrius, *bellitudo*, "prettiness," is formed like *magnitudo*, "greatness."

14 sausage

Paul. Fest. 32: a *botulus* is a type of sausage that got its name from its connection with *bolus*, "catch of fish."[1]

[1] The etymological connection is untenable: *botulus* is a loanword from Sabellic, while *bolus* comes from Greek; besides, a fish sausage would be unheard of.

15 binominis

16 bellule

225 **17** custoditio

18 fucilis

19 Hannibālem, Hasdrubālem, Hamilcārem

20 pilleum quem habuit deripuit eumque ad caelum sustulit

tollit *codd.*, sustulit *Bothe*

496

15 having two names

Paul. Fest. 32: *binominis* refers to a person with a double name, like Tullus Hostilius.

16 prettily

Paul. Fest. 32: *bellule,* like *belle,* is a diminutive adverb from *bene*, "well."

17 protection

Paul. Fest. 54: *custoditio* is the trouble taken over "watching over" (*custodire*) something.

18 deceptive

Paul. Fest. 82: *fucilis* means "deceptive," as if it were *fucata*, "made up (with cosmetics), fake."

19 Hannibal, Hasdrubal, Hamilcar[1]

Gell. 4.7.1–2: according to Valerius Probus, Plautus and Ennius accented the penultimate syllable in the oblique cases of the three words cited.[2]

[1] Hannibal was the most famous Carthaginian general; Hasdrubal was his brother, and Hamilcar, his father.

[2] In classical Latin, the accent falls on the antepenultimate, but Valerius Probus is likely to be right for early Latin.

20 he snatched the felt cap that he had and took it up to the skies

Non. 325: *pilleum*, "felt cap," also has a masculine by-form, *pilleus.*

21 *** sed leno egreditur foras;

230   hinc ex occulto sermonem astu sublegam

231 **22** arte despecta furtorum, rapiens propalam

231^a **23** (sc. Plautus) inducit inter multos amatorem positum dicentem quod solus sit.

24 a primo mani usque ad uesperam

25 meminens

26 sed quid illaec mulier est?

.

21 *** but the pimp is coming out. I'll cunningly take in his conversation from here from a hidden spot

Non. 523: *legere* can mean "steal, filch."

22 having scorned the art of thieving, looting openly

Amm. 15.3.3: Prosper behaved in the way expressed by a writer of comedies.

23 Among many other characters, he (sc. Plautus) puts a lover on stage who says that he is lonely.

Serv. *Aen.* 4.82: when the queen says that she is *sola*, "lonely," she means that she is without her lover, as a queen cannot be truly alone.

24 from early morning till evening

Serv. *comm. Don.* 4.428: when an adverb like *mane*, "early," turns into a noun, it receives inflections.[1]

[1] The adverb *mane* actually started out as a noun, so this phrase is an archaism rather than an innovation.

25 remembering

Serv. *comm. Don.* 4.441: *meminisse*, "remember," does not normally have a participle, but such a participle is attested in Plautus.

26 But what is that woman?

Sacerd. *gramm.* 6.449–50: using a neuter pronoun for a human results in a solecism.[1]

[1] The use of the neuter is normal if a definition is asked for.

235 **27** haec praesepes mea est

28 reboo

29 ita semitatim fugi atque effugi patrem

30 butubatta

31 illibus

240 **32** cette patri meo

33 autem fac

500

27 this is my stable

Sacerd. *gramm.* 6.472: *praesepe*, "stall for cattle," is neuter, but has a feminine by-form, *praesepes*.

28 I call in answer

Prob. *cath. gramm.* 4.38: in Latin verbs only the vowels *a, e,* and *i* occur before the first-person ending *-o; reboo* is not a real exception because the base verb *boo* (I call) is a Greek loanword.

29 in this way I fled by the side roads and escaped my father

Char. *gramm.* 282: *semitatim*, "by the side roads," is an unusual adverb.

30 nonsense

Char. *gramm.* 315: the interjection *butubatta* means "nothing" or "nonsense."

31 to those people

Explan. in Don. *gramm.* 4.545: Plautus does not use *illibus* instead of *illis*.

32 give it to my father

Cledon. *gramm.* 5.59: the imperative *cedo*, "give/say," has a plural form, *cette*.

33 but do it

Cledon. *gramm.* 5.74: in ancient writers *autem*, "but," can occupy the first position as well as the second.

34 autem haec mulier

35 aequiter

36 asperiter

245 **37** flocci pendo quid rerum geras

38 cistellam mihi offers cum crepundiis

    effers *PR*, offers *codices ceteri*

39 pudens qui facit spes in alias ***

40 lolligunculos minutulos fabulare credas

34 but this woman

Context as xxxiii.

35 fairly

Prisc. *gramm.* 3.70–71: Plautus used the adverbial ending *-iter* in cases where one would expect *-e*.

36 harshly

Context as xxxv.

37 I care little what you're doing

Fulg. *serm. ant.* 38: *flocci* means "nothing."

38 you're offering me a box with recognition tokens

Fulg. *serm. ant.* 50: a *cistella* is a "little chest" and *crepundia* are "pretty things for children."

39 someone feeling ashamed, who does *** toward other hopes

Ars Ambros. p. 150. 225 Löfstedt: impersonal verbs like *pudet*, "feel ashamed," do not normally form present participles; *pudens* is a bad form.

40 you'd believe him to be talking tiny squid[1]

Osb. e 184B.: *lolligines* are small fish.

[1] Because of the syntax of the passage, *fabulare* is unlikely to be a second person singular medio-passive; perhaps it is the infinitive with an unusual active ending.

METRICAL APPENDIX

STICHVS

arg. 1 + 2 ia^6
1 as^{hemi}
1^a-3 pros
3^a c^r
4–6 v^r
7–8 an^2
8^a c^r
9 v^r
10 pros
10^a c^r
11–14 pros + c^r
15 c^r + c^r
16–17 an$^{4\wedge}$
18–28 an sy^{22metr}
29–32 an sy^{8metr}
33–38 an sy^{10metr}
39–47 an sy^{20metr}
48–57 ia^6
58–154 tr^7
155–242 ia^6
243 extra metrum
244–58 ia^6

259 extra metrum
260–73 ia^6
274 ia^8
275–77 ia^c
278–79 ia^8
280 tr^8
281 ia^8
282 ia^4
283–87 ia^8
288 tr$^{4\wedge}$
288^a ia^6
289–90 ia^8
291–92 ia^c
293 tr^7
294–99 ia^8
300 ia^6
301 ia^8
302 tr^8
303–5 ia^8
306 tr^7
307–8 ia^8
309–13 an sy^{18metr}

314–18 an^4$\wedge$

319–22 an sy^{8metr}

323–25 an^4$\wedge$

326–27^a an sy^{8metr}

328–29^a an sy^{8metr}

330 an^4$\wedge$ + c^r

331–401 tr^7

402–504 ia^6

505–640 tr^7

641–72 ia^6

673–82 ia^7

683–722 tr^7

723 extra metrum

723^a–61 tr^7

762–768 ia^6

769 ia^8

770 ia^7

771–73 v^r

774–75 ia^7

TRINVMMVS

arg., 1–222 ia^6

223–31 ba^4

232 ba^2

233–34 ia^7

235 an^4

236 v^r

237–37^a an^2

237^b–38 an^4$\wedge$

238^a tr^4$\wedge$

239 cr^c + cr^c

239^a ia^4 + adon

240 an^4

241 an^4$\wedge$

242–43 an^4

244 cr^4

245 cr^2 + cr^c

246 c^r + pros

247 cr^2 + cr^c

248 ia^4 + adon

249 cr^2 + ith

250 cr^2 + cr^c

251 cr^2 + c^r

252–54^a tr sy^{10metr}

255 v^r

256–59 an^4

260 v^r

261–69 an sy^{22metr}

270 an^4

271 an^4$\wedge$

272 an^4

273 an^4$\wedge$

274–78^a an^4

279 cr^2 + cr^c

280 ia^4 + adon

281 cr^4

282–82^a ia^4

283 cr^4

284 v^r

285–86^a ia^4

287–88^a an sy$^{9\text{metr}}$

289 an^4

290 an^4∧

291 an^4

292–98 an sy$^{14\text{metr}}$

299–300 an^8

301–91 tr^7

392–601 ia^6

602–728 tr^7

729–819 ia^6

820–39 an^8

840–42^a an sy$^{8\text{metr}}$

843–997 tr^7

998–1007 ia^6

1008–92 tr^7

1093–114 ia^6

1115–119 an^4

1120–189 tr^7

TRVCVLENTVS

arg., 1–94 ia^6

95–100 ia^4∧ + c^r

101 v^r

102–11 an^8

112–13 an^4∧

114 an^7

115 ia^4

116 cr^c + cr^c

117–18 cr^2 + cr^c

119 ia^4

120–21 thy

122 tr^4∧ + cr^1

123 cr^c

124–26 an^4

127 cr^2 + tr^2

128 an^4∧ + c^r

129 v^r

130–208 ia^7

209 c^r

210 ia^4

211–12 ba^4

213–16 ia^8

217–23 ia^7

224–27 ia^6

228–36, 232–33 tr^7

237–40 ia^7

241–47 ia^6

248–49 ba^4

250 ia^6

251–55 ia^7

256–321 tr^7

322–447 ia^6

448–53 an sy$^{11\text{metr}}$

454–64 ba^4

465–550 tr^7

551–52 ba^4

553 an^8

554–55 ba^c + ba^2

556–57 wil

558 an^8

559–60 tr^8

561–65 tr^7

566 an^2 + an^4

567 an^4∧

568 an^4

569–70 ba^4

571 tr^8

572–73 an^8

574 ba^4

575–80 tr^7

581 ia^4

582 cr^4

583 an^7

584–85 cr^4

586–87 tr^7

588 cr^4

589 cr^2 + cr^c

590 ?

591 cr^4

592 cr^c + cr^c

593 tr^7

594 tr^4∧

595–96 tr^7

597 an^2

598 an^8

599–602 cr^4

603–5 an^8

606–7 an^7

608–11 an^8

612–14 an^7

615 an^8

616 an^7

617 an^8

618–19 an^7

620 tr^7

621 tr^8

622–25 cr^4

626 tr^7

627–28 tr^8

629–30 tr^7

631–98 ia^6

699–710 tr^7

711 an^8

712 ba^4

713–14 an^4 + c^r

715–18 ba^4

719 ia^8

720–21 ba^4

722 ia^6

723 cr^4

724 ia^6

725 cr^4

726 tr^8

727 tr^7

728–29 v^r

730–968 tr^7

VIDVLARIA

1–16 ia^6	fr. xii–xvi tr^7
17–fr. ii tr^7	fr. xvii ia^6
fr. iii–17^g ?	fr. xviii ia^7 ?
18–55 ia^6	fr. xix ia^7
fr. v–68 tr^7	fr. dub. i–ii ?
69–fr. xi ia^6	fr. dub. iii ia^6

FRAGMENTA

1 tr^7	40 ba^2 + ba^c
2 ?	41 ith
3–4 ia^6	42 c^r
5 tr^7 ?	43–44 ia^7 ?
6 ia^7	45 ?
7–8^a ?	46–48 ia^6
9–12 tr^7	49 ?
13 ia^6	50 tr^7
14–15 ?	51 ?
16 ia^6	52 ia^6
17–18 ia^4∧	53–56 tr^7
19 ia^7	57–59 ?
20 ia^8	60 tr^7
21 v^r	61 ?
22–31 ia^6	62–64 tr^7
32–34 ia^8	65–66 ia^6
35 an^4 ?	67–68 tr^7
36 ?	69 ?
37–38 ia^6	70 tr^7
39 ?	71–73 ia^6

74 ?	127 ia^6
75 ia^8	128–29 tr^7
76 ia^7	130 ?
77 ?	131 tr^7
78 ia^8	132 ?
79 tr^8	133 tr^7
80–81 tr^7	134–39 ?
82–86 ia^6	140–41 ia^6
87–88 ?	142 tr^7
89 tr^7	143–45 ia^6
90 ia^6	146–47 tr^7
91–92 tr^7	148 ia^6
93–94 ia^6	149–54 ?
95 ?	155 tr^7
96 ia^6	156–62[a] ?
97–98 ?	163–64 ia^8
99–102 ia^6	165 ia^6
103–4 ?	166–67 tr^7
105–7 ia^6	167[a]–71?
108 tr^8	172–75 ia^6
109 $cr^2 + tr^{4}$∧	176–78 ?
110 ?	179–80 ia^6
111 ia^6	181–82 ?
112–14 tr^7	183–84 tr^7
115–16 tr^8	185 ia^6
117–18 tr^7	186–90 ?
119 ?	191 ia^6
120 ia^8	192–201 ?
121 ?	202 ia^6
122 ia^6	203–4 ia^8
123–26 ?	205 tr^7

METRICAL APPENDIX

206 ?
207–9 ia[6]
210–27 ?
228 tr[7]
229–30 ia[6]

231–36 ?
237 ia[6]
238–48 ?

INDEX OF PROPER NAMES

The index is limited to names of characters in the plays and of persons, towns, countries, peoples, deities, and events mentioned in the plays. Names for which established English forms or translations exist are listed under the English forms, for instance, *Jupiter* or *Underworld*.

INDEX OF PROPER NAMES